Henri Rohan

The memoires of the Duke of Rohan

A faithful relation of the most remarkable occurrences in France

Henri Rohan

The memoires of the Duke of Rohan
A faithful relation of the most remarkable occurrences in France

ISBN/EAN: 9783337225117

Printed in Europe, USA, Canada, Australia, Japan

Cover: Foto ©ninafisch / pixelio.de

More available books at **www.hansebooks.com**

THE MEMOIRES OF THE DUKE of ROHAN·

OR,

A FAITHFUL RELATION Of the most Remarkable

Occurrences

In *FRANCE*;

Especially concerning those of the Reformed Churches there.
From the Death of *HENRY* the Great, untill the Peace made with them, in *June*, 1629.
TOGETHER
With divers Politick Discourses upon Several Occasions.

Written Originally in *French*, by the Duke of ROHAN
And now Englished by *George Bridges* of *Lincolns-Inne*, Esq;

London, Printed by *E.M.* for *Gabriel Bedell*, and *Thomas Collins*; and are to be sold at their Shop, at the Middle-Temple Gate in *Fleet-street*. 1660.

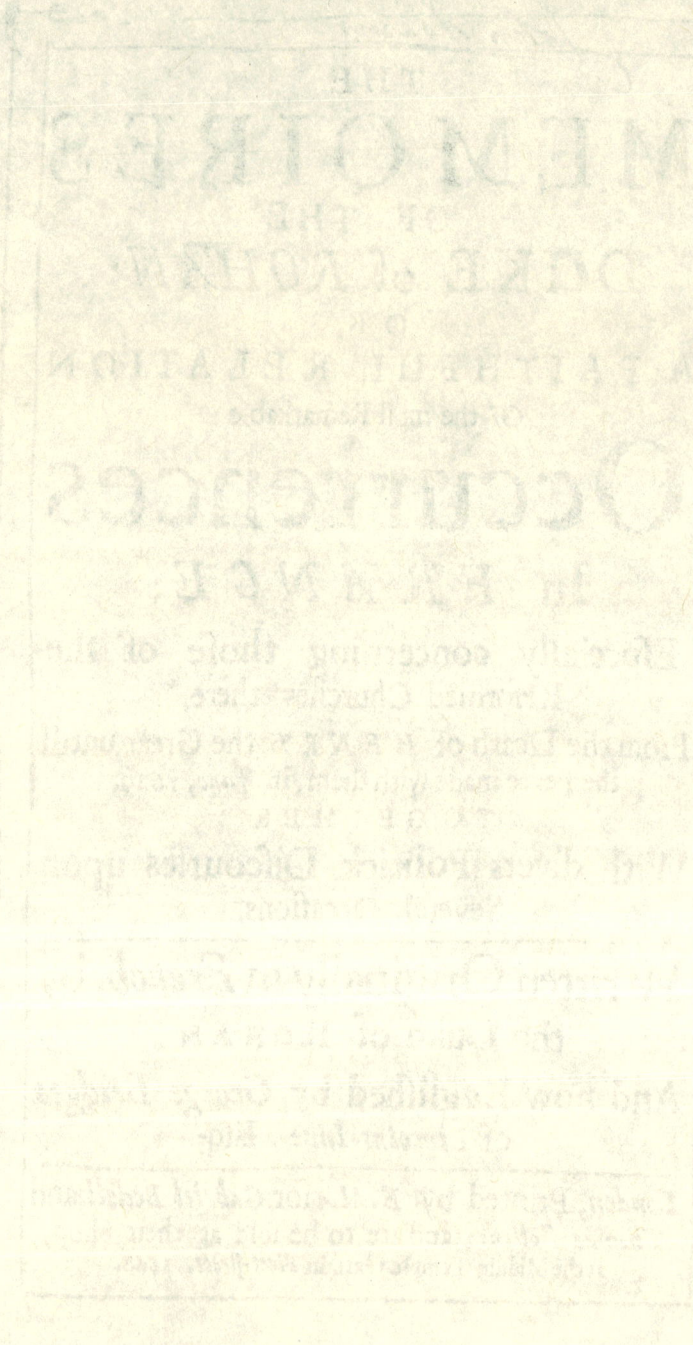

To the Right Honourable,

JAMES,

Lord-Marqueſs of *Ormond*, Lord-Lieutenant of *Ireland*, Steward of His Majeſties Houſhold, Knight of the moſt Noble Order of the Garter, and one of His Majeſties moſt Honourable Privy Councel, &c.

My LORD,

O pretend an Ignorance of Your Perſon, which your Loyalty, (the only Embelliſher of all other Vertues) has rendered ſo Eminently Famous, and thence frame an Apologetique Preface, to uſher in this Addreſs to Your Lordſhip, would be a Crime greater than the Preſumption, and an unpardonable Offence againſt that Goodneſs, which never frowned on the meaneſt payment of that Tribute Your Merits juſtly challenge from all

A 2 Men:

The Epistle Dedicatory.

Men: 'Tis that, My Lord, which imboldens me, Humbly to present Your Lordship with this Translation of a Modern History, written Originally by the Duke of ROHAN, a Prince, whose Valour, and other Rare Accomplishments, not inferiour to the most Eminent of his time, had rendered his Reputation as clear, as great, had they not been unfortunately employed against a Party, in which his King was interessed (Religion it self having not power sufficient to Authorize Armes, raised by Subjects against their Soveraign) for one which payed all his services with Calumny and Detraction.

But far from me be the presumption to direct Your Lordships Judgement of his Exploits, either in the Camp, or Cabinet; either of his Sword, or Pen; which I was principally induced to publish in our Language, by some passages tending to the Vindication of our late incomparable King, and Martyr, from no less false, than foule aspersions concerning *Rochelle*, (His care and diligence to order their relief, being here acknowledged by persons more concerned, than our pretended Propagators of Religion, the *Rochellers* ruine being chiefly occasioned by their own Inconstancy, refusing to admit those succours when come, which they before, even with tears implored, and their own intestine divisions and factions) with which His Blasphemous, and Rebellious Subjects, first sought to wound His Fame, that with more security they might im-
brew

The Epistle Dedicatory.

brew their Hands in His most Sacred Blood: And knowing how zealous an Assertor Your Lordship has alwayes shewen Your Self, both of His Rights and Innocence; and how indefatigable, (though with the hazard of the dearest Treasures, both of Your Life, and Fortune) Your Industry has been, for the restoring of His Majesty, (by God's Miraculous Providence now Reigning over us) even in those times, when Treason having usurped the Throne, Rewards and Punishments were with such prodigious Impiety misplaced, that Loyalty was daily crucified, when Villany was cherished, and advanced; nor were our very thoughts exempt from the Tyrant's barbarous Inquisitions; I could not more justly offer it to the Patronage of any, than Your Lordship; together with him, who, with Your Lordships pardon, humbly begs the Honour to subscribe himself,

My Lord,

Your Lordships most Humble,

Most Devoted,

And most Obedient Servant,

GEORGE BRIDGES.

THE AUTHOR'S PREFACE TO THE Reader.

THIS *Treatise presents you with the History of three Wars sustained in* France, *in defence of the Reformed Churches there; the occasion of the first was* Bearne; *that of the second, the not observing the Peace made at* Montpellier; *and that of the third, was the hope to save* Rochelle: *But our sins fought against us; for instead of profiting, we were hardned by the chastisements God sent us. In the two first Wars, the divisions appeared but as scattered sparks, which in the last united to make a general conflagration, there being no place, where Corruption had not seated it self, and Avarice excluded Piety; so that instead of expecting any overtures from our enemies, every one prostituted himself to sell his Religion, and betray his Countrey: Our Ancestours would have crushed such children in their Cradles, had they thought they would have proved instruments of ruine to those Churches which they had planted in the midst of Flames, and cherished in despight of Torments; and who by their indefatigable pains, and perseverance, had left them possessors of a glorious*

Repose;

The Author's Preface to the Reader.

Repose: *Nor will our Posterity easily believe themselves descended from such Noble Grandfathers, and such Infamous Fathers, if they look not higher, to wit, to God, who raises, and abates the Courages of men, according as his good pleasure is to discover his Wonders to his Church, in raising it from the dust; when the powers of the world conceive it buried there, and depressing it again, when Pride, and an Abuse of his Graces, are the only Product of them.*

And here I speak to you Princes, and Common-wealths, whom God hath honoured with his Knowledge, blest with his Favours, advanced to the height of Dignity, and even satiated with Riches; take warning by us, and boast not your selves in the Arme of flesh, and the greatness of your Forces; in the height of your Prosperity beware a Fall; for then are you nearest danger: Many of you have with dry Eyes, and lethargique Arms, been Spectators of our Tragedy, without contributing any thing to our relief; and we our Selves, have seen the Ships, and Armies of others ingratefully promoting the ruine of those, who relieved them in their necessity: God will not fail to do his work without you, when the time of our deliverance shall come; He is nearer to us in our Adversity, than you are to him in your Prosperity; if we are obliged to implore his Favour, you are much more to prevent his Judgments. Let the examples of others be your instruction, and while it is yet time, consider from what source your blessings flow, and give the honour and glory of it to him, to whom it is only due. In the mean time, prepare your selves to see here, without any disguise, the naked truth of what passed in our late trouble.

I have begun this History at the death of Henry *the* Great; *for that during the minority of the* King, *his* Son, *the Maximes laid down by the* Father, *for the Government of* France, *were changed, and the foundation of the persecution of those of the Reformed Religion laid,*

which

The Author's Preface to the Reader.

which had like also to have proved the subversion of all Christendome, *and given its Monarchy to the house of* Austria.

I leave it to Posterity, to the end, that after my death, the truth of things which I have seen, may not be obscured, either by the Fables of Flatterers, or the Invectives of our Persecutors: I have done it, without any the least Fiction, or Passion, and shall leave every man his liberty to judge of it, as he shall please.

THE
Memoires
OF THE
DUKE of ROHAN:
OR,
A true *Narration* of the most remarkable Accidents in *FRANCE*,

From the death of *Henry* the Great, until the Peace made with those of the Reformed Churches there, in *June* 1629.

The first Book.

Containing the troubles during the minority of the King.

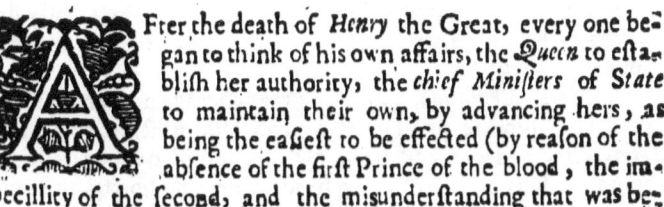Fter the death of *Henry* the Great, every one began to think of his own affairs, the *Queen* to establish her authority, the *chief Ministers of State* to maintain their own, by advancing hers, as being the easiest to be effected (by reason of the absence of the first Prince of the blood, the imbecillity of the second, and the misunderstanding that was between the third and them:) and the other great ones to raise themselves

selves from that abject condition, the precedent raign had cast them into. Amid'ſt all which, hatreds were frequent, and the moſt ſubtle among them made uſe of the paſſion of others to ruine the authority of thoſe that eclipſed theirs.

He that received the firſt ſhock, after the Regency was ſettled on the Queen, was the Duke of *Sully*, who by his ſervices had acquired the honour of *Principal Confident* to the former King, and purchaſed the ill-will of moſt others: For a vertue, eminent, as was his, accompanied with the favour of his Maſter, is alwayes attended on by envie, a vice as frequent among men, as unworthy thoſe who pretend any profeſſion of honour. Many were very zealous for his ruine, and that for different reaſons; The Chancellor *Villeroy*, and the Preſident *Janin*, to confirm their own power in the government of the State, and take from among them a Man, whoſe exactneſſe in the diſcharge of his Offices was their ſhame, ſo clear-ſighted to diſcern, and ſo bold to diſcover their faults; The Count of *Soiſſons* out of ſome particular hatred he bore him; The Marqueſſe *d' Ancre* for fear he ſhould nip his budding fortune; and all the other Grandees, becauſe they thought him too good a mannager of the Publick treaſure; And the Prince of *Conde* when he came to the Court, by the inſtigation of the Marſhal *Boüillon*, who bore him an inveterate malice, and drew on the Prince with hopes of confiſcating his goods: A powerful motive to ſet that Prince on work.

The chiefeſt means they uſed to remove him from the helme, were, to raiſe a jealouſie in the Queen of the auſterity of his humour, who oppoſed her in her liberalities; and to perſwade her, that, having need of the Popes favour to ſtrengthen her authority, ſhe could not ſuffer one of the Reformed Religion, to have any hand in the Government of the State; Prevalent reaſons with a Princeſs, who was a Forraigner little verſed in State matters, jealous of her authority, and diſtruſtful of all ſorts of people: But in the end experience diſcovered it to be the ruine of the State; For the Grandees grew up to a height that diminiſhed the Royal power; the Treaſuries were drained, the Arſenals ſtrangely diſperſed, and the compariſon of that miſerable condition of *France* with that flouriſhing one, the Duke of *Sully* left it in, clearly demonſtrates, how highly prejudicial to the State, was his removal from his employments in it.

The Marſhal *Boüillon*, a man of great courage and underſtanding, able to procure great good, and no leſſe miſchief to a *Common-wealth*, and who had been alwayes curbed by the late King, who was jealous of him, finding himſelf now at liberty, uſes all manner of inventions, to make himſelf thought uſeful, and neceſſary:

fary: The first was to endeavour wholly to possesse the spirit of the Prince of *Conde*, whose kinsman he was, and to perswade him to become one of the Reformation, by that means to make himself the Chief, and Protector of a party, that was then very considerable; and with such industry carryed he on his Plots, that the Queen conceived great suspitions of him; and therefore to divert this blow, sought after him, who as soone as he had made his conditions with her, effaces the desires he had infused into the Prince, to imitate the vertuous actions of his Ancestors; shewing him the thornes were in the way to honour, the perils, hardships and adverse accidents are met withal, in the pursuit of it; In short, the misery and poverty that accompany it, which proved most effectuall reasons to disswade him from a designe so contrary to his nature.

The Duke of *Rohan* in the mean time, who was Colonel of the *Switzers*, was commanded away to the siege of *Julliers*, taking with him a Regiment of the *Switzers*, and having the command of the French Army in the absence of the Marshal *de la Chastre*, who was the Lieutenant General. At his return from this expedition, he finds how cruelly they oppresse his Father-in-Law the Duke of *Sully*; and that, after they had taken from him the *Bastille*, to dispose of the treasure in it, and his command of the *Finances*, to rob *France* with fuller liberty, they were now resolved upon his utter destruction, so to deprive him of all means to resent such indignities: But seeing that it was beyond their skill by any ordinary wayes to blemish the administration of any of his Offices, the Marshal *Bouillon*, who had infected the Prince of *Conde*, and the Count of *Soissons* with the same malitious intention, contrived this designe for his ruine, *viz.* to procure a General Assembly of those of the Religion, which was granted to be held at *Chastellerant* on the five and twentieth of *May*, in the year 1611, in which he promised himself power enough to cause the Duke of *Sully* to be entirely abandoned, so that without any fear of those of the Religion, he might be arraigned before Commissioners impowered for his trial; and moreover, that by his industry he should so order the Assembly, and all the affairs of the Reformed party, that he should make himself the only man considerable: To bring this Project to passe, he vailes it with a pretence of much affection to those of the Reformation, and large promises of an *Amelioration* in their affairs; and communicates it to the Marshal *de Lesdiguieres*, and *Du Plessis Mornay* in particular, by *Bellugeon* an attendant of *Lesdiguieres*, who when he had been with them, returnes with these following Instructions from *Du Plessis*.

1. That

1. That the Provinces be exhorted to choose for Deputies, the best qualified and most sufficient persons.
2. That besides those, others of eminency among them, be also desired by letters to that purpose to be there.
3. That the Deputies may have power to adhere to the plurality of voices, and that the Assembly be not dissolved, till they have received full satisfaction.
4. That the demands of the Provinces be all founded expresly, or upon consequences deduced from the former Edicts and Concessions.
5. Amongst others, that the Edict of *Nantes* be revived again, and observed as it was made with us, but since abridged in many things without us.
6. That our Grants for the places of security be made good to us, and the entire number of the Garrisons restored us, half of which have been wrested from us.
7. That the places we have lost, either by the Governors change of their Religion, or otherwise, be also given back to us.
8. That all the places of security be continued to us for ten years at least, and that they be paid quarterly, fully, and upon the place; and that no money be upon any pretence whatsoever, removed from the places of receipt, till the said quarter be satisfied.
9. That it may regularly be obtained also, and had for provisions for vacant Governments, considering the abuses which are, and may be there committed, to the prejudice of our safety.
10. That we may be permitted to repair and fortifie all such places, as time has thrown into decay, and which for want of reparations will become wholly unuseful to us: And that complaint be made, that under pretence of these Governments, we are refused all other Offices and Dignities, contrary to the expresse Article of the Edict.
11. That no resignations of such places of security be allowed of without the consent of the Churches, which are therein most concerned: The like also for Presidents, and Counsellors of the Chambers.
12. That we may have free liberty as before, to compose, print, sell, and disperse all manner of books concerning our Doctrine.
13. That if there be any Town, whose place for the exercise of their Religion is too remote from it, the King be petitioned to grant one nearer, that being under the eye of the Magistrates, they may be lesse subject to the insolency of the People.

14. That

Book I.   *The Memoires of the Duke of* Rohan.

14. That the Article concerning burying-places, which makes way for so many Barbarisms, may be reformed.
15. That the Pensions allowed the Churches, considering the great number of them, may be augmented.
16. That the Jesuites may not have any residence in our places of security.
17. That those Preachers and Friers, who teach, that all those who communicate with those of the Reformed Religion, or that serve and assist them, are damned, may be punished, as seditious disturbers of the publick peace, and infringers of the Edicts, by which their Majesties have published their intentions, to reunite the affections of their people.
18. That we may be allowed two Masters of request, to be paid by the King, for the first time, and one Notary in every Parliament, or at least in the places of security, and to be payed by us.
19. That some place of security be demanded, as well in the Provinces where there are none, as where there are many of the Religion. But that it be referred to the prudence of the Assembly, to consider how far this demand be pressed.
20. That we may have a Grant for a General Assembly to be held every two years, for the renewing of our Deputies General.
21. That it be expresly specified, that we may have two Deputies General in Ordinary at Court at the Kings charges, but to be nominated by the Assembly.
22. That the Provincial Deputies may addresse themselves to the Deputies General without any previous applications to be made to the Governours of the Provinces.

These Instructions were sent abroad among the Provinces, where every one according to the extent of his power, and credit got them received, and resolved on. The aimes of these Gentlemen were diverse; that of *Du Plessis* was sincere, that of the Marshal *Lesdiguieres* (as the whole course of his life has discovered) tended only to his own interest; as also that of the Marshal *Bouillon*, who made use of the power of others to convert all to his own advantage: For having filled the Provinces with hopes of bettering their condition, and made them enter into most strict resolutions for that end, discovers all at Court, shews them to *Villeroy*, and to the Embassadors of *England* and *Holland*, to whom he also pretended much zeal for the Reformed Religion: And after this takes a journey to *Sedan*, that he might the better give the Court leisure to foster fears of the issue of this Assembly, and finde out meanes to render it ineffectual: His desires in this met a wished success; for at his return he treated fully with *Villeroy*, and having made his conditions for the Government of *Poictou*, worth three hundred thousand Livers, either for himself, or to be disposed of as he should order, and a hundred thousand Livers augmentation upon the Taxes of the common people, which by his appointment were disposed to several particular persons: he promises to change all the resolutions of the Assembly, and give it such an issue, as should highly content the Queen; which he confirmed by an irrefragable Testimony; for revisiting the aforesaid Embassadours, and particularly *Arsens*, he begins a discourse concerning those of the Reformation, quite contrary to his former before his Voyage to *Sedan*, viz. That during the Kings Minority they were better entertain a little patience, than thoughts of bettering their condition, and by that means justly purchase the Kings favour; that for his part he went to the Assembly with thoughts tending only to peace, and wholly bent to endeavour a submission of all to the pleasure of the Court. This much astonished *Arsens*, who conceived now that his composition was made, which he dissembled not at all to his friends: When he had made this progress, his favourites and creatures seconded it with discourses of the same nature, the better at a distance to dispose the people to a compliance with his desires: And because *Chastelleraut* was within the Government of the Duke of *Sully*, whose ruine he thirsted after, he caused the Assembly to adjourn from thence to *Saumure*, the goverment of *Du Plessis*, that he might the more oblige him to a conjunction with him.

Before the Session of the Assembly, he informs *Du Plessis* by several persons of quality that he would not be President of it; that though they elected him, yet would he not accept of the charge, and that it was his desire, he should impart this his resolution to all he should see; for that he thought it very improper for any of the great ones to undertake it. This extreamly pleased them all, especially the Dukes of *Rohan* and *Sully*, who now cast their eyes upon *Du Plessis*, and assured him that they would carry it for him: But the Marshal *Bouillon*, coming the last of all, and after they had waited for him a day beyond the time prefixed, (though not without much murmurings, for that his mischievous designes began now to be discovered) visits *Du Plessis*, and tells him, that notwithstanding what had been said concerning the Presidentship, he now desired their nomination, for that he knew the Duke of *Sully* had with much boasting threatened to prevent him of it; that it was a thing that his many services

Book I. *The Memoires of the Duke of* Rohan. 7

vices to the Party had merited of them; and that in case they refused him the honour, he would be gone the next morning: This change of his minde wrought no alteration at all in the resolutions of the Dukes, who found the greatest part of the Provinces disposed to their inclinations; so that whatever suit or parties the Marshal *Boüillon* could make, he had the voices but of six Provinces, and *Du Plessis* of ten; who when he took his place, had *Chamier* a Minister, chosen for his assistant, and *Desbordes Mercier* for Secretary. This election so nettled *De Boüillon*, that returning to his Lodging he brake forth into words of disgust, and threats of vengeance against all those that had hindred him of the Presidentship; finding well by this Essay, that he was now like to faile of all he had promised himself from the Assembly: However, obliged both by prudence, and the importunate sollicitations of those that were equally friends to them both, he reconciled himself to the Duke of *Sully*, whom he had before declared to be his greatest enemy.

The first thing the Assembly took into their consideration, was the disorder committed at *Chastillon*, contrary to the express Orders of the Marshal *Boüillon* and the *Sieur Frere* Commissioners appointed by the King for that particular affaire, for which the Marshal pretended so high a displeasure, that having dispatch'd thither *Beauchamp*, one of his Gentlemen, to enquire into the truth of the matter, he declared as his opinion, that it was fit the Assembly should choose *Senas* for their Deputy, to be sent to the Court with full instructions, and a strict charge to declare, That they would not treat of any thing with the Kings Commissioners, before reparation were made for that wrong: But that violent heat quickly abated; for he presently excused himself from medling any further in it, because his Commission was expired.

After this the Kings Commissioners had audience, who in all their discourses pretended, that the preservation of those of the Reformed Religion was involved with, and necessary to that of the State, assuring them of their Majesties favour, that they would graciously receive all their Remonstrances and Petitions, cause their Edicts and Concessions to be observed, put those that had hitherto been neglected, in execution; and interpret to their advantage, what was obscure in them. And lastly, That they left it to the choice of the Assembly, either to put their Papers into their hands, or send them to the Court, protesting, that which way soever they took, they should have a quick and favourable dispatch.

From these fair promises sprung no less fair hopes; and according

B 4

any thing concerning them: 'But going to the Assembly, advised them to make their addresses by Deputies to the King, to whom they would do them all good Offices; which was concluded on. At the election of the Deputies, there happened a great stirre, occasioned by the opposition of contrary factions, which made the Assembly resolve not to draw up their Instructions and Commissions, before their nomination; that so they might either inlarge or restraine them according to the conditions of the persons chosen, who were *La Cafe, Courtaumer, Ferrier* the Minister, *Mirande* and *Armet*, who had no power to conclude any thing, but only to debate the propositions; and having explained them, to give an account of all to the Assembly, who would return them their resolutions thereupon: This restriction pleased not all the Deputies, much less the Marshal *Bouillon*, who now plainly perceived, that his design was broken.

While they were preparing their papers, there fell out two particular things worthy the observing. The first was on the several oppositions the Marshal *Bouillon* made to an Article, which the Duke of *Sully* as earnestly pressed, *viz.* That the Assembly should interess themselves in his cause, for that they endeavoured to deprive him of his offices for no other cause, but of his Religion, in which the Marshal proceeded so farre, as an attempt to make the son renounce his Obligations to his Father-in-law, which he violently pursued; especially one time going to visit him being sick, telling him that it was impossible, but that in the administration of those great charges he had borne, especially in that of the *Finances*, when he was Comptroler of the Exchequer, there should be found some faults committed; though not by him, yet by his Officers and Servants; and that if the King should issue out a Commission to examine his actions, neither the Assembly, nor any other of the Reformed Religion ought to be offended at it; no, though the Commissioners should do him wrong, since it would be by the ordinary wayes of Justice that he received it, and that he thought the Duke of *Rohan* so honest a man, a true *French* man, and so great a friend to peace, that he would be nothing moved at it. This speech was but ill-received, and no better answered by the Duke, who told him, that the Duke of *Sully's* important services deserved a better recompence, than to be exposed,

Book I.   *The Memoires of the Duke of* Rohan.   9

as a prey to those that had disserved the State; that his actions in discharge of his Offices, free from all corruption, and misdemeanour, could not, by reason of his qualitie, be inquired into, but by a Court of Peers; and that if he were otherwise dealt withal, all his kindred, and especially he, his son in Law, with all their friends, would engage in his cause; so that after several Sessions, the Assembly proceeding to a determination of that Article, so much urged by the Provinces also, advised the Duke of *Sully* not to accept of money in lieu of his Offices, and especially, not to quit that of Grand Master of the Artillery, promising withal, that if for that end they should use any undue, unlawful, and extraordinary procedures against him, they would publickly Declare that they looked on the Duke of *Sully's*, as the same with the general interest of the Churches, and of Justice; and that therefore they were resolved by all just and lawful means to assist him: And of this the Deputies general had an express charge given them in their instructions.

The other was concerning *Berticheres*, one of the Deputies for the lower *Languedoc*, a Gentleman of quality, and of good parts, who in the raign of the late King, who was displeased at him, by reason of his practices, and intelligence with the Constable *Montmorency* Governour of that Province, was somewhat unhandsomely turn'd out of his governments of *Sommieres*, and *Aiguemortes*; to which having in vaine sought to be restored, he conceived this a favourable opportunity to make the Assembly embrace his cause, for that they were both places of security; and, though they were in the hands of Gentlemen of the same Religion, yet he presumed they were persons, that had not given so great Testimonies of their zeale for the good of the Churches, as he had done; and that though he had been constrained to accept of a recompence for his Command, yet was it only for that of *Sommiers*; but for *Aiguemortes* he never received any thing; and that since his services to their party had drawn upon him this prejudice, it was but reason that they should own the Justice of his Cause: And forasmuch as he had brought with him Writings to verifie what he alledged, he moved the Assembly to appoint Commissioners to examine them, and make their report to them, that they might consider of them.

It is to be observed that this *Berticheres* made a great profession of friendship to the Duke of *Sully*, who had done him many good Offices to the late King, so that he desired some of his chiefest friends for Commissioners, who made so favourable a report of his business to the Assembly, that in spight of the opposition made by the Duke of *Bouillon*, who stood for *Arembures*, to whom the

the Government of *Aiguemortes* was given, it was so well received by the Assembly, that the Deputies residing at the Court, were commanded to use all diligence in his behalf, it being a thing of general concernment, and of great consequence. When he had obtained this, he goes to the Court, where he steers a new course, and to arrive at his aimes, promises most powerfully to assist the Court-party, upheld by the Duke of *Boüillon*, in the Assembly, and by this means got a quick and satisfactory dispatch for his re-entry into *Aiguemortes*: Moreover in this journey he made the Constable his friend, who embraced his cause with the same fervour, as if it had been his own proper concernment, and then returned to the Assembly: The issue of this affair shall be seen in its proper place: But let us now return to the general affairs.

When the Deputies of the Assembly were come to the Court, their first dispatch thence brought news of their fair reception, especially by the Queen, (who commanded them to put their papers into the hands of *Boïssise*, and *Bullion*, Counsellors of State) and of the favourable answers they had at several audiences received from the Council: But this was soon clouded by another message from them quite contrary to the former, which informed the Assembly, that the promise to have their Propositions answered, and returned into their hands, was now interpreted to be after the nomination of the Deputies general, and dissolution of the Assembly: This highly displeased them who had already divulged among the Provinces, the good hopes they conceived from the first intelligence the Deputies gave them: But, forasmuch as it was a thing contrary to the use and custome of the Kings Council, in affaires of all sorts to send back the Deputies unanswered; and that in all their discourses with them there was no mention of any such conditions, the Assembly unanimously resolve not to dissolve before they had received an answer to their Articles; which the Marshal *Boüillon* seem'd to approve of, and promised his utmost assistance to procure them a handsome returne concerning it.

But there was a great difference between the Letter, he shewed the Assembly, and that which he sent away, which intimated his opinion, that at least some of them should see the answers to their Propositions before their dissolution: But the assiduous endeavors of the Deputies proving ineffectual, they returned to *Saumure*, where *Ferrier* in the name of all the rest, made a relation of the particulars of their whole voyage, by which they perceived that *Bullion* was coming after with their Propositions answered; but that before his arrival their Majesties desired the Deputies general might be nominated; which notwithstanding was suspended.

When

Book I. *The Memoires of the Duke of* Rohan.

When *Bullion* came, he confirmed what the Deputies had reported, protested to many upon his damnation, that the Propositions were most favourably answered; terrifies some with threats, whiles he fills others with hopes; and to encrease both their feares, and hopes, he shews the Patents he brought with him for the augmenting the pensions of *Parabere,* and others, and the Orders to cancel those of the Dukes of *Rohan* and *Soubize.* The Marshal *Bouillon* for his part, employes all his Art to winne the Deputies of the Assembly by hopes of a general deputation, and by the power he had to dispose of the Tax imposed upon the common people now raised to an hundred thousand Livers more, the better to enable him to corrupt more men: The resolution also of the Assembly to send new petitions to their Majesties, that they might receive their answers before they dissolved, gave him an opportunity to play the notable Politition: For though there was a very good understanding between the Marshal *Bouillon* and *Bullion,* yet pretended they a difference in their opinions; the one assuring them, that it would be but lost labour to importune the Court any more; the other encouraging them to it with promises of good successe; but his chief design was to weary some with delayes, that he might have the better opportunity to draw others to his party; and in the mean time covered all his projects with a pretence of zeale, that the simpler sort having lesse suspicion of him, might the more easily be intrapped: But failing in this attempt, he resolved with *Bullion* and his friends, to perswade their Majesties to write a letter (of which he sent them a draught) peremptorily commanding the Assembly to dissolve, revoking the Licence granted for their meeting, and declaring null all their past or future Acts: And forasmuch as their Majesties were informed, that all the Deputies did not agree in this obstinacy and disobedience, they commanded those Deputies that would obey to proceed among themselves to the election of six Deputies, who should receive from the hands of *Bullion* the propositions with their answers; which Letter was to be brought by one, that knew well enough how to play his Game. *Bellugeon* the Marshal *Lesdiguieres* his Agent, was made choice of for this employment, a fit Instrument to execute such a Commission, being a crafty fellow, void both of honor and honesty, whose subtle pate was alwayes busied about things conducing only to his own advantage.

Before he began this goodly journey, he takes his leave of the Assembly, falsly pretending, it was only to see his friends and kinred in *Berry*; and then goes out of the Town upon an ordinary Hackny, but soon after takes post: which being certified to the Assembly, as also his treacherous practices at *Paris,* together with

with the calumnies he aspersed the Duke of *Rohan*, and his friends withal, he was by them declared unworthy to be re-admitted to this, and for the future to any other Assembly: But forasmuch as he had the honour of being a servant to the Marshal *Lesdiguieres*, they referred his further doom to him. This censure infinitely vexed the Marshal *Bouillon*, who employed all the power he had to get it revoked, declaring that it was by his command that he had undertaken this journey, but all in vain; which so incensed him against the Duke of *Rohan*, that they forbore to speak one to the other for a long time after.

It was not long before the effects of this voyage were seen; for the Letter for their dissolution contrived at *Saumure*, but dispatched from the Court, came, and soon after *Bellugeon*, who declared that they should now receive full satisfaction: But when the Marshal *Bouillon* went up to the Castle, and shewed the Letter to *Du Plessis*, and *La Force*, endeavouring to gain their approbation of it, and the contents of it were fully understood by them, then were they filled with amazement and displeasure; which *Bouillon* perceiving, he thought it convenient that *Du Plessis* should impart the substance of it, to such of the Assembly as he thought fit, that together they might contrive some means to compose all differences. *Bullion* also promises to deferre the delivery of the Letter, out of a seeming desire to seek out some way for an accomodation; and to that end desires a conference with *Du Plessis*, which being yielded unto, after some discourse, they agreed that in case they should proceed to a nomination of six Deputies, and rest satisfied with the answers were given them, he (although he had no Commission for it) should undertake to procure them satisfaction from their Majesties upon the foure or five principal Articles, as, concerning the Chamber of Edicts at *Paris*, Provision for Vacant places, the payment of the remaining part of Nine score thousand Crowns, and the restoring of those places of security were taken from us; and all this to be done before the dissolution of the Assembly; to which as *Du Plessis* was ready to make his report of this conference, *Bullion* sent him word, that he was informed, and that by very good intelligence, that there were some, who intended to take advantage of his discourses the day before; wherefore he retracted them, and desired he might be permitted to go into the Assembly to have the *Queenes* Letter read, and discharge his duty to the Commands he had received from Her.

This sudden change clearly discovered, that the end of this conference was only to amuse the honest party in the Assembly, the better to surprize them before any thing was agreed on; or that they

they were prepared for what they were to do, either in order to their diſſolution, or the Deputation, and cheat them of the thanks and benefit of their pains: But both *Boüillon* and *Bullion* too, were not a little diſmayed when they ſaw, that when upon the reading of the Letter *Berticheres* roſe up, and ſaid, That for his part, he would obey, and that it was fit that thoſe that were of his opinion ſhould likewiſe declare themſelves; all of them with one voice cryed out, that they were more reſolved upon obedience than he, but that the buſineſſe ſhould be further diſcuſſed, when the Commiſſioner was withdrawn, which was accordingly done.

But here it is to be obſerved, that notice being taken of the conſultations which were commonly held night and day in the Marſhal *Boüillon's* Lodgings, by five and twenty of the Aſſembly (which were all he could draw to a confederacy with him) where *Bullion* alſo was often preſent, the reſt of the Aſſembly, to the number of fifty, with one conſent conceived it fitter to yield to the neceſſity of the times, than to make a diviſion, which would inevitably force them to accept for Deputies general, perſons wholly devoted to the Court faction, and that they were better ſeek out ſome other way to redreſs their evils.

The Marſhal *Boüillon* perceiving that the reſolutions taken up by his *Antagoniſts*, had fruſtrated his hopes of procuring ſome creatures of his own to be choſen Deputies general, makes his applications by *Proxy*, to the Duke of *Rohan*, for his conſent to the reſtoring againe of *Bellugeon*, and ſharing the Deputation general between them two: In which the Duke of *Sully* alſo intereſſed himſelf, and ſo farre prevailed with the Duke of *Rohan*, that he cauſed an interview between them at his Lodgings, where the Marſhal entreated him to abate his rigour towards *Bellugeon*, which he promiſed him to do: But as for ſharing the Deputation, he was ſo averſe from the very mention of it, that at the meeting on the day appointed for their election, the Duke of *Sully* openly blamed him for his obſtinacy, telling him that he would ruine all by his wilfulneſs: But the iſſue diſcovered the contrary: For having aſſured himſelf of ten Provinces, he makes them agree to elect the ſix Deputies that ſhould be nominated by the Miniſters of thoſe provinces; which ſucceeded according as he had deſigned it; for not one of thoſe the Marſhal would have promoted (to his extream diſcontent) were ſo much as named. Thoſe that were choſen, were *Montbrun*, *Bertheville*, and *Rouvray* for the Nobility; and *Manald*, *Boiſſeul*, and *Milletiere*, for the Communalty: As for *Bellugeon*, though the Duke of *Rohan* no more oppoſed him, yet was there much difficulty to revoke his cenſure; many

ny times was it debated; at length, when a good part of the Assembly were risen, those that remained, razed it out of their Records: The Regulations for the Assembly were signed also, but theMarshal entred aProtestation under his hand and seal,not to acknowledge the Ministers for a third estate, or order.

And hence sprang the Original of all our mischiefs and divisions; For the Marshal takes his journey to the Court, to receive a recompence for his services, and revenge himself upon all those that had opposed his designs, principally the Duke of *Rohan*, who feared him least, and had withstood him most of any; wherefore he layes a plot to out him of his Town of *Saint John d' Angely*, of which he was Governour, and place therein *La Roche-beaucourt* the King's Lieutenant in his roome,alledging, that if he were once deprived of that retreat, he would be unable to attempt any thing: On the other side, the Duke of *Rohan*, and his brother, at a Consultation held at *Saumure* before their departure thence, with those that were of their opinion,concluded that every one of them should give their respective Provinces an account of what had passed, and instigate them by particular Deputies to the Court, to make new Remonstrances of their aggrievances, which they so happily performed, that in spight of the contradictions of the Commissioners appointed for the execution of the Edict, the years following there came to *Paris* Deputies from twelve Provinces.

In the mean while the Duke of *Rohan* goes to divert himself at his houses in *Britany*, and so to the Assembly of Estates of that Province ; At his return from thence he was informed of the conspiracies laid at *Saint Johns* in prejudice of his authority; to discover which, and also to apply convenient preventions, he sends thither Haulte *Fontaine*,from whom receiving advice of the necessity of his presence, he hasts thither with all *speed*, and as he passed through *Poictou*, gave his friends intelligence of all, and sent *Loudriere* to *Rochel*.

His unexpected arrival much daunted his enemies, who neverthelesse sent for *Roch-beaucourt* to come speedily to their relief; but the Duke of *Rohan*'s friends, flocking in every moment, grew to such a number, as that *Roche-beaucourt* durst not stir, but contented himself with giving the Court an account of what passed: Upon which information the King dispatches away *La Fontaine* to the Duke, in appearance to know what was the matter, but in effect to confirm by letters, and encourage the *Partisans* of *Rochebeaucourt*, which the Duke, having treated him nobly, learnt out of *La Fontaine*, whom he returned with a faithful promise to wait upon their Majesties, with a free account of all his actions, upon their first commands, which within a few dayes after he received;

And

Book I. *The Memoires of the Duke of* Rohan.   15

And prefently fets forward to the Court, taking with him, among others, *Roche-beaucourt,* and *Faucault,* whom he greatly fufpected; and leaving in Saint *John Haulte Fontaine* with all neceffary Orders and Inftructions, that at his return, he might not finde his own gates fhut againft him.   Being arrived at Court, he fhewed the Queen by feveral inftances, that he had behaved himfelf like an honeft man at the Affembly of *Saumure,* and that he had oppofed the Marfhal *Boüillon,* for that he knew, that he took part with thofe of the Reformed Religion, for no other end, but to advance his own Interefts, and render himfelf more confiderable both of the one fide, and the other, and that had he compaffed his defignes, fhe would have been the firft would have felt the effects of his arrogance: But there were no eares open to his juftification, (it being the conftant humour of Princes not eafily to be reafoned out of opinions, they have been prepoffeffed withal) fo that feeing the time for the Election of a new Major for the Town of *Saint John* drew near, and that his abode at Court was to no purpofe, he pretended that his brother was fick, upon which having got leave to be gone, he took poft that very night; which fell out well for him; For the Marfhal *Boüillon* having notice the next day of his departure, was very earneft to have him purfued, and brought back again; but he made fuch hafte, as it was impoffible to overtake him.

As he paffed by *Parc* in the lower *Poictou,* he took *Soubize* along with him, advertifed his friends in *Poictou* of what had happened, and went to *Saint John,* whither *Foucault,* a Captain of the Garrifon, whom he had taken with him to *Paris,* being fent away from the Court, was come before him, and had fecretly affembled the Major and fome others of that *Cabal,* to out the Duke of the Government, and for that end offered them two thoufand men; which the Duke having notice of, prefently upon his arrival at *Saint John,* he commanded *Foucault,* who was then about three or four leagues thence, to return thither no more, and at the fame inftant fent away *Tenis* to their Majefties, to informe them of the juft caufe he had, not to allow the faid *Foucault* any more acceffe to *Saint John.*

The time for the Election of the Major being at hand, which is alwayes the Sunday before *Palme Sunday,* comes *Claverie* from the Court with an exprefs, which fignified, that by reafon of the divifions of the Town, it was the Kings pleafure, for the repofe of it, and the avoiding of factions there, that the old Major fhould be continued, and that this precedent fhould not for the future any way impair the Priviledges of the Town; whereupon the Duke of *Rohan* remonftrates to his Majefty, how that he was mif-informed of the

the condition of the Town, and of what confequence it was, both to his fervice, and the publick peace, that, according to their ancient cuftome, they fhould proceed to Election of a new Major, hoping that this would be affented to, and for that reafon fent his Secretary with this letter to the Court.

Now the Marfhall *Boüillon* rightly imagining, that the Duke of *Rohan* would oppofe the continuation of the old Major, as a thing highly prejudicial to him, engaged the Royal authority in it to the uttermoft, that fo he might either ruine him by his voluntary fubmiffion, or by obliging the King to force him to a complyance; So that two dayes after the arrival of *Claverie* comes *Saint More*, a younger brother of *Montauzier*, and brother in law to *Roch-beaucourt* with another, and ftricter expreffe to the fame purpofe: But the Duke of *Rohan* knowing, that his own ruine would affuredly be the confequence of the loffe of *Saint John*, conceived it leaft dangerous for him to fecure the Town, and feared not to refufe all thofe Orders as prejudicial to the King's fervice, and to proceed to the Election of a new Major, according to the ufual cuftome of the Town, out of three of the Corporation, whofe names were fent by Deputies, conftituted for that purpofe, to his Majefty, to make choice of which of them he pleafed; and for the fecurity of the place, the Keys were, in the interim, put into the hands of the firft Alderman.

The report of thefe things caufed a great buftle at Court; *Tenis*, and *Onglepied*, whom the Duke fome few dayes before, had fent thither, were committed prifoners to the *Baftille*; his mother, wife, and fifters were forbid to go out of *Paris*; and Propofitions were alfo made of drawing down an Army to befiege him; On the otherfide the Duke, well knowing the power of his enemies at Court, and that he was to expect a violent perfecution from them, took great care to make all thofe of the Reformed Religion in *France* fenfible, that the hatred conceived againft him, was occafioned only by the refolution and conftancy he had fhewed to the good of their affairs; that his, and the loffe of *St. John*, would draw after them their deftruction alfo; that if their adverfaries found this eafily accomplifhable, they would not ftop their courfe in fo fair a roade; and then prepares himfelf the beft he could to make a brave refiftance. But at length when all things were more maturely deliberated, the King's Council thought fitter to commit this bufineffe to a Treaty, and *Themines* was fent to the Duke to determinate the difference in a peaccable way: The refult of his negotiation was, That, for eight dayes the Keyes of the Town fhould be left in the hands of the old Major, that they fhould proceed to the nomination of three, out of which the King fhould

make

make choice of one; and, that after this Election *Roche-beaucourt* and *Foucault* should be permitted to return again to execute their charges, provided, notwithstanding that the latter should presently quit the Town again.

Themines sent this agreement to the Court, where at first it was well enough liked of; but when it was communicated to, and scanned by the Dukes enemies, it could by no means be approved of: But *Themines* had orders sent him, to insist upon the return of *Roche-beaucourt* and *Foucault*, before the new Election, which the Duke of *Rohan* consented to; and thus, for the present, was mitigated the heat of this affair, though the persecutions against the Duke of *Rohan* and his party continued in their former violence; especially at Court, where the Marshal *Bouillon* endeavoured, first to corrupt the Deputies, then to make divisions among them; and last of all to destroy their authority: And when the Provinces sent their Deputies to the Court to remonstrate their resentments of the ill impressions were given their Majesties of their loyalty, to vindicate themselves from the calumnies vented against them, and to obtain a grant of all their just demands, so necessary to their subsistence: The Marshal *Bouillon* perceiving, that neither his confederacies in the Provinces, nor the Commissioners purposely sent in to them, could hinder the deputations, turns now his whole endeavours to render their Negotiation fruitless, alledging, that it was a diminution of the Kings authority to give audience to an Assembly convened against his will; that, if their requests were yeilded to, and satisfaction given them that way, it would disgust the loyal part of his subjects, and reunite the now disjoyned Provinces with the Complainants; and openly discovering also great displeasure, that they should repay all his services with slights, and envie; imputing unto him, upon all occasions, what ever mischief befel them: So that, though he could not prevent their audience, he frustrated the contentment they hoped thence, telling the Deputies general freely, that what he did, was in revenge of the affronts he received from the Assembly at *Saumure*.

These things passing thus, the Marshal *Bouillon* continues his ill offices to the interests of those of the Reformed Religion in general, and those of the Duke of *Rohan* in particular; and having obtain'd the Ambassadorship extraordinary for *England* to get the alliance with *Spaine* approved of there, feeds himself also with hopes by the means of that imployment, there to procure a dislike of the actions of the Assembly of *Saumure*: But the Duke of *Rohan* found an opportunity, by a Gentleman that attended on the Marshal in the voyage, to give the King of *England* a true information of all things; so that as to that particular, the answer he he received, was, that if the Queen should be induced to infringe the Edicts made in favour of those of the Reformed Religion, so that it were manifest, that they were persecuted for their Religions sake; his Majesty required, in that case, that neither the League lately made with *France*, nor his present confirmation of the same, should be understood to their prejudice: For Nature teaches every one, when he sees his neighbour assaulted for a quarrel which relates to himself, to foresee what he may expect from the issue of it. As for his part, the King of *England* exhorted the Marshal to a reconciliation with the Duke of *Rohan*, to whom also he intimated his pleasure in that particular: In reference to which, the National Synod then held at *Priuas*, endeavoured it also, and for that end, besides the Deputies general, chose *Du Moulin*, and *Durand*, Ministers, and *L' Isle-gro lot* an Elder, whose care and pains in it were so effectual, that the sixteenth of *August*, in the year 1612. the Marshals Boüillon, and *Lesdeguieres* signed these ensuing Articles, viz. *That they would hearken to a sincere reunion, promising to submit their own particular interests to the common welfare of those of the Reformed Religion, by an Oblivion of all past injuries: That they would freely renounce all resentments, and animosities against any persons, and for what cause soever: That they would love and honour every one according to his ranke and quality, giving them upon all occasions, all testimonies of friendship, as far as the duty of true Christians, and faithful Subjects of the King should oblige and permit them.* They farther also protested, *that they desired nothing more, than by a firm Union and concord to see the Kingdom of God advanced, and the Churches flourish in a happy peace, under the obedience of his Majesty; and, moreover, to imploy all their power, that the authority of the Synods be not invalidated, nor the Discipline infringed; and that they would not favour, nor any wayes assist any particular persons or Churches, that by unjust or prejudicial means should separate from the Union, and conformity to the Doctrine and Discipline received in the Churches.* This Protestation was also signed by the Dukes of *Rohan, Sully,* and *Soubize, La Force,* and *Du Plessis*; to which they desired might be added these following Articles; viz. *To cause this Act to be signed by the Governours of all places of security, and other persons of consideration in the Provinces, and that by the way of Conference; and, that a Clause might be inserted, by which they should oblige themselves to observe, as well all Politique, as Ecclesiastical order, and to restore and confirm the authority of the Deputies general in their charges.*

But for all these goodly appearances, the persecutions against those

Book I. *The Memoires of the Duke of* Rohan. 19

those of the Religion, and the Duke of *Rohan*, ceased not; which enforced them at last, upon the grievances of the Province of *Xaintonge* to call an Assembly of five Provinces, according to the regulation of the Assembly of *Saumure*.

Whiles these things were a doing, there hapned a new accident, which hastned the Assembly: *Berticheres*, supported with the power of the Constable, the Decree of the Assembly of *Saumure*, and the favor of the Court, would needs repossesse his government of *Aiguemortes*: But the Province, advertised of his demeanour by *Saugeon* (whom the Duke had sent thither purposely with a character of him) so ordered that affair, that, in spight of the Constable, they maintained *Arembures* in it, and kept *Berticheres* out; which so incensed him, that he made *Saugeon* a prisoner at *Ville-franck* in *Rouergue*, which was more than he could do in his own government. When the Duke of *Rohan*, and the Province of *Xaintonge* heard this, they avowed the voyage, and owned the cause of *Sangeon*: The Assembly also met at *Rochel*, notwithstanding the ill usage, and traverses occasioned them by the Marshal *Bouillon*, who showed himself more their enemy, than all the Kings Council beside (notwithstanding his engagement passed to the King of *England*, and the Deputies of the National Synod) and instigated the Clergy of *France* to go to the *Queen*, and hinder her giving any favourable answers to those of the Religion, supposing that such rigor would force them upon extremities, & would make them appear guilty of a desire of war, and give him an occasion to interpose as a mediator for them at Court; that so, he might render himself useful to both parties, and whatever happened, still make up his own reckoning.

On the other side, *Du Plessis* tired with these persecutions, from which he himself was not exempted, and fearing what the issue of these disturbances would be, interposes for the composing of them, and comes to *Rochel* accompanied with *Rouvray*, one of the Deputies general, and brother to his son in law, bringing with him a draught of some Articles, not signed: But the successe of his negotiation, not answering his expectation, he withdrew again, and with him, the Province of *Anjou*, (one of the five assembled) Neverthelesse, the other four continued well united, and by Messengers, desired the Duke of *Rohan's* presence at *Rochel*, to consult with them about what was to be done: When he came, it was resolved, that they should send a Gentleman to the *Queen*, in the name of the Provinces, to accept, for the present, the offers had been made them, referring the pursuance of the rest to the Deputies general. But hearing, in the mean time, of the commotions at the Court, of a bold action committed in the assassination of

C 2　　　　　the

the Baron *de Luz*, to the great displeasure of the *Queen*, and violation of her authority; the Assembly took the boldness to send *Le Parc*, *d' Archiat*, and *Cressonniere* to their Majesties, with protestations of their loyalty, and offers of their service, choosing rather to submit to their pleasures in accepting the offers made them, than to augment the present troubles by their importunities: *Bessay* also made a Speech to the same effect, in the behalf of the Duke of *Rohan*; and all were well received at Court: Thus ended this Assembly, which though continually traversed, as is before related, brought more benefit to the Publick, and comfort to the Duke of *Rohan*, than that of *Saumure*.

The *Articles* agreed on (and pretty well observed) were,

1. That the King's Atturneys should have Orders to receive the Attestations of the Ministers, without compelling them to add the Epithet, *Pretended*, to the Reformed Religion.
2. That the Ecclesiastical persons should be permitted the enjoyment of the same liberty, they had in the raign of the late King.
3. That they have a Toleration of Provincial Councils, for the ordering of their Politick affairs, as in the late Kings time.
4. That the Ministers, as well as other Ecclesiastical persons in *France*, may be exempted from the payment of all Taxes and Subsidies, and that all necessary provisions to this effect, be given them.
5. That all the Edicts be published anew, together with a Declaration, confirming all Grants, Favours, and Concessions of the late King, with an Act of Oblivion, and a Decree, that all proceedings commenced against those of the Reformed Religion become null, and as if they had never been.
6. That the Inhabitants of *Rochel* be permitted to enquire into the occasion of what hapned at *Couldray*; and be also freed from the jealousies they may justly derive from the two near approach of the Ships, and that, to that end, they be commanded to ride farther from the shore.
7. That the Remonstrances of the lower *Languedoc* be received concerning *Aiguemortes*; that provision be made for it; and that, in the mean time, the place be committed to the care of *Chastillon*.
8. That the razing of *Vessieres* be suspended, and the Remonstrances of the Province of *Languedoc*, concerning that particular, be received.

9. That

Book I. *The Memoires of the Duke of* Rohan. 21

9. That nothing be changed in the *Mas d' Agenois* in the lower *Guienne*, and that *La Vessiere* be replaced there.
10. That the Count of *Panias* be desired by letter, to continue the Captain *Pre* in his command under him, in *Mansiete*.
11. That the troops which are in *Xaintonge, Poictou,* and the places adjacent, be removed.
12. That *Roche-beaucourt*, and *Foucault*, be sent out of *Saint John*.
13. That the one of their Companies shall be given to the Duke of *Rohan*, and the other to the King's Lieutenant, which shall be placed there, in the place of *La Roche-beaucourt*, but with the approbation and good-liking of the Duke of *Rohan*.
14. That the Office of Serjeant Major of the place becoming void, either by death, or demission of the Officer, it shall be supplyed as the Duke shall please.
15. That the pensions of the Dukes of *Rohan*, and *Soubize*, shall be paid, both the arreares, and what shall for the future accrue.
16. That no violence be done to the friends or servants of the Duke of *Rohan*; that those that had pensions shall receive them, as before the Assembly of *Saumure*; and that no injury be done to the Baron *de Saugeon*, but that he be restored to his liberty.

Whiles the Court raised these tempests in the Provinces, it self was not free from commotions. The Marshal *d' Ancre*, who had ingrossed the whole favour of the Queen, bred, and cherished divisions among the great ones, lest their union should obstruct his advancement; so equally ballancing all parties, that neither could over-poise the other, and continually fomenting envie and jealousies among them, lest their reconciliation should prove his ruine: They on the other side suffering themselves to be hurried on by the violence of passion, rather than led by the calmer conduct of reason, so that all the Princes of the blood were seen in opposition one against the other, and those also of the house of *Lorraine*, according as their present enjoyments, or hopes of future favour moved them: But at length the Prince of *Conde* upon the Queens refusal to give him *Chasteau Trompette*, raised a party of discontents, under pretence of reforming the disorders in the government of the State; The Marshal *Boüillon* the main contriver of this Party, managed it with such artifice, that he caused the Prince, the Dukes of *Longueville, Nevers, Maine,* and others, to absent themselves from the Court, whom he himself followed the last of all, and with the Queens consent too, upon the hopes he had given her

her of reducing all thofe Princes; And with fuch dexterity handled he the affair, that he became both the Author and compofer of it; in which there was one very remarkable thing to be taken notice of, which was, that he imparted the whole bufineffe to the knowledge of the Duke of *Rohan*'s moft faithful friends, and concealed it from his own, whom in other things he had alwayes trufted; for that he very well knew the corruption and falfhood of the one, and the integrity and fidelity of the other.

The Prince with his Partifans retired to *Mezieres*, a Town belonging to the Duke of *Nevers*, near *Sedan*; The Duke of *Maine* who was Governour of the Ifle of *France*, with the Towns of *Soiffons*, *Noyons*, and the Caftle of *Pierrefons*; the Marqueffe *de Ceuvres* with *Laon*; all very confiderable places, together with the Duke of *Longueville*, Governour of *Picardy*, with all the friends and fervants they could mufter in their governments joyning to the frontires of *Germany*, and *Flanders*, with the reft of the difcontents in *France*, made up a very formidable party; to which I fhall not adde, that upon the retaining of thefe Male-contents from the Court, the Duke of *Vendofme* being apprehended in the *Louvre*, and there detained prifoner; a few dayes after made his efcape, and got into *Britany* his own government, where he made great preparations alfo.

Things being in this condition, the *Prince* writes a letter to the *Queen*, whofe contents were nothing but complaints of the diforders committed in the State under her authority; that the Princes of the blood, Dukes, Peers, and Officers of the Crown were excluded from the Publick affairs, which were managed by three or four only, who to maintain their own height, fowed divifions among the Nobility, lavifhing the treafures, and at their pleafure, difpofing of them, the Arfinals and Frontire Garrifons, which were intrufted in the hands of ftrangers, who were in no wife refponfible for them; that they defired an Affembly of the States General, according to the Cuftome, during the Minorities of their Kings, in which the *Queen* fhould finde a legal provifion made for the fupport of her authority, the prefervation of the Lawes, and reforming all abufes that obftructed the admininftration of them. He writes alfo to the Parliament of *Paris*, and all the Grandees not yet confederated with him, to invite them to a Conjunction with his Party; and to the Deputies general alfo, telling them that thofe of the Religion were not forgotten in his Remonftrances; He fent alfo *Le Maretz* Lieutenant of his guards, to the Duke of *Rohan* to court him to arme in his behalf, protefting that he would not liften to any agreement, but with his confent: But the Duke who on the one fide knew very well the credit the Marfhal
Bouillon

Boüillon had gained among his most intimate confidents; and on the other, remembring the continual ill offices he had received from him ever since the Assembly of *Saumure*, and being not unjealous that the war was only declared in words, whil'st in truth they were already entred into a Treaty, resolved to send *Haultfontaine*, in whom he reposed great confidence, along with *Manetz*, to make a discovery of the true posture of the *Prince* his affairs; and in the interim made his addresses by letter to the Queen, assuring her, that he would continue united with the whole body of those of the Religion, to whom if she pleased to vouchsafe some satisfaction, she should reclaime her discontents at an easie rate.

In the mean while the *Prince* came to *Saint Menehould*, a strong place within the government of the Duke of *Nevers*, which he had secured; and there also arrived *Hault-fontaine*, where, instead of a war proclaimed, he found a Treaty well advanced; He was received with much honour, and admitted also to their Counsels; Upon his arrival, it was given out, that he came with an offer of eight thousand foot, and two thousand horse from his Master, on purpose to hasten the Treaty, and yet was he sent back to the Duke with an assurance that there should be none, and a request to raise armes: But *Hault-fontaine* assured him that the Peace was concluded, and that *Amboise* was to be given to the Prince, *Menehould* to the Duke of *Nevers*, and a round summe of money to the Duke of *Boüillon*, and that an Assembly of the States general was promised; which in a short time after was performed: And thus did their own private interests intercept their regard to the consideration of the publick.

The Duke of *Vendosme*, who, after his escape, had levied many men in *Britany*, and engaged himself in the fortification of *Blavet*, was much troubled to see himself thus forlorne: He sent *Roche Giffar* to the Duke of *Rohan*, with earnest perswasions to joyne with him, which were well mixed with faire promises in favour of those of the Religion: But all could extract no other answer from him, than that the best counsel could be given him, was to digest, as well as he could, his dereliction, and in time, to comply, lest his obstinacy should draw upon him an inevitable ruine. But this advice had no operations upon his resolutions; though the Prince, when he came into *Poictou*, added his perswasions too, and endeavours to approve of his precipitation of the peace: The Prince was also very serious to see the Duke of *Rohan*, who to satisfie him in that particular, came to *La Roche des Aubieres in Anjou*, where he shews him, how he had been forced to shuffle up a peace the best he could, for that the Marshal *Boüillon*, ambitious of all the thanks and profit, had debauched and seduced most of his party (speaking well indeed of none but the Duke of *Nevers*) so that he was constrained to accept of *Amboise*; That he hoped to procure an Assembly of the States General, in which his party would be the most prevalent, for that every one in their Province, stickled hard for him; and that it was there, the affairs of the Kingdom should have a redress, and the Nobility enjoy their dignities, or else that they should have more forces, and a better pretence for a War; that though he had cast off many Gentlemen and Souldiers, yet he regarded not that much; for that he knew, *France* was alwayes well stored with discontents.

To which was answered, that the States would rather oppose his designs, and instead of augmenting, lessen his authority; for that the fear of evil, and hope of good, the most prevalent motives upon the affections of men, were from the *Queen*, not him; and that the reason, why many refused to take Armes, though he commanded them, was, because he himself did not, but had made his peace; for which he was upbraided both by the Duke of *Rohan*, and his brother; of which he excused himself the best he could, with many large protestations of friendship to them, and a high approbation of the Counsel they had given the Duke of *Vendosme*; and thus was their interview terminated: After which, the Prince to make his advantage of all, wrote to the President *Janin*, that he had desired a meeting from the Duke of *Rohan* for no other end, but to break off the confederacy between the Duke of *Vendosme* and him.

This being past, all parties were very industrious to procure a nomination of such Deputies in the Provinces, for the States General, to be convened at *Paris* the winter following, as were most devoted to them; And in the mean while the *King* and *Queen* took their journey towards *Britany* to reduce the Duke of *Vendosme*: When they came to *Poictieres*, *Villeroy* dispatches to the Duke of *Rohan* one *Villette* (whom he knew to be a friend of his) to let him know, that their Majesties passing within twenty Leagues of him, would take it ill if he neglected to come and wait upon them, assuring him of a fair reception; and that it was such an opportunity to set himself right againe with them, as in prudence he ought not to let slip: Upon this encouragement he went thither, where, after a very good welcome given him, they engaged him to be present at the States of *Britany* to be held at *Nantes*, where all their propositions were answered with a free assent to them, whether they concerned the Deputations for the States General, or the Duke of *Vendosme*, who was forced to pre-

present himself before them, and wholly submit himself to their pleasures. This done, they returned thence, it being presently after the Autumn, to *Paris*, whither a general curiosity carried every one to see what would be the issue of the States General. The Prince was in very good intelligence with the strongest party in the Parliament, occasioned rather by their hatred to the present government, than by any influence from his vertue or good conduct; for had his life and actions been in any degree proportionable to his pretences, and Remonstrances, he would have much disturbed the Queens government.

Come we now to the States, who assembled at *Paris* about the latter end of *October*, in the year 1614: where all things passed according to the Queens desire, who notwithstanding dissolved them, without giving them any satisfaction at all: The Prince was faine to yield up *Amboise* againe, which he had gotten at the Treaty of *Saint Menehould*; and that by the advice of the Marshal *Boüillon*, who thought by shewing the power he had over the first Prince of the blood, who only might lawfully question the actions of the Queen, to render himself so acceptable and considerable, that of necessity he should be employed in the management of the publick affairs: But remembring that his services had been less recompensed than his disservices, and that men stood in awe of that aspiring spirit, so apt and ready for any great undertakings, he resolves to imploy it again to mischief; and taking occasion from the ill propositions made in the States, from the treacheries discovered there, by a presumption to establish the Papal in prejudice of the Royal Authority, from the Decree made by them for the consummating the Marriages with *Spaine*, from the prodigious greatness of the Marshal *d'Ancre* universally envyed, and maligned, especially in *Paris*; and from the discontents the Deputies the States carried back into their provinces, all which things he so dexterously ordered for his purposes, that from that foundation he raised a *broülliery* of that importance, that even those that thought not at all of meddling in it, were insensibly engaged in the party.

The better to arrive at his aimes, the Marshal *Boüillon* drew into the confederacy with the Prince all the Grandees of the Kingdome, whom either some particular injuries received, or envy (the basest, yet most common vice of all) had discontented; handles the Parliament of *Paris* so handsomely, that the greatest part of them favoured his design, prevailed so farre upon the English Embassadour, that he incited his Master to countenance his party, and made *Rouvray*, *Desbordes-Mercier*, and *Bertheville*, Deputies General from the Assembly of those of the Religion, persons of great abilities, and good repute, his own; shewing them the remedies he would apply to the disorders of the State, the advantages should thence accrue to those of the Religion in general, and themselves in particular; to wit, to the one the place of Embassadour into the *Low Countreys*, to the other the revenue of a Counsellor in the Chamber of Edicts; and to the third, the Deputation General; all very perswasive arguments.

When he had thus disposed his affairs, leave was granted for an Assembly to be held at *Jergeau*, the fourth day of *April*, which place was judged improper for a free debate, and attaining the ends proposed; wherefore it was removed to *Grenoble* the fifteenth of *July*, one thousand six hundred and fifteen, upon the instant request of the Deputies General, and the Provinces, and the assurance the Marshal *Lesdiguieres* gave the *Queen*, that he would order all things so, that she should have no cause to feare the issue of it; which place, though the vast power, and well-known humour of the Marshal might cast some umbrages of suspicion on it, could not however be refused, because that *Dauphine* was a Province, in which those of the Religion were most numerous and powerful, and where without danger they could not be disgusted.

Whiles these things were in agitation, great care was taken to incense the spirits of the *Parisians*, and with such effect, that the Parliament set forth a Declaration, inviting the Prince and Peers to joyne with them in their Consultations; which though they were checked for, yet desisted they not, but proceeded to the presenting of very bold Remonstrances to the King himself, whose substance was, that he ought not to begin the first yeare of his Majority with such absolute commands, nor accustome himself to such actions, which good Kings, as himself, very rarely had recourse to, and after an exaggeration of the great and signal services of their Court ever since its first establishment, and that all the weighty and most important affaires of the State were managed by their Counsel, or that the Kings had repented it, they remonstrate the displeasure they had to see that the Late States should endeavour to subvert the Fundamental Law of the Kingdome, by rendering the Soveraign power of the King doubtful, and problematick; that for the suppression of such pernicious Maximes, and that his Soveraignty which he holds only and immediately from *God* himself, be not upon any pretence whatsoever subjected to any other power, it were necessary to ordaine, that the Original Laws of the Nation, and the occasional decrees founded on them be renewed and put in execution; and those held for enemies to the State, that would subject the Royal Authority to

any

any forraign domination: Moreover they remonſtrate alſo how neceſſary it were to continue the ancient Alliances, and forraigne Confederacies renewed by the late King; that the King ſhould be alſo adviſed by the Princes, Officers of the Crown, and veterane Counſellours, perſons experienced and intereſſed in the State, and that none be permitted to receive penſions of forraigne Princes or States: That all Officers be protected in the diſcharge of their duty: That for the future no ſurvivances or reverſions of Offices be granted: That the Military commands be not Vendible: That the governments of provinces, ſtrong places, and principal Military commands be not conferred on ſtrangers: That for the conſervation of the dignity and ſplendour of the Romiſh Religion, without derogating from the Edicts of pacification, and for the preſervation of the priviledges of the *Gallick* Church, and rectifying the abuſes crept into it by means of *Suffragans* and *Coadjutors*, there be not ſuffered any multiplication of new Religious orders; and that Biſhopricks be conferred on perſons of good Families, and ſuitable qualifications, both for age and vertue: That the courſe of Juſtice be free, and all obſtructors of it puniſhed; and that the Kings Council upon applications made to them, may not abrogate any decrees of the Parliament; but that thoſe who would ſue for relief againſt them, do it by the uſual and Legal wayes: That no pardon be granted to any Murtherers: That Edicts and Ordinances againſt Duels be obſerved: That the decrees of the Kings Council be more ſtable, and not reverſeable upon every occaſion, either for money or favour: That the exactions and irregularities committed in the Chanceryes of the Parliaments, and Preſidial ſeats, and Taxes raiſed without verification in Parliament be ſuppreſſed: That all ſocieties of Counſellors of Eſtate, Intendants, and other Officers of the *Finances*, or Exchequer, together with all partnerſhips, be forbidden: That all publick gaming, and tippling-houſes be ſuppreſſed: That proviſion be made againſt the abuſes of treaſurers, and the offendors puniſhed; and that the exceſs of rewards be moderated: That the Government of the Exchequer be intruſted but to a few perſons, as in the time of the late King: That the profuſion of the treaſures may be compued from this; that the Revenue is greater now, than in the late Kings time, who ſpent every yeare in buildings and other expences, now taken off, three millions of Livers; and laid up two millions; that if thoſe five millions had been laid up every yeare ſince his death, there would be in the Treaſury twenty millions; beſides the fourteen millions he left there, which, to the great regret of all good *French* men, are now conſumed; extravagancies of ſuch a nature, as will quickly

ſend

send *France* a begging, if not remedied; which cannot be but by a strict inquiry into the actions of those that have been guilty of these male-administrations, of which they know their Majesties to be intirely innocent: Wherefore they most humbly implore their leave, to put in execution their decree made in *March*, one thousand six hundred and fifteen, promising to disclose to them things of great concernments to the State, which are yet hidden from them; by means of which, provision may be made for prevention of all these disorders: But in case that the evil Counsels, and crafty Artifices of persons interessed herein, shall hinder these Remonstrances of a faire reception, the said Parliament solemnly protests, That for the discharge of their consciences, for the service of their Majesties, and preservation of the State, they shall be obliged hereafter to nominate freely the Authors of these abuses, and lay open to the world their wicked comportments, that remedies may be applyed in due season, when the affairs will more conveniently admit of them, and his Majesty shall please to take better notice of them.

This Remonstrance wrought the designed effect, procuring the Parliament a sharp check, and affectionating them so much the more to the Prince his party: Hence ensued great animosities and very liberal discourses of all sides; and presently after, came Letters from the *Prince* to the *King*, the *Queen*, and all the Grandees both of the Court and Parliament, together with his Declaration, which resuming the business from before the War of *Saint Menehould*, complaines of the irregularities in the elections of the Deputies for the States general, of the elusion of the Article proposed by the third Estate or Commons, for securing the life and authority of the King, against the designes of the Pope; of the excessive Offices and exorbitant power of the Marshal *d' Ancre*, and his extravagancies in the administration of them, presuming to deprive the Princes of their governments, and procuring Laws oppressive to the people, for the satisfying of his own avarice, and ambition, disposing of all the Offices of the Kingdome, as well Ecclesiastical as Temporal, infringing the liberty of the States, to which the Prince was forbid an access, causing the Parliament of *Paris* to receive a smart reproof for their Remonstrance; concluding the marriages with *Spaine*, without communicating the business to those it ought to be imparted to, by such practices slighting and deserting the Ancient *Allyes* of the Crown, and among others the Duke of *Savoy*; who, to the great dishonour of *France*, is suffered to be trampled in the dust; causing a refusal of the propositions made by the Nobility to the States, for the observation of the Edicts of Pacification; attempting to induce

power: The Prince and further demanded, that before they proceed to a consummation of the marriages with *Spaine*, some course be taken for regulating the Counsels, and reforming, and composing the abuses and disorders in the State: About which, he had several conferences with *Villeroy*, to amuse and intrap him, rather than out of an intention to contrive any remedies for them: At length upon the Summons given him by *Pontchartraine*, to the voyage into *Guienne* to consummate the Marriages, foreseeing thence the wrack of his hopes, and pretences of a good Reformation, he declares that the Armes he had raised, had no other aime than the preservation of the Kings authority, and the glory, and honour of the Nation, inviting all good *French* men, both of the one, and the other Religion to joyn with him, and all the Ancient *Allyes* of the Crown, to favour him in so good a design.

When the Prince had published this Declaration, he made his Levyes in *France* and *Germany*, and took his Canon at *Sedan*: The King also raised an Army of ten thousand Foot, and fifteen hundred Horse, Commanded by the Marshal *de Bois-Dauphin*, to oppose the discontents, and with other Troops sets forward towards *Guienne*, attended on by the Duke of *Guise*, who was to conduct *Madame* the Kings sister to the Frontieres of *Spaine*, and there to receive the *Infanta*, and waite on her back to the King.

In the mean time the *Prince* earnestly sollicites the Assembly at *Grenoble*, by his Agent *La Hay*, who delivers them his *Manifesto*, and shews them the advantages would redound to those of the Religion, in case the Assembly would comply with him in reforming the State, and opposing the matches with *Spaine*; and further engages himself not to conclude any thing, but by their advice. The Prince his party, nor their adherents, durst not open their mouths to second this motion; But yet the others imagining that from so important an opportunity they might with good reason derive strong hopes of obtaining some favour from the King, they deputed *Champeaux*, *Desbordes-Mercier*, and *Mailleray*, to him, who found him at *Tours*, and presented to him five and twenty Articles of greatest consequence to their Interests, humbly supplicating him to vouchsafe them some satisfaction thereupon. Of these Deputies, *Desbordes-Mercier* was of the Prince his faction, the other two were of the same opinion with the Duke of *Rohan*, who

thought

thought the first equally affected to him with the others; of whose abilities being very conscious, he reposed an entire confidence in him: He received Letters from him from *Poictiers*, which gave him notice of their dissatisfaction, and urged him to a conjunction with the Prince, assuring him that the Assembly would be well satisfied with it, and also do the like themselves: The other two Deputies governed by this, joyned in this intelligence, informing him moreover, how much their Majesties slighted the Assembly, so that adding to this, the refusal made him of the Survivance, or Reversion of the Government of *Poictou*, (to which his father-in-law had given his consent) contrary to the solemne promises passed to him for it; together with the perswasions of his brother the Duke of *Soubize*, who was well affected to the Prince, he began to stagger a little: Besides, in his return to *Saint John*, from *Saint Maixant*, where he had been to see the Duke of *Sully*, he met a Gentleman belonging to the Count of *Saint Paul*, who desired his assistance to oppose the Marriages with *Spaine*; and was seconded by *Saint Angel*, *Savignac*, and *Doradour*, who in the name of all the Governours, and Nobility of the Religion, sollicited the same thing, and chose him for their General, confirming him with an assurance, that the Count of *Saint Paul* would deliver up *Fronsac* to *La Force*, as a pledge for the performance of his word.

The accumulation of all these things, to wit, the hope of Redeeming himself from the neglect and slights lately thrown upon him; the sollicitation of his brother, together with the desire he had to serve those of the Religion, overpoised his former resolutions, and sent him into *Guienne*, where he found that the Count of *Saint Paul*, with the Romish Catholicks, had made their peace, and a great confusion among those of the Religion; nevertheless, having gotten together *La Force*, *Boisse-Pardaillan*, *Chasteau-neuf*, *Favas*, and *Pamissant*, with others of the Religion, it was resolved, that they should make use of the leasure afforded them by the Kings stay at *Poictiers*, occasioned by the sickness of *Madame* the Princess, to prepare for a War; feeding themselves with hopes to raise an Army of six thousand Foot, and five hundred Horse, which at their first Rendezvouz amounted but to six hundred Foot, and fifty Horse; nor could all their power ever bring more, than two thousand men together; so that the King easily, and without any interruption got to *Bourdeaux*, whence the Queen Mother dispatched *Chesnay* to the Duke of *Rohan*, with very fair offers, upon condition that he would joyne with her: But neither he, nor *Bois-de Cargois*, who was deputed from the Assembly with the like Commission, could get any

other

other anſwer from him, than, That he would not faile to make good his word, where he had engaged it: But this failing, the Queen endeavours to take off *La Force*, and *Boiſſe-Pardaillan* from him; As for the former, he conceived himſelf oblig'd to the defence of *Bearn*, and the other perſiſted in his integrity.

The Duke of *Rohan's* chiefeſt care now was to engage in the party he had embraced, all the Towns, and Communalties of the Religion, together with the Aſſembly General, whom by expreſs Meſſengers, he advertiſes, that upon the refuſal of favourable anſwers to their propoſitions, and the earneſt ſollicitations of their Deputies, he had now declared in *Guienne*, and his brother in *Poictou*, perſwading them to own their actions, and adhere to the Prince: The Duke of *Soubize*, who had ſtaid at *Saint John* during the Kings abode at *Poictiers*, immediately after his departure, makes his levyes in *Poictou*, and *Xaintonge*, and ſuddenly took the field with four thouſand good Foot, and five hundred Horſe, which were very opportunely ready to receive the Prince at his arrival there.

In the mean time the Duke of *Guiſe* conducts the *Princeſſe* towards *Spaine*, and brings thence the *Infanta*; whoſe voyage afforded the Duke of *Rohan* the opportunity to ſeize upon *Lectour*, by the aſſiſtance of *Fonterailles*, who let him into the Town, where, when he was entered, he beſieged the Caſtle, and forced it to ſurrender, before the Duke of *Guiſe* could relieve it, or the Aſſembly of the higher *Languedoc* interrupt his deſign: From thence he marches to *Verdun* and *Mauvoiſin*, which he could by no means draw to his party; and thence to *Montaubane*, which, though with much reluctancy, he got to declare for him: In this March he met with the Duke of *Candale*, who diſcovered to him his intention of embracing the Reformed Religion; after mutual complements they part, and the Duke of *Rohan* keeps on his way towards *Languedoc*, to the Aſſembly, who by reaſon they had not the freedome they expected at *Grenoble*, were adjourned to *Niſmes*, where his dexterous endeavours had ſuch happy ſucceſs, that maugre the power of *Chaſtillon*, which the vertue of his Anceſtors had acquired him; he deſtroyed all his credit with them, made himſelf be acknowledged General of the *Sevenes*, and ſo prevailed upon the Aſſembly, that all the oppoſition *Chaſtillon* could make in it, or in *Languedoc*, could not hinder their conjunction with the Prince; whoſe *Partiſans* ſeeing themſelves backed by the Dukes of *Rohan*, *Sully*, and *Soubize*, at that time carried all before them; and *Desbordes-Mercier*, *Cruſel*, and *Novialle*, were deputed to carry the Act of Union to the Prince, and get his signature to the Articles agreed on: whose substance was,

> To oppose the reception of the Council of Trent; and the marriages with Spain.
>
> To procure a reformation of the Council, and an observation of the Edicts made in favour of those of the Religion; and that they should not desert one another, lay down their Armes, nor hearken to any pacification, but by a mutual consent.

At *Montauban* heard the Duke the first news from the Prince, though he had dispatched several Messengers to him; and thither he sent him word, That, notwithstanding the opposition of a strong and well-marshalled Army, he had passed the Rivers of *Marne*, *Seine*, and the *Loire*; and that having gotten the start of the adverse Army, he was now marching to joyn with him in *Guienne*, desiring him to march towards the *Dordoigne*, and for the security of his passage, possess himself of some places upon that River; which he quickly did, taking among others, *Soüillac*, one of the best passes on it, and beating up the Quarters of the Count of *Lauzune*'s Regiment that was barricado'd in two great Villages.

But the Prince, instead of that, took the way of *Poictou*; where he very seasonably met with the Duke of *Soubize*; for he was very weak in Foot, and his whole Army so harassed, that had not the Town of *Saint John* received him, and the Duke of *Sully* at length, with much ado joyned with him, causing also all the places he held in *Poictou* to declare for his party, he would have been but in a sad condition.

In the mean while their Majesties return towards *Tours*, the Duke of *Guise* commanding the Army of the Marshal *de Bois Dauphin*, and the Duke *d' Espernon*, with another, having the charge of their conduct: All these conjunctions with the Prince, raised him from the contempt he lay under, to so considerable a height in the opinions of his Adversaries, that he is now sued to for an accommodation.

Now it is to be understood that the Marshal *Boüillon* and the Duke of *Mayne*, being more strictly ligued, and of greater intimacy with the Prince than any of the whole party besides, and consequently more sought after by the Court, resolved to have a peace, and purchase their own conditions at the expence of the whole confederacy: In order to which, a Cessation of armes is agreed on, and the Town of *Loudun* made choice, of for the place of Treaty; Invitations were sent also to the Assembly General,

Book I.   *The Memoires of the Duke of* Rohan.   33

to draw as near to them as *Saint Foy*, where the Marshal *Boüillon* was in great reputation : But the Duke of *Rohan* being advertised by his brother of all their plots, discovered to his friends in the Assembly the whole mystery, and let them know, that it were expedient the Assembly should instantly remove to *Rochell*, where their authority would be greater, and their strength more considerable; and that for his part he was resolved to go to the Treaty, though not summoned to it, leaving *Boeße Pardaillan*, in his absence to command in *Guienne*.

Before we proceed to the particularities of the Treaty, there are two very observable things to be taken notice of. The first was the Duke of *Nevers* his arming, without declaring for either side, but pretending as a Mediatour to enforce both parties to an accommodation, out of an apprehension he might give them to sway the ballance on that side he should incline to : A thing feasable by the King of *England*, or of *Spaine*, but a ridiculous attempt for him. The other was nothing more Judicious, and that was a resembling action of the Duke of *Vendosmes*, who by the King's Commissions had raised a considerable force, but joyned not with the Prince till after the truce; so that, he served for nothing but to inhaunce the conditions of that party he declared for, and frustrating himself of all means to make his own, being of himself not considerable, attracts to himself the *odium* and malignity borne to the whole party.

At this Treaty there were present of the Kings part, the Marshal *Brissac*, *Villeroy*, the President *d' Thou*, *d' Vic*, and *Pontchartraine*, who sedulously sought by sowing divisions among them, to weaken the confederates, and consequently lessen their conditions : The Prince, weary of the War, pretends nothing but a desire of peace, renouncing in appearance, all further thoughts of the publick affairs, and demanding only a satisfaction of the interests of particular persons, but resolving principally to find his own there too : He had ingaged to the Duke of *Vendosme*, not to consent to any peace, unless he had the Castle of *Nantes* given him : To the Duke of *Longueville* he promised the *Cittadell* of *Amiens*, and to those of the Religion, a confirmation of the Edicts : But when the Duke of *Mayne*, and the Marshal *Boüillon* were arrived at their ends, they quitted all thoughts, but how to make the rest relinquish theirs, to effect which, they used all manner of Artifices, the most crafty and pregnant inventions could furnish them with : But the admirable constancy of the Assembly General at *Rochell*, and the firm union between the other Grandees, threw insuperable difficulties in the way to their designs.   D   But

But in the mid'st of these transactions, the Prince falls desperately sick, which caused a great confusion among them all, and made them more sollicitous to have this affair dispatched: The Duke of *Sully* was desired to go to the Assembly, and represent to them the dangers, that attended the present condition of things, whence he returned, with a full assurance of their good inclinations to peace; which three dayes after, they confirmed by ten Deputies they sent with an express charge to supercede all former demands, that might retard the conclusion of the Treaty; confining themselves to an obtention only of all expedients, necessary to confirm and secure to them their former Concessions: Among which were the continuation of the Assembly where it was, untill the verification of the Edict; the disbanding of the Armyes; the restitution of *Tartas*; and the dispatch of the Commissioners appointed to put the Edict in execution, according as the Duke of *Sully* had promised them in the Princes name; which he clearly made appeare by his instructions, when the Prince receded from the aforesaid promise: But the King's Commissioners encouraged under hand, insisted eagerly on the dissolution of the Assembly, which had like to have broken all, had not the Duke of *Sully*, pregnant in evasions to prevent mischiefs, firmly persisted in his endeavours to compose the business, offering another Writing to the Commissioners, which they approved of, and desired him to procure the Deputies of the Assembly their assent to it also, which, with the assistance of the Dukes of *Rohan*, *Cazdale*, and *Soubize*, he so happily endeavoured, that they assented to it, upon condition, that there might be an alteration of some termes; And forasmuch as the Commission of the Deputies was too restrictive, they joyntly sent an express to Remonstrate to the Assembly the necessity of terminating this affaire, and to that end desire such an enlargement of their power, as should oblige them to ratifie what they should conclude in their names, and with the advice of the Grandees of the Religion: The Duke of *Sully* thinking he had now finished all, carries the said Writing to the King's Commissioners, with whom were present the Dukes of *Nevers*, *Maine*, and *Bouillon*, who all confirmed it, and after them the Deputies also: But when he returned with it againe to the Commissioners, they denyed what they had done; but yet as the Duke was going from them, they recalled him againe, and after much contestation came once more to an agreement: After which they all met at the Duke of *Nevers* his Lodgings, who treated the whole company at Dinner; where the King's Commissioners, for the third time, so altered the Writing, that there was nothing left of its first

design

Book I. *The Memoires of the Duke of* Rohan.

design; for which reason the Duke of *Sully* would no more trouble himself with it.

Whereupon the Prince caused the Grandees to be called to sign the Peace; he was yet so ill that he could neither understand it, when it was read, nor comprehend the difficulties yet to be surmounted: Nevertheless he called the Duke of *Sully* to know what hindered the signing of it, which being told him, he calls *Villeroy*, and having whispered something to him very softly, presently declares to the Duke of *Sully*, that *Villeroy* had given him the Writing just as it was at first designed with the advice and consent of the Duke; and without expecting the Answer of the Assembly, or any reason to the contrary, signed it: Whereupon the Duke of *Bouillon* had many sharp contests, real, or pretended, and delusory, with *Villeroy*, for that he desired that the English Embassadour, who had been a great instrument of the Peace, should sign it too, which the other opposed as a thing neither handsome, nor honorable for the King to suffer.

This precipitate signing of the Peace by the Prince, occasioned great and general murmurings among the rest of the Party, that saw themselves thus deserted by those that were the Authors of the Warre: And the Duke of *Bouillon*, to enhaunce the price of the services he had done the King, bitterly inveighs against the Assembly, branding them, and all that should abet them, with the name of Rebells; offered to march against them, and declared that he should esteem for enemies to the State, all those that upon any pretence whatsoever, should refuse to signe the peace; But neither his, nor the threats of the Commissioners prevailed ought upon the others constancy. And because this brangling was a disturbance to the Prince, the whole company removed to the Countess of *Soissons* Lodgings, where every one, all other difficulties being cleared, to avoid disputes for the precedency, subscribed his approbation apart, and none, but the Prince, and the Deputies, signed the Declaration.

But when all was done, this War wrought no alteration at all in the publick affairs, but what was procured by those of the King's party, who made use of this occasion to revenge themselves upon their enemies: So *Villeroy*, and the President *Janin*, whom the Chancellour *de Sillery* had formerly put by, that he might have the sole administration of all affaires, caused the seals to be taken from him, and committed to the President *Du Vair*: But *Villeroy* nothing advantaged himself hereby; for the Marshal *d' Ancre*, conceiving a jealousie, that at the Treaty he held correspondence with the contrary party, to out him of the *Cittadell* of

Amiens, caused his Office of Secretary of State, to be given to *Mangot*.

When this business was thus concluded, every one departed, but diversely affected, and very ill satisfied one with another; and the next day came the full power from the Assembly to their Deputies to conclude the Peace. The Marshal *Boüillon*, and the Duke of *Trimoüille*, to insinuate themselves the more into the King's favour, engaged themselves to the Commissioners, by an Act under their hands and seals, to rout the Assembly, and all that should presume to justifie them, in case they refused to dissolve, after the six weeks prorogation accorded them, was expired.

If the number of the discontents on the Princes side was great, it was not less on the other: The favour of the Marshal *d' Ancre* was more insupportable to those, that upheld, than those that opposed him: and he also perceiving himself more tyrannised by his creatures, than his enemies, made the late reconciled party believe he would enter into a firm and strict amity with them; which the Duke of *Guise* suspecting, he also, to cross the Marshal *d' Ancre*'s aimes, seeks after an union with them too: And in order to it, makes his applications to the Marshal *Boüillon*; who fed him still with very fair words, and hopes, that in case he failed of his end at the Court, he might have a good occasion to intangle it in new perplexities.

Some dayes before the conclusion of the Peace, it was proposed in the Prince his Council, that the Grandees of his party should enter into an inviolable League amongst themselves, that two of them should alwayes in their turns, reside at Court, whilest the others kept at a greater distance from it; and that every one of them should embrace the particular interests of the others; The Marshal *Boüillon* rejected that Proposition, as unseasonable, for that, having occasion to dis-oblige the greatest part of them, he foresaw this might discover his intentions; and besides, he was yet desirous to derive his advantage from the merits, and esteem of his services: But after the Treaty was concluded, himself renewed the former proposal, which was then also as unseasonable, because their minds were now too much varied from what they were, and they so jealous one of another, that every one steered his course by his own particular interest.

The Prince went to take possession of the government of *Berry*, given him in exchange for that of *Guienne*; The Duke of *Mayne*, and the Marshal *Boüillon* to the Court, to try how the pulses beat there, but principally to reap the fruit of their services; The Duke of *Sully* to his government of *Poictou*; The
Duke

Duke of *Rohan* to *Rochell*, to inform the Assembly of what had passed at the treaty of *Loudun*, and to procure a nomination of good Deputies general: But the Court *Caball* being united with the Prince his faction, and the hopes of favour, gratifications, and pensions, he gave to those that should incline to his will wholly governed them, so that *Bertheville*, and *Mainald* were chosen.

The Duke of *Rohan* seeing how he was hated at Court, and that the success of all things thwarted his projection, resolves to make an Essay upon the Duke of *Sully* for the government of *Poictou*, of whom when he had obtained a demission of it, his Patents were prepared, according to the tenor of the Articles of the Treaty, upon condition that he should go to receive them at Court, which he resolved to do; and there delivers himself freely to the *Queen*, telling her, that the slights she had thrown upon him, had induced him to let her Majesty know, that he was neither voide of resentments, nor destitute of power; that, it was true, he had served and obliged a most ingrateful person, which he was very sensible of, and that if she pleased to vouchsafe him a pardon, and amnesty for his actions against her, and admit him again to her favour, he vowed that except the party of the Religion, he would devote his most faithful services to her, against all the world besides; of which offer and protestation she testified her belief by her acceptance of it.

But to return to the Marshal *Bouillon*; he employed the uttermost strength of his whole abilities to gain an admission to the helm of State, declaring that he was the only man could, at his pleasure, rule, and dispose of the Prince, who was also the only person could prejudice the authority of the *Queen*, and that consequently his satisfaction, and employment would free them from any further apprehensions, whatsoever: But the Marshal a' *Ancre*, who had ingrossed all the power, being the only Favourite, and intended to change the whole Council, to place therein creatures of his own, thought it not convenient to suffer the introduction of such a one; which the other perceiving, stuffs the Princes head with new jealousies, to prevent his returne to the Court.

There were the Countess of *Soissons* of the one side, and the Princess of *Conde* of the other, that extreamly rejoyced at the report of the Prince his intentions to return thither; but all (so jealous were they one of another) agreed to divert him from them, unless it was by their means that he came; which he knowing very well, waved them all, and by the mediation of *Rochefort*, and the Arch-Bishop of *Bourges*, secretly made his peace

peace with the *Queen*, fixing himself upon her, and to protect the Marshal *d' Ancre*, with the exclusion of his own party; provided he might be solely intrusted with the management of the publick affairs, and made Chief of the Council of the Revenew.

Coming to *Paris* against the good liking of those afore-mentioned, he was welcomed with loud acclamations, and applauses, and resumed a great power in the State: The Duke of *Rohan*, with the *Queens* permission, gave him a visit; and sharply reproached him for signing the Peace, without expecting the Commission from the Assembly; which he excused, saying, that he was induced to it by an apprehension he had, lest the Duke should hinder their granting it; and when he afterwards understood that he was restored to the *Queens* favour, he told him he was very glad of it, for that he had now brought no other resolutions with him, but to enjoy himself, mind his own affairs, and no more to intermeddle in any factions, but entirely to adhere to the *King*, the *Queen*, and the Marshal *d' Ancre*: And when the dissatisfaction of the Great ones, and principally of the Marshal *Boüillon*, who was supposed to have an absolute power over him, was objected to him; his answer was, That he now very well perceived his drift, and the subtleties he used to perswade him, that the welfare of the State consisted either in peace or War, according as he was pleased, or displeased, and that he would no more stoop to that Lure.

On the other side, the Marshal *Boüillon* though he saw himself quite cast off, despairs not, but for fear of exasperating him, covers the displeasure he had conceived against the Prince, with a seeming approbation of all that he had done; and that his Counsels might be of greater validity with him, draws the Duke of *Guise*, with his brothers, and the Duke of *Nevers*, into an union with those of his party; taking advantage of the Parliaments, and *Parisians* hatred against the Marshal *d' Ancre*, and by the means of *Luines*, who now began to be the sole Favourite, exposes him to the King's also; and communicated to many of the prime Nobility his design to secure the Court by the death of the Marshal *d' Ancre*, who had bartered away the King's Lieutenancies in *Picardy*, and the Citadel of *Amiens*, together with that of *Normandy*, which the Duke of *Montbazon* had, and reserved to himself the government of *Peronne*, *Montdidier*, and *Roye*: The Duke of *Longueville*, enraged to see himself disappointed of *Amiens*, and the rest of *Picardy*, pursues his design, loudly proclaims to the world his discontents, and the Intelligence he held with the Town of *Peronne*, enters it, and

possesses

possesses himself of the Castle, before any one could stir to prevent him. Mangot, the new made Secretary of State in the place of *Villeroy*, is sent thither by the King, but to no purpose, for that the Castle was already delivered: At his return from this successeless voyage, the King, being advised to handle this businefs with all gentlenefs possible, sends the Marshal *Boüillon*, who made two journyes thither, but brought not back the satisfaction, was desired; and indeed his own particular aime was to confirm the Duke in his conquest, to the end that he might engage him, and his friends, in the design he still pursued. And one day, having assembled the chiefest of his Confederates, to consult about the killing of the Marshal *d' Ancre*, the Duke of *Maine*, who was supposed to be the most zealous in the businefs, offered to kill him himself, provided that the Prince would be there, and that it was necessary to know his resolution therein; the Marshal *Boüillon* replyed, That they ought to beware of that, but that he would undertake to make the Prince avow the action when it was executed, but that it was dangerous to impart it to him before, and that he should not by any means have any notice of it, till it were ready to be put in execution, that he might not have leafure to retract: But the obstinacy of the Duke of *Maine* carried it, and the Prince when he was acquainted with what they had resolved on, whether it was, that he feared the issue of it, or that for this once he would be a man of his word, that very Evening let the Marshal *d' Ancre* know, by the Arch-Bishop of *Bourges*, that he could by no means abandon the Duke of *Longueville*, and that he revoked the promise he had made to protect him: Whereupon the Marshal, the same night posted into *Normandy*; and there seeing himself forsaken by the Prince, and many of the Great ones, combined to assault him in the Court it self, contrived how he might prevent them: Informs the *Queen* by some of his Confidents, that the *Prince* deceives her, that the Marshal *Boüillon* amuses her, that many of the great Nobility were resolved to devest her of her authority, and that the businefs was already come to such a point, that she had no other remedy left her, but to seize upon their persons; on which she resolved, with *Mangot* the Bishop of *Lucon*, and *Barbin*, creatures of the Marshal: And on the first day of *September*, upon a *Thursday* at noon, was the Prince arrested in the *Louvre*, by *Themines*, who for that action was created Marshal of *France*; and that which is very remarkable in this, is, That upon the same day of the moneth, and of the week, and at the same houre was he born: They thought to have surprized the Duke of *Maine*, and the Marshal *Boüillon* there also; but the

for-

former lodging near *Saint Anthony*'s Gate, had opportunity enough to escape; and the other being that day gone to a Sermon at *Charenton*, was advised by his friends to return no more; so they went to *Soissons*, and the Duke of *Guise* and his brother took the same way also; The Duke of *Vendosme* also fled towards *La Fere*; The Duke of *Rohan*, who at the very beginning of these commotions had quitted the Prince, was not however without his fears, when he saw him carried away by *Themines*, and that immediately upon it *Saint Geran* came to enquire after him from the King. This arrest caused a great tumult in *Paris*, which was encreased by the Prince his Mother, and many Gentlemen, who animated the people of the Suburbs of *Saint Germaine* to plunder, and raze the Marshal *d' Ancre*'s house, which they found so sweet an employment, that the pillage of it lasted two dayes; and indeed great prudence was it, not to oppose them in the heat of their fury: For the next day *Crequi* Colonel of the Regiment of the Guards, with one company of them, and another of the Citizens, easily took them off from the prey, which in the height of the hurly burly would have proved a greater difficulty.

Their Majesties gave notice of this Mutiny to those of the Nobility that remained in *Paris*, and likewise to the chiefest of the Council; among whom, the Duke of *Sully* spake his mind freely, and declaring his dislike of the action, advised them to compose those differences by the intervention of the Pope his *Nuncio*, and other Embassadours, but so, as that the full power to determine all should remaine still in the King, and the Queen his Mother. But this Council was disapproved, and the way of force made choice of: In the mean while the Marshal *Boüillon* sets all his wits on work, to engage the Duke of *Guise* somewhat further, offering to make him chief of a party, where he should command all that durst dispute the place with him: tells him moreover, that what they did, was to restore the first Prince of the Blood to his liberty, and take the King out of the hands of the Marshal *d' Ancre*, against whom the general hatred had evidently appeared by the burning and pillaging of his house in *Paris*, even before the King's face; that if they should speedily gather together their friends, and fire all the Mills about *Paris*, they should cause a greater insurrection there: But when he saw that these perswasions prevailed nothing upon him, and that he was treating for his return to Court, where he was offered to Command the King's Armyes; he then moved to have him stopped; which the Duke of *Mayne* would not give way to.

Thus

Book I.   *The Memoires of the Duke of* Rohan.   41

Thus all the Councils of the Marshal *Bouillon* were rejected, though they were very good; For, in extremities, things will not admit of tedious deliberations, and ballancings of future events; and many times a rash attempt closely pursued, meets a fortunate success, when circumspection (in such a case) ever fails: Which clearly appeared here; for the Queen having drawn the Duke of *Guise* and his brothers, changes the Officers of State, giving the seals to *Mangot*, the Office of Secretary of State to the Bishop of *Lucon*, the Intendancy of the *Finances*, or Treasurership to *Barbin*, appeases all popular tumults, and by a Declaration, verified in Parliament, criminalizes all that had absented themselves; Raises several armies, and gives the command of that in *Champagne* to the Duke of *Guise*, that in the Isle of *France* to the Count of *Auvergne*, and having made *Montigny* Marshal of *France*, and Governour of *Berry*, sends him thither, who secures the Province, and makes himself Master of the Tower of *Bourges*: The Marshal *de Souvre* does the like to the Castle of *Chinon*, which by the treaty of *Loudun* was given to the Prince. In the beginning of the yeare One thousand six hundred and seventeen, the Duke of *Guise* stormes some places held by the Duke of *Nevers*, which, without any great resistance made, he takes, and then prepares for the siege of *Meziers*. The Count of *Auvergne* also takes *Pierrefons*, and marches towards *Soissons*: And the Duke of *Maine* attempting to beat up the Quarters of the Duke of *Rohan*, Colonel of the light Horse-men, in *Villiers-Cotrets* received a shrewd repulse: In the mean time the Marshal *Bouillon* retires to *Sedan*, where he endeavours to strengthen himself with some forraign assistance: Thus were the affairs of the Princes but in a sad condition, even then when their deliverance appeared by the death of the Marshal *d' Ancre*, which occasioning a change of the whole face of things, it will not be impertinent, in this place to insert a particular relation of it.

The unlimited power of Favourites is the ruine of a State: For either they change it themselves for their own ends, or else they give the ambitious opportunities to attempt it, or at least are they made the pretences of all the disturbances that happen in it: For seven years had the Marshal *d' Ancre* furnished *France* with such pretexts, and that great people, whom the raign of *Henry* the great had accustomed to a subjection to the government of their King himself, universally hated him, imputing all their mischiefs continually to him; So that his death filled every one with hopes of an amelioration: But those quickly vanished, when they saw *Luynes*, a man of a mean extraction, cloathed

thed with his spoiles, and at the first rise advanced to greater authority; who by the pas-time, and delights he shewed the King in Hunting, and by his low submissions had raised himself to the highest place in the affections of a King, who was then but fifteen years old: A Prince very singular, and jealous of his authority; which yet he understood not at all, and more apt to believe the worst, than the best: It was a matter of no great difficulty to perswade him, that the Marshal *d' Ancre* aimed at a power would prejudice his, and that the Queen Mother was consenting to it, that she might continue the rains of Government, as in his Minority, in her own hands; For the insolencies which alwayes accompany great Favourites were exreame in the Marshal *d' Ancre*; and the Queen Mothers neglect of her sonne too apparent: So that *Luynes* having before hand dealt with *Deagent* the chief Deputy of *Barbin*, who was Intendant of the *Finances*, caused him that night to entertain the King with a discourse of the mischievous plots were contriving against him; and out of hopes of some great advancement, he made his treachery against his Master the foundation of the designe: *Marcillac*, his Associate, was he who had formerly betrayed the Prince to the Queen, and now betrayes her to the King: *Desplans* an ordinary Souldier in the King's Guards, had a share in this employment too, for that he had been a servant to *Brantes*, who was brother to *Luynes*: In short, in the contrivance of this design were employed only base and infamous persons; but to *Vitry* Captaine of the Guards was the execution of it committed, who was commanded to kill the Marshal, and for recompence, was promised to be made Marshal of *France*; which accordingly he performed as he was entring the *Louvre*: At the same time were arrested also the Marshal *d' Ancre*'s Lady, *Mangot*, the Bishop of *Lucon* and *Barbin*, and then were the Chancellour *de Sillery*, *Du Vair*, Keeper of the Seals, *Villeroy*, and the president *Janin* sent for to resume their Offices. After this were the Queenes guards taken from her, and some of the King's appointed to wait on her: A Gallery also that led from her Chamber to a Garden she had caused to be made, was broken down; nor was she suffered, without leave, to see any thing, but the sad conversion of her authority and liberty, into a low and despicable condition, and miserable servitude.

Expresses were sent into all parts to give notice of this change, all hostility ceases, every one returns to the Court, where all strive, who should soonest and most impudently renounce that, which but four and twenty hours before, they adored; It being the

Book I. *The Memoires of the Duke of* Rohan. 43

the property of generous souls only to follow those in their adverse, whom they honoured in their more prosperous fortune; The Duke of *Rohan* got leave to visit the Queen-mother, the strength of whose constancy was still superiour to the violence of her pressures: And then, seeing himself regarded with a frowning eye, and taking small pleasure to see those he had so lately fought against to be the only welcome persons, goes into *Piedmont*, where he arrived a little after the taking of *Verseil*, and passing the Summer there, he saw an action worthy to be observed, and related. *Don Pedro de Toledo*, after he had taken *Verseil*, which had endured a long siege, to refresh it, divided his Army into *Montferrat*, and the Dutchy of *Milan*, and quarters it about *Alexandria*, a Countrey abounding in corne, and all manner of necessaries: In the meane while the Duke of *Savoy's* Army recruited, and the Treaty of peace was still continued by the mediation of the Cardinal *Ludovisio* on the Pope's behalf, and *Bethun* on the King's; several conferences had they with *Don Pedro*; In the interim of which, the Marshal *Lesdiguires*, who commanded the relief sent by the King to the Duke of *Savoy*, to defend his States, but not to attempt upon the Duchy of *Milan*; having sent to discover how the *Spanish* Army lay, made a proposition to beat up the Quarters of two thousand men, that lay in *Felissan*, a Village that was but slightly barricadoed, and seated in the middest of all the other Quarters: proving by many reasons, that, though at sifirst ght the designe might seeme very hazardous, yet really was it not so, for that marching that way one night with all his forces, at break of day he beat up that Quarter, which hindered the *Spanish* Armies rallying, and was the reason that those he had left behinde him, having no retreat, were utterly lost. This motion took the wished effect; For the Duke of *Savoy* having appointed his Rendezvous at *Ast*, marched by a private way, which avoided *Nice* and *La Roque*, and came to *Felissan*, which was instantly begirt, and forced, for they had no need of the Canon, which *Shomberg* Marshal of the Camp, was bringing up with the Rear-guard, with which he was commanded to take in a Castle, to secure the provisions, which he did: The next day was taken a place called *Quatordeci*, in which were four hundred souldiers: The same day the Duke of *Savoy* gives the Duke of *Rohan* three hundred horse, to cut off some Cavalry of the enemies, that were coming from *Alexandria*: As he was marching to execute that designe, he discovers 300. horse and 1200. foot marching from *Cazal* to *Alexandria*; He makes towards them with his whole party, but, notwithstanding he used all diligence possible, he could not reach them before it was

dark,

dark, and that the enemy had sheltred himself in a very advantageous hold; A proposition was then made for the incamping round about them, and sending that night for two thousand horse, that might be ready there to defeat them by break of day; and I believe this project might have taken; But the consideration of leaving the rest of the Infantry at *Felissan* in the middest of the enemies Quarters, who might easily beat them up, caused them to resolve upon a retreat: So that after a dayes stay at *Felissan*, they marched towards *Nice*, which they surrounded, and in twice four and twenty hours, was the Town forced, and the Castle surrendred, in which were near two thousand fighting men: The next day finding *La Roque* quitted, they pursue those that were of the garrison, who were all *Switzers*, whom they overtook, and made prisoners: Thus in the space of one week, were taken four thousand five hundred of the enemies army; which being so weakened: and the Duke of *Savoy* finding himself to be more than twenty thousand strong marching men, had designed to enter in to the Duchy of *Milan*; when lo, from *France* comes the conclusion of the peace, with a Command to the Marshal *Lesdiguieres* to get the Duke of *Savoy's* assent to it, which he effected: But return we now to the affairs of *France*.

    Luynes seeing that so short a time had vested him with the entire spoyls of a most eminent Favourites seven years toyle, having the sole influence upon a young Prince of fifteen years old, whose Mother he had mortally offended, being himself but of mean parentage, and without any support in the Kingdom, not studied, nor any way versed in State affairs, and yet governing all with a most absolute authority, makes use of *Deagent*, and *Modene* as his chief Counsellors: And the next care he had, was to impose a Confessor upon the King, of an immediate dependance upon himself, so to awe him by their superstition (a powerful engine to work upon the spirit of a young Prince) and to place about his person petty inconsiderable fellows, who amused him with childish toyes, and kept so close a siege about his person, that none could be admitted so much as to speak to him in private: After this he caused the Queen-mother to be conveyed to *Blois*, where she was most strictly guarded: And then, that he might enrich himself with her wealth also, proceeded to the arraignment, and trial of the Marshal *d' Ancre's* Lady; in which he used such unlawful sollicitations, and took such unusual courses to procure her death, that at her execution, the former hatred of the *Parisians* against her was far exceeded by their passionate commiseration of her present calamities; caused *Mangot* to be confined to his own house; the Bishop of *Lucon* to be relegated

Book I.   *The Memoires of the Duk of* Rohan.   45

gated to *Avignon*, and *Barbin* was sent to the *Bastille*; and then marries the Duke of *Montbazon*'s daughter to strengthen himself with an Alliance not obnoxious to envie; having for that reason refused the Duke of *Vendosm*'s sister.

When he had ordered these things after this manner, he caused to be convened at *Rouen*, the most eminent of the Nobility, together with the principal officers of the Parliaments (called the Assembly of *Notables*) that without parting from the King at all, he might put himself in possession of the government of *Normancy*; where the disunion of the Grandees, their infidelity, and pusillanimity, together with the base and servile spirits of the Officers and Deputies of the Parliaments, present at this Assembly, confirmed the Authority of this upstart Favourite, so that every one yeilding to his yoak, he began now to think himself sufficient to dispose even of Fortune her self.

The Duke of *Rohan*, who was now allyed to him by his wife, who was of his family, courts him too, among the rest, endeavouring to reconcile him rather to the Queen, than the Prince, who from his Prison had already sent him Overtures and premises, that in exchange of his liberty, he would support him with his assistance, and fixe him in an impregnable condition; He told him, that he could not long, keep them both prisoners; that he that was there before, his advancement could have no colour to lay his restraint to his charge; and that it was an easie matter to hinder his deliverance, that the Queens condition was different, who one time or other would escape from him; for though she were kept also under guards, yet was it with more respect, and not as prisoner; and that such guards were not so secure : He added moreover, that if the Prince regained any power in the State he would be a more dangerous opposite than the Queen-Mother could, that he was of a good wit, quick, highly ambitious, and covetous; that though he was not of a vindicative nature, yet was he not obliging neither, nor had he the least friendship for any one; that being not able to detaine them both still in prison, it was necessary he should strengthen himself with the assistance of one of them; and that however he had displeased the Queen, yet would she prove his surer prop, for that she was not so prone to intermeddle with the affairs, as the Prince was; and the jealousies that were between the King and the Queen (which he knew well enough how to mould to his own advantage) would be his security against them both ; *Luynes* seeming satisfied with these arguments, encouraged the Duke by all means to mediate this reconciliation; who having a servant named *La Ferte*, who was an intimate friend of *Larbins*, had by that means an

op-

opportunity to let him know the service he intended to the Queen his Mistresse, to which the Duke of *Montbazon*, *Luynes* his Father-in-law, was also much inclined. *Barbin*, (by the means of *Bournonville*, Governour of the *Bastille*, where he was a prisoner) gave the Queen intelligence of what had passed, advising her to write letters to the King, *Luynes*, and to the Duke of *Montbazon*; to the first, full of complaints of vindication of her self, and of respect; to the other two to do her all good offices to the King: the draughts of which letters were first carried to the Duke of *Rohan*, who amended them, and corrected the acrimony of some expressions in them: But the Bishop who was to carry these letters, in whom *Barbin* greatly confided, proved false, and most perfidiously betrayed the whole plot; yet, according to the instructions he received from *Deagent*, made he several journeys to the Queen, but with treacherous purposes to work the ruine of her, and all else that had a hand in this businesse: But seeing that this design tended only to a reconciliation, and yeilded no colourable pretences to ground any accusation on, they flie to subtilties; and in *Bournonville's* name, desire a Ring from the Queen, as a testimony of her acceptance of his service, for that being brother-in-law to the Marshal *Vitry*, he could not otherwise believe she could have any good thoughts of him: The Queen, though somewhat surprized with this demand, yet could it not raise any jealousies in her, for that the Bishop who was employed in all these errands, was a creature of *Barbins*, made some difficulty to part with the Ring he desired, as unwilling to give any thing that was not worthy of her, but promised to have one bought purposely at *Paris*; But he importuned her so much, that she took one from one of the Ladies attending her, and gave it him: The Bishop carries it to *Deagent*, who kept that, and caused another to be made just like it, which he conveyed to *Bournonville*, as if she had voluntarily, and of her own accord sent it him: After this they infused jealousies into the King, that the Nobility had a design to surprize the *Louvre* to introduce the Queen, and restablish her in her former authority, and that all that were of the conspiracy, wore a blew Ring on their finger, which was the cognizance of the party: And *Luynes* one day shuts the Duke of *Rohan* into his chamber, where he entertained him with discourses, that the King was certainly informed that he was alwayes much devoted to the Queens service, that he knew all his machinations for that end, and the secret negotiations of *La Ferte*; but of regard of his alliance to him, he had prevailed with the King to pardon him, and therefore now it was fit he should tell him all: This proposition was with much disdaine rejected by the Duke, who replyed, that he was no Informer, and that he was glad they knew his actions which had no other aime than the King's service; that he confessed he was a servant to the Queen-Mother, and that it was the duty of every good Frenchman so to be.

After all these contrivances, and many others which never came to my knowledge *La Ferte* was taken prisoner, and committed to the *Bastille*, confronted with *Barbin*, and both of them were brought to their tryal; and notwithstanding the importunate sollicitations made in favour of them, and were admitted of purposely to intangle more people, the result of all was, the depriving *Bournonville* of the *Bastille*, the perpetual banishment of *Barbin*, and of *La Ferte* for five years, who, notwithstanding never stirred at all from his Master.

These violent procedures filled the Queen with great fears and jealousies, and made her more solicitous to free her self from this captivity, being now well assured that the hopes *Luynes* gave her of it, sometimes by *Cadanet*, sometimes by *Modene* were but only to amuse her, especially when she saw that the negotiation of *Arnoux* the Jesuite and the King's Confessour came to nothing; this Jesuite made the King solemnly swear at Confession, never to dislike what *Luynes* did, nor to meddle himself with any State affairs.

The consideration of all these things made her at length resolve to work her enlargement; and to effect it, by the advice of the Marshal *Bouillon*, she made choice of the Duke *d' Espernon*, whom she knew to be a man of great power, valour, and prudence: But he was displeased with her, and came to Court with full intention to side with the King; he must therefore be brought about; which the Queens servants deriving much advantage from the Favourites ill conduct, very dextrously performed: And first, they terrifie *Luynes* with the great power, and haughty humour of the Duke *d' Espernon*; qualities not tolerable by one who aimes at a general adoration: On the otherside they exasperate the Duke, who was of a rouchy nature, and unaccustomed to a base and servile subjection: The first occasion they took from his attempts to promote his youngest sonne to a *Cardinalat*, for the which he was the first upon the Roll, and received all possible assurance of it, but was put by, by the contrivances of *Villeroy*, who preferred *Marquemont*: But *Villeroy* dying immediately after, he continues his pursuit, with great hopes still: But the Cardinal *de Retz* having made *Deagent*, and by that means gained *Luynes*, carried it; but not without obliging himself by promises unworthy a person of quality, with poor and infamous submissions, which he still so religiously observed, that being afterwards made Pre-

sident

fident of the Council, he seemed rather to do the duty of a Deputy to *Deagent*, than of a Cardinal.

This was opportunely seconded by another occasion derived from the Keeper of the Seals, *Du Vair*, who, hurried by his own pride, or the instigation of those that were desirous of new troubles, would needs take place at the Council-table, of all the Dukes and Peers of *France*: The Duke *d' Espernon*, as the most ancient that was then there, complains, in the name of all the rest, of it to the King, who took it ill from him, and the interest of the Gown-men, was preferred before that of the Peers of *France*: This stomached him so, that he brake out into many bitter invectives, even against the King himself; so that it was no hard matter to perswade him that there was a designe to send him to the *Bastille*, considering the late Presidents before his eyes: The Queens servants, (who would not discover any thing of their intentions to him while he remained in *Paris*) so handsomely improved his jealousies, that one morning very early, and without taking leave of any body, he goes thence to *Metz*. When he was there, *Ruccelay*, the chief contriver, and manager of the whole project begins with him, by moving a reconciliation between him, and the Marshal *Boüillon*; and then imparts to him the Queens designe, with her request to him, to procure her liberty, with many large promises annexed to it, of which, in such cases none are sparing: The almost insuperable difficulties and dangers of this enterprise, together with the ingratitude, the usual recompence Princes reward great services withal, at first startled, and caused some hesitation in the Duke of *Epernon*: But then the glory would attend the execution of so high and noble a designe, the indignation he conceived at the small regard was had of him, together with his desire of revenge, (passions predominating in all great courages) overcame all the suggestions of his fears: When he had resolved on it, he proceeds in it with that caution, secresie, and good Fortune, that having made all necessary provisions for *Metz*, where the King, purposely to keep him at a distance from the Court, where he feared him, amused him with pretended and imaginary designes, he passes through *France* into his governments of *Xaintonge*, and *Angoulmois*, and there effected the Queen-Mothers deliverance, on the one and twentieth of *February* one thousand six hundred and nineteen, who came from *Blois* to *Loches*, a place belonging to the Duke, who there went to receive her with two or three hundred Gentlemen, who all conducted her to *Angoulesme*.

This escape of the Queen caused a great confusion at the Court, where it was conceived that her party was much more numerous, or that it might quickly swell to a bigger bulk; wherefore great preparations were made for war, that the ensuing peace might be more advantageous: The command of the Army to be sent against the Queen was given to the Duke of *Mayn*; who was thought to be the most an enemy to her, and most faithful to *Luynes*; and because it was conceived that it would be acceptable to him, to him also was committed the charge of the negotiation of *Bethune*: Sollicitations were also made in the behalf of the Bishop of *Luçon* (who till then had remained in exile in *Avignon*) for his return to the Queen, and inforced with promises made in his name, by his brother in Law *Pont Courlay*, to incline the Queen to such a peace as should shoot with the King's desires, and also to sowe jealousies between the principal authors of her deliverance; in which he failed neither of his endeavours, nor successe. For *Rucelay*, who had as largely contributed to her liberty as any one, left her in discontent, and drew with him the Marquesse of *Mauny*, and *Themines*, who afterwards proved one of the greatest enemies to the Queen, who found her self but in a bad condition to engage in a war, by reason that many envied the gallant action of the Duke d' *Espernon*, few would submit to his imperious humour, and every one believed that all would end in peace, and were therefore unwilling to imbarque in an affair, by which they should gaine nothing but the King's displeasure, and hatred, whilest others carried away the glory of the enterprise: For which reason also the Duke of *Rohan*, being sought to, by the Queen, sent her word, that he was much troubled that he was not privie to, and imployed in the beginning of her designe; which if he had, he would have served her most faithfully: But being at Court then when she made her escape, he was commanded by the King to his government of *Poictou*, to preserve it in peace; that, for his part he would do her no harme, but advised her to make a peace, in which he was confident *Bethune* would serve her; and that being in full liberty, and security, she would have more favorable conveniencies to raise a greater number of servants and friends than at present: *Schomberg* did cleare otherwise for to endeare himself beyond the other Zealots for her ruine; he laid a plot to blow her up by firing the Magazine at *Angoulesme*, which was happily discovered, and prevented. At length was a peace concluded, and near *Tours* was the interview between the King and the Queen-mother; to whom was given the government of *Anjou*; and for her better security, the Castles of *Angiers*, *Pont de Cé*, and *Chinon*.

Come we now to the affairs of *Bearn*, the sourse and rise of all our evils, which will retract our view as far back as the death of the Marshal *d' Ancre*, after which *Du Vair*, Keeper of the Seals, being restored to his Office; upon the sollicitations of the Bishops of *Bearn*, and imagining he should do so eminent an action, as would gaine him such reputation at *Rome*, would advance him to the dignity of a Cardinal, he procured an order of the King's Council, for restoring to the Ecclesiastiques of that Countrey their goods that were formerly aliened by authority, and had for fourty, or fifty years been imployed for the maintenance of their Ministers, Academy, and the Garrison in the Fort called *Navarrins*. *La Force*, then Governour of that Countrey, was at Court at the same time, and mainly opposed the Order, shewing the difficulties would obstruct it, and the inconveniencies might arise from it; which I conceive he did with very sincere intentions: But being over-powered, turns his desires to his own private advantage, and promises to promote the execution of it, upon condition he might be made Marshal of *France*, which was promised him: But either the difficulties he met withall, or rage to see himself laughed at at Court, made him resolve to stand it out against all; In which he met with great opposition in the Countrey, occasioned by those of the house of *Benac*, backed with the Count of *Grammond*, his deadly enemies, and by the politick practices of the Court, so that he was now hated by all parties for not doing what he might for the satisfaction of either.

The Duke of *Rohan*, who was his friend, patronized him still at Court, and, seeing that the Kings Commissioner *Renard* cast all the blame of the ill successe he had in his voyage upon *La Force*, used all means possible to compose the businesse, shewing that if the Province of *Bearn* should addresse themselves to the Reformed Churches of *France*, their particular might grow into a general cause, from whose circumstances might arrive some accidents not easie to be remedied, and that it was the wisest course to quench this fire before it were throughly kindled: That it was most reasonable (since the thing was begun) that the King should receive satisfaction, and the Countrey also should be secured; and that partial persons were most unfit to be imployed in it: These reasons were the better relished, for that they already began to discover several Assemblies in the Provinces, and to fear the event of them: And now were things in so fair a way, that the Duke of *Rohan* had obtained a re-imbursement of the like sum of money restored to the Ecclesiastiques, to be had out of the next receipts; and in case of non-payment, permission was granted to the Countrey to seize again upon the goods of the Ecclesiastiques. But for as much as *La Force* found not his advantages in this accommodation

Book I.   *The Memoires of the Duke of* Rohan.   51

tion, he was easily induced to reject it, complaining to the Court, that to discredit him thus, was the way to disable him for any future services, and to those of the Religion, that it was an introduction to the ruine of the Reformed Religion in their Country: And notwithstanding that all the Churches of *France*, were, upon good deliberation, satisfied wi h this agreement, yet never could the people be induced to it, so that the dispute lasted till the Convocation of the General Assembly of those of the Religion at *Loudun*, the three and twentieth of *May*, one thousand six hundred and nineteen.

Luynes in the mean time did all the ill offices he could to the Duke of *Rohan*, endeavoured to criminalize him, for buying the government of *Maillezais*, of *Aubigny*, and of a private house in *Poictou* which was very strong, and which he compelled him to pull down; having, but a little before it was razed, engaged some in an attempt to surprize it; and though those that had undertaken it, were taken as they were ready to put their designe in execution, yet ordered he things so, that he could not have justice done upon them: After this, having released the Prince from the *Bastille*, to strengthen himself with his power against the Queen, and the Prince declaring himself an open enemy to the Duke of *Rohan*, the Duke resolves to adhere entirely to the Queens service, of which he went to *Angiers* to assure her; and understanding of the party was raising for her, he advised her not to stay there, but to remove to *Bourdeaux*; that her most faithfull servants were the Dukes of *Mayne*, *Espernon*, and *Rohan*; that being there, she would have a powerful Parliament to declare for her, and that there she was secure from any invasion before she had an army ready to dispute the field; that if she stayed at *Angiers*, and that if *Pont de Cé* were taken from her, she and her whole Party would be lost without one blow striking; that she ought to give the greater confidence to this Council, because it was to his own disadvantage, for that being so near the King, he was like to be the first would suffer.

To this she answered, That she much approved of his Reasons, but that if she should follow his advice, it would give the Duke d'*Espernon* suspitions that she intended. to put herself wholly into the hands of the Duke of *Mayne*: Besides, the hopes the Countesse of *Soissons* gave her from *Normandy*, built upon her Sonne-in law the Duke of *Longuevill*, who was lately made Governour of that Province, and was Master of *Dieppe*, and the Grand Prior who held *Caen*, and both of them had great correspondences in *Rouen*, prevailed so upon her, that she would by no means budge from *Angiers*: But desired that the Assembly at *Loudun* might be

E 2   continued,

continued, which might have been effected, but then it muſt have been by making ſuch a diviſion as at *Saumure*; when the Duke of *Rohan* had conferred about it with the chiefeſt friends he had in the Aſſembly, and among others, with the Count of *Orval*, his brother-in-Law, who was very powerful among them, they concluded to accept of what the King offered, *viz.* Within ſix moneths to give the Aſſembly ſatisfaction in the affair of *Bearne*, and the reſtitution of *Leetour*, one of their cautionary Towns, which if not performed, then ſhould the Aſſembly convene again within one moneth after, and that at *Rochel*: This very well pleaſed the Queen, to whom it was farther manifeſted, that this new Convocation, being in ſpight of the Court, to be in the moſt conſiderable Town of their party, where none but the moſt reſolute would come, and firmly binde the Aſſembly to her, together with all the Reformed Churches in the Kingdom; But withal they deſired her, that in caſe any peace was made, they might be ſatisfied concerning their two demands touching *Bearne*, and *Leetour*, which ſhe promiſed.

Now, ſo violent and tyrannical was the government of *Luynes*, that it had wearied all the world, and even his beſt friends alſo, as the Duke of *Main*; for whom, a little before, he had procured the Government of *Guienne*, in exchange for that of the Iſle of *France*; and, not ſatisfied with this, he gives it to the Duke of *Montbazon* his father-in-law, and ſeizes upon that of *Picardy* with all the Fortreſſes there, and in lieu of it gives that of *Normandy* to the Duke of *Longueville*. Moreover, he and his two brothers were made Dukes, and Peers of *France*; and all vacant Offices, Eccleſiaſtical Benefices, and Penſions were ingroſſed by theſe three brethren, and diſtributed among their poor kindred that flocked in to them, from the parts about *Avignon*: So that jealouſie, and envie, together with the badde adminiſtration of the publique affairs had rendred them ſo odious, that every one betook himſelf to the Queens party; Even the Prince of *Piedmont*, to whoſe marriage with Madam the King's ſiſter, he had, not long before occaſioned; *Luynes* ſeeing himſelf charged on every ſide, but ſupported by the Prince, perſwades the King to prevent the Queen his Mother; and whiles by divers meſſengers, he entertains her with hopes of an accommodation, and corrupts, and ſeduces her followers; he makes freſh levies of ſouldiers; which ſhe perceiving, does the like, and by the Vicount *Sardigny* ſends a letter to his Majeſty to let him know, how ſhe is conſtrained to provide for the ſecurity of her perſon, to ſave her ſelf from the fury of her enemies, who abuſing his authority, imploy it to ruine her. This, with the advice of the Prince, haſtens the King into

into *Normandy*, to secure that Province, which was in a tottering condition, and much enclined to the Queen; but his Presence, though accompanied with but a small force, soon settled all: *Rouen* is secured, *Caën* yeilded, *Alencon* also, and all the Nobility submit. This happy and unexpected successe makes him proceed to *Mans*, and thence straight to *Angiers*; Great was the confusion this caused in the other party, especially in the Bishop of *Lucon*, who not suffering the Queen-mother to go where her greatest forces lay, for fear lest she should get out of h's tuition, makes her resolve upon a pitiful defence in a town of no consideration, and an enemy to her party, that so intangling her in a necessity of submitting to an inglorious Accommodation, he might make her own peace upon better termes; which he did, and from that time he ever held intelligence with the King's party. Moreover the Duke of *Retz*, whether it was, that his Uncle the Cardinal *de Retz* had gained him before, or whether his apprehension of the danger had altered his mind, most certain it is, that seeing the King's forces ready to fall on upon the works of *Pont de Cé*, of which he had undertaken the defence, upon an imaginary discontent that a peace was concluding without his privity, he suddenly quits them, and with all his troops repasses the *Loire*; Thus was *Pont de Cé* taken, and the Queen who had thirty thousand good men ready in *Guienne, Poictou, Xaintonge*, and *Angoumois*, was vanquished by five or six thousand only, and reduced to a necessity of accepting such Articles as her enemies pleased to vouchsafe her; according to which, and her own particular order, the Dukes of *Maine*, *d' Espernon*, *Rohan*, and *Soubize* laid down their Armes.

THE
Memoires
OF THE DUKE of ROHAN:

The second Book.

Containing a Relation of the Warre against those of the Reformed Religion in France.

AND now are we arrived at the sourse of all our evils, and fatal commencement of the Warres against those of the Reformed Religion. The King, having thus happily put a period to this War, goes to *Bourdeaux*, where he suppresses the authority of the Duke of *Maine*, and commands the *Bearnois* that the late Decree be put in execution: But they, neither knowing how to obey him, nor defend themselves, oblige him in person to a voyage into *Bearn*: And there it was they first began to slight and laugh at the performance of their parol engagements; For the next day after their arrival, and a solemne promise made to the *Bearnois* to preserve their priviledges entire, were they totally devested of them, by the re-uni

on of *Bearne* to *France*, and changing, contrary to the engagement of their faith given the Governour of *Navarrins*.

Moreover it is to be known, that the Deputy general *Favas*, who was in pursuit of the government of *Lectour* in the behalf of his son, the more to induce the Court to yeild to his request, threatned to send to those at *Rochel* to convene the Assembly general, according to the power given them by the Assembly at *Loudun*: But seeing, that prevailed not to compasse his designe, and not considering how unseasonable it was, he writes to those of *Rochel*, from *Bourdeaux*, to cause the said Convention, advising them also to repair their fortifications; And thus are the publique continually swallowed up by private Interests.

When the King was returned to *Paris*, the Assembly general meets at *Rochel*, and *Favas* still followes the Court, to finde some means to accomplish his desires; His Majesty in the first place, forbids the holding of the said Assembly, next commands their dissolution, and lastly declares them Traytors: The chief of those of the Religion, conceiving that great prejudice to them would attend their obstinacy, were of opinion that they were best to dissolve upon certain conditions, of which they had hopes given them from the Court: But the Letters which *Favas* sent thence, together with the particular discontents of *La Force*, and *Chastillon*, by reason of the hard usage the one received in his Offices, and a desire the other had to have more, occasioned the continuance of the Assembly; whence the King took a pretence to prosecute his designes to the uttermost, to which, the basenesse, and treachery of the Governours of the Cautionary Towns facilitated his accesse.

It is to be observed, that before the Kings departure from *Paris*, the Dukes of *Nevers* and *Maine* were in great discontent retired into *Champagne*, and the Count of *Soissons* to *Fontevault*: The Duke *de Luynes*, that he might not leave such thorns in his back, was very desirous to reconcile them; and to move them to it, *Favas* was sent to informe the Dukes, that he was now going to the Assembly with full satisfaction to all their demands, and that it would be prudence in them to comply, before the determination of that affair; the like speech was made to the Count of *Soissons* by *Villarnoul*, which wrought all their returns to the Court, and occasioned the reconciliation between the Cardinal *de Guise*, and the Duke of *Nevers*.

After the reducing of these Princes, the assurance *Villarnoul* gave of *Saumur*, the defection of the Governours of the Cautionary Towns in *Poictou*, the revolt of *Pardaillan* with a part of *Guienne*, that of *Chastillon* in the lower *Languedoc*, and that by the

presence

presence of the Duke *de Lesdiguieres* they were assured also of *Dauphine*; the King sets forth, not to a Warre, but a certaine Victory: The Duke *de Luynes*, lately made Constable of *France*, goes with him, who so absolutely possessed his Masters favour, that in the progress of this Warre, we shall see, not the intentions of the King, but the Treasons and disloyalties of this Upstart executed, who having by that means crept into a fortune, ruled all with a Soveraign power which he continued even to his death, leaving the King's Council such a Copy, whose imitation would prove the ruine of the Kingdom.

The first testimony of the lubricity, and insincerity of their words, was given at *Saumure*, which, to the violation of the Faith engaged in his Patent, was taken from *Du Plessis Mornay*: The same successe also had all the Townes in *Poictou*.

The Dukes of *Rohan*, and *Soubize* his brother, who had opposed the convocation of the Assembly, and earnestly endeavoured their dissolution, when convened, seeing such a rout, resolved not to abandon the party: The Constable, who was their kinsman, many times sent to try their pulses; but neither his promises, nor threats, made the least impression on their consciences, or fidelity: The last Messenger was the Colonel *Arnaud*, who brought them Letters from the King, full of perswasions to quit their resolutions, and intermixed with menaces of an inevitable ruine in case they obstinately persevered in them; and withal to let them know that the first siege would be that of *Saint John d' Angely*: But this journey had a double end; for, in case he prevailed not upon the two brothers, he had Orders to conferre with the Major General *Auriac*, who was then at *Saint Julian*, about a quarter of a League from *Saint John*, with four thousand men, to cause him to put in execution a design he was entred on, by means of the intelligence he had with the Captaines, *Galloix*, and *Vaux*, and two of the inhabitants, whose names were *Masures*, and *Roquier*, who had promised, if he would approach with his Troops, and fall in upon the Suburbs called *Mata*, and thence make up straight to the Gate, they would be ready there, with their confederates, and keep it open; which *Auriac* attempted the very next day after *Arnaud*'s departure from *Saint John*: But the presence of the Dukes of *Rohan* and *Soubize*, both which were yet in the Town, prevented their success; *Soubize* was resolved to abide a Siege; and *Rohan* three dayes after went to *Rochelle*; from whence he brought and put a thousand men into the Town, with above an hundred Gentlemen, besides two Barques laden with all manner of provisions; and then went back to *Guienne*.

He

He was desired by the Assembly to reconcile *La Force* and *Pardaillan*, to which the former was very much inclined, but the other would not so much as see the Duke of *Rohan*, by which he clearly perceived his engagement to the Court: *La Force* desired *Rohan* to take a view of the Communalties of the lower *Guienne*, that he might the better take order for the security of the division the Assembly had allotted him. From thence he goes to *Bergerac*, *Saint Foy*, *Clerac*, and *Tonneins*, and thence to *Nerac*, where the Chamber, or Court of Justice yet was, but must be removed, before they could secure the Castle, where the Court sate, and where the President, a *Romanist*, lodged; who after many contests, at length withdrew with one Gentleman, whom the Duke of *Rohan* gave him for his Convoy as far as *Marmande*: But the President made but an unhandsome return of this civility: For when he returned to *Tonneins*, he gave *Vignoles* intelligence of it, who about a League from *Tonneins* lay in ambush for him, with six or seven score Gentlemen Voluntiers armed at all points, and three other Troops, who let them pass, and then the first Troop followed their Reare, the second marched up to flanck them, and the third, which was the strongest, between the other two; that they might be ready to relieve the other upon all occasions: The Marquess *de la Force*, who commanded *Rohan*'s light Horsemen, was left to make good the retreat, with thirty of *La Force* his guard, whom he caused to alight from their Horses, and thirty other Horse, among which there were but ten *Cuirasses*: The Marquess advertises *Rohan* and *La Force*, that the enemy marched towards him, whereupon they face about, and advance, commanding him to charge them: But the first Troop instead of receiving the charge, flew off towards *Vignoles*; when presently half of *La Force*'s Guards gave them a Volley, which killed and hurt about five or six Men and Horses, which made them keep off at a Musquet shot distance from them. The second Troop, which flanked them, perceiving a little Ditch between them and *Rohan*, fell off, as the first did: Which *Vignoles* seeing, advanced not at all with the third, so that without any further interruption, they kept on their way to *Tonneins*: Among the Troops of *Rohan*, and *La Force*, were there but fourteene *Cuirasses*; and of Gentlemen, and their servants, not above seventy six Horse.

After this, *Rohan* left *La Force* who very exactly knew the Countrey of the lower *Guienne*, and went from *Nerac* to *Montauban*, fetching a compass of above five and thirty Leagues, by reason that the Marshal *Themines* lay in his way, and arrived there on the eighteenth of *July*, One thousand six hundred and

Memoires of the Duke of Rohan. 59

Montauban he received intelligence that *Nerac*
Duke of *Maine*, who commanded in to him
ill the Nobility of *Guyenne*: La *Force* at the
in attempt upon *Caumont*, surprizes the Town,
to the Castle; The Duke of *Maine* having a
olyes to releive it, and to continue the Siege of
iich he had a fortunate success; and the Duke
rt *Themines*, lies down before *Septfons*, a
himself; and when he had drawn him thither,
indred Voluntiers, he retired to *Realville*, and
la Roque: whence, after three or four dayes
ew away againe, and the Duke went to *Mon-*
e the adjacent Countrey from the ravage and
the Marshal, who followed him thither, where
n them some light skirmishes, of no great con-

ike of *Rohan* remained at *Montauban*, came
he rendition of *Saint John*, and also of *Pons*,
Chasteau-neuf, of the revolt of *Pardaillan*, the
and also of *Bergerac*, by the treachery of
'anissault; of the taking of *Nerac* by the Duke
vas drawing towards *Gascony*) which was fol-
e loss of *Lectour*, *Leyrac*, *Mas de Verdun*, *Mau-*
e-Jourdan; all which places the Governours
up into the hands of the Duke of *Maine*. Nor
iemselves better in the lower *Guienne*: For
inquin, *Puymirol*, and divers other places
their Governours; and, which is most predi-
it was then with the Assembly general, at *Ro-*
d his sonne to give up to the King *Castel-Ja-*
, two cautionary places, and remote from the
twelve or fifteen Leagues. In short, of all
e, no place made any semblance of op-
, which was well fortified and manned,
omprising the Inhabitants) three thousand figh-

osses made the Duke conceive, that seeing there
y resistance made in La *Force*'s division, he
iave the Royal Army upon him: Wherefore
ovide for *Montauban*, marks some of the out-
be fortified, makes up the Regiment of the
ten Companies, reduces the Inhabitants into
all things fitting for a long Siege, and resolves
astres, thence into the lower *Languedoc*, to
raise

raise up their dejected spirits there, and prepare some relief for Montauban.

He departs thence attended on by his own guards, and accompanied by the Count d' *Orval* and his, fords over the River *Tarn* near the Isle of *Albigeois*, where he met with some opposition; at this pass, was the Captain of his guards wounded; the Captain, with some of the Count d' *Orval*'s guards, and one of his Mules were killed, and his Gentleman of the Horse, had his Horse hurt: Thus passed they to *Castres*, whence the Count d' *Orval* returned to *Montauban* to expect the Siege.

In the mean while, the Duke of *Rohan*, that he might lose no time, sends to the *Sevenes*, and the lower *Languedoc*, for a supply of four thousand men, and he himself goes as far as *Millaud*, where he understood by the Messengers he had sent thither, that though the people were generally well inclined, yet would the Artifices of the disaffected prevail over their good intentions, unless he himself advanced to the *Sevenes*.

Chastillon, at the same time, sent *Briquemaut* to the Duke of *Rohan*, to invite him to a conference, which he accepted of, and to that end advanced as far as *Saint Hippolyte*, where the said *Briquemaut* returns againe to the Duke from *Chastillon*, to let him know, that he very much wondred that he should enter into the division allotted him, and that he suspected it was with a design to prejudice his authority: It was answered him, That certainly he had no good memory, and withal was shewn him the Letter he had written to the Duke, that the only expedient to drive him out of the *Sevenes*, and stop his passages into the lower *Languedoc*, was, not to impede the succours he had demanded, which rather than faile of, he would encounter all difficulties whatsoever: that if he was desirous of an interview, he was very ready to satisfie him; and that if he would in person go to the relief of *Montauban*, as he had offered, he was confident, they two would be able to procure the peace of the whole Kingdom.

In short, after he had strugled with many difficulties, he drew at length four thousand Foot out of the lower *Languedoc*, and the *Sevenes*, and, with his own money raised a thousand more, with which he returnes againe towards *Millaud*, from whence he sent Orders to *Malauze*, *Leran*, and *Saint Rome*, who in his absence commanded; the first in *Albigeois*, and *Rouergue*; the second in *Foix*; and the third in *Lauraguais*, to make ready the forces of the *Colloques*: He sent to *Castres* also, and upon his march caused all necessary provisions of meal, and bread, for the nou-

rish-

Book II. *The Memoires of the Duke of* Rohan. 61

rishment of his Souldiers to be made ready.

In the mean time the King having besieged, and by reason of their intestine divisions for want of a Commander in Chief, taken *Cleras*, and seized upon all the places about *Montauban*, except *Saint Antonin*, sate down with his Army before *Montauban* on the one and twentieth of *August*, One thousand six hundred and twenty one, (where *La Force*, with his two sons, were gotten in) and sent the Duke of *Angoulesme*, with fifteen hundred Horse, and foure thousand Foot, to lie upon the River *Tarn*, and intercept the relief was preparing for *Montauban*; who made as if he would besiege *Lombez*, a place, about half a League from *Realmont*, where there was a Castle that commanded the Town, and held alwayes for the King. The Duke of *Rohan*, receiving intelligence of it from *Malauze*; and also of the conspiracy in agitation for the delivery of *Castres*, with all speed sends away *Boyer*, one of his Colonels, with a thousand foot, and a faithful promise to follow him suddenly with the rest of the Army.

When *Boyer* came to *Castres*, he found that *Malauze* had drawn his main Body to *Realmont*; whither his coming also, with this supply, raised the Duke of *Angoulesme* from before *Lombez*; whereupon *Malauze*, instead of expecting the arrival of the Duke of *Rohan*, as he had commanded him, but suffering himself to be carried away with the importunity of the multitude, goes with one piece of Canon, which he drew out of *Realmont*, to besiege a Church that was Garison'd and Fortifi'd, called *La-Fauch*, which as *Boyer* was viewing he was slaine, and the Duke of *Angoulesme* at the instant the Church was surrendred, came and inclosed the rest of the party with his whole Army: After severall charges and skirmishes, in which *Balauze* behaved himself with much Gallantry, and *Saint Rome* also, in rescuing him, (for he charged through the mid'st of the enemy, with fifty Gentlemen (many of whom he lost) they capitulated to march off with their Armes, all but their Canon; and, for the space of six months not to beare Armes for the party: Thus were all the forces with their Chiefs, and all the Nobility of *Albigeois*, and *Lauraguais*, disabled from any service for the remaining part of that, and untill *March* the year following.

The Duke of *Rohan*, for his part, loses no time, but advances with his Troops, and while his Rear-guard was marching up to him, draws the Canon out of *Millaud*, takes *Saint George* a small, but well inclosed place, and *Luzanson* a private house lying between *Millaud* and *Saint Afrique*, in which there was a Garison that extreamly incommoded his passage; and

had

had continued till he had cleared the whole way, had not the intelligence he received of the defeat at *Fauch* diverted him; that made him double his pace, so that he came very opportunely to *Castres*; for *Lombez* was surrendred, *Realmont* was in Treaty, and the whole Countrey in a drooping condition: He cheered them up the best he could; yet all he could do, was not sufficient to get thirty Gentlemen, nor two hundred Foot together in all the upper *Languedoc*; So that his whole dependance was only on those he brought with him from the Lower *Languedoc*, and the *Sevenes*.

Another fear also perplexed him, lest in his absence, *Chastillon* should recall his Troops, to prevent which, he opposed against him an Assembly of five Provinces, viz. The Lower *Languedoc*, the *Sevenes*, *Vivaretz*, the Upper *Languedoc*, and *Dauphine*, who impowered him to detaine the supplyes he already had, and to raise more in case he had occasion for them.

Things being in this condition, the Duke sends to discover what Fordes were passable and not guarded, furnishes himself with good guides, and formes his design to relieve *Montauban*, at the same time, by the way of *Ville-nouvelle*, by *Saint Antonin*, and of *Ville-Bourbon* by *Carming*. The first of which is five Leagues distant from *Montauban*, the other ten; so that he intended to put in his greatest relief, consisting all of Foot, on that side; and the lesser, composed of *Dragoons*, and threescore *Reformado's* only, on the other.

In the interim of these actions, the Constable *Luynes* seeing that his Embassies sent to the Duke of *Rohan* by *Saint Angel* and *Saludie*, could not move him, nor the perswasions of the Duke of *Suly*, and *Lesdiguieres* those of *Montauban*, who still replyed, That they would do nothing without the advice and consent of their General, resolved at length to give them leave to send their Deputies to him (who were conducted by *Desplans*) to try if that might produce an accommodation, who came just as the relief was ready to march: And very opportunely too; for the Duke understanding by them, that they wanted nothing but men, and that if they had but a thousand, or twelve hundred more, they were confident they should be able to hold out all that Winter, he promised them that, within eight dayes they should have the recruit they desired, gave them the Word, and Signal, and so they returned.

The Duke of *Rohan* had five hundred *Dragoons*, whom with hopes of pillaging the Countrey up to the very Gates of *Thoulouf*, he had encouraged to advance towards *Phylaurens*, *Cuc*, and *Carmaing*,

Carmaing; but when they were all met at their appointed Rendezvous, he sent them orders, by one of his Gentlemen to march directly to *Montauban*, which orders were not observed; either by reason of too much consideration, or apprehension of the danger, though there were less on that, than on the other side.

As for the other relief, commanded by *Beaufort*, one of his Colonels, it was better ordered: He marched from *Castres* in the evening, with about a thousand or twelve hundred men, comes to *Lombez* about one of the clock in the morning, where he stays till the next night, then fordes the *Tarn* at *Grave*, marches all night, and the next evening about five of the clock comes to *Saint Antonin*, without any ill *rencontre* at all: There he stays all the next day, and in the evening sets forward towards *Montauban*.

But the falseness of the guides he had taken up at *Saint Antonin*, who betrayed him, forced him to return thither againe: Three dayes after they sent him a guide from *Montauban*, who safely conducted him over the River *Veyrou* at a Forde, and brought him very well within half a League of the Town; whence, notwithstanding the several parties both of Horse and Foot he perpetually met with between that and the Town, and the many Redoubts and trenches that obstructed his passage, he vanquished all those difficulties, and put seven hundred men, and nine Colours into *Montauban*: But *Beaufort* himself came short of it, being taken in this brave action: And it is to be observed, that this relief which consisted all of Foot, marched every day almost eighteen Leagues in an enemies Countrey, forded through two dangerous Rivers, and passed through the mid'st of two Royal Armies that lay in wait to defeat them.

The Duke of *Rohan* took a double course to prosper the design of this relief; one was by sending *Calonges*, and *D. s-Isles* with *Desplans* to consult with those before *Montauban*, about some way of accommodation; the other was, by marching at the same time that *Beaufort* did, with forty Colours of Foot, and those few Horse he had, towards *Lauraguais*: So that when the Duke of *Angoulesme* was ready to pursue *Beaufort* with all his Cavalry, he received intelligence that the Duke of *Rohan*, with the greatest part of his forces, was upon his march for *Lauraguais*, which put such a Dilemma on him, that he knew not which way to turn; and in the mean time *Beaufort* passes through the mid'st of his Army, and the Duke of *Rohan*, the day following, return'd to *Castres*, and sent back his Troops to the places whence he had drawn them.

Calonges

Calonges and *Des-Isles* were in the King's Quarters, when these supplies got in, and thence returned to *Castres* with *Desplans*, who from the Constable carried the Duke of *Rohan* an invitation to an interview, which he accepted of; and notwithstanding the disswasions of the people of *Castres*, and almost every one that was about him, he went to *Villemur*, and had a conference with him at *Reviers*, about a League from *Montdisban*, where after an exchange of many complements, the Constable led him aside into an Alley, and there began with him in this manner; I am much obliged to you that you have reposed such confidence in me; it shall not at all deceive you; you are no less secure here than in *Castres*: Being entred into your allyance, I cannot but be studious of your prosperity; deprive me not of the opportunity, during the favour I enjoy, to augment the splendour of your house. You have relieved *Montauban* even before your Soveraign's face, a glorious and heroick action; but abuse it not: It is high time for you to mind your own and your friends advantage; the King will never consent to a general peace; see therefore that you make conditions for your friends and servants, and let those of *Montauban* know that they have but a short reprieve from their ruine; that the Forts and Lines drawn about them, have barred up alwayes to their further relief that, unless they now accept of reasonable termes, to wit; either a Cittadel, Garison, or Demolition of all their fortifications, you will utterly desert them: As for *Castres*, and the rest of the places in your division, propose what you please, and it shall be granted; and for your own particular, a blanck is offered you; insert your own conditions. In vaine may you hope for any assistance from *Germany*; they have more need to crave, than lend aide; or from *England*; you know the peaceable humour of that King; or from within our own Kingdome; the Queene Mother has all her support from *Spaine*, *Rome*, *Savoy*, and the *Jesuites*, who are no friends to the *Huguenots*; and as for *Monsieur* the Prince, a piece of money swayes him any way; As for *Monsieur* the Count of *Soissons*, I have received Letters from him and from his Mother, who is ready to send him in to the King: As for the other Grandees of *France*, I doubt not but you receive encouragement from them; but 'tis with intention to purchase their own ends at your expence. I have, with much difficulty, hitherto hindred the confiscation of your estate and Governments, I cannot longer oppose it; you must either resolve to fall under a certain and ignominious ruine, or to advance your house to a greater height than it ever yet knew: For if you persist in your obstinacy, the King will rather yield to all those of the Religion,

ligion besides, that he may have the satisfaction of making an example both of your person and family: But if you will now credit me, you shall break through these dangers with honor, and the favour of your King, and obtain whatever you shall desire, as to your own fortune, whose encrease I so much desire, as that it may be a support to mine.

To which the Duke of *Rohan* answered, I should be an enemy to my self, if I desired not my Prince his favour, and your friendship; I shall never refuse either goods or honours from my Master, nor from you the Offices of a good Kinsman: I very well consider the danger I am in, but I beseech you also reflect upon yours; you are mortally and universally hated, for that you alone ingross that which is the object of every ones desire: The ruine of those of the Religion is not so near, but that they may afford leasure enough to the Male-contents to tame their parties, and those that will not openly declare for us, will yet comply in any thing that may tend to your destruction. The beginnings of the Warres against those of the Religion, have commonly been with great disadvantages to them, which yet the restless and volatile humour of the *French*, the discontents of those that ruled not, and strangers have many times repaired: If you can obtaine a peace for us from the King, before the like mischiefs happen againe, it will be much for his honour and advantage; For having subdued the party without the least check, without any appearance either of divisions within, or relief from without, he will oblige his conquered, and manifest to the world, that 'tis not the Religion he persecutes, but the Professours of it; for their pretended disobedience, will break the neck of all other factions, and, without any prejudice received, will return a feared and honoured Conquerour: This will also redouble your credit with him, and seat you in a condition above the reach of any attempt whatsoever: But if you drive things on to the extremity, and this torrent of prosperity continue not its course, as it is like to finde a bay at *Montauban*, every one will re-erect his spirits, depressed by the businefs of *Pont de Ce*, and our later losses here, and infinite perplexities will you be involved in: Consider that you have already gathered all the fruits, that either your promises, or threats can produce, and that what is left of us fight for a Religion we believe to be the true one. As for my part I have already considered of the loss of my estate, and Offices, which if you have retarded out of respect to our alliance, I am obliged to you for it, but am fully resolved, and prepared for all extremities, being solemnly engaged by promise, my conscience also commanding me, not to hearken to any but a general Peace.

This Conference, because they would not admit of a general Treaty, proving ineffectual, the Duke of *Rohan* returned to *Castres*. The difficulties at the Siege of *Montauban* dayly encreasing, the Constable listened to the better dictates of his second thoughts, and renewed the Treaty: But the unsteadiness of his spirit, too fickle to perfect any thing, and the contradictions he met with from those that desired a continuation of the War, intangled him still in delayes, till the King was necessitated to raise the Siege of *Montauban*, on the eighteenth of *November*, One thousand six hundred twenty one, where *La Force*, and the first *Consul Dupuy*, a man of great authority and courage ordered all things so exactly for the defence of the Town, and execution of the publick resolutions, that they may worthily claime a great part in the honour of preserving the place.

The Duke of *Rohan* in the mean while, had sent his troops into the County of *Foix* upon the sollicitation of *Leran*, who with them took in some Castles, and afterwards laid Siege to *Vareilles*, which was relieved, and he, in some disorder, retreated to *Pamiers*: But seeing the King's Army now at liberty, having quitted the Siege of *Montauban*, he took care to provide for those places were most in danger; and remanded his Forces from *Foix*: *Saint Florent*, one of his Colonels, and a Kinsman of the Constables, to make his own conditions, had intended to seize upon *Saint Espuel*; and in pursuance of that design, and that he might with less difficulty be received into the Town, with his Regiment, counterfeited a Letter from the Duke of *Rohan*; But the Consuls, forewarn'd of his purposes, refus'd to let him in; so that the stay he made thereabouts, gave the enemy an opportunity to prepare an Ambascade for him between *le Mas* and *Revel*, where in the night time he was totaliy defeated, without any resistance made of his side.

Mirambeau the eldest son of *Pardaillan*, perceiving that his father had compounded for *Monheur*, and *Saint Foy*, and that he was to deliver them up to the King as he marched by, enters and seizes upon *Monheur*, the news of which hurried his father thither, who treats him very severely; and thinking he had now entirely secured that place, returns to *Saint Foy* to make sure of that also: But God would not suffer his treachery to escape longer unpunished, raising up *Savignac* of *Nisse*, who lay in wait for, and slew him in an Inn in *Gensac*; whereupon *Mirambeau* in *Monheur*, and *Terbon* his brother-in-law in *Saint Foy* declared for the Party of the Religion: The King, having intelligence of this alteration, sends speedily to block up *Monheur*, and marches after in person with the rest of his Army, besieges and

Book II. *The Memoires of the Duke of Rohan.* 67

and takes it upon composition; During this Siege the Constable dyed of sickness; his death wrought a great change in the Court: The Queen-Mother, seeing her self rid of her deadly enemy, begins to cheer up again; The Prince also returns to the Court, in hope now to Paramount it there; every one aims at the vacant place, and all remembrance of the designes contrived in the Constables life time was buried with him.

The Cardinal *de Retz*, and *Schomberg*, usurp the management of the State affairs, the Prince came to wait upon the King at *Poictiers*, who joyned with them, and so potent was their party grown, before they came to *Paris*, as that the endeavours of the Queen-Mother, and all the Ancient Ministers of State, were nothing available to incline things to any propensity to peace. The Duke of *Lesdiguieres*, upon some commotions raised in *Dauphine* by *Montbrun*, immediately after the Siege of *Montauban*, got leave to go thither, and takes order for their suppression. The Duke of *Rohan* also sent back all the Troops he had out of the lower *Languedoc*, and the *Sevenes*, whither we must now reflect, to see what this interim produced there.

Chastillon proposes to the Assembly of the five Provinces, the recalling of their Forces, upon pretence to relieve the lower *Languedoc*, which yet was no way invaded, but they rejected the proposition; so that, this invention taking no effect, as to prevent the Duke of *Rohan* of new supplies; he causes a new levy to be made (at which he was not present himself) which the Assembly gave way to, upon the engagement of the Captains to wait upon him, in case the Duke of *Rohan* should command them, which yet they refused to do upon his summons, saying, That they owned no General but *Chastillon*, but trifled away their time in besieging *Alzon*, a paltry Town of no importance. In short, *Chastillon* in all things, and places, opposed the authority of the Assembly, who, in requital (with the assistance of the people) devested him of all his power, forcing him to quit *Montpellier*, and retire to *Aiguemortes*, while they detained his Son, and Mother-in-law. *Berticheres* who was chosen Lieutenant of the lower *Languedoc*, adhered to the Assembly, who having tasted the sweetness of their authority, would by no means hear of a General, but continued their government till the latter end of the year, that the people began to find it insupportable; which they perceiving, elected the Duke of *Rohan*, who immediately set forward towards the Province, and came to *Montpellier* on *New-years-day*, 1622.

At his arrival there the Duke found the Provinces of the lower *Languedoc*, and the *Sevenes*, engaged in such broyles against the Assembly of the five Provinces, that he was necessitated to spend the whole month of *January* in endeavours to compose them: The Provinces declared that the Assembly had exhausted their treasures, of which they were resolved they should render them an account; and that, since there was a General chosen, they ought no longer to prolong their Session.

The Assembly on the other side, maintained, That they ought no account to any but to the Assembly general, from whom they derived their authority; that they ought to continue in full power, till a final determination of all affairs; that the General ought to have no other Council but themselves; and that to them belonged the sole management of the *Finances*; that they were Superiour to the particular Provinces, who had nothing to do to supervise their actions, nor had they power of themselves to summon any Conventions; and perswaded the Duke to interdict them, as themselves, before his arrival, had intended to have done: But he, seeing the Province of the *Sevenes* was already convened, and that the lower *Languedoc* was resolved upon the like course, endeavoured to get the Assemblies allowance of it, who instead of assenting to it, because they foresaw it would much impaire the continuation of their Session, resolved on other wayes to prolong it. And first of all they used all possible means to possess themselves of the Castle of *Sommiers*, backed by *Berticheres*, who pretended a right to it, and addressed themselves to *Chastillon* for his assistance: But defeated of their purposes by the diligence of the Duke of Rohan, and the Castle secured, they turn their applications to the Duke de *Lesdiguieres*, to whom they described the Duke to be an ambitious person, desirous to perpetuate the War, that he might continue his power; and declaring also, that they had rather submit to a peace with the King upon any terms, than to his Tyranny; and that if he intermedled further with them, he should be taught to know the limits of his power; But he refusing to hearken to them, and all their other attempts failing of the success they aimed at, they send Deputies to the *Sevenes*, and the lower *Languedoc*, where the Duke was, who to prevent a further rupture (which proved a matter of great difficulty, so much were the Provinces of *Languedoc* incensed against the Assembly) got them to allow of the actions of the Assembly of the five Provinces, to receive their Deputies into their protection; that there should be no peace concluded without provision for their security, but that they should forbear to Act as an Assembly, till the business were fur-

further determin'd by the Assembly general, to whom all parties were to send their reasons; and that two Deputies of the Assembly of the five Provinces, should be of the Duke of *Rohan*'s Council.

It is to be observed, that after the Duke's arrival at *Montpellier*, the Assembly that sate there, before his face, disposed absolutely of the *Finances*, and of all other affaires, made Laws, gave pass-ports, and protections; and in all that time referred nothing to his Council of War but one quarrel to be pieced up there; And when the Duke proposed to them a Convention of the States of all *Languedoc* to be held at *Millaud*, to consult about the raising of money, and to provide for the administration of Justice, they stiffely withstood it, because they feared it was to abrogate their authority.

When they had occasion to send to the Assembly general, the Duke moved that they would send joyntly with him and the other Provinces; but they were still for several Deputations, being resolved to calumniate him, what they could; which they did sufficiently by their Envoy *Babat* a Minister, who recounted the wonders they did, before the Duke came among them, who had since confounded all by his ambition; that, he pursued his own, at the expence of the publick Interest; that having ruined *Foix*, and *Albigeois*, he would do as much to the lower *Languedoc*, where he began to fix himself, and play *Rex*; that they were better fall into the hands of the King, and entirely submit to his will, than to be subject to this Duke; and that at length they should be faine to recall *Chastillon*: That they should beware of coming under the power of *Soubize*, who desired nothing more than the dissipation of the Assembly general, and had already written to the Duke, that it was composed only of seven or eight pitiful Rascals; and for conclusion, that if they would but impower them to continue their Session, they would curb the Duke well enough.

After the Convention of these Provincial Assemblies, the Duke of *Rohan*, considering, on one side, the preparations made by the Duke of *Montmorency* to invade him, the Levyes of the Duke of *Guise* in *Provence*, for the same purpose, *Chastillon*'s plots to undermine him, and the Levyes of the Duke *de Lesdiguieres* to invade *Vivaretz*; And on the other, the miserable condition he found the Provinces, he came to serve in, by reason of the many needless armings *Chastillon* had made there, to the great discouragement of the Souldiery, and ruine of their friends, Countrey, whence the Troops never stirred, exhausting of their treasures, and stores of Salt, aggravated by the impossibility of recovering more, by reason of *Aiguemortes*, which intercepted their Commerce, he resolved with all speed to hasten his Levies.

    Blaccons Lieutenant of *Vivaretz* being in the mean while hard beset by the Duke of *Lesdiguiers*, sollicites the Duke of *Rohan* for a supply of five hundred men, and withal, that he would make haste to follow them with his whole forces: Those of *Bedarieux* and *Gignac*, likewise demand some relief, for that the Duke of *Montmorency* had suprized *Lunas*, and forced *Gressissac*, both private houses, besieged *Fougeres*, and threatned also the above named places: The Duke, having no Forces on Foot, and two Armies upon his hands, excluding the Troops of *Provence*, goes to the *Sevenes* to try if he could thence pass five hundred men into *Vivaretz*; but at the straights near *Villeneufve de Berg*, were they repulsed, which obliged him to send to the Duke of *Lesdiguieres*, to see if he could by any means retard his advance: But, notwithstanding his Remonstrances, and the dead of Winter besides, he continues his march with six thousand Foot, and five hundred Horse; to make a Bridge over the *Rhone*, between *Bay* and *Pousin*, besieges *Pousin*, and batters it, which abides his assault, *Blaccons* gets in to it, and behaves himself bravely in the storme; at length, the place being ready to be lost, by the mediation of him, whom the Duke of *Rohan* had sent to the Duke de *Lesdiguieres*, was yielded to him, upon condition, that if the peace (they were now in Treaty on) were not concluded, he should again restore it to those of the Religion; that he should forthwith withdraw his Army, and should not make any further attempts in *Vivaretz*, nor *Languedoc*: And he for his part promised, as soon as possible, to send the President *Du Cros* to proceed in the Treaty for a Peace.

    The Province of *Vivarets* Assembled at *Privas*, approved of all, and wrote to the Duke of *Rohan*, in favour of *Blaccons*, that he would confer on him the Government of *Bay*, which he granted.

    The Duke, thus freed of the Army of *Dauphine*, thinks now of Victualling *Gignac* (which was well near starved, by reason of a Church well fortified, and strongly garison'd by the enemy, distant about a Musket shot from the Town, the whole Countrey round about them being enemies also) and advancing with his Army to oppose the progress of the Duke of *Montmorency*: In order to which he came to *Montp*ll*er*, where he presently fell sick of a Feaver, which lasted him fifteen dayes; In the mean while the President *Du Cros*, that at the beginning of his Malady came to see him, was cruelly assassinated in the Town, and *Berticheres*, by his order, Victualled *Gognac*.

Book II.   *The Memoires of the Duke of* Rohan.   71

Having recovered his health, about the beginning of *March*, and speeded his Levies, he took the field, before he was well able to endure it, *Berticheres* made a motion to attach the Tower *Charbonniere*, that opening that passage they might have Salt by that way, and consequently money to defray part of the charges of the War; *Saint Blancart*, Governour of *Peccaix*, seconded the Proposition, so that, that designe was concluded on; *Chastillon* presently had notice of it, and the Duke of *Rohan* was informed that *Berticheres* had faithfully promised him that he would ruine all his troops: Wherefore the Duke resolved to refer this businesse to a farther debate; at which he urged against *Berticheres* the difficulty of the siege; *Saint Blancart* thereupon stood up, and said, That unlesse they resolved on it, he would comply with *Chastillon*, there being otherwise no possibility of their subsistence; so that he was constrained to yeild to it; and in the meane while he makes an attempt on *Beaucaire*, which succeeding not, by reason of the extream coldnesse, and tempestuousnesse of the night, it was executed in, he returned to the Tower *Charbonniere*, where he found that instead of advancing, they were driven off, and that they had suffered *Chastillon* to fortifie several intrenchments he had made upon a Causey, which at first might have easily been forced, but would now require more than a moneths time to take them. Moreover, they had drawn off those souldiers the Duke had lodg'd between *Aiguemortes* and *Charbonniere*; all which he well considering, without imparting his resolution to *Berticheres*, sends to block up the Castle of *Montlaur*, that hindred the intercourse between *Montpellier*, and the *Sevenes*, and afterwards went in person to the siege of it, with intent to draw off the Duke of *Montmorency* from *Bedarieux*, who spent so much time in taking of *Fougeres* that he could not come early enough before *Montlaur* was taken by assault.

Immediately after this action was over, the Duke *de Lesdiguieres*, impowered by the King, invites the Duke of *Rohan* to a personal Treaty for a Peace, which he assented to, leaving his Army under the command of *Berticheres*; At *Laval*, between *Barjac*, and *Saint Esprit* was their interview, where they agreed on Articles to be treated on, and the Duke of *Rohan*, in his own, and the name of the Provinces of his Division, appointed *Calongues*, *Des-Isles*, *Dupuy* of *Montauban*, *Du Cros* of *Montpellier*, and *La Borée* of *Vivaretz* for their deputies: Both he, and the Duke *de Lesdiguieres* joyntly advertise the Dukes of *Bouillon*, *Sully*, *Trimouille*, and *Soubize*, *La Force* also, and the Assembly general of this Treaty, that they might all send their Deputies to joyn with those of the Provinces; informing them withal, that as concerning *Saumure*,

F 4   and

and the places of *Poictou*, they could not conclude any thing, but must remit them to other things to be terminated by the King himself: We must now leave the Deputies on their journies, to take a view of what passed in the lower *Languedoc*.

The Duke of *Rohan* returned to his Army, which he found at *Castelnau* near *Montpellier*; The Duke of *Montmorency*, with *Chastillon*, who was now joyned with him with his *Gens-a' armes*, or horse men compleatly armed, and those of the Duke of *Guise*, which he had sent for out of *Provence*, had besieged *Courvousée*, two leagues distant from *Montpellier*, which the Duke of *Rohan* had resolved to relieve, but the place being yeilded the next day, he encamped at *Saint John de Vedas*, and *Salle-neufve*, and the Duke of *Montmorency* at *La Veruve*, *Fabregues*, and *Sauffan*; a small river called *Mouffon*, parted them, so that for six dayes together, both armies played only with their Canon one upon another, after which the Duke of *Montmorency* retires to *Ville-neufve* a small Town upon the Lake. The Duke of *Rohan* the same day drew off to other quarters also, and in his march summoned *Sauffan* in which was left a Garrison, which yeilded the next morning.

Berticheres, whether it was that he feared the losse of his goods, or that he desired to ruine the Dukes Army, or that really he had received such intelligence, comes and tells the Duke, that for certain the Duke of *Montmorency* had passed the Lake, and was marching towards Saint *Gilles*, an Abbey belonging to *Berticheres*, and a very convenient place for a Magazine; beseeching him to allow him fifteen hundred foot, and an hundred horse to prevent him, and that according to the intelligence he should receive from him, the rest of the forces might be in a readinesse to follow him; which the Duke granted him; and in the meane while, with two thousand men he had left, goes to besiege *Saint Georges* : But the Duke of *Montmorency* hearing that *Sain Georges* was besieged, and that the Duke of *Rohan*'s army was divided, returns to relieve it, takes up his quarters at *Saint John de Vedas*, a league from *Saint Georges*, and by discharging of two piece of Canon, gives them a signal of the succours he had brought, and that very night essayed to put in two hundred men, who were briskly repulsed. The next day the Duke of *Rohan*, leaving three hundred men to continue the siege, made choice of a very advantageous place to fight in, and there stayed all the day; and in the interim, sent with all speed to *Berticheres* to command him back. That evening came *Blacquiere* to him, with a Regiment out of the *Sevenes*, and the next day *Malauze*, with fourscore horse from the upper *Languedoc*, and *Berticheres* stayed not long behinde; so that the Duke being

now

now three thousand foot, and three hundred horse strong, in the very sight of the Duke of *Montmorency*, raises his batteries, and takes the place, which was yeilded upon composition, the defendants lives only saved.

Berticheres was the second time like to have been the occasion of another great fault, by his obstinate affirming that the Duke of *Montmorency* was retreated to *Ville-neufue*, and had left five hundred men at the Bridge of *Veruve*, which might be easily cut off. The Duke of *Rohan* was of a contrary opinion, averring, that if he himself were gone off, he would not have left those foot to the slaughter; the other desirous to evidence what he had affirmed, leads him towards the Bridge, where they found some forlorne parties of Musquetires in the ditches, which they soone made them quit: But *Rohan* perceiving that *Berticheres* had engaged a Regiment too far, commands all his forces, both horse and foot, to advance, and two field-pieces to be drawn after them; *Berticheres* closely pursues his designe, commands *Blacquiere*'s Regiment to storme the trenches at the Bridge, and another Squadron to second them: But this being but an extempore project, and executed without any precedent deliberation, was also without successe: For *Blacquiere*, and his Serjeant Major *Randon* being slaine with Musquet shot, the whole party retreated in disorder; and at the same instant the Duke of *Montmorency* drew all his Army into *Battalia*, firing two field-pieces on our men; *Rohan* made him the like return from his side, and all the remaining part of that day was spent in *Canenades*, and light skirmishes; the river *Mousson* still separating the Armies, who in the evening drew off to their quarters: There were ten or twelve slain on either side; and the Duke of *Montmorency* the second time retired to *Ville-neufue*; whence, leaving his Troops in Garrison in the adjacent places he went to *Pezenas*; which the Duke of *Rohan* having notice of, takes with him provision for two dayes, and with two Culverins marches that night to *Gignac*, blocks up the garrison'd Church adjoyning to it, raises his battery in the open day, and after the first Volley took it upon capitulation, and having demolished it, returns towards *Montpellier*; taking his way through the Valley of *Montferrant*, where he took and dismantled *Mattelais*, and other little places, and fortified Churches, which yeilded his souldiers good booty, which was the reason that some of the Troops of the *Sevenes*, finding themselves so near home, forsook him.

Montpellier thus freed from the inconvenience of the enemies Garrisons, made *Usez* desirous of the like benefit. Thither the Duke of *Rohan* marches, and upon composition takes *Cerniers*, a Castle whose situation did indifferently secure it from any battery, and

and *Saint Suffret* by assault: But as he thought to have made a farther progresse, he was prevented by a request from the principal inhabitants of *Nismes*, to come to their Town, to suppresse a Sedition lately raised there; which with all diligence he did, leaving to *Berticheres* the charge of his Troops, the greatest part of which deserted their colours, so that there were not left a thousand men together, *Portes*, having gotten together near two thousand men besieges *Pruzillac*, a paltry place, which had before been surrendred to *Berticheres*, who put in to it the Colonel *Beauvois*, who having handsomly defended it for two dayes, was at length forced, for want of powder, to give it up.

Chastillon at the same time comes before *La Tour l' Abbé*, near *Peccaix*, and belonging to *Saint Blancart*, which, either by the Cowardize or Treachery of *Bousauguet* who commanded it, was within the space of twice four and twenty hours, surrendred; So that *Rohan*, who had rallyed some troops for that end, had not leasure to relieve it, nor means any longer to keep his forces together, with which he had marced up and down for three moneths together without any pay, and made many sieges, both by reason of the refractorinesse of his Colonels, and the approaching harvest, a season, in which the poor of the lower *Languedoc* gaine their whole subsistence.

To return to *Nismes*, It is to be observed that *Brison* had been protected and gratified by the Duke of *Rohan* more than any other, out of hopes he had to win him that way: But he, being of a nature on which no obligations could prevail, ingrateful, and presumptuous, had, notwithstanding [designed to possesse himself of *Nismes*, to make his own conditions withal; pretending a most transcendent zeal to their cause, and losing no opportunity to asperse the Duke with calumnies, openly declaring that he had betrayed *Pousin* to the Duke *de Lesdiguieres*, and was the sole cause of the losse of *Vivaretz*. He conspired also with the Deputies of the Assembly of the five Provinces, who, instead of returning to their own homes, went from town to town irritating the people against the Duke of *Rohan*; and having now made sure of *Brison*, and his assistance in *Nismes* were resolved upon the first opportunity to reassemble there, to oppose the authority of the Duke of *Rohan*, who being informed that they were all met at *Nismes*, with intention to begin again their Assembly, sent one of his Gentlemen to forbid them, and to command the Deputies of *Vivaretz* to return to their Province, shewing them withal the Deposition of *Babat*, wherein the Deputies had most basely scandalized him, which *Brison* stoutly opposed; but found not the people any way inclineable to be led by his passion; So that, the Deputies were

forced

Book II. *The Memoires of the Duke of* Rohan. 75

forced to be gone, and *Brison* to wait upon the Duke to excuse this procedure.

Whil'st he was upon his journey, the principal inhabitants of *Nismes*, making good use of his absence, took occasion to procure a Declaration of the general Council of the Town, that the Government of *Brison* was no longer supportable, that *Rohan* should be requested to approve of this result of their deliberations, and that they might be permitted to live under the sole authority of their own Consuls, till a more urgent necessity should require a Governour, and that then they would accept of any one he should please to place over them; and that he would with all speed repair to their town to prevent any disorders might survene: Whereupon he went thither, and there approved of and ratified this act of their Council. At the same time was there held an Assembly at *Nismes* to take order for the securing of their harvest; to whom *Brison* addressed his complaints; But the Assembly waved them, and approved of the determination of the Council, and the Dukes confirmation of it: *Brison* seeing he could not this way arrive at his aimes, goes to *Montpellier*, and in all places endeavours to stir up the people against the Duke of *Rohan*, attempting also by means of his Confederates to raise a sedition in *Nismes*; which the Duke having notice of, sends the Lieutenant of his Guards with a command to arrest him, where ever he should find him, who, after some time spent in the search of him, at length arrests him in *Usez*.

When *Nismes* was thus secured, order was taken for the levying, and paying of a sufficient number of Souldiers to preserve the Countreys about *Montpellier*, *Nismes*, and *Usez* from the spoyle, and ravage, the Duke of *Montmorency* had orders from the King to make in those parts, and also to send some supplies to *Montauban*.

After the holding of this Assembly, it was thought fit that another should be convened in the *Sevenes* for the same cause; and forasmuch as the Duke of *Montmorency* already began to burne, and waste the places near. *Montpellier*, *Rohan* to prevent farther mischief, left *Laudez* his Quartermaster-General with a Brigade of horse: upon the first approaches of *Montreal* Major-General to the Duke of *Montmorency*, at a contest about a Farme-house, the Adjutant seeing his son too far engaged, goes with some Musquetires to disengage him, whereupon *Montreal* charges him with above an hundred horse; but *Laudez* came very opportunely to his rescue, charged, and wounded *Montreal* with his own hand, made him flie, and pursued him fighting up to his own body, which was in so tottering a condition, that had *Saint Andre* the

King's

King's Lieutenant of *Montpelier* made use of that opportunity to charge them, he had utterly routed the whole party.

We must now return to the otherside of the *Loire*, and the Deputies the Duke of *Rohan* had sent to the Court: Those that were desirous of Peace, endeavoured to keep the King at *Paris* to expect those Deputies, of whose speedy arrival the Duke *de Lesdiguires* had given notice; for that the Chancellour, and the President *Janin*, who were unfit for travel, could not otherwise be present at the Council, nor consequently be able to withstand the violent motions of those who were inclined to a prolongation of the warre, which they perceiving, omitted no inventions to withdraw the King from *Paris*, and on *Palm-Sunday* carried him by stealth, out at a back gate of the *Louvre*, just as if they were running away with him, to keep his *Easter* at *Orleans*; whence, without staying for the Queen-Mother, he goes down the River as far as *Nantes*; the fortunate successe of the Duke of *Soubize* obliged him to take this course; who with two thousand men, in the middest of all the Duke d' *Espernon*'s forces, in *Xaintonge*, and *Angoulmois*, of the Count de *Rochefoucaults* in *Pictou*, and *Saint Lukes* in the Islands had seized and fortified the Isle of *Oleron*, taken *Royan*, the Tower of *Mournac*, *Saugeon*, and several other places, totally defeated *Saint Luke*'s Regiment, and at noone-day forced *La Chaume*, and took *Les Sables*: In short, he struck so great a terror into the Countrey, that had not the King's arrival prevented him, he had absolutely made himself Master of the field: But before the arrival of the Duke of *Rohan*'s Deputies, the condition of affairs in *Pictou* being much altered by the defeat of *Riez*, the retaking of *Royan*, and the Treaty commenced by *La Force*, they were remitted to the Queen-Mother, who stayed at *Nantes*, and from thence to the Chancellour at *Paris*, so that they returned without having effected any thing: The King keeping on his way in *Guienne*, concludes the Treaty with *La Force*, who for a Marshal of *France* his staff, and two hundred thousand crowns gave up *Saint Foy*, which he had injuriously gotten, and detained from *Terbon Pardaillan*'s son in law: And he, and his sons gave up all the Offices, and Governments they enjoyed, without the privity of the Assembly general or the Duke of *Rohan*.

While this Treaty was in agitation, *Tonneins*, after a handsome defence, was surrendred to the Duke d' *Elbeuf*; and *Luzignan* made a particular composition for *Clerac*, which he yielded also, so that the King came to *Saint Antonin* without any other opposition: The Inhabitants of *Montauban*, mindful of the good Offices they had received from those of *Saint Antonin*, though they feared they should disfurnish themselves of Souldiers,

ers, sent thither *Saint Sebastien* a Captain in *Beaufort*'s Regiment, with what Souldiers they could spare to command the place: But his being mortally wounded, in an assault made upon some out-works, which were carried by main force, together with the springing of some Mines, so terrified the Inhabitants, that in great confusion, and so suddenly yielded they the Town, that two hundred men, which they desired from *Montauban*, conducted by *Salce*, and *Rousseliere* found the place taken, where they were quietly let in by the enemy who stabbed many of them, before the rest could perceive that the place was lost. But at length discovering their error, they saved themselves the best they could; *Salce* and *Rousseliere* were taken, and not released but by the Articles of Peace.

Those of *Montauban* fearing that from *Saint Antonin* the next visit would be to them, sollicited the Duke of *Rohan* for a Governour, and some supplies of men, who sent them *Saint André de Montbrun*, who with great courage, and equal fortune made way for himself and five Hundred Men into the Town.

The King's approach to the higher *Languedoc* greatly disheartned the whole party, and gave those that were false among them an occasion to renew their intelligences; Every Town in particular, sent the same harsh message to the Duke, that unless he presently repair thither, the whole Countrey will be given up. This cast him into many anxious perplexities; for if he goes not whither he is called, the Countrey is lost; and if he does go, he leaves the lower *Languedoc* to a manifest hazard, where his absence would give *Chastillon* an opportunity to revive his factions and conspiracies: And on the other side the Duke *de Lesdiguieres* presses him with reiterated summons to a second interview: At length he resolves to relieve those that were most necessitated, excuses himself to *Lesdiguieres*, sends a renfort of Souldiers to *Monpellier*, to preserve their fields from ravage, by reason that the Duke of *Montmorency* had received a recruit of five Troops of light Horse, which *Zamet* brought him from the King's Army, and gives order for the levying of a thousand men for the higher *Languedoc*; whither as he was going with his own attendants only, *Chauve*, Minister of the Church of *Sommiers*, a man of exemplary piety, and singular eloquence, comes to him at *Saint John de Gardonnenque*, and tells him that he knew, and that by very good information, that *Chastillon*, much displeased with himself for his former actions, was sore troubled to see the imminent ruine of those of the Religion, whom, but for the affronts he had received, he had never deserted; and was confi-

dent,

dent, that if he were handsomely dealt with, he would return again to the party, to the great advantage of it, both by reason of the consideration of his person, especially in *Languedoc*, and of the consequence of the Town of *Aiguemortes*, which was in his hands. This was a device of *Chastillon*'s confederates, who, knowing the reputation of this Minister, had abused him with these hopes, that the Dukes refusal to admit of him, might furnish them with more specious pretences on which to ground their detractions and new calumnies against him ; which the Duke very well foreseeing, answers, That he was so farre from diverting his good intentions, or hindring a work of so general concernment, as the regaining such a person to their party, that, on the contrary, in any thing tending to their advantage, he would meet him more than half way: As for the command conferred on him, by reason of the other's absenting himself from the Province, as he had never sued for it, so neither was he so fond of it, as not to yield it up, whenever the Province that gave it him should think fit to revoke it ; and that he wished with all his heart, that he would seriously and in good earnest, comply with his duty to his own, and the publick Interests ; that for his part, he was contented with the command assigned him by the general Assembly at *Rochell*, in the upper *Guienne*, and the upper *Languedoc*, whither he was now going to provide against the dangers the King's approach gave them cause to feare, leaving the way open for *Chastillon* to return to those he had before forsaken: However the duty he owed both to his imployment, and conscience, obliged him to say, that there were yet many things in this case to be considered, and that the Province ought maturely to weigh, and every one in particular strictly to examine the importance and consequences of this affair, and principally *Chauve* himself, both by reason of his profession, and the charge he had now undertaken: But that the infallible tryal of his sincerity would be, whether he would effectively deliver up into the hands of the Province, the Town of *Aiguemortes* ; for that if his pretences to serve the party were real and sincere, he would make no difficulty of it, but if feigned and fallacious, he would never dis-possesse himself of it : *Chauve* very well approved the motion, believing he would accept of it ; and so returned.

The Duke foreseeing that in his absence this businesse would be moved again, gave an especial charge to *Dupuy* (whom he left his Agent in that Province) to take great heed, that nothing passed there, to the prejudice of the publick or his Interest; to which end he gave him sufficient power, and instructions, tending,

ding chiefly to this, that if this proposition were started in any Assembly whatsoever, and that they should proceed to Treat on it without the precedent condition, to wit, that the Garison of *Aiguemortes* should be first restored to the disposal of the Province, he should oppose it; and if they Treated on those termes, he should see that there were no foul play used, and that nothing were concluded without a previous performance of that condition.

This done, he proceeds in his journey to the higher *Languedoc*, and arrives there just upon the taking of *Saint Antonin*, and so opportunely, that he prevented the Rendition of *Lombez* and *Realmont*, and revives the drooping and almost decayed spirits of the whole Countrey, in which he lost nothing but *Carmaing*, *Saint Espuel*, and *Cucq*; the first by treachery, the other two by reason of their weaknes were quitted by the inhabitants, and afterwards fired, as the Army marched by.

The King seeing, that the Countrey resumed their courages, advances further, carried on with the hopes the Duke of *Montmorency* and *Chastillon* gave him, and chiefly of *Montpellier*, sending all his Ammunition down the *Rhone* to the lower *Languedoc*; *Blaccons* revolt, who sold *Baye* to the King for twenty thousand Crowns, having opened the passage of that River: The Duke of *Rohan* on the other side gets before them, and enters *Montpellier* at the same time the King got into *Beziers*; leaving a thousand Foot with *Malauze* to assist him against the Duke of *Vendosme*, whom the King had left with an Army in the higher *Languedoc*, as he had also the Marshal *Themines* with other Troops about *Montauban*.

About the same time came a Gentleman to the Duke of *Rohan*, from the Duke of *Boüillon*, with credential Letters, importing also his resentments of the miseries of those of the Religion; that he thought a Peace would have been concluded at *Saint John*; and afterwards at *Montauban*, that, since that he understood that he and the Duke *de Lesdiguieres* were in Treaty about it, that he advised him to conclude it upon any terms, provided it were general; for that being not able to dispute the field with the King, for want of forraign assistance, their destruction, though it might be retarded, would yet be inevitable, and that the longer the peace was deferred, the more disadvantageous would it be: Nevertheles if it was our ruine, that they had inalterably decreed, that he would take the field with what forces he could make, to assist the party by a considerable diversion of the enemy; that he was in Treaty with Count *Mansfeld*, and that he desired three things of the Duke: First, that he would in-impower him to Treat with Forraigners: Secondly, that he, and the Provinces under his command, should oblige themselves to bear an equal share of the charge of the Levyes: Thirdly, that no Peace should be concluded without him; all which Propositions were assented to, and the Gentleman returned well satisfied, having also received a faithful assurance, that if the peace were not made by the first of *September*, it should not be concluded without him, provided that within the time limited he were certified of his acceptance of the conditions.

In the absence of the Duke of *Rohan* from the lower *Languedoc*, the Council of that Province, composed at that time of the Deputies of the three Towns of *Montpellier*, *Nismess* and *Usez*, imagining that since *Saint Antonin* was taken, they might be the next the King would invade, and that though the fortifications of *Montpellier* were already well advanced, yet was it unprovided of men and provisions, conceived it necessary to assemble the whole body of the Province, to order all; and *Lunel* was the place designed for the Assembly to be kept at; where when all the Deputies with *Dupuy* were met, and had debated, and resolved on what concerned the victualling and securing of *Montpellier*, and other places in case they should be besieged; the adherents of *Chastillon*, of which there were many present, having made their party, thinking to make their advantage of this opportunity, produced againe the Articles for his re-establishment: The Deputies of the three Towns, voluntarily, and of themselves opposed this overture, for fear of falling into the hands, and under the command of one, they had so highly offended, by devesting him of his charge; Protesting to the Assembly, that if they assumed any other debate than what concerned the executing of the Decrees already past, for the relief of *Montpellier*, and other places, they would utterly desert them, and disavow all their future determinations; *Dupuy* in obedience to the command he had received, seconded this opposition, which *Berticheres* (Moderator of the Assembly, as being the Duke's Lieutenant General) also much countenanced, alledging, that they had no power to Assemble, in the absence, and without the permission of their General; and that though they were now convened, yet was it with his good leave and approbation, and upon the present exigency of affairs, of which they had given him an account, and that this necessity being now taken off, they ought to forbear the debate of other particular matters, till his return.

Nevertheless the confederates aforesaid resolutely persisted in their design, renforcing every day their sollicitations, with hopes to procure at length a resumption of the suspended debate,

and

Book II. *The Memoires of the Duke of* Rohan. 81

and to carry it by plurality of voices, or at least by this means to take off *Lunel*, *Aimargues*, and *Mauguio*, which adhering to *Chastillon*, would raise his esteem at Court; of which when the Deputies of the three Towns, and *Dupuy* had notice, they resolved, that at the first mention of it, they would object the interest of the Province of the *Sevenes*, which being a part of the Generality of the lower *Languedoc*, it must needs be prejudicial to the common repose of both the Provinces, to determine that affair, without the others intervention or privity; wherefore they sent a true account of all that had passed to the Council of that Province then sitting at *Anduze*, together with their advice concerning what they conceived ought to be done by them in the behalf of their Province: The same Deputies also, with *Dupuy*, went to *Bertichezes* to make sure of him, who faithfully promised to continue immoveable in his opposition. In the succeeding Sessions there were still some words thrown out by *Chastillon's* friends, concerning that subject, but they passed unregarded. In the mean while came the Deputies from the Assembly of the Province of the *Sevenes*, who made a large Remonstrance of the injuries their Province would receive from the change they would introduce in their proceedings, that it was an unheard of procedure, and that their Province could never suffer; that that of *Languedoc*, should by it self presume to abrogate the Decrees of the Assembly of the Circle, or five Provinces, in which the Deputies of the Assembly of the *Sevenes* had a joynt concurrence of Votes with those of the lower *Languedoc*; and moreover represented to the Assembly their own Interests, and the inconveniences would ensue their submitting themselves to the power and conduct of a man, whom they had so highly provoked, by the suspicions they had of him; and in the last place protested, That in case the Assembly should proceed further, in the absence of the Duke of *Rohan*, or without his consent and approbation, they would absolutely disclaim them.

This opposition of the Deputies of the Council of the *Sevenes*, seconded by those of the three Towns, grounded upon their own, and the large Commission, and power of *Dupuy* something cooled the heat of those sollicitours, which yet in a short time after they resumed again; and importuned *Chauve* anew, to prosecute what he had begun; which he would by no means undertake, without imparting it to *Dupuy*; who after he had remembred him, upon what terms he had parted with the Duke of *Rohan* at *Saint John de Gardonnenque*, tells him that he wou'd consider of it, and then give him his answer; and in the mean time had a conference about it with the Deputies of the three Towns, who thought

G it

it not unfit that *Chauve*, as of himself, and without any particular Commission, should sound *Chastillon*'s inclinations, to discover whether he would yield to that condition of delivering up *Aiguemortes* into the hands of the Province, which was then very opportunely met, to receive both it, and him, with all assurance he could desire of an Amnesty, and the continuance of their respects to him: It being most apparant, that *Chastillon*, who they knew desired nothing more than to intrude himself among us, only to render himself more considerable, and his Interests more favoured at Court, would never disfurnish himself of the only means left him, to procure a performance of the promises made him, and that thus they should also make him desist from his pursuit. When they had given *Chauve* their answer in these termes, he approved of it; and promised to comport himself according to their directions; and thereupon had a conference with *Bansillon* the Minister of *Aiguemortes*, who highly magnified the advantages this re-establishment of *Chastillon* would produce to their party in general: To whom *Chauve* replyed, That it would be impossible to efface the impressions *Chastillon*'s procedures had left in the whole Province, unless he supplied them with the means he had in his hands, by yielding up the Town of *Aiguemortes* to their disposal; which if he would do, they would evidence the contentment they had, to see a person of his quality return into the way from which he had digressed, by their promptness to serve and honour him, as they had formerly done: This discourse pleased not *Bansillon* at all, who told him, that he conceived that *Chastillon* neither would, nor ought to consent to this Proposition; that he had good reason to take heed of falling into those snares he knew were spread for him; for that having devested him of all power, they might the more easily dispose of him at their pleasure, or at least pay all his former service with the cold recompence of Oblivion, or neglect; and that therefore he conceived the Treaty absolutely broken: Upon which, as *Chauve* was about to leave him, he told him, that he would give *Chastillon* an account of all, and him an answer the next day at the same place; which he did, and in effect conformable to his own preconceptions; which absolutely cleared the judgement of *Chauve*, and many others also, when he had given the Assembly a Summary of this conference.

In the mean while the Deputies of the three Towns incessantly sollicited *Dupuy*, to press the Duke of *Rohan*'s return, representing to him the condition of the Province, and the danger it was in of being ruined by the divisions sprung from this late Proposition, and the delay his absence occasioned in the progress of their

their affaires: Whereupon *Dupuy* resolved, to make a journey himself to the Duke of *Rohan*: But yet he would not leave the Assembly, before he had gotten a promise from *Berticheres*, that there should be no more mention made of the aforesaid re-establishment for eight dayes, by which time he should return again from *Nismes* whither he pretended he was going; but in the mean time he goes by great journeys towards the Duke, whom he found at *Pont de Camares*, who having received from him an account of all passages, quitted all other things to return with all possible speed to the lower *Languedoc*: When he was come to *Mirveis*, he sent a Gentleman, with command to travel night and day to the Assembly, to let them know that he was within two days journey of them, and desired them to suspend all further debates concerning their affaires, till his arrival.

This unexpected news surprized the Assembly so, that instead of continuing their consultations, they went to meet him as farre as *Sommieres*, where when he had learned of them, what order they had taken for the raising of Souldiers, and supplying the Garisons with necessaries, he ratified what they had done, and so dismissed them.

Thus ended this tentative of *Chastillon*'s friends to restore him to a repute with the Party: After which *Rohan* went to *Montpellier*, where he turned fifteen or sixteen of his chiefest Confidents out of the Town, and ordered all things necessary (as before he had done at *Montauban*) for a siege, both for ammunition, victuals, and the fortifications.

It is to be observed, that in the Duke's absence, *Americ* the first Consul of *Montpellier*, and *Carlincas* his Kinsman, took occasion upon a defeat of two or three companies, near to *Perolles*, which *Saint André* had sent thither, while the enemy was plundering the Countrey thereabouts, to accuse him to the people, who had already a jealousie of him; and *Berticheres*, though his father-in-law, instead of assisting him, helped to thrust him out of the Town; not out of any affection to the cause, but of a pestilent ambition raigned among them; every one labouring to raise his own advantages upon the ruines of others, and better their conditions by delivering *Montpellier* to the King: But the seventeen dayes stay the Duke made there, and the discovery he made, by a Messenger of the President *Faure*, taken neare *Nism's*, that *Berticheres* Treated with the King, together with some Colonels, who were ordered for the defence of *Montpellier*; and the execution of *Bimayt*, who was one of them, reduced things to a better posture; But yet these disorders retarded the Levyes, so that of foure thousand Souldiers designed ed for the defence of the Town, they got in but fifteen hundred.

It is moreover to be noted, that the Duke of *Rohan* seeing the great want of Ammunition in the Province of lower *Languedoc*, and of time, and means to fortifie all their Garisons, proposed the dismantling of them, and the reducing of their forces to *Montpellier*, *Nismes*, *Usez*, and *Sommieres*; which the people then rejected, but have since, though too late, repented it; for their obstinacy drew upon them the loss both of their Estates and Liberties; for whiles they vainly trifled away their time and labour, in fortifying so many places, neither of them was fortified or defended as it ought, but both they, and the reliefs sent to them, which in the other places would have been of great use, were now made wholly unserviceable.

The King seeing that the care and diligence of the Duke of *Rohan* had defeated all the designes of those that would have delivered up *Montpellier* to him, staid some time at *Beziers* to expect his Ammunitions, and to recruit his Army: And in the mean time sent the Marshal *de Praslin* to besiege *Bedarieux*, which he took, and dismantled; and then sent the Duke of *Montmorency* to take in *Mauguio*, which the inhabitants knew not how to defend, nor yet would they quit it, nor spoyle the wines, as the Duke of *Rohan* had commanded them.

The Prince of *Condé* about this time came to the King's Army, and thence went to besiege *Lunel* and *Massillargues*, within half a League one of another, and sufficiently stored with all necessaries, there being in *Lunel* two Colonels besides the Governour, who all joyntly wrote to the Duke of *Rohan*, that if he would send them in but five hundred Souldiers, they would give a handsome account of the place: The Duke, when he had setled *Calonges* in *Montpellier*, and left *Dupuy* his Agent there, in his name to provide all things requisite for the defence of the Town, went purposely to prepare the desired supply, and sent them in eight hundred men; but much to their regret; for the next day, though they had not suffered any the least extremity, and that the breach made was not considerable, they yielded themselves with all their Arms, and Baggage. Those of *Massillargues* had done the like but a few dayes before: But the Articles of *Lunel* were violated even before the Prince of *Condé*'s face; for when the Garison marched out, they were beaten, disarmed, stript, and a great part of them killed or maimed; and in this lamentable posture went they to *Nismes* and *Sommieres*, on which they brought so great a terror, that upon the appearance of the enemy before *Sommieres*, in which there were fifteen hundred

dred men, they did even as bad as those of *Lunel*; and, which is a most shameful thing to be related, the Captains took two thousand Crowns, to leave their arms to the enemy.

The Town of *Nismes* alarmed by these sad accidents, sent Messengers to request a visit from the Duke of *Rohan*, which he willingly condescended to, but first got together as many Souldiers as he could at *Anduze*, which he left under the Command of *Charce* his Lieutenant General in the *Sevenes*, and of the Adjutant General, who when they saw the Duke of *Montmorency* return to the *Sevenes*, drew into a body about a quarter of a League from *Anduze*, at a Pass not easily accessible, which they fortified; and had not their care and diligence in furnishing *Sauve* and *Aletz* with two valiant and expert Commanders, and a thousand, or twelve hundred Souldiers, drawn out of *Saint Hyppolite*, and the places adjacent prevented it, those two Towns had been also lost: So that the good posture they were in, together with the Duke of *Rohan*'s obstructing of *Montmorency*'s provisions, which came a great way off, forced him, after a successeless voyage, to return again.

In the mean time the Marshal *Themines* plundred all the Countrey about *Montauban*, burnt all their Countrey houses, and obstructed their Vintage: But all this hindred not *Saint Andre de Montbrun*, their Governour, from drawing out his Canon, and battering, and taking many Castles, among others, *Ramie*, and *la Bastide*, and storing his Town with Corne and Wine for a whole yeare: He had also several Skirmishes with the Garison of *Montech*, and others also, and still came off with honour and advantage.

The Duke of *Vendosme* also with seven thousand Foot, and five hundred Horse, sate down before *Lombez*; *Malauze* comes to *Realmont* with intention to relieve it; but conceiving it not tenable against such a force, by reason of the weakness of the Town, and that the Castle which commanded it, was Garison'd by the enemy; contented himself after a long Skirmish, with drawing off the Souldiers, as well inhabitants, as strangers; and abandons the town, which was burnt. From *Lombez* the Duke marches to besiege *Briteste*, a little place, weak of it self, and commanded almost on every side: Thither *Malauze* sent five hundred men under the Command of *Faucon*, one of *Sesigny*'s Captains, who behaved himself very gallantly: He endured the Siege a month or more, beat them off in four or five assaults, was twice relieved with fresh supplies of men and powder, by *Malauze*, whose main body lay at *Saint Paul* and *Miatte*, about a League and half from *Briteste*, and never had more than two thousand Foot, and two hundred Volunteers on Horse-back, with whom, and by the means of the brave resistance of the besieged, he did so well, that the Duke of *Vendosme*, being commanded by the King to come, and joyn his Forces with the Army that lay before *Montpellier*, raised the siege after he had spent two thousand Canon bullets on them, and lost fifteen hundred of his men; and those within the town three hundred.

The departure of this Army, freed the whole Country from much harm, and greater fears; and invites us to return to the lower *Languedoc*, where the Duke *de Lesdiguieres*, having exchanged his Religion for the honour to be made Constable of *France*, conceiving himself more capable now, than heretofore, to procure a Peace, sollicites the Duke of *Rohan* to another interview, who seeing the hopes he had grounded on the Count *Mansfield*, who was gone into *Holland*, had failed him, the more willingly complies with his desires. They met at *Saint Privas*, where they agreed on all things, except the King's entry into *Montpellier*; whereupon he obliged the Duke to a journey to the Town, to propose it to them, with all possible assurances, they shou'd desire, to testifie, that they intended not the least infringement of their liberties: But this to be done without any cessation of Arms, nor was the Duke allowed more than two dayes stay there, to perfect this negotiation; who, considering the danger *Montpellier* was in, unless supplied with a new renfort of Souldiers; for that the works being not finished, their defects were to be made up with an addition of more men, sends express Orders to his Adjutant General *Sorle*, to draw twelve hundred men, out of the two thousand he had with much adoe detained at *Anduze*, and by the Valley of *Montferrant* conduct them to *Montpellier*, the night ensuing the evening that he should get in there: But when the Captains and Souldiers knew that they were to be locked up in *Montpellier*, they all deserted the Adjutant, who came thither accompanied only with fifteen.

Those of *Montpellier* would by no means admit of the Proposition concerning the King's entry into their Town, fearing a suppression of their liberties, by reason of the Prince of *Conde's* animosities against them; which the Duke perceiving, encourages them to stand bravely upon their defence, assuring them that he would provide for their relief, in which, for his part, he omitted nothing that might forward it: But as there is a vast difference between the promises and payment of money, so instead of ten days, within which time he thought to have sent them aid, notwithstanding his journeys to *Nismes*, *Usez*, and the *Sevenes*, not with-

without manifest hazard of his person, could he not, under five weeks, get four thousand men together; nor those neither without engaging himself by promises to most of the Captains; that they were not to be sent to *Montpellier*, but only that the consideration of their numbers might procure them a more advantageous Peace: So great was their consternation; and those that were desirous to get thither, were yet deterred by the apprehension of the difficulties, which really were very great; the King having then an Army consisting of twenty thousand Foot, and three thousand Horse; for the Constable, and the Duke of *Vendosme* had now joyned their's with the other Forces; besides, so great a way were they to go, and such difficult passes had they to get through, that it was impossible to approach within three Leagues of the Town, without encountring the King's whole Cavalry; and moreover so great a scarcity was there of Provisions, that they could not keep the Troops together, more than eight or ten dayes: Those of *Montpellier* of the other side, could no longer subsist for want of men, by reason of the excessive duty they were on, and therefore every moment sent they most important Letters for relief: To which may be added also a new Summons sent him by the Constable, who had before left the Court in some discontent for that he could not prevaile to obtain a Peace; yet now at his return was he in higher esteem, both by reason of the Forces he had brought with him, and that the Prince, in his absence, had nothing advanced the Siege: All which the Duke considering, and that he was utterly destitute of hopes of any Forraign assistance, having newly received a Letter from the King of *England* pressing him to conclude a Peace, and seeing no probability of any good to be done at home; every one being weary of the War, and labouring to purchase his own particular safety, with the expence of the publick Interest; that the first Town should fall off, and embrace a particular Treaty, would totally frustrate all endeavours for a general Peace; that the least cross accident should happen to *Montpellier*, or the relief intended for it, would be irreparable; that the King could not want men, the Duke of *Angoulesme* being then at *Lions* with a recruit of eight, or ten thousand; and that, without a miracle, *Montpellier* could not be preserved: Moreover, seeing that there were about the King two powerful parties; the one pressing the conclusion of a Peace, the other, the continuation of the War; and that the former could not subsist without a Peace, no more than the other without a War; and that the Chief of the latter, to wit, the Prince of *Condé* had deserted the Court upon the Composure of former differences, he he conceived that those that promoted the Peace being alwayes neare the King, would take care to see it faithfully observed: This made him resolve upon another conference with the Constable, at which the Duke of *Chevreuse* was present; where all was concluded acco:ding to the Declarations and Breviates drawn up to that purpose: Which when the King acquainted the Prince of *Condé* with, he left the Court; and the Duke of *Rohan*, with the Deputies of the *Sevenes*, *Nismes*, and *Usez*, went to *Mon'plier*, where they all confirmed the Peace; the substance of the principal Articles of which was, as followeth:

1. A Confirmation of the Edict of *Nantes*, and of all Declarations and Articles Registred in the Parliaments.
2. A restoring of both the Religions to the places, where they were formerly exercised.
3. A re-establishment of the seats of Justice, Offices of the receipts, and Officers of the *Finances* to those places and towns where they were before the troubles; except the Chamber of the Edict of *Guienne*, to *Nerac*.
4. Prohibitions to hold all Assemblies concerning civil affairs without leave, but an allowance of those relating to Ecclesiastical affairs only, as *Consistories*, *Colloques*, National, and Provincial *Synods*.
5. A Discharge of all Acts of Hostility according to the tenor of the seventy sixth, and seventy seventh Articles of the Edicts of *Nantes*.
6. A particular Abolition for what happened at *Privas* before the troubles.
7. A cleare Discharge of all Persons liable to any accounts, and Officers, according to the seventy eighth, and seventy ninth Articles of the said Edicts of *Nantes*; as also of all Judgements, given against those of the Religion, since the Commencement of the present commotions, according to the fifty eighth, fifty ninth, and sixtieth Article of the second Edict.
8. A Confirmation of all Judgements, given by Judges of the Religion, Constituted by the Superiours of the Party; both in Civil, and criminal matters.
9. A free Discharge of all persons of both Parties, without ransome.
10. A restoring of all persons to their Estates, Liberties, and Priviledges, Offices, Honours, and Dignities, notwithstanding any former Gifts or Confiscations.

11. And

11. And more particularly the King doth Declare, Ordaine, and Decree, That for the future there shall be no Garison kept, nor Cittadel built in the Town of *Montpellier*; but that his Majestie's pleasure is, that the charge of the Town shall be in the hands of the Consuls, and that there be no innovations there, except the demolishing of the late fortifications.

12. That all the fortifications of *Rochelle*, and *Montauban*, remain intire; and the moiety of those of the Towns of *Nismes*, *Castres*, *Usez*, and *Millaud*.

The end of the Second Book.

THE

THE
Memoires
OF THE
DUKE of *ROHAN*:

The third Book.

Containing a Relation of the second Warre against those of the Reformed Religion in France.

He Peace thus concluded, the Prince gone from the Court, and his Faction, by his absence, and the death of the Cardinal *de Retz* quite decayed, every one began to have fair hopes of its continuance; and that, grown wise by our former miscarriages, we should now renounce all future thoughts of Civil broyles, and mind the Protection of the ancient Allyes of the Crown: But the beams of favour now reflecting solely on *Puizieux*, a man of a hot spirit, and whose whole ingenuity consisted in tricks and fallacies, he became more studious of his own, than his Masters greatnesse (a vice incident to all favourites) being carefull to raise himself some props at *Rome*, and very unwilling to give *Spaine* the least disgust;

So

So that all Leagues with other forraigne Princes, were made with such respect to those two powers, as if we stood in fear of their displeasure: Nay, and to sooth the Popes *Nuncio*, who had alwayes opposed the Peace, at the very beginning of it, would undertake to shew him, that it was not made to abate the persecution, but to promote the ruine of those of the Reformed Religion. For immediately after the King's entry into *Montpellier*, the sense of the general Grant was inverted in most places of it, notwithstanding the several Remonstrances the Duke of *Rohan* made to oppose it: Nor were the Souldiers drawn away from *Montpellier*, though promised to be done immediately after the King's departure; then was it put off, till his return from *Provence*, then, till he came to *Avignon*, and lastly till he should be at *Lions*; whence the Duke of *Rohan* having followed him to all those places, urging their departure very earnestly, and perhaps too boldly, telling the King they should desist from farther razing the fortifications, if he revoked that command, returned with a Letter to *Valence*, commanding him expresly to do it. Nor did they forbear in their march through *Dauphine* to seize upon all the places that were in the hands of those of the Religion, though they had served the Kings party, the only recompence they had for fighting against their consciences, nor were any but those only, that were possessed by the Constable, exempt from this violence, which yet he preserved with much difficulty, for had not the Marshal *Crequi* engaged to deliver them up after his death, they had then gone the same way with the rest. At *Lions* the Deputies of *Rochelle* came to wait upon the King, whence they carried back Letters to *Arnaud* Governour of *Fo't Lewis*, commanding him, that within eight dayes after the *Rochellers* had performed what the Articles had enjoyned them, as concerning the demolition of their fortifications, he should cause the said Fort to be slighted also: but *Arnaud* received another of the same date, but a cleare contrary sence.

When the King went from *Lions*, towards *Paris*, the Duke of *Rohan* returned to *Languedoc*, really and sincerely to execute, what ever had been promised in the name of those of the Religion, touching that part of their fortifications they ought to slight. Going to *Montpellier*, he found the Consulate of the Merchants changed, of which he complains to the Court, but in vaine: He delivers the Kings Letter to *Valence*, who promised to obey it; from thence he goes to *Nismes* and *Usez*, whom he presently sets on work; thence to the higher *Languedoc*, *Montauban*, *Foix*, and *Rouergue*, where at a conference with the Duke of *Ventadour*, the Count of *Carmain*, the President *de Caminade*, and the Count
                                                                                                    d' Aquien

d' Aquien, Commiſſioners, as he was for the demoliſhing the fortifications, all things were agreed on between them and he for his part inſtantly ſet about them, delivering up alſo all Forts, and Towns that had been taken in the Warre, reſtoring alſo the exerciſe of the *Romiſh* Religion to thoſe places, where it had been formerly uſed.

Notwithſtanding all which *Valencé*, who, beſides the four thouſand men were in *Montpellier*, had four or five Regiments more, and three or four troops of light horſe, had deſigned to ſurprize, with theſe the *Sevenes* under pretence of taking up quarters there, and by means of ſome correſpondencies he had gotten among them; of which when the Duke had notice, from the principal Communalties of the *Sevenes*, who ſent him their complaints of this infringement of the Peace, he wrote to them back again for anſwer, that he knew it was not the Kings pleaſure, and therefore that they ſhould not receive them; and to *Valencé* that he ſhould forbear thoſe quarters till his arrival, leaſt otherwiſe it ſhould prejudice the eſtabliſhment of the Peace: The Duke of *Ventadour*, the Count *de Carmaine*, and the Preſident *de Caminade* wrote to him to the ſame effect; which he regarded not, but proceeded in his enterpriſe, the Towns of *Sauve*, and *Gange* receiving his Troops, but all the other places, upon the Duke of *Rohan*'s Letter refuſed them: The Duke when he had put things in ſuch a forwardneſſe in the higher *Languedoc*, returns to *Montpellier* according to the agreement between him, and *Valencé*: But he was no ſooner entred the Town, than made a Priſoner, and kept with a ſevere guard upon him: This cauſed a great aſtoniſhment in many, who could not imagine that this ſhould be done without order; but being known at Court, it was not approved of there, for fear leſt it ſhould prove too great an obſtruction to the raiſing of the fortifications; ſo that his liberty was preſently ordered.

Whiles the Duke was under this reſtraint, *Valencé*, contrary to the Articles of the Peace, divides the Conſulate of *Montpellier* between thoſe of the Religion and the Papiſts, and to effect it, uſed all manner of violence to the old Conſuls, detaining them as priſoners one whole night in his own lodgings.

The Court gave the Duke of *Rohan* no better ſatisfaction concerning this, than the former breach of the Peace; receiving, inſtead of relief, advice, that to avoid the ſuſpitions the lower *Languedoc* had of him, he ſhould remove to the higher, to execute the remaining part of his Commiſſion: For *Puyſieux* brother-in-law to *Valencé*, having caſhiered *Schomberg*, and reſtored the Chancellour his Father, was now the only powerful man, and by

drawing

drawing false glosses upon all the actions of *Valencé* improved them all to his advantage, and upon all occasions thwarted the affairs of the Duke of *Rohan*, clouding all his attempts with injurious and sinister interpretations and jealousies: And yet upon the answer the Duke sent that he would not leave *Nismes*, nor the *Sevenes* till they were rid of those Troops that lay upon them, he quickly received an order to dismisse them: After which he departed towards the lower *Languedoc*, leaving those of *Nismes* very much unsatisfied of him, out of a perswasion that he was of intelligence with the Court, and privie to all the violations of the Peace, and that his imprisonment was not real, but a delusory trick to palliate his other practices; The usual recompence persons of quality and honour derive from services done to the people.

When he came to *Millaud* he was informed, that the Duke *d'Espernon* had written to all the Towns held by those of the Religion in *Roüergue*, to send him Deputies both of the one, and the other Religion, and that they should not proceed to the Election of their Consuls, (who are usually chosen at *Whitsuntide*) before they had from him known the King's pleasure therein; this caused a great confusion among them; but by the advice of the Duke of *Rohan* they proceed, notwithstanding, to their Elections, at the accustomed time, according to the Declaration of Peace, which imports, that in the Consulary Towns, held by those of the Religion, nothing shall be innovated; and then sent their Deputies to the Duke *d'Espernon* to know what his pleasure was: Avoiding by this means, the injury intended to the Peace, and them in this particular.

This done, he goes to *Castres*, where he fixes his residence, and thence sends the King a perfect account of the entire execution of his Commission; humbly beseeching him, that, according to his Royal promise, the disgarrisoning of *Montpellier*, the demolition of the Fort *Lewis*, and the re-establishing of the Chamber (or Court erected in favour of those of the Reformed Religion) at *Castres*, might be no longer deferred: But instead of receiving Justice thereupon, contrary to the Act of Pacification, verified in several Parliaments, without any restrictions, or limitations, the engagements given underhand and Seale, re-iterated by several Letters, the Answer given to the Propositions of the Deputies general, and his Majesties answers to the Committee of the Parliament of *Thoulouze*, concerning the Chamber of *Castres*, the Garrison in *Montpellier* was continued, and a Citradel also was erected there, the Fort *Lewis* was re fortified, and the Chamber was removed to *Bezers*: But this was not all; The Temples, or Churches of those

of

Book III. *The Memoires of the Duke of* Rohan. 95

of the Religion were still detained from them; The Parliament of *Thoulouze* made an Ordinance for dividing the *Consulate* of *Pamiers*, between those of the *Reformed*, and those of the *Romish* Religion; vexes and torments particular persons, by imprisoning their persons, and sequestring their estates for things they had, according to the tenor of the Declaration, been indempnified for: In short, the pressures of those of the Religion, since the Peace, were far heavier, than those they suffered in the time of the war. The Duke of *Rohan* continues his sollicitations at Court; and declared his mind so freely, that he was forbid any farther to mention of their affairs, it being the King's pleasure that they should addresse themselves to the Deputies general, who also promised with all speed possible to send Commissioners into the Provinces to put the Edict in execution, and redresse all their grievances.

In the mean while the Galleys remained still at *Bourdeaux*, and the Duke of *Guise* came up with his Ships to the Isle of *Re*, which gave a great alarm to *Rochelle*, and made the Duke of *Soubize*, and the Count *de Laval*, to retire also to the Town: But this fear was quickly over; the Duke withdrawing thence, and sayling with his Ships towards *Marseilles*, followed by the Galleys, whose absence had much prejudiced the trade of *Provence*, imboldning the Pyrates so, that they took and carried away their Merchandizes even in sight of *Marseilles*. But the King discovering much displeasure against those that fled in to *Rochelle*, the Count *de Laval*, went to make his Apology at Court: But the Duke of *Soubize*, conceiving that way not honorable for him; and that his abode in *Poictou*, or *Britany*, could not be with any security, goes directly to *Castres*.

But let us now look after the Commissioners sent into *Languedoc* to put the Edict in execution; *Favier*, Counsellor of State, and *Saint Privat*, were sent on this imployment; but, to make short, did nothing, either in the upper, or the lower *Languedoc*, tending to the case of those of the Religion; but remov'ng to *Pamiers*, fell into a division concerning the businesse of the Consulate there, and each of them sent his opinion, and reasons to the Court: And thus passed the year one thousand six hundred and twenty three.

In the beginning of the year 1624. *La Vieuville*, whom the Chancellour had advanced to the Super-intendance of the *Finances*, not enduring that his Benefactor should be his Competitour in favour, amongst other things complains of the disservices he and *Puisieux* had done the State, in preferring the interest and advantage of *Rome*, and *Spaine*, before that of *France*; and that

the

the acceptance of the Articles of Peace touching the affair of the *Valteline*, by the Commander *de Sillery* Embassadour at *Rome*, and brother to the Chancellour, was occasioned by instructions, which he (unknown to the King) had received from *France*, to that purpose: Whereupon the King, as easie to believe the worst, as hard to believe the best of any one, resolves to deprive them of their Offices, and gives the Seals to *Alligre* Counsellour of State, and *Puiseux* his Office of Secretary of State, was shared among his other companions; and *Vieuville* remained the only Favourite; who to improve their disgrace to his further advantage, caused all the Embassadours to be changed, placing creatures of his own in their rooms; and had like to have framed a Criminal Process against the Chancellour; who in a little while after dyed of grief and age; and the Keeper of the Seals was promoted to his place.

After this, the new Favourite, changing the former Maximes, that he might the better discover the male-administrations, of those whose disgrace he had procured, caused the Treaty of the *Valteline* to be disowned; obtaines another more advantageous to the State; sets on foot the Marriage of *Madame* the King's Sister, with the King of *England*; renews the Leagues for the recovery of the *Valteline*, and rescuing it from the oppression of the *Germanes*: To which end *Bethune* was sent Embassadour extraordinary to *Rome*; the Marquess *de Cœuvres* to the *Valteline*; *Mansfield* into *Germany* with considerable Forces; and the Constable with the Duke of *Savoy* against the *Genoeses*. This disposition of affairs gave fair hopes of great matters, which indeed had very prosperous beginnings.

And that there might be a good stock of money to carry on the Warres, an Inquisition into the *Financiers* was thought very expedient. And because *Beaumarchais Vieuville*'s Father-in-law was the chiefest, and wealthiest among them, they resolved to disgrace him first: And in order to it, first of all they scattered little Pasquils against him; afterwards they dealt more boldly, and plainly with him, and every one, prognosticating, from the violent prosecution of his Father-in-law, that himself was not like to continue long; took liberty to exhibit accusations against him also, so that at length the King commanded him to be arrested, and sent to *Amboise*, where he was kept till he made an escape, without ever knowing the cause of his Imprisonment, and is now at his own house in full liberty, and security.

To this Favourite succeeded the Cardinal *Richelieu*, who owed his first introduction to State employments to his predecessour *Vieuville*. See how faithfully these Favourites serve one another;

other: The King recalls *Schomberg*, and sets at liberty the Marshal *d' Ornano*, who by the instigation of *Vieuville* had been a little before committed to the *Bastille*. The support the Cardinal had from the Queen-Mother, made his favour more lasting than the others, and encouraged him also to greater insolencies: For the King having a great aversion to the Queen, his Wife, and no less a jealousie of his brother, the Duke of *Anjou*, conceived that the Queen his Mother, would be of great use to him, to moderate, and compose these domestick jars, which more disturb the Palaces of great Princes than all their other affairs besides.

The Cardinal who now grasped the whole power of *France*, continues the Treaty begun with Forraign Estates, and consummates what his Predecessours had left imperfect. But *Arnaud*, Governour of *Fort-Lewis*, dying, and *Toiras* succeeding him in his commands, favoured by the Cardinal, and *Schomberg*, conceives greater hopes of ruining *Rochelle*, than ever *Arnaud* did; which were so earnestly embraced, as if they had not at the same time undertaken a War against the King of *Spain*: So that the *Rochellers*, sadly reflecting upon the encrease of their persecutions, and that the preparations to block them up by Sea were near perfected, and that the Forraign Engagements, nothing lessened the contrivances against their Town, apply themselves to the Dukes of *Rohan* and *Soubize* for their advice, and assistance; who were perplexed with many doubts about it, by reason of the divisions, and other defections they had experimented in the former Wars, and that they were fearful of displeasing the *English* and *Hollanders*, because of the League lately made by them with the King, conceiving that from them they were to expect either their preservation, or their ruine: Nevertheless the necessities of the *Rochellers* forced them upon a design, which the Duke of *Soubize* undertook the management of on *Blavet*, and the ships that were there preparing for the Siege of *Rochelle*, hoping that upon his success in the Attempt, the Allies, and Confederates of *France*, would more easily incline the King to an Accommodation with the *Rochellers*, as well for the difficulties would obstruct the pursuit of his intentions against them, by reason of the losse of the Ships destined to that purpose, as also for his desires to continue the grand design of the League.

Upon this ground the Duke of *Soubize* about the latter end of the yeare departs from *Castres* to go into *Poictou*, where very secretly he makes ready five small Vessels; with which, notwithstanding the perfidiousness of *Noüailles*, to whom he had intrusted the knowledge of the whole design, and who a little before it was ready for execution had discovered it; he resolved either to carry the Fort, or perish in the attempt. In the beginning of the year 1625, he sets saile from the Isle of *Ré*, with three hundred Souldiers, and an hundred Mariners, which gave the great Ship called the *Virgin* so brave a charge, that after some resistance, he himself boorded her the third man, with his sword in his hand, took her, and, presently after, all the rest.

After this he lands his Men, with a resolution to attempt the Fort, which upon *Noüailles* information, was newly reinforced with fifteen or sixteen piece of Canon, and a stronger Garison.

The Duke of *Vendosme* who was Governour of the Province, and had made great preparations to block up the Duke of *Soubize* in the Port of *Blavet*, presently rallies up two thousand Foot, and two hundred Gentlemen, to force him in the Port, and with an Iron Chaine, and a Cable, as big as a mans thigh, stops the mouth of it, which was very narrow and close adjoyning to the Fort; So that *Soubize* for three whole weeks was locked up in it, having nothing to guard his ships, and man the Town of *Blavet* (whose advenue, which was very straight, he had cut off) withal, but the above-said number of three hundred Souldiers; and was reduced to such an extremity, that the day before he got off, his great Ship called the *Virgin*, endured a battery of six pieces of Canon, and received an hundred and fifty shot.

Whiles he lay in this perillous condition, the wind, that had been, till then, still against him, changed, and *Soubize* seizing the opportunity, sent some *Shalloupes* mann'd with good resolute Souldiers, who, though all the while exposed to the fury of two thousand Musquet shot, with Hatchets cut asunder the chain, and the Cable, that barred the Port; By this means he got out with fifteen or sixteen ships, and lost but only two which were run aground on the Sands: In this Equipage he recovered the Isle of *Ré*, where having mended his ships, and gotten together about fifteen hundred men, he seizes on the Neighbouring Isle of *Oleron*, where he staid to compleat his Army.

The Duke of *Rohan*, at the same time had also made way for some attempts in *Guienne*, *Languedoc*, and *Dauphine*: But the Secretary *Montbrun*, as he was travelling with some overtures from the Duke to his friends, was taken at *Villeneufve* neare *Avignon*, and discovered all, which dashed the greatest part of his designs, and caused the three sons of *Montbrun* to retire to *Anduze*.

Book III. *The Memoires of the Duke f* Rohan. 59

Presently was the news spread abroad, that *Soubize* his project was discovered, and broken; and the long time he was shut up in the Port of *Blavet*, greatly perplexed the Duke of *Rohan*, who had no other news of him, than what the common rumour brought, but saw him disowned by the Town of *Rochelle*, by the Deputies general also, and by all the persons of quality, that were of the Religion, at *Paris*, who more favouring the Court faction, endeavour'd to make all our Towns disclaim him.

During this interval nothing was attempted: The two Eldest of *Montbrun*'s sonnes, discouraged at these unhappy beginnings, make their peace, renounced the Duke of *Rohan*, and go into *Dauphine*, but the youngest named *Saint André*, the most resolute of them, came to *Castres*, and did what he could, though in vain, to encourage, and retain his Brothers in the Party.

The Chamber at *Beziers*, and the Presidial of *Nismes* also, together with all Officers of our Towns, make goodly Acts of disavowal, which they sent to the Court: But at length when the news came of *Soubize*'s gallant and fortunate Sally out of the Port of *Blavet*, and that he was absolute Master of the Sea, they began to think otherwise of him, than as of a Pyrate; and the Baron *Pujols* was sent from *Paris* to the Duke of *Rohan*, the Colonel *Revillas* from the Duke of *Savoy*, and after them came the Baron of *Coupet* also from the Constable, to mediate an accommodation, to which the Duke was really enclined, and clearly did what lay in him to promote it, out of a desire he had to serve the King in his Wars in *Italy*: But either the perpetual and malicious contrivances at Court, against those of the Religion, or the bad Instruments employed in the Treaty, or the indisposition, at that time, of the late King of *England*, and late Prince of *Orange*, to assist us, or all these things together, frustrated the negotiation of the success it might have otherwise had, and prevailed so with our Towns to make them disclaime the Duke of *Soubize*, that the Duke of *Rohan*, who till then would not stir, was now enforced to take up arms, to shew, that it was no defect of power, (as they imagined) but his zeal to pacifie and compose things, that had hitherto restrained him.

The first day of *May* he began with an attempt upon *Lavaur*, but coming an hour too late, he miss'd of his aimes there: yet was not this expedition wholly successeless, for in it he wrought all the Towns of *Lauraguais* to declare for him; and at his return to *Castres*, he found that according to his order, the Marquess of *Malauze* was turned out of *Realmont*, which about a month before he had possessed himself of: And here it is to be observed,

H 2 . that

that *Malauze* was sought after, as far as *Auvergne*, to be made Head of a party against the Duke of *Rohan*, for that the Town of *Rochelle* was divided, and the Common Council refused to joyn with *Soubize*: So that the Deputy of the Town, in all negotiations, spoke only as from the common people, which party, the Magistrates, and Principal Inhabitants, still opposed: So that a very hard task had the Duke of *Rohan*, to reconcile, and unite the Town of *Rochelle*, and the other Corporations of the Religion, with *Soubize*. And forasmuch as it was very requisite he should go to bring about the *Sevenes*, and the lower *Languedoc*, where the Deputy of *Rochell.* could not have audience; he convoqued an Assembly of the higher *Languedoc* at *Castres*, by which being chosen for their General, he raised some Troops, established a Committee of the Assembly to order all affairs in his absence, and then sent *Saint Andre de Montbrun* with a Commission to be Governour of *Montauban*, which after much reluctancy, at length declared also for the party.

This done, he goes thence with six hundred Foot, fifty Horse, and four score *Harquebusiers*, and marches towards *Milland*: When he came to *Saint Afrique*, he was met by *Couvrelles*, sent from the Town of *Rochelle*, and *Soubize*, to inform him of the entire conjunction of the whole Town with *Soubize*, and that, according to the Articles of Agreement, they had sent Deputies to the Court, desiring us to do the like, and to this end *La Faye Saint Orse* had brought the King's pass-ports for the principal Corporations; to which his Majesty was at length induced, after he had in vain essayed to divide the Dukes of *Rohan* and *Soubize*, and bring them to several Treaties.

When the report of this news was also brought to the Council, and that *Couvrelles* had represented to them the great divisions of the *Rochellers*, and the factions sprung up amongst them, how extreamly desirous they were of peace, upon what hard conditions they had joyned with *Soubize*, and the ill order they took for their Navy, they conceived they had now no time to throw away upon tedious debates; and that (though *Rohan* liked not of their procedure in Treating with the Court) since *Rochelle* had begun, it was expedient, to shew that the party was well united, and ready to follow their example. *Le Clerc*, and *Noaillan*, were chosen Deputies for *Montauban*, *Dorson*, and *Madiane* for *Castres*, *Guerin* for *Milland*, and *Forrain*, and *Milletiere*, for *Rohan*, who desirous to extract what advantage he could out of this opportunity, to insinuate into the *Sevenes*, makes use of the King's passe-ports to induce them to call an Assembly at *Anduze*; which happily succeeded: From *Milland* he he draws his Forces to *Saint John de Breüill*, which made a flourish, as if they intended to stand it out: but when they saw him in a posture ready to storme their Fort, they instantly changed their note, and submitted. Hither came to him three Deputies from *Vigan*, to dissuade him from marching thither, for that he would finde the Gates shut against him; to whom he gave no other answer, but that he would try whether he should or not: The next day he continues his way, and two Leagues from *Vigan*, met another messenger to the same purpose, who also added, in case he advanced, threatnings of effusion of blood: But this prevailing nothing on him, his adversaries courage failed them, and they drew back; So that without any difficulty he got to *Vigan*; whose gates thus opened, cleared all the way as farre as *Anduze*.

Whiles he was on his march, the Presidial of *Nismes*, and also the Chamber of *Beziers*, used all their skill (but to no end) to alienate the affections of the people of the *Sevenes* from the Duke; who having resolved on a journey to *Nismes*, was yet loth to put it to a hazard, without first sounding the inclinations of the Inhabitants, for fear lest so publick an affront, as a refusal to his face, should ruine his whole affairs. To this end he sent thither *Saint Blancart*, who having conference with some of his friends in the Suburbs, their advice was, that the Duke should suspend his coming thither, and that they would send their Deputies also to the Court, that the Town of *Usez* should do the like, with instructions conformable to those of the *Sevenes*; which accordingly they performed, choosing *Castanet* for *Nismes*, and *Viguier*, *Goudin*, and *Boisleau*, for *Usez*.

The Duke of *Rohan* seeing, that he was excluded out of the Towns of *Nismes*, *Usez*, and *Alez*, convoques an Assembly of the *Sevenes*, at *Anduze*, the most numerous he could, where yet there were many wanting, from many of the Churches, especially of the *Colloque* of *Saint Germaine*, where the Marquess *des Portes* mainly opposed him; and after he was declared General of that Country, he sent *Caillou*, *Du Cros*, *Puyredon*, and *Pagesy*, Deputies to the Court.

While these things were in agitation, the Marshal *Themines* brought four thousand Foot, six hundred Horse, and Canon too, and with them a great terrour also upon the Countries of *Lauraguais*, and *Albigeois*; whereof the Duke being advertised by redoubled messages, he sends back the Marquess of *Lusignan*, with all the Forces he had brought with him, and with all diligence hastens his levies of Souldiers, to be commanded by *Freton*,

Saint Blancart, and *Valescure*, in which his endeavours met with such unhappy traverses, that instead of four thousand men, which was the number he aimed at, he could muster but half the number: Whiles these men were raising, he sent his Scouts towards *Sommieres*, resolving to attempt it with seven or eight hundred common Souldiers, upon this supposition, that *Valance* would not run the hazard of drawing out of his Garison, to relieve it, that it would be a means to make *Nismes* publickly declare for him; and that if he could have but twice four and twenty houres time, the whole Countrey would come in to him, and raise him to a condition able to force the Castle: But, as it is a dangerous thing to presume on the defects of others, instead of relying on a mans own strength, the event clearly deluded his preconceptions; For though he had taken the Town, *Nismes* would not stirre to his assistance, nor could he get relief from the *Sevenes* time enough; *Valence* at the same time sent twelve hundred men, out of his Garison, to relieve the Castle, who from three of the Clock in the afternoon, till night, fought with *Saint Blancart*, who had lodged himself, with three hundred men only, in a place of such advantage, that he could be no way forced, nor yet could he hinder the entry of the relief into the Castle, by reason of the extream largness of the advenue: Which the Duke perceiving called off *Saint Blancart* into the Town; resolving, that night, to draw off with the whole party also, which he did, carrying with him his wounded men; and among others *Freton*, who was wounded with a Musquet shot in the knee, of which he afterwards dyed: *Saint Blancart* in this conflict, when the relief enter'd the Castle, lost three Captaines, and some other Officers.

After this, the Duke thought on nothing more, than hastning his Levies, that he might be in a condition to relieve the higher *Languedoc*; and taking order that his affairs in the *Sevenes* might not be prejudiced in his absence; to prevent which, he left a Committee of the Assembly, to direct the management of them; in which he engaged all that had any interest in the places of greatest consequence, and left *Chavagnac* his Field Marshal to command all the Souldiery in that Countrey.

While these things were in agitation in the *Sevenes*, and the lower *Languedoc*, the Marshal *Themines* drew near to *Castres* to plunder, and spoyle the Countrey, which put the Council the Duke had left there, in such a confusion and feare, that they durst not give order for any thing at all, but left the whole burthen upon the Dutchess of *Rohan*, who contrary to the natural and more tender disposition of her Sex, shewed so much care

and

Book III. *The Memoires of the Duke of* Rohan. 103

and resolution in all things, that, every one deriving courage from her example, the Marshal received several losses, being worsted in every skirmish before the Town; where *Nougarede* an old Gentleman of the Country got much honour.

In the mean while the Marquess of *Lusignan* marches towards *Castres*, with those Forces the Duke had given him to conduct thither; which when the Marshal had intelligence of, he drew off his Cavalry, and part of his Infantry, to fight him; whom he found lodged in *Croisette*, a Village two Leagues distant from *Castres*, where he stormed him, but found him so well Barricado'd, and resolute upon his defence, that after a furious assault, he was faine to retire with much loss, many of his men being slain and wounded; which when he had done, the Marquess of *Lusignan* retreated as farre as *Brassac*, and the next day, taking another way, marched with all his Troops into *Castres*, at noon day, Drums beating, and Colours flying, and without any opposition at all. This renfort, with some skirmishes that passed to the Marshal's disadvantage, made him, seeing he could do no further mischief to the Town, resolve to retire to *Saint Paul*, and *la Miatte*, which were sufficiently manned: Neverthelefs *Saint Paul* made no resistance at all, but was taken in the open day without any battery raised, or siege formed, and the Souldiers all marched off to *La Miatte*, which they yielded also upon composition not to bear arms for six months.

This was the only check the Marshal *Themines*, by chance, gave us in *Lauraguais*, and *Albigeois*, where, when he had fired the aforesaid places, he made as if he would besiege *Realmont*. But understanding that the Duke of *Rohan* was come hither with above two thousand men, which he brought from the *Sevenes*, whose passage at *Larsac*, where he had designed to fight him, since he could not prevent; he draws off all his horse and foot, marches up almost to *Castres*, firing all as he went, passes by *Brassac*, endeavouring to gain a commodious field for his Cavalry, between *Cauve* and *Viane*: But *Rohan*, having intelligence of it, makes such haste, that by incessant marches night and day, he got to *Viane*, before the other could be on his way thither; from whence he sent the Regiment of *Valescure* to *Cauve*, and his own guards, and the Captain *Dupuy* with his Carabines (for that his foot was so tired they could not march) to *Brassac*.

The Marshal having now lost all hopes of preventing the Duke, and taking *Brassac*, goes forward, burning some Villages in his march, and comes with his whole strength, both of Horse, and Foot, in sight of *Viane*, where having drawn them up in Battailia,

lia, and seeing that the Suburbs of *Viane*, called *Peirefegade*, which lies at the bottom of the Town, and is divided from it, by the height of the hill, was not at all fortified, falls into it with all his Forces, takes, and fires it, and then retires to his Quarters: In this assault there was one Captain slain, another taken, and about five and twenty, or thirty Souldiers killed and wounded, *Saint Blancart* also had a light hurt; and the souldiers that were in the Suburbs drew up to the Town.

The Dutchess of *Rohan*, who by several messengers had sent to informe the Duke, of the Marshal's design to stop his passage, omits nothing on her part, but sends to all the Garisons, appointing them a Rendezvouz at *Brassac*; which the Duke having notice of, he departs that evening, and comes to *Brassac*; where finding fifteen hundred Foot, and two hundred Horse; he resolves, the next night to send out to discover the posture of the Marshal's Army, which lay at *Esperance* between *Brassac* and *Viane*, and according to the intelligence he should receive to fall into his Quarters the night following, with all his Troops, *Saint Blancart* by the way of *Viane*, and he himself by the way of *Brassac*. The discovery made, and the Scouts returning with intelligence that the Army lay there in great disorder, and in a place of great disadvantage to the Horse, the design to beat it up was concluded on; but the very day preceding the night it was to be put in execution, either upon notice given him, or that he foresaw their intentions, or that provisions failed him, he quitted those Quarters, and taking his way towards *Vabres*, went to lodge at *La Bichenie*: The Duke also rallyes all his Forces, and marches towards *Croissette*, and *Roque-courbe*, from whence he sent five or six hundred men into *Realmont*, and then divides all his Troops about *Castres*, to observe the posture of the enemy, who when they had refreshed themselves for some dayes about *Lautree*, march towards *Lavaure*, and there prepare for a march into *Foix*: The Duke goes into *Lauraguais*, puts some men into *Britefte*, sends the Regiment of *Fieton* to *Revel* and *Sourire*, and that of *Montluz* and *Valesure*, to *Realmont*, and as soon as he saw that the enemy steered his course towards *Foix*, he commanded *Saint Blancart*, who was then at *Puylaurens*, thither with five hundred chosen men.

Lusignan, in the mean time, being informed that the Regiment of *Lescure* had taken up their Quarters in the Suburbs of *Teillet*, goes instantly to beat them up; breaks through their Barricado's, kills, and wounds about an hundred, takes one Captaine, and forces the rest to flie for shelter to the Fort; but had he come by night, as he did by day, not one of them had escaped;

ped; for there was a very great diffention between *Grandval*, who commanded the Fort, and *Lefcure*, to whom he would never have opened his Gates in the night time; which was the reafon that induced *Lufignan* to this attempt, in which *Valefcure*, and *Montluz*, two Colonels were wounded, but not much: After this the Duke of *Rohan* returns to *Caftres*, whither he commands *Lufignan* alfo; rallies what Forces he had, takes with him one piece of Canon, and Marches towards *Realmont*, both to give the enemy a diverfion, and to enrich his Army with Booty.

The firft place he fell upon was *Sicurac*, which endured five and twenty, or thirty Canon fhot, but after he had fired the Town through the breach, they were faine to yield. This march of his made the whole Countrey look about them; The Duke of *Ventadour* got together about two hundred Horfe, and two thoufand Foot; The Marfhal *Themines* alfo hies thither, with all his Horfe, and the Regiment of *Normandy*; but both the one, and the other, being informed that the place was taken, went back again; and the Duke continues his courfe towards the Mountain of *Albigeois* and *Rouergue*, leaving his great Canon at *Realmont*, and taking with him only two little field pieces, that carried a Ball about the bignefs of an Orange.

Thofe of *Foix* in the interim, fent him word, that the Inhabitants of *Caumont*, *Lesbordes*, *Samarac*, and *Cameradé*, were refolved to fire their own Towns, and retire, the former to *Mazeres*, the other to *Azil*, for that they wanted Souldiers to defend them; whereupon the Duke commanded thither *Boiffiere* Lieutenant Colonel of *Freton*'s Regiment, with five hundred men, many of whom, when they heard they were to go to *Foix*, forfook their colours, fo that he went with two hundred and forty only, who got very well thither.

And here we may not pafs over in filence a generous action of feven Souldiers of *Foix*, who refolved, in a poor mudd walled houfe called *Chambonnet* near *Carlat*, to wait for the Marfhal *Themines*, and his whole Army, whom they there kept at a Bay two whole dayes; and after they had, in feveral affaults, killed forty of his men, feeing their ammunition was fpent, and that he was drawing down his Canon upon them; they confulted how they might, the night following fave themfelves; to which end one of them goes out to difcover how they might avoid the Courts of Guard; which when he had done, and as he was returning, the Centinel of the Houfe efpying him, and taking him for one of the Enemy, fhot at him, and broke one of his Thighs; Neverthelefs he gave them an account of his difcovery, fhews them the way, and very instantly urged them to make their escape: But his brother, who was also the man had wounded him, almost mad with grief, resolves not to leave him, and tells him, that since he had been the unhappy instrument of his disaster, he would be his companion in what fortune soever befell him: The good nature of one of their Couzin *Germains*, moved him also to a resolution of embracing their destiny; so the other four at the request of these, and under favour of the night, after mutual embraces, save themselves; whiles these three, placing themselves at the door, charge their Musquets, with patience expect the light, and then most valiantly receive their enemies, of whom when they had slain a good number, themselves dyed freemen: The names of these poor Souldiers deserve a place in History, their action being not inferiour to the most memorable, Antiquity can boast of.

But to return to the Duke of *Rohan*, who marches along the frontires of *Rouergue*, and takes a small Fort called *Roque Ciziere*, in which he left a Garrison; the same day he goes to another, called *La Bastide*, which he found deserted, as also some others which were pillaged, and burnt: From thence he goes to *la Cauve*, and in his way thence towards *Augle*, takes and burns some other small Forts; and then makes a descent into the Valley of *Mazavel*, where he goes on firing more Forts, up as far as *Saint Pons*: And as he would have continued this progresse, in revenge of those places the Marshal of *Themines* had fired in his absence; he received intelligence from *Bretigny*, Governour of *Foix*, and from *Saint Blancart* also; that the Marshal *Themines*, and the Count *de Carmain*, Governour of the Province, had invested *Azil*, with an Army of seven thousand foot, six hundred horse, and nine peece of Canon; that there were in it seven hundred souldiers, people of the same Countrey, which they had sent thither, under the command of Captain *Carboust*, and Captain *Vallette*, both experienced old souldiers; that they could not conjecture, what would be the issue of the Siege, for that the place was but weak, and the assaults most furious; but yet was it of that consequence, that if it should miscarry with those which were in it, there would not be men enough left to maintain the lower *Foix*, both by reason of the weaknesse of *Pamiers*, which would require a very strong Garrison, and also of the Intelligences the enemy had in it: But if he could spare them a recruit but of five hundred Men, they would engage themselves to keep the lower *Foix*, and would do their uttermost to preserve *Azil*.

This

Book III. *The Memoires of the Duke of* Rohan. 107

This Intelligence diverted the Dukes resolutions, who thereupon sent *Lusignan* with a party of Horse and Foot, to convoy the Canon back to *Castres*, and thence to *Realmont*, while he himself with the residue of his Troops, with much difficulty convoys six hundred Souldiers to *Revel*, where when they had staid a day to receive some pay, he sent them under the command of *Valescure* into *Foix*, who conducted them very well thither; and then returns to *Castres*.

The difference between the Baron *de Leran*, and *Bretigny*, much perplexed the Duke of *Rohan*, for that, being Master of *Carlat* (which was but a League distant from *Azil*) it was in his power either to promote, or impede its relief: Whereupon he sent *Villemore* and *Orose*, Captains of his guards, to make him sensible of the injury he did himself, in obstructing the relief of *Azil*, by denying his Souldiers admittance into *Carlat*, commanding them withal, in case the Baron would not submit to reason, publickly to declare to the people of *Carlat* the cause of their coming; which they so handsomely ordered, that he was compelled by the Inhabitants to yield to the Duke's commands, and to receive whatever Souldiers should at any time be sent thither, by his order, which proved no small advantage to *Azil*, and indeed was the only cause of its preservation.

While things were thus carried on in *Foix*, the Duke d'*Espernon*, with fifteen hundred Horse, and four thousand Foot, advances towards *Montauban* to ravage the Countrey thereabouts; and *Soubize*, to divert him, makes a descent into *Medoc*, where he took some Garisons: But understanding that *Manti*, with the Admiral of *Zealand*, named *Haultin*, were coming against him with forty good Ships of War, he re-imbarques, meets, fights, and defeats them, sinks five of their Ships, of which the Vice-Admiral of *Zealand* was one, and kills them more than fifteen hundred men.

The news of this defeat, made them change their note at Court, and whereas before they protracted the Treaty in expectation of the issue of this fight, now, seeing it proved to their disadvantage, they conclude it, and send Deputies to the *Rochellers*, to receive their acceptance of it: *Forain* also goes to them from the Duke of *Rohan*, who, considering the indisposition of the King of *England*, and the Prince of *Orange*, towards their party, advised them to accept of that peace their Naval Victory had purchased them; to which *Soubize* adds his perswasions also; but the *Rochellers* very indiscreet in that particular, and according to the humour of people as insolent in prosperity, as dejected in adversity, refuse to hearken to it, without a present demolition of the Fort.

In

In the mean time the King takes great care speedily to repair his Fleet, and obtains of the King of *England* seven great Ships; So that the delayes the *Rochellers* used in concluding the Treaty of peace, gave their enemies opportunity to corrupt some of the Captains of *Soubize* his Fleet, and among others, his Vice-Admiral *Fozan*: At the same time also the Duke of *Montmorency* resolves upon a descent into the Isle of *Ré*, and to make an attempt upon *Soubize* his Fleet which lay in the *Foss de l' Oye*, a Road joyning to the Town of *Saint Martin de Ré*; a rash and senseless enterprize in appearance, which yet treachery made feisible, and purchased it a far different Character.

Then came *Milletiere* and *Madiane* to *Rochelle*, with the Articles of peace agreed on at *Fontainbleau*; but it was then, when *Soubize*, who was in the Isle of *Ré*, sent them word thence, that the King's Navy were sayling towards him, and that with all speed they should transport themselves into the Island: At first, every one laughed at this Message, nay, and there were some in *Rochelle* offered to lay great wagers, that the *English* and *Dutch* Ships were called off again: *Soubize* reiterates his Messages, and for the last time summons them to his assistance: There were then in *Rochelle* eight hundred Gentlemen well mounted, and about eight or nine hundred Souldiers, of *Soubize* his Army, with the greatest part of his Officers, and among others the Counts of *Laval*, and *Loudriere*: Upon this last summons they all make ready to imbarque; but the Maior diverted them, perswading them that they were better to expect the morning, than run the hazard of the evening Tide, and so made them lose all opportunity to transport themselves; For the next morning appeared thirteen of the King's great Ships in the Road, which prevented their passage over: *Soubize* seeing himself thus abandoned, lands all his Foot, which were not above fifteen hundred Souldiers, leaving only an hundred in his great ship called the *Virgin*; commands his Admiral *Guiton*, and his Vice-Admiral *Fozan*, not to stirre out of the Road, where they were secure, but there to wait his further Orders; And then divides his Army into three Squadrons, to secure those three places, which he conceived most obnoxious to danger, and where he thought it most probable that the enemies should attempt to land: But, notwithstanding all his care, he could not dispatch time enough, before *Toiras* had landed three thousand Foot, and fifteen hundred Horse; whereupon he resolved to draw all his men into a body, and fight him the next day, which accordingly he did: At the first onset he routed the Avantguard, and slew about three or fourescore of the most forward of them; but being relieved by

the

the main body, *Bellesbat* who commanded *Soubize* his left wing, instead of seconding him, faced about, and plunged himself, and the whole party he commanded in the Marshes: This much encouraged the Enemy, who now oppressed *Soubize* on all sides, whose Major General *Verger-Malague*, and some of his Captains being slain, the rest fled in such confusion, that all the Art and Industry of *Soubize* could not rally them againe; who yet that day, even by the confession of his enemies, justly purchased the reputation of a worthy Commander, and valiant Souldier. The remainder of his Troops he drew off to *Saint Martin de Re'*, where he made account to transport them againe to his ships, and once more try his Fortune in a battaile at Sea; But there he found, so great a terrour had possessed *Guiton*, that contrary to his expresse command, he had turned out the hundred Souldiers left in the *Virgin*; and that *Fozan*, with some Captains, combined in the same conspiracy with him, to intimidate the rest, had runne aground the best ships, and that the rest, seeing themselves thus betrayed, and abandoned, shifted every one, the best he could, for himself; all but the *Virgin*, in which there were only five Men left, but very resolute, who seeing foure of the King's ships making towards them, resolved to stand it out against all extremities: The enemy came up to, grappled with, and boorded them, whereupon the Master, whose name was *Durand*, leaps into the powder with a lighted match, and blows up all the five Ships together, in which there perished seven hundred thirty six men.

In this accident there was one thing very remarkable, concerning one *Chaligny* a Gentleman of *Poictou*, and his son, who were two of the five left in the Ship: The father, before the firing of the Magazine, being wounded, and disabled to save himself by swimming, commanded his son to shift for himself, who, with much reluctancy, at length obeyed him; but the good man, being in the protection of God, was as well preserved, as his Sonne; for being, by the force of the Powder, carried up into the aire, he chanced to fall into a Shalloup of the enemies, without receiving any further harm at all, and was afterwards ransomed.

Soubize finding his affairs in so broken a condition, leaves his Major General *Le Parc d' Archiat*, at *Saint Martin d' Re'*, and in a Shalloup gets to the Isle of *Oleron*, where he provides the best he could for the preservation of it, leaving five hundred men in the Fort, which he furnished with all necessaries, and then, with seven of his ships, which had retired thither, sets out to sea, and out of the reliques of his late Fleet, gets together two and twenty Ships, with which he passes into *England* to repair them: After which, *Le Parc d' Archiat*, made an honourable composition, which was also well observed, and drew off all his men from the Isle of *Ré* to *Rochelle*; But those that *Soubize* left in the Isle of *Oleron* yielded themselves basely, a thing not unusual after such routs; for it is not given to all men, to have their courages of an equal temper in adversity and prosperity.

This fatal accident did not so much deject the spirits of the *Rochellers*, as it elevated theirs at Court: For when *Milletiere* and *Madiane*, returned thither with the *Rochellers* acceptance of the peace, they would not endure any further mention of it; but to break them by a division, continued their old project of granting a peace to the higher and lower *Languedoc*, excluding *Rochelle*, and *Soubize*.

While these things thus passed in those parts, they of *Azil* held out beyond the expectation of their friends, and the hopes of their enemies that besieged them, who from a battery of Nine Guns sent them in three thousand shot, and made three indifferent large breaches: But the enemy preparing to give them a general, and furious storme, *Bretigny*, and *Saint Blancart*, who had several times relieved them, resolved, now at this last push, to Rack all their powers for them; The conduct of this relief was undertaken by *Saint Blancart*, who got in to them with three hundred and fifty men, forcing, in his passage, a Court of guard which kept a Bridge, with the loss of one man only: The arrival of this renfort silenced all disputes, among the besieged, concerning the command, which before had occasioned some divisions among them; but all acknowledging *Saint Blancart* for their Superiour, he so well ordered all things, that after the expence of eighteen hundred Canon Bullets within the space of three dayes, the Marshal *Themines* gave them a fierce assault with his whole Army, commanding also five hundred Reformado's to dismount, and serve on Foot (there being many hundreds of people that had placed themselves on the tops of Mountains to behold this fight:) Thrice was he repulsed with the loss of above five hundred men; Within the Town the Captain *Vallette* who commanded at one of the breaches was there slaine, some other Officers too, the besieged lost, together with seventy or eighty Souldiers slaine and wounded: But above all, either friends or enemies, *Saint Blancart* there Renowned himself, both by his prudent care and vigilance in repairing the breaches, and his Valour in defending them, being alwayes ready in person at all places of greatest danger; in this action surpassing even himself: The Marshal

shal now thinks of nothing, but how to draw off his Canon; in which having spent two whole nights, and many of his Souldiers, which he lost in the Attempt; he drew off with the Fragments of his shattered Army towards *Lauraguais*.

This small success, together with the effect the Duke of *Rohan*'s continual sollicitations wrought upon the people of *Nismes*, inducing them to declare for his party, relevated his affairs out of the drooping condition they were in: Some of our Deputies then attending the Court, were about the same time sent to the Communalties to procure their acceptance of the peace, excluding *Rochelle* and *Soubize*, which many ill affected zealously promoted, especially at *Castres*, where they had resolved to assent to it upon those terms: But *Rohan* arriving there in the nick, and urging their former resolutions to the contrary, made them alter their intentions, and then summoned an Assembly at *Millaud*, where the Towns of *Nismes* and *Usez* appeared by their Deputies; and all unanimously made an Act of acceptance joyntly with *Soubize* and *Rochelle*, and sent it to the Court.

The Duke who several times had experience of their endeavours to surprize him, under pretence of Treating, stops not there, but goes to *Nismes*, and *Usez*, where he was received with great acclamations of joy; and having confirmed his Party in *Aletz*, by sending thither *Marmeyrac*, a Gentleman of the Country, to head them upon occasion, departs one night from *Nismes*, and comes the next morning, by ten of the Clock, to *Aletz*, where at first he found the gates shut against him, but the industry and diligence of *Marmeyrac* quickly got them open, so that now there was not any place in the lower *Languedoc*, or the *Sevenes*, that had not declared for the Duke of *Rohan*, who convened an Assembly of the *Sevenes* at *Aletz*, both to assure himself of the Town, and also of the *Colloque* of *Saint Germain*, which the continual sollicitations of the Marquess *de Portes*, and his faction, had still kept off from him; which obliged the Duke, in the interim, before the meeting of the Assembly, to make a step thither, where his presence was of great use, both to procure Deputations for the Assembly, and the conjunction of that *Colloque* with the others.

At the beginning of the Assembly the Dutchess of *Rohan* dispatched *Villette* to the Duke her Husband, with intelligence, that, upon the assurance many Communalties had given of their readiness to accept of the offered peace, with the exclusion of *Soubize* and *Rochelle*, the Court party stiffely persisted in their former resolutions, not to admit of any other, and had sent back
some

some of their Deputies to declare their adherence to them; and that therefore it would concern him, to have a vigilant eye upon their actions: This message had a sinister sence put upon it, and the Marquess of *Montbrun*, who a few dayes before came to *Nismes*, on purpose to insinuate himself into the affections of the people, found no better expedient to effect it, than vailing his intentions with a pretence of much zeal to the Religion, by forging scandalous accusations against the Duke of *Rohan*; which when he had notice of, and that *Du Cros* was come with the final determination of the Court, not to grant any peace, but with the exclusion of *Soubize*, and *Rochelle*; he took him with him to *Nismes*, convoqued a second Assembly at *Millaud*, and caused *Nismes*, and *Usez*, in his presence, to nominate their Deputies, and resolve in no wise to desert *Soubize* and *Rochelle*; from thence he went to *Vigan*, where he also caused Deputies, of the like resolution with those of *Nismes* and *Usez*, to be chosen for all the *Sevenes*; and with them all proceed together to *Millaud*.

While he was thus busied about these affairs, he receives news of *Soubize* from the Dutchess of *Rohan*, which assured him, that, within three months, the King of *England* would send a very considerable relief to *Rochelle*, desired him to make it known to the party, and to order things so, that they desert him not. When he came to *Millaud*, he understood that the higher *Languedoc* had determined to accept of the peace, excluding *Soubize* and *Rochelle*, and that, had not the presence of *Lusignan*, and *Saint Blancart*, as they returned from *Foix* with the Troops of the *Sevenes*, very opportunely prevented it, they had sent their acceptance to the Court. This intelligence made the Duke carry on the Assembly as far as *Castres*, where when he had assembled the Province anew, and received the resolutions of those of *Montauban*, to the same effect with those of the Provinces of the lower *Languedoc*; and the *Sevenes*, he inforced the former to retract their late intentions, and to confirm the other Act of acceptance, including *Soubize* and *Rochelle*: But to effect this, he was obliged to some extremities, securing the persons of seven or eight of the most eminent Citizens, whom he dispersed into divers places of *Rouergue*, and the Mountain of *Albigeois*; publishing a Declaration of what he had done, as also the reasons moving him thereunto, together with the Decrees of the said Provinces, which were approved by all, except the Town of *Puylaurens*, who resolved to stand upon their Guards, and not to open their gates to any of either side; protesting notwithstanding that they would not dis-unite from the party of the Religion.

When

When their affairs were brought to this pass, the Deputies were sent back to the Court with the final determination of the Provinces not to abandon *Rochelle*: And a few dayes after their departure, arrives a Messenger from *Vivaretz*, who informed the Duke, that *Brison* had taken *Pousin*, and some other places of less importance, and that all *Vivaretz* had declared for his party, and did beseech him to advow the taking of those places, and to confer the Government of *Pousin*, and the whole Province upon *Brison*, which he condescended to.

Not long after, the Dutchess of *Rohan* sends the Viscount *Roussille* to her husband, with intelligence that the Earle of *Holland*, and Sir -- *Carleton* extraordinary Ambassadors from *England*, and *Arsens* extraordinary Ambassadour from the States of *Holland*, were arrived at Court to sollicite the King to sign the League, and make us accept the peace, which she believed was already well advanced, and that she desired, if possible, to hear from him before it were concluded; to which the Duke replied by the same Messenger, that above all things the Deputies should endeavour to preserve from demolition, the fortifications of *Pousin*; that that being obtained, and the *Rochellers* contented, the Communalties where he was, would rest very well satisfied: But besides the aforesaid Ambassadours, those of *Venice* and *Savoy*, in short, all that were interessed in the League, out of the hopes the King would sign it, interposed their mediation also, to hasten the peace; which the Ambassadours of *England* by a Deed in writing, in the name of the King their Master, became sureties for the entire observation of; against which the Deputies of the Communalties having nothing to object, the peace was accepted by them, on the fifth day of *February*, eight dayes before the return of the Viscount *Roussille*.

Whil'st the Duke was busied in composing the disorders of the higher *Languedoc*, he was alarmed by reiterated messages, that *Nismes*, unless his sudden presence prevented it, would be certainly lost, by reason of the divisions happened since the arrival of the Marquess of *Montbrun*, and his brothers there; who with many Artifices, and great diligence, had gained the populacy to them, and by seditions, and tumults, attempted to ingross the power of the whole Country, which the most eminent of the Nobility withstood, so that the matter was now come to a formal quarrel, which, but by his presence, was not appeasable; this made him hasten his instructions for the higher *Languedoc*, where he leaves the Marquess of *Lusignan*, with four companies of strangers, whom he quartered in *Castres*, and then posts away to *Nismes*; where at his arrival, he met first of all with the Baron D' *Aubais*, whom

the

the lower *Languedoc* had deputed to the Court; and afterwards with *Montmartin*, the Deputy General, who brought with them their late acceptation of the peace, and were now come to have it ratified; *Mainald* the other Deputy General, *Du Candal*, and *Mailleray* were sent to *Rochelle*, *Novillan* to *Montauban*, and *Madiane* to the higher *Languedoc*. *Montmartin* sollicites the Duke of *Rohan* to ratifie it at *Nisms*, but by no means would he consent to any particular ratification; but summoned an Assembly to be held at *Nismes*, in which the Act of acceptance should with a general consent be confirmed on the fifteenth day of *March* following; deferring it to a longer term, that he might in the mean time hear from *Rochelle*; in which interval, *Montmartin* goes to the higher *Languedoc*, to hasten the Deputies of that Province to appear at the time appointed: But he found that at *Montauban* the peace was already accepted, and that, without expecting the Convocation, all the higher *Languedoc* had also ratified it, sending their Deputies thither for forme only. The day before the Session of the Assembly, the Duke was informed of the *Rochellers* confirmation of it also; so that there remaining only the lower *Languedoc*, and the *Sevenes* to do the like, the Assembly drew up a general Act of Ratification, which *Montmartin* and *Aubais* with the Deputies of the Duke of *Rohan* carried to the Court; in this act only the Province of *Vivaretz* was not compriz'd, for that then they must surrender *Poufin*, which our Deputies could not preserve, because they had no Commission to make any demands concerning it before the peace was concluded; which was occasioned by the negligence of the Deputy of that Province, that gave not notice of the taking of *Poufin*, till many dayes after the departure of our Deputies towards the Court.

Thus was our peace concluded, where we must observe, that the King, out of fear of the supplies the Duke of *Soubize* had procured in *England*, taking occasion from, and making very good use of the discontents of the English Ambassadours, sent *Botrù* into *England*, who so well managed all, that during his Embassy, which lasted but three weeks, he obtained a *Renvoy* of new Ambassadours thence to *France*, to conclude all things concerning the League, upon condition they should enforce the Deputies of the Religion to accept a peace, upon very ambiguous and uncertain terms, especially for the Town of *Rochelle*; who, in regard they had no hopes of any considerable relief from any other party were of necessity obliged to be submissive to them. The Deputies also of the particular Provinces, to shew that they of the Religion prefer'd the advancement of the grand design of the League before their own security, and to remove out of the way the pretence of the Kings Counsel for not signing it, while the War continued in *France*, did the like: But so resolute was the demeanour of the Dutchess of *Rohan* towards the English Ambassadours, and the Cardinal *Richelieu*, to whom he protested, that unless the Ambassadours interposed in it, nothing should be concluded, that, after she had neatly broken a particular Treaty of the *Rochellers*, carried on by their Deputies, whom the Court-party, and the Duke of *Trimoüille* had drawn over to them, she prevailed so far upon them all, that contrary to their former resolutions, they interessed themselves in it. This shelter'd her from the malice of her enemies, and the Deputies from any blame that might be imputed to them from their Communalties, and also obliged the King of *England*, seeing that the peace was accepted by his advice, to see it faithfully observed, to which his Ambassadours more strictly bound themselves by a formal Deed, signed, and sealed with their own Arms; so that the conclusion of our peace was an universal joy both to the Court, and all Forraign Ambassadours there residing; but fifteen dayes after, when contrary to the solemn protestations made to them concerning that particular, they saw also this Treaty in the *Valtoline* was concluded by the King, & the King of *Spain*, they were clouded with no less discontent; especially the English, when they perceived, that betrayed by delusory hopes, they had been made the instruments, to oblige us to accept a peace so much to our disadvantage.

Thus did the French, in cousening the English, and all the Princes interessed in the League, deceive themselves also, having done nothing in this affair, that tended not to the advantage of *Spain*, the oppression of the Allies of the Crown, and the great detriment of *France* it self.

This is an account of the passages in the second War; in the progress of which *Rohan* and *Soubize* were opposed by all the Grandees, even of the same Religion, whom either too much envy, or too little zeal, had aliened from their party, by all the Officers of the Crown, and a great part of the most eminent of every Town, whom their own covetousness, and the allurements of the Courts had blinded; as for the Forraign Nations, the *English* and *Hollanders* contributed their Ships, and *Germany* it self stood in need of the assistance of others; so that it is no great wonder if a better peace could not be obtained; but yet was it much more advantageous than the former, forasmuch as those of the Religion preserv'd their Fortifications, and got the King of *Englands* caution for the performance of it; God will assist us more powerfully, when our entire conversion to him makes us more capable of his favour.

The End of the third Book.

THE Memoires OF THE DUKE of ROHAN:

The fourth Book.

Containing a Relation of the third Warre against those of the Reformed Religion in France.

After the peace was thus accepted by those of the Religion, *Brison* only, who had not taken up Armes till towards the end of the War, seeing that a submission to the Treaty of peace would divest him of *Pousin*, a place upon the *Rhone*, which, not long before, he had surprized, refused to be comprised in it; encouraged thereunto by the Constable *Lesdiguieres*, who at his return out of *Piedmont*, being in some disfavour at Court, and unwilling to return thither, but catching at all employments that might colour his abode in his own Government, made very good use of this occasion, which he so well improved, that having spun out this affair for some months, he at length procured

for an ample Pardon, and forty thoufand Crowns, in lieu of that place, which was yielded up by him, and afterwards, by the King's command demolifhed.

This was the laft Act of the Conftable's life, which fuddenly after the termination of this affaire, crowned with many dayes and much honour, he yielded up at *Valence* : He was a Gentleman of *Dauphine*, who by his valour, prudence, and good fortune, having paffed through all the leffer charges of the War, had advanced himfelf to the higheft : And had not fo conftant and uninterrupted a courfe of profperity, effaced, towards his latter end, all fhame in him, fo that, he difhonoured God, by his domeftick, and infamous debauches, fullying his houfe with Adulteries, and publique Incefts, he might have juftly been parallel'd with the greateft Perfons, Antiquity can boaft of!

From this amicable compofure of our Inteftine differences, fprung faire hopes of the duration of our peace; which in a fhort time alfo withered: For it was contrary to the intention of thofe that aimed to raife their fortunes upon the ruines of thefe of the Religion: Amongft whom the Marquefs *de Portes* was the moft violent, who favoured by the command he had in the lower *Languedoc*, left no way uneffayed to force the people upon fome defperate courfe; of whom he exacted contributions as in the time of the War, though by the Articles of the Treaty, they were entirely abolifhed : But this being not enough to provoke a people harraffed with fo many and yet fmarting mifchiefs, and covetous to enjoy the fmall repofe they poffeffed, they fly to another invention; which was to ground a jealoufie upon the Duke of *Rohan*'s ftay at *Nifmes*, which many, out of a defire, either to conferve an old ill paid penfion, or to purchafe a new one, fomented with frequent calumnies, no week paffing without fome new accufations exhibited againft him, upon which, and the facility they propofed to themfelves of expelling him the Town, they refolve to make him the object of their malice, furthering their defign by an occafion taken from the annual elections of the Confuls for *Nifmes*, who are alwayes chofen at the later end of the year.

Whiles they fo induftrioufly labour his ruine here, they are nothing lefs remifs to procure it in the other Provinces, and indeed over all *France*, ftriking at him by the National Synod, appointed to be held at *Cafires* as a place moft animated againft the Duke, for that during the laft War, he had ufed fome feverity towards fome perfons of quality in that Town, that would have betrayed him. Thither was fent Commiffioner *Galand*, a perfon son without contradiction of very great abilities, but withal mercenary, and void of shame, or conscience, with instructions to disapprove the Duke of *Rohan*'s late engagement in armes, to disadvow his forraign Intelligences, and, if possible, to get him excommunicated.

The Duke seeing two such strong batteries raised against him, and threatning more danger than the War it self, prepares to defend himself against their violence: And forasmuch as that of the Synod seemed to be of greatest consequence, he endeavoured to secure himself against it, by procuring, in several Provinces of *France*, the election of such persons for Deputies, as were men of an inflexible integrity both to the Party and himself too, and draws up a Declaration, remonstrating chiefly the just cause he had to use such proceedings against those he had formerly expelled the Town; for that he knew that to be the principal crime they had to charge him with in the Synod: And forasmuch as the Town at a publick consultation had ordered their gates to be kept shut against him, and that he feared the like usage from them to any should come from him, he very privately made choice of another Minister, in the room of his own Chaplaine, to communicate his Declaration to his friends, and to entreat *Beaufort* the Deputy of the *Sevenes* to deliver his Letter, which he had written to the Synod, with charge, that neither the one, nor the other should discover themselves, but when it might be very seasonable; which happened well to him; for they were prepared to refuse admittance to any that should come from him; nay, *Marmet* his Chaplain, though he protested, that he came only about an affair of particular concernment to himself, could not be permitted any longer stay there, than of four and twenty houres.

On the fifteenth of *September*, in the year 1 6 2 6, *Chauve* was chosen Moderator, *Bouteroüe* Assistant, *Blondel* Pastor, and *Petit* an Advocate of *Nismes* Scribe. And now *Galand* bestirres himself against the Duke of *Rohan*, whose enemies in *Castres* are no less diligent in preparing the venome they had to poure out against the Duke in the Synod, animated also thereunto by the Commissioner *Galland*: But all their designes vanished into air: For the Deputies being before sufficiently satisfied with the reasons moving the Duke to proceed against them in that manner, made them not dare to present any bill against him to the Synod; who nevertheless could not conceale the displeasure they had conceived against those of *Castres*, with whom they disclaimed any future reconciliation; so that they were now become a general abomination; and the only way to ruine any affaire, was to offer it to *Galand*'s recommendation; And thus ended the Syned, where, by the Kings command, (that he might abridge those of the Religion, of their liberty of convening any Generall Assemblies) were chosen the Deputies General: The six nominated, were the Count *de la Suze*, the Marquess of *Galerande*, and *Beaufort* for the Nobility: and for the Commonalty, *Texier*, *Dupuy* Deputy of *Burgogne*, and *Bazin*; of whom *Galerande* and *Bazin* were accepted.

This affair thus terminated, we must now reflect upon the Consulate of *Nismes*. The Presidial, or Soveraign Court of the Town, according to the humour of many Corporations, not brooking the Duke of *Rohan* so near them, joyned with a Party composed of many persons of Note in the Town, whom the Court faction had invited, and drawn over to them: But finding themselves yet too weak, by ordinary and Legal wayes, to promote to the Consulate Creatures of their own, they resolve to engage the Royal power in it, and to effect it by wayes unusual and destructive to their own Priviledges, and contrary to the Articles of the late Peace. To which end, they send privately to the Court, where they obtain a Commission directed to the Chamber of Edict in *Languedoc*, to go and order the said Election of the Consuls; and that nothing might be omitted to forward their design, the Duke of *Montmorency* is sent from the Court into his government, who passes by *Nismes*, where he encourages those of his Faction, which he strengthens with the neighbouring Nobility; and those he could not win to his Party, he forces to absent themselves from the Town, till the business was determined: And for as much as the Marquess of *Montbrun* towards the latter end of the former war, had gained some credit among the Populacy, he was also sent for out of *Dauphine*; for they hoped not only to make such Consuls as should be at their devotion, but upon the Dukes opposing himself against it, to hale him out of the Town, dead or alive: These things thus prepared, the day of Election comes; the Marquess of *Montbrun* also arrives at the time appointed, so do *Monsac*, *DeSuc*, and the two *Deans* (or Seniour Counsellors) of the Chamber, who were nominated Commissioners for this affair; who declaring their charge to the Deputies of the Town, receive for answer, their fixed resolutions, to maintain the Priviledges of the Town: The Common-Council of which meet according to their accustomed manner, in the morning to proceed to the said Election; whither the Commissioners go also; but finding the doors of the Town-house shut, are fain to return to their lodgings, where they declare against the proceedings of the Common-Council, and send

about

about the Town to assemble the Inhabitants for a new Election; some refuse to stir, others go, but without any commotion in the Town were obliged to retire again.

Now the new Consuls enter not into their Office, till a moneth after the Election; so that the Court had leasure to send a Prohibition to those that were elected, forbidding them to meddle with the Office, and enjoyning the old ones to continue the exercise of it, till it were otherwise ordered: notwithstanding which, when the first day of the year was come, the Baron *d' Aubais*, *Genoyer*, *Saguier*, and *Pelssiere*, according to the usual manner took possession of the Consulate; where we shall leave them in repose, to look further back upon the affairs, and view their propensity to new imbroylments.

When the Peace was concluded in the year 1626, it was conceived, that the Cardinal *Richelieu*'s thoughts would be wholly bent on forraign affairs, of which he gave some semblant evidence: The Prince of *Piedmont*, then at Court, was nominated Leiutenant-General of the Kings Armies for forraign Parts; then hoped the *Venetian* Ambassadours, they should now see *Italy* freed from the *Spanish* oppression; the *English* that they would recover the *Palatinate*; and preparations were making (but in words only) for all these designs; of the reality of which if any one seemed to doubt, it was confirmed by a thousand oaths: But when a few dayes after the signing of the Peace with those of the Religion, unknown to all the Confederates, was signed also that of *France* with *Spain*; then brake forth complaints and discontents of the one side, seconded by excuses of the other, every one casting the blame upon another, especially upon *Fargis* Ambassadour in *Spain*, whose Wife, as if he had exceeded the limits of his Commission, was made to sue out his Pardon: but these pretences could not salve the distempers of the Confederates interessed in the League, which some of them afterwards upon occasions did discover.

The cause of this sudden and unexpected peace, was attributed to a desire the Cardinal had to live some time in quiet, that he might the better secure his own greatness, and that nothing might obstruct his pursuit of the design against *Rochelle*, where he intended to do great matters; or else to some Jealousie he had conceived of a new party, to be raised in *France*, under the command of the Duke *Anjou* to ruin him; but whether it was the one, or the other, or both together, certainly the occasion of these ensuing factions, gave him fair colours for any design.

The Queen Mother desirous to marry the Duke of *Anjou*, would needs consummate the Match, desired by *Henry* the great, between

tween him and the Princess of *Montpensier*, which he was absolutely averse from; whether this aversion proceeded from himself, or the suggestions of others, not desirous this treaty should take effect; which encouraged many to joyn with him. But the Prince of *Condé*, and his Wife, whom this marriage threatned with a remove so many degrees from the Crown, as the Duke of *Anjou* should have Sons; The Count of *Soissons* for the same reason, and out of hopes he had to marry that Princess himself: The Duke of *Longueville* out of Jealousie of the Duke of *Guise*, whose Sons were all Brothers to the Princess *Montpensier*; The Duke of *Vendosme* upon the same consideration, to which his Brother the Grand Prior of *France* added his discontents against the Cardinal, who had deluded him with promises of the Admiralty of *France*, which afterwards under another title, he reserved to himself; many of the chief Nobility out of particular Interests; The Queen who feared the others fertility would prejudice her in the King her Husbands and his Subjects affections; and the King himself induced by several apprehensions, opposed it: See here very considerable obstacles to be removed.

Nevertheless the Queen-Mother, who with good reason grounded on her own, & the Interest of the State, was very zealous for this marriage, despairs not, but begins her design with an attempt to gain the Colonel *d'Ornano*, who was formerly the Duke of *Anjou's* Governour, and continuing still his Favourite had a great influence on him: To this end, she gets him made Marshal of *France*; but what ever promises these honours extracted from him, they quickly vanished, as soon as he saw the Princess of *Condé*, whose beauty and attractions raised in him so much love and vanity, as totally blinded him; so that being caressed and sued to of all hands, he lost himself in that Maze of felicity: the better to carry on his own designs with her, he pretends to the Queen-Mother that his services are wholly bent to effect her desires, and procure her contentment, when really the charms of that Princess had drawn him entirely to her devotion; 'Twas she also governed the Queen, proposing to her the disrespect and contempt the Children of the Duke of *Anjou* would bring upon her; and that if he must needs be married, her Sister the *Infanta* of *Spain* would be a more convenient match for him: But all this while this Princess hoped that having clearly gained the Marshall *d'Ornano* to her assistance, she should in the depth of this Labyrinth find out a way to conduct her own Daughter to the Dukes bed. See here three Parties in one, the Queens, and those of the two Princes of the blood, all which, though for different reasons, and which they concealed the one from the other, conspire to impede this

match:

match; and so strenuously prosecute their desires, that the Duke of *Anjou* absolutely refused her.

At the same time there hapned a private quarrel which was seconded by many other: *Chalais* Master of the *Wardrobe*, having in a Duel slain *Pontgibault*, younger Brother to *Ludde*, Nephew to the Marshall *Schomberg*, and a Favourite of the Duke *d' Elbeuf*, caused a great division in the Court; the Duke of *Anjou*, the Count of *Soissons*, and the *Grand Prior*, undertook the protection of *Chalais*; the Duke *d' Elbeuf*, with the whole family of *Guise* (except the Duke *de Chevreuse*) favoured the House of *Ludde*; this division lasted all the Winter; at length, *Chalais* having obtained his Pardon, and sensible of his obligations to his Protectors, gave himself up wholly to their Interests, and was of great use to continue the Duke of *Anjou* in his obstinacy against the marriage with the Princess *Montpensier*; The Princess of *Condé* also diffident of the sufficiency of her power with the Queen, perswades her to engage the Dutchess of *Chevreuse* in her party, for that her own Interests lying with the other Party, she feared lest otherwise she should divert her: But her will was easily brought to a compliance with the Queens; the sense of her great obligations to her, making her promise to sacrifice all her Interests to her commands and service. On the other side, the Queen-Mother passionately prosecutes the accomplishment of the Marriage; especially the Cardinal, hoping that to effect it against so many and great oppositions, would enlarge the Princess of *Montpensiers* obligations to him so, that his power would suffer no diminution, though misfortune should alien even the Kings affections from him; the Princess of *Conti*, Sister to the Duke of *Guise*, and all their family bestir themselves mainly to the same end, and by the means of the Duke *d' Elbeuf*, who was a Friend of *Baradas* the Kings Favourite, or else of some other persons who engaged themselves in it, the King was also brought about to rellish the match too, out of an apprehension infused to him, that those three factions pretended only a rupture of the marriage, whereas, in effect, their design had no other aim but his ruin, to clap him into a Monastery, and marry the Duke of *Anjou* to the Queen: This impression made him now as zealously promote, as he had formerly opposed the marriage; earnestly importuning his Brother, and sending to the Marshall *d' Ornano*, who returned large protestations of obedience to his commands, but that as yet he could not discover any disposition in the Duke for it: Thus for some time was the Marshall caressed and sued to by all parties.

In the mean while, the opposite Party strengthen themselves
with

with a supply of all such as hated the Cardinal, especially the Duke of *Savoy*, who, (desirous to repay him the ill office he had lately received by the conclusion of the peace with *Spain*, which exposed him to the inconvenience of a war with *Genoa*, and the hatred of *Spain*,) by his Ambassador the Abbot of *Scaglia*, proposes to the Duke a match with the Princess of *Mantua*, and by the same instrument instigates him to rid himself of the Cardinal, as the only obstacle to all his designs; but the Prince of *Condé*, and the Princess his Wife, seeing the King varied in his, had not courage enough to persevere in their resolutions for the Party they had undertaken, though they were most engaged to prevent the marriage; but indeed so great a propensity was there in their natures to treachery and falshood, that without any difficulty was this change wrought in them: the one hoping to gain a piece of Land, called *Dun-le-roy*, and was a part of the Crown-land, to joyn it to his Dutchy of *Chasteau-Roux*; and the other, that she might not totally leave the Court the seat of her pleasures and contents; and the better to act their parts, the Prince comes to *Valery*, not far from *Fountainebleau* where the King then was, whither the Princess also makes several journies; after which the Marquess of *Brezé* Brother-in-law to the Cardinal, makes three voyages thither also, but very privately; to whom, as 'tis said he gave an account of all passages, adding to, rather then curtailing the relation of any particular, according to the custom of all Informers, that by such means hope to inhance the price of their discoveries.

About this time were intercepted several packets going into *Spain* and *Savoy*, which occasioned the securing of the Marshal *d' Ornano*, who was yet somewhat more ceremoniously dealt withall then ordinary, in regard of his Master: The King one afternoon commands the Regiment of his guards into the *Basse* Court at *Fountainebleau*, under pretence of exercising before the Queens; but instead of returning to their quarters, they possesse themselves of all the advenues of the village, which was also surrounded by the Cavalry: And the King going very early to bed, not long after rose again, sent for the Queen-Mother, the Cardinal, the Chancellour, and the Marshall *Schomberg*, with whom he resolved upon the Arrest, which was executed by the Captain of the Guard.

Whereupon the King sent instantly for the Duke of *Anjou*, to let him know that the reason of his imprisonment was, because he knew that instead of serving him according to his duty, the Marshall infused bad Counsels into him: at which the Duke was highly displeased, and to as little purpose discovered he his disgust

Book IV. *The Memoires of the Duke of* Rohan. 125

gust both in words and gestures, flies in great fury at the Cardinal, demanding of him, if he had been privy to this design, who told him that indeed he was not ignorant of it; the same demand makes he to the Chancellour, who for not daring to advow the action, lost his seals a few dayes after, and was banished the Court.

After this Arrest of the Marshal, was *Chaudebonne*, a Domestick of the Duke of *Anjou*'s sent to the *Bastille*, as also *Modene* and *Deagent* for their old faults: The Count of *Chasteau-Roux*, and the *Chevalier de Jars* were also banished the Court, suspected for having so great a dependance on the Queen and the Count of *Soissons*. The Marshal was sent to the *Bois de Vincennes*, and all the places under his Command seized on, the most considerable of which was *Pont Saint Esprit* in *Languedoc*: The report of this, made all the Princes and Great ones then at *Paris*, and in no little amazement at this accident, return to their attendance on the Court.

The Duke of *Anjou* persists still in his discontent, and is more averse then ever from the marriage with the Princess of *Montpensier*; But being yet destitute of any safe retreat, he is inforced to cover his displeasure with a dissembled accommodation with the Cardinal; and hunting often about *Fountainebleau*, resolves one day to go towards *Fleury*, and dine with him, who then lay there; but having notice of the Dukes intentions, and that it was only to do him a discourtesie, departs thence before day, comes to *Fountainebleau* just as the Duke was rising, and gave him his shirt.

This little discovery rouses the Cardinal, and makes him very sollicitous to provide against the storms impending over him: he understands moreover, that all contrivances against his life come from *Savoy*, that the Abbot of *Scaglia* is the chief Instrument imployed in it; that the Queen made use of the *Dutchess* of *Chevreuse* to animate the Duke of *Anjou* against him, that the Grand Prior irritated by a private discontent, is also one of the most violent against him, whereupon he resolves to ruine those he could, and to rid himself of the rest the best he could.

This was the ground of his irreconcilable hatred against *Savoy*, of the ruin of the Grand Prior, *Chalais*, & the Dutch. of *Chevreuse*. To compass his design, and prepare his way to the Government of *Britany*, which he coveted for its good Ports, and the conveniencies to execute this new office of Superintendent of the Sea, which he had introduced to succeed the suppressed Admiralty of *France*; he suggests to the King, that the Duke of *Vendosme* grew too potent in *Britany*, considering his pretensions to that

Dutchy

Dutchy in the right of his Wife, and the alliance he was entring into with the Duke of *Retz*, who was very powerful in that Province, and Master of two of the most considerable places in it; that the Grand Prior, the most zealous of all the Duke of *Anjou*'s Partisans, was his brother; that it might be one day a most secure retreat for the Duke, and of dangerous consequence to all *France*, considering its situation both so near to *England* and *Spain*; and that it would be expedient to provide timely preventions against such fatal accidents. This made the King resolve upon a journey thither, and to prepare himself for it, the whole Court removed back to *Paris*; but the better to conceal the intended voyage, they pretended only a journey to *Blois*; Nevertheless the Grand Prior rightly conceiving that a further progress was designed, offers to seek out his Brother, and bring him to justifie himself against all accusations whatever; provided he might be secured by an engagement of their words, not to be injured in his person: this he imparts to the Cardinal, who approves of his design, fils him with hopes, but no promise of security, advising him to procure that of the King, which he does, and so departs for *Britany*.

The Duke of *Anjou* was very unwilling to this Journey, but finding no evasion for it, at length resolves upon it: All the Court go, except the Count of *Soissons*, and the Princess of *Montpensier*, whom the sickness of their Mothers stayed behind. The King being at *Blois*, thither came the Duke of *Vendosme* and his Brother: For two dayes together the King made them infinite caresses, which the third night he closes with an Arrest by the Captain of his guards, and then sent them both Prisoners to the Castle of *Amboise*.

After this was done, the Cardinal, who had all this while stayed at one of his houses near *Paris*, comes to *Blois*, openly commiserating the misfortune of the Grand Prior, but not his Brother, in which the whole Court sympathize, for that the one was beloved, but the other hated; and that which most moved their compassion, was, that the Grand Prior had most innocently been the Instrument of both his own and Brother's disaster. The resolution for the voyage into *Britany* is continued, and also to press the Duke of *Anjou* to the marriage, who still opposed it: But some of his Party, fearing lest at length he might recede from his resolution, advise him to quit the Court: Some counselling him to take the way of *Rochelle*, others that of *Metz*: Moreover they send to the Count of *Soissons* for *Balagny* and *Boyer*, two trusty persons, the one to be his conductor towards *Rochell*, if they took that way, and the other to treat with his Uncle the

Duke

Duke of *Villars* Governor of *Havre*, that they might secure that Port to receive the forraign succours promised them. But as 'tis usual in all dangerous enterprizes, mens hearts failing them, instead of executing their designs, they raise difficulties to overthrow them, so hapned it in this; For instead of going themselves, they sent a Gentleman belonging to *Chalais*, to the Duke of *Valette* to know whether he would receive the discontents, and by that means gave him opportunity to evade a business, in which, had they surprized him, he had without resistance been engaged: For conceiving by this message that they were not well resolved, he sent them word, that the place belonging to his Father the Duke *d' Espernon*, he must first send to know his pleasure, before he could return them any other answer: This very well pleased those that disswaded his departure, especially *Chalais* who was of a mild temper, and naturally averse from faction; to which his friends had never inclined him, had not his spirit been too flexible to withstand their solicitations; so that seeing the trouble and danger still increase, he grew very desirous to dis-entangle himself of the affair, and to that end, intreats the *Commandeur de Valencé* to assure the Cardinal, that he would renounce the Duke of *Anjou*'s Interests, and become his servant; The Cardinal who desired nothing more, receives and cajoles him so handsomly, that he engages him by promise, to discover all the Dukes designs to him: This lasted a few dayes; but the inconstancy of his humour, which yet was nothing mischeivous, hurrying him to another change; he repents of his promise, will discover nothing, and raccomodes himself with the Duke of *Anjou*; requesting the *Commandeur* to revoke the promise he had given the Cardinal in his behalf, who excuses himself of the employment, foretelling him, that it was the next way to a Prison or worse; But *Chalais* notwithstanding, persisting in his resolutions, got some other to carry his intentions to the Cardinal, who nothing relished the message, which recalled to his mind the business of *Fleury*, and gave him some Jealousies that it was the Dutchess of *Chevreuse* that had regained him, and therefore he thought it now time to dispatch him: Wherefore he causes him to be arrested and sent Prisoner to the Castle of *Nantes*; and Commissioners of the Parliament of *Britany* were appointed for his trial; at which he confesses, and accuses, what, and whom they please; thinking by that means (being little versed in criminal proceedings) to save himself, confirms also some flying reports of his engagement to kill the King who was helping him to bed; but he was condemned and executed for this only, that being a Domestick of the Duke of *Anjou*'s, he had advised his Master to retire from the

Court:

Court: But after all these weaknesses, seeing how ineffectual they had been to save his life, he dyed with much courage and constancy; At the same time also was *Marcillac* apprehended, and devested of his Government of *Sommieres* in *Languedoc*; *Troncon* and *Sauveterre* were also banished the Court, for presuming to disswade the King from the intended marriage: To which the Duke of *Anjou*, during those procedures, was anew urged; and his Favourites being already won, the Duke upon hopes of the Marshal *d' Ornano's*, and *Chalais* liberty, at length resolves upon it, and falling from one extremity to another, suddenly and privately marries the Princess of *Montpensier*, (who was purposely sent for from *Paris* with a gallant train) loves and caresses her, and now cannot live without her. Hereupon his Appanage was assigned him, to wit, the Dutchyes of *Orleans* and *Chartres* (wherefore for the future we shall call him the Duke of *Orleans*) together with the Earldom of *Blois*; great in appearance, but seated in the heart of *France*, without any good place within the whole circuit of it, and of a very small revenue, his chiefest assignations for the maintenance of his house being out of the Treasury, that so they might at pleasure be taken from him.

The marriage thus consummated, they proceed notwithstanding to the execution of *Chalais*, inquiring also after informations against the Duke of *Vendosme*, especially whether he held not Intelligence with the Duke of *Soubize*, during the war in the year 1625. Commissioners also were appointed for the trial of the Duke, and his Brother the Grand Prior; but the one objecting the Priviledge of his Peerage, and the other of his Cross of *Malta*, they were at last sent to the *Bois de Vincennes*, without any further proceedings against them; only the Dukes houses in *Britany* were razed, and he was deprived of his Government of that Province, which was conferred on the Marshal *Themines*. 'Twas thought the reason that diverted the Cardinal from the design he had upon this Government, was, that having placed into *Brest*, one of the fairest and securest Ports of all *France*, one *Sourdeac*, a creature of his own, out of hopes to secure it to himself; the King without his privity, conferred that command upon a Souldier of mean quality, which vexed him so, that abandoning all future thoughts of the other, he resolved upon the purchase of *Hauvre de Grace* in *Normandy*.

Upon the Confession of *Chalais*, Messengers were also sent to *Verger*, a House of the Prince of *Guymenés* to confine the Dutchess of *Chevreuse* there, but she escaped that confinement by her departure before to *Paris*, where being informed of what had passed, she recovered, by great journies to *Lorrain*.

The

Book IV. *The Memoires of the Duke of* Rohan. 129

The voyage of *Britany* having thus succeeded, the King returns to *Paris*, where the Count of *Soissons* durst not expect his arrival, but grown wise by the misfortune of others, travels into *Italy*, where the Court-hatred pursued and persecuted him; For Letters were sent to *Bethune* Embassadour extraordinary for the King at *Rome*, that he should take care the title of *Highness* was not given him; to which *Bethune* having no other passion then for his Masters service, answers, that he would never be guilty of such a crime, but that if the Count of *Soissons* had offended the King, he ought to punish him in *France*, and not in that which would so much intrench upon the honour of the Crown; and that he would rather quit his employment, then do such a disservice both to his Master and Family.

When the Court came to *Paris*, not a word was spoken of the Dutchess of *Chevreuse* her removal; *Sardigny* and *Bonœil* were confined to their own houses, one being accused for advising the Count of *Soissons* to leave *France*, the other for his too great propensity to the Queens service. Attempts were made also to take the *Chevalier de Jars*, which having notice of, he prevented by his flight into *England*: About this time also the Marshal *d'Ornano* died of the Stone, whose death occasioned several discourses.

We will now leave the Duke of *Orleans* to comfort himself with the embraces of his new Wife, for the losses and misfortunes of his servants; and the Cardinal to refresh himself awhile, after having dissipated so thick, and menacing a cloud, as hovered over his head, to come to the affairs of *England*; whither the Abbot *Scaglia*, four moneths before, was gone in quality of Ambassadour extraordinary, and carried together with his Masters, his own particular passions, both being unanimously bent to spare nothing, that might purchase them a sound revenge upon the Cardinal; There he found the Duke of *Buckingham* of the same humour, whom he encouraged to procure the banishment of all the *French* attending on the Queen of great *Britany*, for that they cherished their Mistress in some froward humours, which many times occasioned differences between the King and her, alledging that *Spain*, *France*, and *Savoy* would be sufficient presidents to warrant the action; recounts the numerous factions and discontents he had left in *France*, the ill usage of those of the Religion, in whose Interests the King himself was engaged, as being surety for the observance of the last treaty of peace, and assures him of his Master the Duke of *Savoyes* complyance and fidelity upon all occasions; All these perswasions joyned with the urgent sollicitations of the Duke of *Soubize*, in the behalf of those of the Religion, moved the Duke of *Buckingham* to perswade the King his Master private-

K   ly

ly to send a Gentleman to the Duke of *Rohan* to inform him of his deep resentments that those of the Religion had by his means and intervention been deceived, that he now saw clearly, that instead of restoring *Rochelle* to its liberty, preparations were makeing to oppress it, and that he desired to know also what persecutions they suffered in *Languedoc*; that it was expedient they should address their complaints to him, that, being Caution for the late peace, he might have just occasion to demand reparation for the infractions of it, which if it was refused, he protested that he would employ the whole strength of all his dominions, and hazard also his own person to obtain an exact and punctual observation of the Edict for peace: But that since it was fitting, for the better Justification of his procedures, to begin with such formalities, he desires that he would send him over a Gentleman, by whom he might be fully informed and directed how to proceed.

The Duke who saw no humane means to preserve *Rochelle* but by relief from *England*, received this Message with all respect and honour; and informed the Gentleman, that the Communalties of the Religion could not write to the King his Master neither in General, nor in particular without being detected, which would crush the affair in its birth, that he would undertake that office for them all, by sending a Gentleman with a Letter, to implore that assistance of him, he was obliged to give them; who moreover should be fully instructed with the particular in observations of the peace, and what he thought was the most convenient course to be taken in reference to the war: With this answer the Gentleman returned, and a few dayes after, according to his promise, the Duke dispatcht St. *Blancart* with orders to go by the way of *Rochelle*, to see in what condition was the Citadel of Saint *Martin* in the Isle of *Ré*; which he exactly well performed, and after his arrival in *England*, obtained a conclusion of a war for our relief.

In the mean while the Duke of *Buckingham* causes all the Queens *French* Servants (except a Chaplain) to be cashiered, which made so great a noise in *France*, that the Marshall *Bassompiere* was sent Embassadour extraordinary into *England* to compose the affair, and returned thence with satisfaction correspondent to his instructions and intentions: But the two Favourites accord not at all; he of *France* causes the Marshal, being no creature of his to be disowned, and the other procures a dissolution of the treaty.

Not long before, the taking of some *Normande* ships by the *English*, gave another occasion of difference; The Parliament of *Rouen* hereupon not receiving that speedy satisfaction they expected, laid an *Embargo* upon all *English* Vessels in all their Ports,

and

and the *English* upon the reciprocal and fruitless complaints of both Parties, made Prize of all the *French* they met with.

The *Duke* of *Buckingham*, who in all these affairs acted nothing out of affection to religion, or regard to his Masters honour, but only to satisfie his passion for some foolish Amours of his in *France*, upon these two occasions grounds a request to be sent Embassadour to *France*; Thus from the petty follies of the Court, springs the disturbance of whole Kingdoms, most of the mischeifs that infest them flowing from the particular Interests of Favourites; who trampling Justice under their feet, subvert all good policy, change the good Maximes of the State, and make their Masters but properties to support their greatness, wealth and revenge.

The Duke of *Rohan* jealous of this Embassie, sent one of his Gentlemen very privately to *Paris*, to observe the actions of *Buckingham*, and to encourage him in his fornier resolution: But the King would not admit of his Embassie, so that his design of Love being frustrated, he now followes the dictates of his rage, and since he could not see the object of his passion, resolves to shew the King his power, preparing all things for the war; in which, by his present care and assiduity, he redeems his former negligence and remisness; and that he might omit nothing that might further his design, the Lord *Montague* is sent into *Savoy*, and thence to the Duke of *Rohan*, where arriving very privately, he delivers his Credentials from the King, and from *Buckingham*, in whose names he assures him of the great preparations in *England* for our assistance, to wit, of thirty thousand men to be disposed into three several Fleets, the first designed for the Isle of *Re*, the second coming up the river of *Bourdeaux* to land in *Guienne*, and the third in *Normandy*, to give the King a sound diversion there, whil'st he should be busied in *Guienne*; that the Rivers of *Loire*, *Seine*, and the *Garonne* should with good Frigots be kept closely blocked; that the Duke of *Savoy* would make an invasion either upon *Dauphine* or *Provence*, and moreover promised the Duke of *Rohan* five hundred auxiliary horse, and the Duke of *Chevreuse* also the like number; that his desire was, that with those thousand horse, and the foot he should levy in *Languedoc*; he would march to *Montauban*, to rally those of the Religion in *Guienne*, and joyn with the *English* Army, that should make its discent by the River of *Bourdeaux*: To which he replyed, that immediately upon the entry of the *English* into *France*, and not before, he would engage himself to take arms, and procure the lower *Languedoc*, the *Sevenes*, *Rouergue*, and a part of the higher *Languedoc* to declare, and upon his own score to raise four thousand foot, and two hundred horse to march to *Montauban*;

and moreover, if he had half the Cavalry promised him, he would undertake to joyn the *English* Army in any part of *Guienne* whatsoever.

Montague returned satisfied with this answer, and the Duke of *Rohan* began his preparations, which yet he could not make with that secresie, but that the Court had soon an inckling of them; so that his Mother and Sister had been made Prisoners, had they not sought their safety by flying to *Rochelle*, where they did eminently contribute to the defeating of the King's designs there; and as all contrivances against him, were clandestine and underhand, so, for his part did he cherish those of the Religion in their discontents, especially concerning the Consulates of *Nismes* and *Aletz*, whose accomodations he prevented, so that he preserved those Corporations in a firm resolution to dare all extremities, rather then suffer the least diminution of their Priviledges, and all the rest in a condition to adhere to them; And on the other side, the Court faction having interessed the Royal authority in the concern of those Consulates, would not in the least degree recede from their purposes.

When things were in this posture, about the twentieth of *July* comes the Duke of *Buckingham* into the Rode of *Rochelle*, with a brave Armado, in which were ten thousand men, with store of Canon, and ammunition for war, with all sorts of Instruments for Pioneers: which when the *Rochellers* saw, instead of receiving him whom they had so impatiently expected, they shut their gates and havens against him, to prevent the arrival of any one from him, to impart his Commission to them; for the Maior and those in authority were corrupted by the Court Party, and the poor people had neither strength, nor courage to admit him: So that *Soubize* was fain to go on shore in a Shalloup, and landing near to one of the Town-Gates with one of the King of *Englands* Secretaries, his Mother went straight to another, whither when the Duke was also come, she went forth and drew him in by the arm, at which the People much rejoyced, and in great troops followed him to his lodging: When he was thus gotten in, he assembled the Councel of the Town, to whom the Secretary declared the substance of his Message after this manner; That the Duke of *Buckingham* had sent him to let them know, that by the command of the King his Master, he was now come in sight of them with a Gallant Army, ready to land where occasion should require; that that which induced his King to this, was his certain knowledge that the Councel of *France*, (corrupted by the house of *Austria*) conspired the ruine of all Christendom; which manifestly appeared in the affairs of *Germany*, which they have entirely ruined, especially by that permission was given to Count *Mansfields* Army to pass through *France*, which, as he was ready to march, was refused him, and was the destruction of that, and consequently of the *German* Army, in which twelve thousand *English* perished by famine; that since the King his Master had by his Ambassadours mediated a composing of the late War against those of the Religion, and engaged himself for the faithful observation of the Articles of the Treaty, (and that too with the consent of the King of *France*) in which, those of the Religion had submitted to conditions too harsh for their present estate to bear; he had seen their Confederates of *Italy* deserted, and the Armies designed for their defence, employed to block up their Garrisons, and to reduce this Town to a Consumption by Famine, the continual cries of which place, and of the whole body of the Reformed party, having by the mediation of the Dukes of *Rohan* and *Soubize*, reached his ears, and taking notice of the vast preparations at Sea, closely to begirt this Town; and that to that end, by an unrepresidented act of injustice, one hundred and twenty *English* ships, with all their Merchandize, Mariners, and Artillery, were seized on in time of peace; that for these, and many other reasons, compassionating their miseries, and heavy pressures, his promise also to see the Articles agreed on, performed, obliging him, he now offer'd them a powerful assistance both by Sea and Land, in case they will accept of it, and engage in the War with him, protesting not to prosecute any particular pretension or interest whatsoever, save only what was accorded to those of the Religion, for which he became Caution: That in case the Town refuse this offer, the Duke solemnly protests before God, and the world, that he holds his Master fully absolved of all obligations both of Conscience, and Honour; and that for his part, he shall dispose himself to execute the rest of the commands imposed on him by his Master, and that he desires their clear and speedy answer: This Harangue much moved the people, who saw no other re-fourse, nor hopes of deliverance then from the *English* Arms; yet so prevalent was the faction of those that endeavoured the destruction of that poor, and miserable Town, that with much difficulty were they induced to resolve on any thing; at length they sent their Deputies to the Duke of *Buckingham*, to give the King of *England* thanks for the care he took of them, and withall to let him know, that having heard, and well considered of his Message, representing his Majesties good intentions to all the Reformed in *France*, of whom they were but a part; that being bound by their Oath of Union to act nothing but by a general and unanimous consent, they conceived their answer would be much firmer, and more acceptable to the

K 3   King,

King, if it were accompanied with that of the Duke of *Rohan*, and the rest of the Reformed party, towards whom they were now sending with all speed; beseeching the Duke of *Buckingham* favourably to interpret this Protraction of the demanded junction, and be a means that it may not be displeasing to the King of great *Britain*. In the mean time they would address their prayers, and vowes to God for the prosperous progress of his Arms to a plenary execution of the good, and holy intentions of his Majesty.

This answer had like to have drawn great prejudice on them of all hands; from the *English*, to see their great irresolution, and that they should need a spur, who could find no safety but in their courage, and audacity; from those of the Religion, inasmuch as they demanded their advice, not assistance: Thus in affairs of great consequence, Councels accompanied with too much circumspection, are attended on by no less dangers; for they discover so much fear, as raises the courages of enemies, and depresses those of friends: The Duke of *Soubize* sent the Duke of *Buckingham* a particular account of this deputation, and answer, by *Saint Blancarte*, and withall, an absolute assurance of the Town of *Rochelle*.

It is now to be observed, that when *Soubize* left the Fleet, to know the intentions of the *Rochellers*, two things were agreed on between him, and *Buckingham*: First, that the first descent should be in the Isle of *Oleron*, both for the facility of it, there being not above twelve hundred souldiers to oppose them, nor any fortress able to make eight dayes resistance; and also for the conveniencies of the place, abounding in corn, and wine, commodious for the maintenance of their Souldiers and Mariners, easie to be kept, and that once taken, and the *English* Vessels guarding the Sea, would in short time reduce the Isle of *Ré* to great extremities; whereas if they made their first attempt on the other, which was well stored with souldiers, sufficiently fortified to make a good opposition, the success of the attempt would be full of hazard, and the conquest of uncertainty; the other was not to attempt any thing before the Duke of *Soubize* his return: But when *Saint Blancart* came there to acquaint the Duke of *Buckingham* with the issue of his negotiation in *Rochelle*, he found the design varied, a discent into the Isle of *Ré* determined, and ready to be executed, which the Duke of *Buckingham* also, not expecting *Soubize* his return, hastens; whether it was, that he feared lest *Toiras*, who had already three thousand foot, and two hundred horse in the Island, should grow too strong, many of the Nobility, and great numbers of souldiers flocking thither from all parts; or that he was loth

Sou-

Book IV. *The Memoires of the Duke of* Rohan. 135

Soubize should participate of the honour of the action. At this discent there was a smart and gallant combate, the *English*, like a deluge, over-whelming all that opposed them, which greatly terrified the *Romanists*; and had he closely pursued the victory, and gone directly to the Fort, according to the advice of the Duke of *Soubize*, who was by that time gotten thither, he had found it empty both of provisions and souldiers; but the loss of five dayes idly trifled away, gave *Toiras* leisure to rally his scattered men, and to carry all the provisions, could be found in the Village, up to the Fort.

This only fault drew after it many mischiefs on the reformed party; in this fight was slain *Saint Blancart*, (who came thither soon enough to land the second man) deservedly lamented by his party, being a young man, whose piety, courage, and prudence emulously strove to renown him.

This discent of the *English* caused great commotions at the Court, and had a sudden taking of the Fort succeeded it, probably a great alteration of affairs had followed: For the sickness, the King, about the same time, was surprised with, the general discontent of the Nobility at the Cardinals favour; the jealousie of those were but lately engaged with the Duke of *Orleans*; the abode of the *Count* of *Soissons* in *Piedmont*, and the Duke of *Savoy's* known desires of revenge, for his desertion by the *French*, were sufficient grounds for more than ordinary jealousies; and every one impatiently expected to know the fate of the Fort, that they might declare their affections; which the King well knowing, omitted nothing for its relief; fed the Town of *Rochelle* with hopes of an accommodation, provided they joyned not with the *English*, essayed to work upon the Duke of *Rohan* with offers of large sums of money, and dispersed Messengers to all the Reformed Towns, to render odious the discent of the *English*, and to draw from them such Declarations as might secure him against the fear of their conjunction with them; and prevailed with *Montauban* and *Castres* to send Deputies to the other Corporations to disswade them from it, and by this Argument, that *Rochelle* had not joyned with them.

The Duke of *Rohan*, who for a long while before had been acquainted with the Artifices of the Court, and particularly knew their *Partisans* in every Town, fore-seeing well that he could not hinder such Declarations, advises them to insert in them the general clause, under the benefit of the Edicts, and all other concessions, that so he might in convenient season disengage them again, and with hopes of good news from *Rochelle*, engages them not to desert that Town. At length come letters thence, but such, whose

K 4

contents answered not his desires; nevertheless he is obliged to make use of them; but how to extract any advantage out of them, was no small difficulty: If he should send them to every Town, they might occasion divers resolutions to be taken up by them, and possibly contrary the one to the other, which must needs cause great divisions; if before he took up Arms, he should convoque an Assembly, none of the Corporations would dare send their Deputies, for fear of rendring themselves criminal, which would yet be a greater evil; he resolves therefore to conceal the letters he had received, & at the same time to write severally to all the principal Communalties of the *Sevenes*, (and unknown the one to the other, nor mentioning any Assembly) to send their Deputies to him to *Nismes*, to whom he had things to impart that much concerned them in particular; the same desire sent he to *Vsez*; hoping that when he had drawn the Provinces of the lower *Languedoc*, and the *Sevenes* to any good resolution, the rest of the Reformed party, or at least the greatest part of them, would easily follow their example. This invention succeeded well; for all the Deputies came at the time and place prefixed; but the Commission of the Deputies of *Vsez*, being not large enough, and fearing some treachery from that Town, he carried all the Deputies thither, and there formed an Assembly, not doubting, by his presence, to confirm them to his party; this done, he recounts all the breaches of faith during the first War; all the infractions of the Edict of peace, made before *Montpellier*, (which occasioned the loss of that Town) the continuation of the siege of *Rochelle*; the detention of their goods, and the unjust and cruel execution of many innocent persons, which was the cause of the second; which being composed by the intervention of the King of great *Britain's* Ambassadours, they to obtain a condiscension of those of the Religion to the Kings proposals, with the Kings consent, and in the name of the King their Master, became Caution for the performance of the Articles, which being no better observed than the former, the danger of *Rochelle* daily increasing by straitning their Port; the loss of their Franchises, and liberty of Commerce, by the repairing, instead of the promised razing of the Fort *Lewis*; by the fortifying the Islands, and storing them with Ammunition, and other provisions; by the building, collecting, and arming so many ships; by maintaining so many neighbouring Garrisons; by so many attempts upon the Town; by the subversion of the priviledges of *Nismes*, and *Aletz*, depriving them of their liberty of electing Consuls; by the manifold infringement of the Edicts in all points, and places, and towards all persons; that the consideration of all these things had obliged him to remonstrate their

Book IV. *The Memoires of the Duke of* Rohan. 137

condition to the King of great *Britain*, to implore him, according to his Royal promises, to afford us some redress of our grievances; which so prevailed upon him, that after a fruitless tryal of all fair means, he had at length resolved openly to assist us, and to that end had sent the Duke of *Buckingham* with a gallant Army, whose beginnings were very prosperous: But that it was upon condition, that the lower *Languedoc* should joyn with his forces, and not listen to any but a General Treaty, and with the consent of the said King, and of the whole body of the Reformed Party within this Kingdom; adding moreover that the Town of *Rochelle* would not conclude any thing without them: And, with that, shewed them the Letters he had thence, telling them, that, considering the importance of the affair, he had thought it necessary to assemble the two Provinces of the *Sevenes*, and the lower *Languedoc*, that there might be a perfect harmony in their resolutions, which would never have been, had he sent those Letters to all the Towns severally; that, moreover, he could not in time of peace convoque an General Assembly, whose only summons would then have proved its prevention: but that he was assured that the resolutions of those two Provinces would charm all the rest to an imitation: wherefore he conjured them to a serious consideration of the premises, assuring them of his strict and perpetual adherence to them.

Whereupon they decreed that the Duke of *Rohan* should be desired to resume his charge of General of the Reformed Party, to make leavies of Souldiers and all other things he should conceive conducible to their good; that he be desired to form, as soon as may be a General Assembly, to continue during the war, for the direction and management of their affairs, that the oath of Union be renewed, with the addition of their Junction with the King of great *Britains* forces, and also of all other Princes, Lords and Gentlemen, that for the maintenance of this cause have, or for the future shall raise arms, with a subjunction of a promise not to accept of any particular peace, nor to consent or hearken to any treaty, but general, and with the approbation of the whole body of the Reformed Party, and of those Princes with whom they are, or shall be united.

This being done, they all depart: and *Rohan* gives out his Commissions, and, that he might not disgust the People, raises and arms his men at his own expence, appointing a day to make some attempts upon several places: And while he prepares himself for the field, let us reflect upon the Isle of *Ré*, where we left the Duke of *Buckingham*, publishing a declaration to justifie his Masters proceedings, and advancing to quarter his army in the Town of Saint *Martin de Ré*, whence he began to straighten the

Citadel,

Citadel, consisting of four Bastions not yet perfected; and having no out-works to defend it: This place he resolved to reduce, by starving it, presuming they had but small store of provisions in it; and that being Master of the Sea, he might easily prevent the entry of any recruits either of men or victuals; but being something too careless in blocking them up, he contents himself with stopping up the Haven with boats and beams laid a cross it, surrounding the Fort with his Army, and the Island with his Fleet, but disdaining to take a small Fort in the Island, which held for the King, and was seated on one of the best landing places in it: whence afterwards issued all the mischiefs that befel him.

Besides those errors, were committed also these, *viz.* that instead of raising a work towards the Sea, the only quarter to be feared, a very frivolous and useless one was raised on the Land, and three Batteries, but at a distance, rather to affright, than hurt: A Well also was not well heeded, about five and twenty, or thirty paces from the Counterscarp, in which was only thrown a dead horse, and some stones to cover it; but the besieged knowing, of what dangerous consequence that loss would be to them, disfurnishing them of water in the Fort, quickly uncovered it, and having well cleared it, fortified it with a work, which preserved it them during the whole Siege: The Guards also were not well ordered towards the Sea; nor could the re-iterated advice of the Duke of *Soubize* ever induce them to divide their Ships, and place them before the Ports, where they would have much prejudiced the Romish Party. Nay, it was yet worse; for upon very light pretences, every day came one or other from the Fort, to speak with the Duke of *Buckingham*, and discover the condition of his Army; and from that time, by the means of the Baron *De Saint Surin* and *Montaut*, were set on foot on divers Treaties, which were continued till such time, as the Duke of *Buckingham* dispatch'd one of his Nephews to the Court with the said *Saint Surin*, but for what reason, was not known to the Duke of *Soubize*.

Now for the better understanding of this Affair, it is to be known that *Ré* is an Island, lying about a League from *Rochelle*, seven miles in length, and of great fertility, especially in wine, and salt: There are in it, three principal *Bourgs*, or unwalled Towns, of which *Saint Martin De Ré* is one of the fairest of *France*, and seated on the best Rode of all that Coast: There is also a fair Port, which stretcheth it self all along the Town, like a little Arm of the Sea; and it was the mouth of that which the Duke of *Buckingham* blocked up, to prevent the introduction of provisions into the Fort: Between *Ré*, and *Brouage* lies another Island, called *Oleron*, as big, and populous as the other, but much more

Book IV. *The Memoires of the Duke of* Rohan. 139

more fruitful; in which the King had garrison'd a Fort, built there by the Duke of *Soubize* in the former War, but of small consideration; had *Buckingham* seized upon this Island, where almost all the Inhabitants are of the Religion, he had then totally defeated the Fort of *Ré* of all means of relief.

The King about this time falling sick, was constrained to send the Duke of *Orleans* in his place, to command, and confirm the Army, which the Duke of *Angoulesme* had about *Rochelle*, where notwithstanding the *Rochellers* protestations by which they disowned any confederacy with the *English*, yet was their usage nothing better, but they began now to begirt them more closely by Land, to retrench all manner of Provisions: but the main design of the Army chiefly reflected upon the Fort of *Ré*, to recruit that with men, and victuals, in which they spared no expence, neither of men, nor money; so that at several times they got in sufficient numbers to keep it till its entire deliverance.

The *Rochellers*, after they had often, but in vain, renewed their protestations of fidelity and obedience, seeing that all their submissions, neither abated their sufferings, nor the malice of those who thirsted for their ruine, but only fomented divisions among those of the Religion, and furnished the ill-affected with specious pretences to exclaim against the others; at length remonstrate how that they had with-drawn themselves from the Crown of *England*, to subject themselves to that of *France*, the great priviledges they had acquir'd by it, their good services ever since, their immoveable fidelity, in which they had constantly persevered, notwithstanding the destruction of their Trade, the consuming of their Harvests, the devastation of their Countrey, the cruelties exercised upon their Citizens; in short, all those miseries which a licentious Army in many years can inflict upon their greatest enemies; and after this sad repetition of their sufferings, openly declare for the *English*.

As for the Duke of *Rohan*, he also publishes a Declaration, containing the infractions of the two former peaces, the reasons he had to resent them, and makes his Addresses to the King of great *Britain*, who was Caution for the latter; protests that he has no other aime, than at the observation of the Edicts, which once granted, he freely offers to expose himself to a voluntary exile from the Kingdom, that so there might be no ground left for future pretences and jealousies. On the other side, the King also issues forth new Declarations, in which he promises an observation of the Edicts to those that shall persist in their obedience, a pardon to those that had flown from it, if within a certain time they returned to it, denouncing heavy securities against the persons, and

estates

estates of such as shall adhere to the Reformed Party; the Duke of *Soubize* was proclaimed Traytour; and the Parliament of *Thoulouze*, though it has no jurisdiction over the Peers of *France*, condemned the Duke of *Rohan* to be torn in pieces with foure horses, proclaimed him ignoble, and set a price of fifty thousand Crowns upon his head, ennobling those that should assassinate him, which encouraged three or four unhappy Villains to attempt it; but they came short of any other recompence than a Halter, or a Wheel; it being not within the compass of any humane power, without an especial permission of the Divine, either to prolong, or shorten the life of any man.

These light skirmishes of the pen thus dispatched, come we now to the more fatal ones of the Sword; of all the designs contrived, and promised to the Duke of *Rohan* to be put in execution upon divers places, in several Provinces, none took effect, but that of *Corconne*, the management of which, he had committed to the Lieutenant of his Guards, together with one named *De Pize*, (who in a short time after, gave it back to the enemy again) The chiefest obstacle of it was, the peoples refusal to allow of any such attempts, before an open Declaration of the War: So that at the beginning of this, there was not any Paltry Village, or Fort, that stood not upon his Guard; a thing not heard of in the former Civil Wars, when men were more zealous for their Religion, more faithful, secret, and confident of their Commanders, to whom they gave so great respect, that their bare Tickets only were sufficient to engage them in a War, and to attempt the most considerable places of the Kingdom; whereas now the Irreligion and Disloyalty of those of the Religion, is more difficultly opposed, than the malice of their enemies.

About this time, *Montague* sent him an Express, importing, that the intentions of a Discent to be made in *Guyenne*, were altered, and that for this Summer the Duke of *Buckingham* would make no invasion but about the Coast of *Rochelle*; so that the King of great *Britain* discharged him of his promise to march to *Montauban*, leaving him at liberty, to make choice of what place he pleased for this Summers action; but that the Duke of *Savoy*, with whom he was, was of opinion, that he might make a more advantagious progress along the *Rhone*, than in any other quarter, and promised to give the enemy a good diversion in his: But all these designs were projected with reference to the taking of the Fort of *Ré*, of which there was not the least umbrage of a doubt. The Duke of *Rohan* took this Express into consideration, and would willingly have made his first Exploits in those quarters, had he not been necessitated to reclaim the Towns of *Roüergue*,

and

Book IV.   *The Memoires of the Duke of* Rohan.   141

and the higher *Languedoc*, who in his abſence had been inveigled into reſolutions contrary to his, and their determinations alſo ſent to the King; ſo that nothing but his preſence was capable to make them take Arms; which fixed him in his former purpoſes, for which he ſent *Montague* his Reaſons, aſſuring him however, that, if the Duke of *Savoy* would inſtantly take the Field, he would quit all other deſigns to joyn Forces with him; but that otherwiſe it would be expedient to remit that Affair till another time: And ſo, leaving the Baron *D' Aubais*, to command the lower *Languedoc*, and a Council in the *Sevenes*, to govern their Affairs there; he marched with his whole Force, compoſed of four thouſand five hundred Foot, and two hundred Horſe, directly towards *Millaud*; and in his March, took *Pont D' Arre*, a private Gentlemans houſe, and *Arigas* a Church that was fortified, and very much incommoded the Bayliwick of *Vigan*; whiles he ſtayed at *Saint John De Breüill*, *Alterac*, and *Guerin*, two of his *Partiſans* in *Millaud* came to meet, and diſſwade him from that attempt, alledging the difficulties attending it, and that as ſoon as *Montauban* and *Caſtres* had declared, they would do the like.

The Duke told them they had done very ill to come out of the Town, which they had left to the diſpoſal of thoſe that were diſaffected to them; that it would be the ruine of his deſigns, and a Preſident for all the Towns of *Roüergue* to ſhut their Gates againſt him; that he could not begin with *Montauban*, and *Caſtres*; for that *Millaud* lay directly in his way to them; and that he was reſolved with all his Troops to get in, or ravage their whole Countrey; deſiring them to go before, and give them notice of it: But they found how their abſence had encouraged the adverſe party, who having ſhut the Gates of the Town, and thoſe of the Bridge over the River *Tarn*, where they muſt of neceſſity paſs, they could not obtain a re-admittance, but were enforced to return to the Duke with the newes; which yet ſtopped him not, who well ſaw the neceſſity of proſecuting this deſign; hoping that the ſight of him would animate the people to an inſurrection; who failed not his expectation: For having with much difficulty and peril, by reaſon of the depth, and largeneſs of the River, paſſed over ſome of his Guards, who laying at the Gates of the Bridge on both ſides, they at length fell down, and gave him free paſſage to the Suburbs, where taking ſome Horſe, and his Trumpets, and in that Equipage marching round the Town, he ſo excited the people, that under the favour of the night, without any oppoſition, they meet all with their Armes, and forcing the Conſuls to open the Gates, went themſelves to conduct him into the Town.

This ſucceſs made him way into all the Towns of *Roüergue*, and

and of the Mountain of *Albigeois*, except *Braſſac*, and *Saint Felix* Tower, where he left ſome Regiments with *Vacquereſſe*, who had already blocked up this Tower, and having ſprung a Mine, took it upon compoſition; whereupon *Braſſac*, at the end of four and twenty houres yielded alſo: But *Saint Germier*, who carried on his buſineſs at *Caſtres*, behaved himſelf ſo ill, that he ſuffered himſelf, with all his Confidents to be turned out of the Town: This Preſident made *Realmont*, *Briteſte*, and the three Towns of *Lauraguais*; viz. *Puylaurens*, *Revel*, and *Soreze* refuſe alſo to declare; ſo that he was fain to come with his Cavalry to *Roque-Courbe*, a little Town, about one League diſtant from *Caſtres*, and two from *Realmont*; whence he made ſeveral Eſſayes to reduce thoſe two refractory places; at *Caſtres* he prevailed nothing at all; at *Realmont* his perſwaſions met a more civil reception, and their Gates, that refuſed the Duke of *Montmorency*, admitted him; there he placed *Maugis* Governour, who had been moſt active in doing him this ſervice, and very faithful to him in the precedent Wars.

The reduction of this place was ſome enlargement to him; thither he ſummoned the Colloque of *Albigeois*, which he wrought to reſolutions conformable to his own; but before he could advance any farther, *Puylaurens*, or *Revel* muſt of neceſſity be ſecured; otherwiſe it were impoſſible he ſhould adventure to go either to *Montauban*, or into *Foix*, being to march twelve or fifteen Leagues in an enemies Countrey, and that over great Plains too, having the Duke of *Montmorency* attending on him, who had drawn together the whole ſtrength of the Country to fight him, and was alwayes double or treble ſtronger in Horſe than he; it was once in his thoughts to croſs the *Tarn*, but the late abundance of rain had made it unfordable; ſo that having no way but that of *Lauraguais*, and an Army before him, he could not put himſelf upon the hazard of that paſſage without ſome place of retreat. He begins therefore with *Puylaurens*, as a place whoſe example would invite all the reſt; *Terrieux*, and *Mauris*, two, whoſe good ſervices in the former Wars, made him repoſe a great confidence in, promiſed, that if he would give them five hundred piſtols to diſtribute in the Town, they would procure his admittance; but, inſtead of performing what they had engaged themſelves to do, they betray the whole deſign to the Duke of *Montmorency*, to the end he might ſurprize *Caſſagne*, who with his own, and the Baron *d' Aletz* his company, and fifty of the Duke of *Rohan*'s Guards, were commanded to execute it; to whom, when they came to the appointed Rendez-vous, the Traytors ſent word, that it was not in their power to effect what they had undertaken; the others ſeeing

themſelves

themselves far from any retreat, *Cauſſe Caucallier*, who had very good acquaintance, and *Gaillard*, a brother, in *Revel*, who with *Des-Iſles-Maiſons* were carrying on an infallible deſign there, and which wanted only two dayes to be put in execution, fearing the inconveniencies threatned by the great length of their retreat, made a deſperate propoſal to anticipate the time, and attempt it preſently, which they all aſſented to, and ſucceeded ſo well in, that the people of *Revel* ſeeing *Rohans* Livery, imagining he himſelf was there, and *Gaillard's* brother, with ſome other of the Inhabitants, having ſeized upon a Tower, favoured their *Eſcalade*, in which they met with no other oppoſition than ſome ſtones thrown at them: Thus they became Maſters of the Town, the news of which made the Duke of *Rohan* reſolve, inſtantly, and without any further delay to advance.

In order to which he cauſed fourty thouſand loaves to be made, and leaving *Roque-Courbe* came with part of his forces, and lay at *Arifat*, a houſe not above halfe a League from *Caſtres*; the next day he marched to *Narrez*, where he appointed his general Rendez-vous, and quarters that night at *Sajes*, where he had intelligence that the Duke of *Montmorency* with all his troops lay between him and *Revel*, whereupon, to diſencumber himſelf of all the Carts he had to carry it, he diſtributed all the bread among his ſouldiers; and the next day having marched about a League, he diſcovered the Duke of *Montmorency*, with three or four hundred horſe only: whereupon he rallies his men; and in good order marches in ſight of him, keeping on his way to *Revel*, without any rencontre at all, and quartered about a League from *Revel*, where he arrived the next day early. The Duke of *Montmorency* takes up his quarters at *Saint Felix*, and other adjacent places, whence he might get the advantage of the way, whether he took that of *Montauban*, or of *Foix*.

The Duke of *Rohan*, in the meane time, intercepts a Letter written by the Conſuls of *Mazeres*, and addreſſed to the Preſident *de Suc*, importing the inclinations of that Town to joyne with the Reformed party, but that the Duke's preſence was very requiſite to promote the publique Declaration of their intentions; which he took into his ſerious conſideration, and reflecting upon this, that he had yet three dayes march before his Army could reach *Montauban*, no retreat upon the way, that his journey thither was not neceſſary, the *Engliſh* being engaged in other parts, and having good aſſurance of the entire affections of that Town, he thought fit to embrace this offered opportunity of reducing the whole Countrey of *Foix* to his party; This made him reſolve upon that courſe, and, that he might get the ſtart of the enemy,

having

having caused his Souldiers to take bread for two dayes, and quit part of their baggage, he parts from *Revel* at midnight; but by reason of the badnesse of the weather that night, and the incommodious advenews of the Village, where his foot lay, it was day before his Reare could get out of it; so that passing by *Montcaussion*, where a troop of horse of the enemies were quartered, notice of their march towards *Foix* being given, it occasioned a slight skirmish, which yet retarded not the armies march: The same troop followed his Reare at a distance, till they came neare to a little Town called *Soville*, two Leagues from *Revel*, where the Duke of *Montmorency* was ranging his troops in Battalia, as conceiving it the most proper place to oppose the Duke of *Rohan*'s passage, and fight him, by reason of a fair plain beneath it, very advantageous for his Cavalry, in which he was much superiour, and of a little, but very dangerous brook, all whose bridges he had broken down, so that he could not passe but in sight of him.

The Duke whose Army consisted of four thousand foot, & fifteen hundred good horse, made four Battalions of his Infantry, which he ranged in formes of Lozenges, leaving great intervals between them for his Cavalry who faced the enemies army, and could, as they marched, be easily ordered to charge them either in Front, Flanck, or Reare; and his baggage placed he in the middest of the four Battalions, resolving in that order either to passe, or fight him; But enquiring of his guides, if there were no other passage over the brook but that which the enemy possessed, they informed him, that upon the left hand of him there was a Ford near a little Castle, called *de Jean*, where the brook being narrow, there might easily be a bridge made for the passage of the foot: Thither then marched he directly, leaving the Duke of *Montmorency*'s Army on his right hand, and when he had gotten beyond him, very opportunely sends to take the Castle, which two hundred souldiers of *Castelnaudary* were coming to possesse, and would mightily have incommoded his passage. This done he disencumbers himself of his baggage, which he sent before over the brook to the Castle, and having gained a little hill, between the enemy and the brook, halts there, to observe the countenance of the Duke of *Montmorency*, and considering what he were best to do; Once he thought not to quit the advantage of that place, fearing to march over the brook by day, in view of an army that sought all advantages to encounter him, and might suffer as many as they pleased of his men to get over, and then charge the rest: On the other side, considering, that if he stayed there without provisions, in an enemies Countrey, an army attending him, and having five long Leagues to *Mazeres*, he feared it would be too great a burthen for his

his souldiers to support, so that, by the advice of all his Officers, he resolved to expose himself rather to the hazard of a battel, than the miseries of toyle and famine; and when the bridge was made, marched towards it, in the aforesaid equipage. *Auzon* who had the command of a troop of horse, and was nearest the Duke of *Montmorency*'s Army, being placed upon a hillock, that gave him the prospect of the whole Countrey every way, let the Army advance too far before him, before he began to draw off; so that he was charged by two hundred Horse, who pursued him home to his Foot in great disorder, and had like to have Routed them too; but the Duke of *Rohan*'s Guards, who were very opportunely on foot, and ready to relieve him, gave them a Volley, and at the same instant a sharp charge, and repulse; this beginning much animated *Montmorency*'s Army, part of his Cavalry, with his Foot also, advancing with great shouts to the charge; but receiving a second repulse, and two of the Duke of *Rohan*'s Battaillons coming up, with their Pikes charged directly to them, the Foot stayed not to expect them; but flying, cast away their Arms, and quitted the Field; they were closely pursued up to a Work, which hindred our discovery of what was on the other side of it, and saved the enemy from an entire defeat: For the Duke of *Rohan* would not suffer his men to make any confused pursuit, because the Duke of *Montmorency*, who had not yet come up to the charge, was beyond that Work, with above three hundred Horse in Battaila; but commanded *Leques* only to advance, to observe their posture.

    The Duke of *Montmorency*, when he had rallied his Men, drew them off to *Soville*, and there Ranged them again in Battaila, but without any semblance of renewing the Fight: The Duke of *Rohan*, for his part, kept the Field more than a long houre, caused his dead to be buried, and thanks to be given to God; and then, without any interruption, passed the Brook, and kept on his way; but could not reach *Mazeres* till the next day at Noon, after he had been forty houres on horse-back: In this Fight he lost *Causse-Caucallier*, one of his Life-guard, one of his Pages, two Lieutenants of Foot, five or six Souldiers, and had thirty or forty wounded. Of the Duke of *Montmorency*'s party, were left many more, yet was it no bloody Incounter; and it is to be believed that this engagement of his was rather occasional, than before determined; for it seems he had more reason to charge the Duke of *Rohan* in his passage over the Brook, than in any other part: But 'tis easier to correct the actions of others, when a man is out of danger of the blowes, than in the action it self, which requires a prompt and sudden execution, and af-

L   fords

fords not leasure to perpend, and weigh all events. The Duke of *Montmorency* had, at this Rencontre, but three thousand Foot, but he had six, or seven hundred Horse of his own, besides all the Gentry of quality of *Languedoc, Roüergue, Foix*, and some from beyond the *Garonne*.

When the Duke of *Rohan* came to *Mazeres*, all his men oppressed with hunger, lassitude, and want of sleep, for refreshment, he found the gates shut against him, and the Magistrates utterly averse to receive him; but the common people at length took heart, and in spight of the Consuls, and most potent Inhabitants, let him in; where, after he had taken the best order he could for quartering of his Horse, he made provision for his Foot also. When the Duke of *Montmorency* heard of the indisposition of the people of *Foix* to joyne with the Duke of *Rohan*'s Forces; he came and took up his quarters at *Saint Gallelle* upon the River *Cers*, which runs to *Mazeres*, a good league distant from *Saverdun*, whence he sent to inform them, that he was come thither with his Army for their assistance, that they should be of good courage, and not suffer themselves to be caught by the allurements of the Duke of *Rohan*; who for eight dayes together, was oppressed with the extremity of keeping all his Army upon his own expence, and yet could he hardly furnish his Foot with one loaf a day each one; having no other place in *Foix* besides *Mazeres*, and the River *Ricge* swollen to a height, that making it unfordable, cut off all communication with the upper *Foix*: So, that had these inconveniencies lasted but a few dayes longer, he had been in danger of perishing by Famine if he stayed; or by the Sword, if he returned; having no Ammunition to defend himself withall: All these necessities pressing him, he sounded so many Fordes, till at length having found one between *Saverdun*, and *Pamiez*, which the Duke of *Montmorency* could not so suddenly reach, he resolves in this desperate condition, to make an attempt on *Saverdun*, where he knew the people were well-affected to him, and the lower Town being easie to be forced, he hoped that when he had taken that, fear would induce the other to an accommodation with him; which project had a wished success: To this end, he marches by night from *Mazeres* with a part of his Troops, and at break of day passes the *Ford*; but with great difficulty for the Foot, by reason of the swiftness, and extream coldness of the River, which then also was swelled so high, that some of his Souldiers, and many of his Arms were lost in it; so that at last the Horse were necessitated to transport the remaining Foot behind them; which done, he marches strait to *Saverdun*; where first, by a Trumpet he summoned

summoned the Inhabitants to open their Gates; and upon their refusal advances, and, after some Volleys of small shot, which neither slew, nor hurt any one, with the assistance of some honest persons of the Town, Ladders were mounted, and the place entred: The taking of the lower Town, much confounded the ill-affected; some flie, others hide themselves, at length all cry out for mercy; and the higher Town also was surrendred on the 12th. of *Novemb.*1627.

The same day *Faucon*, by the Duke of *Rohan*'s order, with two hundred Men, secured *Montmaur*, a small Town, and Castle lying between *Revel*, and *Mazeres*; but of great consequence for the uniting *Lauraguais*, and *Foix*: This was effected by the intelligence of *La Barte*, whom the Duke of *Montmorency* had highly disgusted.

The Duke vigorously prosecutes these fortunate successes, and upon hopes of some Correspondents in *Pamiez*, on the 22th. of the same Month he shewes himself with his Horse before it, but had no other entertainment than what they sent him from their Musquets; whereupon he determined, the night following, to clap a Petarde to the Wall, to which he was induced by some of the Inhabitants, that had given him a meeting near the Town; instead then of returning to *Saverdun*, whither he was going, he retires to a Covert, half a league from *Pamiez*, forbidding his men to make any fires; thither he commands *Goudin* and *Malmoirac*, with their Regiments, whom he had before ordered to be in a readiness; but those that should have come out of the Town to conduct him to the place, and inform him of the true state of it, came not to the Rendez-vous; nevertheless *Bruel*, one of the Town, Author of this enterprise, and who knew well enough where the Petarde was to be fixed, being with him, he proceeded in the designed attempt, which was executed after this manner. *Cassagne* had the command and conduct of the *Petards*, which were carried by Gentlemen of his own, and some Officers of his Horse, who were seconded by *Leques* with thirty armed Men, and fifty choice Pikes, and Musquetiers; after whom marched *Goudin*, and *Malmoirac*, then the Duke of *Rohan* himself in person: In this Equipage they come up to the Wall, where, notwithstanding the Allarme, and Volleys of shot, the first Petarde was fixed, but the Breach being not large enough, a second was clapped on, which extended it to a sufficient wideness for an armed man to pass; whither the Inhabitants flocking to defend the Breach, *Bazier* the Engineer, took a small Granade, and threw it in through the Hole among them, where it broke, and spoiled the Thigh of one of the Defendants, and dissipated the rest; which gave the Assailants opportunity to enter the Breach; the first that entred, was *La Tour Gerestoux*; the second, was the Baron of *Villemade*, and after them, the whole Party. The taking of the Town in this manner, spread so universal a terrour over *Foix*, that some Forts, well stored with all necessaries, gave themselves up for fear. After this the Duke was received into the *Mas d' Azil*, and *Carlat*, by which means he reduced all those, that were of the Religion in the County of *Foix*, to his party; and probably had done much more, had the *English* enterprizes in the Isle of *Ré* prospered; whom it will be now expedient to look after.

The negligence of the *English*, gave opportunity to thirteen Barks, laden with provisions, to come up to the Citadel, where they arrived the sixth of *September*, about the Morning, and got off again the ninth following, carrying with them all the wounded and unuseful persons: The easie passage of these, encouraged others to the like adventure; but, the Guards being re-inforced by the *Rochellers*, some of them were taken, and severely dealt withall; and on the last of *September*, of fifteen or sixteen Barks which came up, seven were taken, and the rest put to flight.

On the twelfth of *September* came from *England* a Renfort of fifteen or sixteen hundred Souldiers, with a supply of all other necessaries; whereupon the Duke resolved to attempt the little Fort *De la Prée*, and turned some of his Canon that way; but this design was dashed upon a sudden, no man knows why.

On the sixth of *October*, the besieged, pressed by strong necessities, sent out *Monraud* with offers to capitulate, in case they were not relieved with victuals the next day: This obliged us to double our Guards, and, as the winde sate, it was easie to conjecture that the relief could not come but from *Olonne*; whereupon some ships were commanded out to meet them, and prevent their passage; but, instead of that, the Captain of the Guard took another course, and went with his ships to the *Fosse de l' Oye*, while three and thirty Barks, seizing the opportunity, passed without interruption, and nine and twenty of them came up under the Citadel; where yet it is to be noted, that they could not come near the Land, but upon a great Flood, which comes but every fifteen dayes, by reason whereof the *English* might yet with much facility, have destroyed the relief; which though arrived, yet could not be unladen; so that Propositions were made to the Duke, assaulting them on both sides by Land, to fire the Barks with what was in them: which might have been done without any prejudice received from the Castle, by reason of the height of the

Banks

Banks capable to shelter the Assailants: He seemed to approve of this motion, but took no course to put it in act; contenting himself only with trifling away the time in vain attempts to fire them by Sea.

When the relief was gotten in, *Buckingham* calls a Council, who resolve to draw off; so that on the twelfth of *October*, they began to re-imbarque their Armes, and other Ammunitions they had upon the Land: After this he sent for a Gentleman belonging to the Duke of *Soubize*, to whom he declared that the Council of War, considering how well the place was stored with all necessaries, the year so far spent, his Army much diminished, and all his Provisions consumed, had conceived it necessary to draw off; The Gentleman endeavoured to dissuade him from that resolution, shewing him that the Fleet which the Earl of *Holland* was conducting to them, would sufficiently repaire all those necessities; that the relief the Besieged had received could not last long; and that if vigilant guards were kept, they would be soon reduced to their former extremities; that his retreat now he had engaged them, would be the loss and ruine of the *Rochellers*, who would cast all their displeasure and *odium* upon the Duke of *Soubize*, as the Authour of their destruction, and that it would be an irreparable dis-reputation to the King his Masters Arms, to have attempted such an enterprise with so little honour and profit.

To all which Arguments he gave no other answer, than that his Captains would stay no longer; but yet, if the Earl of *Holland* came time enough, with his Fleet, he would endeavour to alter their minds: By which the Gentleman concluding that the Duke was fixed in his resolutions to be gone, gave speedy notice of it to the Duke of *Soubize*, who ever since the middle of *September* had lain sick at *Rochelle* of a *tertian* Ague joyned with a great vomiting, desiring him, if possible, to post thither; which he did, and at his arrival in the Isle of *Ré*, uses all his Art to perswade the Duke of *Buckingham* and his Officers into a better humour, of which they gave him some small hopes; but he, nevertheless, seeing them still carrying their things aboard, assured himself they would not budge from their former purposes.

The King, in the mean time, being recovered of his sickness, comes in person before *Rochelle*; where his presence raised both the number and spirits of his Army, and upon intelligence how the Duke of *Buckingham*'s was lessened, resolves to make a discent into the Isle of Ré under the protection of the little Fort *de la Prée*, which had still held out. On the other side the *English* men's desire to return, having made them very careless of their guards, they suffered seven or eight pinnaces to steal up towards the Fort, and on the sixteenth of *October* they land four hundred men; the twenty seventh there came up ten more, and on the thirtieth five and twenty; whereupon the Duke of *Buckingham* rallies his Men; and, quitting the greatest part of the Trenches, marches by night, with what horse and foot he had, to prevent a discent already made, commanding out a forlorne of *French*, which not being seconded, were enforced to retire. The Merchants of *Rochelle* in the mean time, seeing what preparations were made for his return, instantly sollicite the Duke to give them fifty or sixty tunnes of Corn he had upon the Shore, which he assented not to, till they had no leasure to carry it off, so that they fell to the enemies share: But before his departure, to shew that he had left nothing unattempted, he resolved to make one essay more, which resolution he grounded upon the report of some fugitives from the Fort, who averred that there were but eight hundred souldiers in it, and those too for the greatest part sick; that the Courtain towards the Sea had neither graffe nor Rampart, so that if he mounted his Ladders on that side, it might be easily forced. Without any further information, or battering the Parapetts, he resolves to give a general assault, proposes it to the *French* Officers, desiring them to dispose the *English* Colonels to it, and in case they should stick at it, he would then make use of his power to command them. The attempt thus resolved on, he prepares his men for the storm, assigning the *English* and *Irish* their post on the land side, and the *French* mixed with *English* towards the Sea: *Manuel* conducted the ten first Ladders, but could mount but two, though his party behaved themselves with much gallantry and resolution; (but to attempt to force by *Escalade* above fifteen hundred Men in a Fort with four *Bastions*, well furnished with Artillery, and all other necessaries, was a way eternally to discourage his Souldiers, rather than to lead them on to the purchase of any honour) but leaving many dead, and carrying off more wounded, they were forced to retire.

This repulse, together with the intelligence of the hourly encrease of the forces in the Fort *de la Prée*, hastned the Duke of *Buckingham*'s raising the Siege, and his retreat to the *Bay de l' Oye*, to ship his men with more leasure and security: On the eight of *November* early in the morning the Drums beat for their departure at noon, and scarcely was the Rear Guard got out of the Town, but the King's Army appeared much stronger in Horse, and equal to the others in Foot; having this further

Book IV. *The Memoires of the Duke of* Rohan. 151

ther advantage, to pursue a retreating Army, and seize all occasions which either the incommodity of the passes, or the usual disorders that attend such retreats might favour them with. At the pass *de la Coharde*, they made as though they would have charged them, but observing the good order of the *English*, and the advantage they had of the ground, after a long halt, both Armies marched off, the *English* keeping the plain, and the King's Forces the Sea coast: Beyond this pass was a hollow way, which crossing the Marsh, extended it self as far as the Bridge *de l' Oye:* At the entring of this the Squadrons began to be somewhat pressed, and to stand upon their defence; but the Van, and then the Body being got into it, the Rear-guard, charged by the Marshal *Schomberg*, was easily routed; in which defeat the *English* lost seven or eight hundred men, but the night approaching, favoured their imbarquing of the rest.

In this action the Duke of *Buckingham* committed two great errours; one was, The committing his retreat to the charge of fourscore Horse, which being forced in upon the Rear of their own Troops, broke, and confounded them; the other was, His omission to raise a Fort, or some other defenceable work at the entry of that hollow way, where he had still designed to make his retreat in case of necessity, which would absolutely have secured it.

At his departure, he assures the *Rochellers* of his speedy return to their deliverance, with a more numerous and better fortified Fleet, alledging the inconvenience of the season, and defect of provisions, as the only causes that obliged him to draw off; and promising them a quick and abundant supply of all necessaries for a long defence; and further desires some of their Merchants to follow him into *England*, that they might testifie the integrity of his affection and diligence, and that they might themselves carry back the effects of his promises. Nevertheless when he drew near the Coast of *England*, himself took a fly-boat, sending the *Rochelle* Merchants to expect him at *Bristol*, desiring the Duke of *Soubize* to do the same at *Portsmouth*, where he would be as soon as he; and then steers his course towards *Plymouth*, where the Earl of *Holland's* Fleet rode. When he came thither, he gave order that the ships that there lay ready, and laden with Corn for the *Rochellers*, should be discharged, and the Provisions sold, upon pretence that they would be spoyled; which done he gets before to pre-possess the spirit of the King of great *Britain*, rejecting the blame of the errours committed in the expedition on those were no way culpable; So that when

L 4 the

the Merchants came to exhibite their complaints against him, they were informed, it was the next way to make their condition worse: And when they importuned him for a quick dispatch of the provisions for the *Rochellers*, the Duke of *Buckingham* used no other excuse to answer their sollicitations, than that they were sold; and that which more amazed them, was his carrying away three hundred Tun of Corn, which he might have left them, till they could have been better stored. But notwithstanding all this, the Merchans addressed themselves to the King of *England* himself; to whom they represented their imminent danger, and the great preparations making to consummate their ruine; imploring his Majesty to favour them with a good and speedy recruit of Victuals, that being the greatest want that afflicted them; which once supplied, there was nothing else which they much feared: But if their enemies had leasure to block up their Port, their destruction was inevitable: All which the King answered with promises of a powerful and speedy relief, assuring them moreover, that he would hazard all the Forces of his Kingdom, rather than suffer them to perish.

While they expect the effect of these promises, the *Rochellers* dispatcht their Admiral *Bregneau* with money, and express command to buy Corn, to lade both his own, and those other ships they had already in *England*, and to return with it with all speed: *David*, who was sent after him, with the like Commission, stores his ships with provisions, and very happily got back with them into *Rochelle*: But *Bragneau*, instead of executing his Commission, goes directly from *Plymouth*, where all things were ready for him, to *Portsmouth*, under colour of furnishing himself at a better rate; and yet instead of doing that, goes to *London*, where puft up with vanity derived from the promises of the Duke of *Buckingham*, he minded nothing but an ambitious and covetous pursuit of the honour and profit of the Admiralty of the refugiated *French*, which at length he obtained, by the voluntary demission of it, which the Duke of *Soubize* made of it, in favour of the *Rochellers*, and to ease them of the extraordinary expences they were at; and yet notwithstanding, all the instant, and dayly sollicitations made to him to that purpose, could not induce him to be gone, till the difficulties of the passage grew so great, that he was at last forced to wait the departure of the other Fleet preparing for their relief.

This was the issue of this expedition of the Duke of *Buckingham*, in which he wracked both his own and his Countreys honor, consumed much of the *Rochellers* provisions, and ruined the party he came to relieve.

The

Book IV.   *The Memoires of the Duke of* Rohan.   153

The hopes this Victory gave the King of carrying the Town, made him more intent upon the Siege: The whole winter he spent in investing it by Land with Forts, Redoubts, and lines of Communication, and straightning it at Sea by a Bar extending from the point of *Coreilles* to *Fort Lewis*, in which he spared neither cost nor pains.

The Bonfires the *Romanists* made throughout the whole Country of *Foix*, gave the Duke of *Rohan* the first light of these misfortunes, the certainty of which was afterwards confirmed by an express from the Duke of *Soubize*, who encouraged him still with hopes that, the next Spring they should return in a condition to wipe off the stains this affront had cast upon them.

At the same time the Duke of *Rohan* received two several Advertisements from the lower *Languedoc*; one was, that the Marquess *de Portes*, who had many confederates in the *Colloque* of *Saint Germain*, having corrupted the Garison in the Castle of *Florac*, and gotten them to declare openly for him; *Montredon*, chief of the said *Colloque*, haste thither, and calling in the whole Province to his aide, had besieged the Castle, and in sight of the Marquess *de Portes*, who was come with two thousand men to relieve it, sprung two Mines, stormed, and forced it to surrender: The other was, that the Prince of *Condé* was coming down the *Rhone* towards the lower *Languedoc*, and that *Brison* was in Treaty with him about the Province of *Vivaretz*, which he sought by all means to intimidate; urging the Duke of *Rohan's* absence, and at so great a distance from them as an argument to inforce his design: This made him consider that it was best to preserve what they were already Masters of; conceiving that if he wintered in *Foix*, he should bring a famine on the Countrey, which had already had but a bad year, and was so little, and so remote from their other quarters, that if the Prince of *Condé* on one hand, and the Duke *d' Espernon* on the other, should joyn with the Duke of *Montmorency*, he should be blocked up on all sides: That if he went to *Montauban* it would be to small purpose, for that the *English* were now gone, and the Winter was come on, and moreover that there was no possibility for him to return thence again; so that he conceived the securest way was, to return towards the lower *Languedoc* to oppose the Prince of *Condé* there, and so preserve that Countrey.

But before his departure, he convened the *Colloque* of *Foix*, settles *Beaufort* in the Government of it, to the great satisfaction and joy of the Inhabitants; leaving with him his own Regiment

ment (which consisted yet of eight hundred men) and his own Troop of light Horse-men; makes *Rousseliere* Governour of *Saverdun*; took order for the fortifying of some places, of which there were three very considerable, to wit *Mazeres*, *Saverdun*, and *Carlat*; and as for the *Mas d' Azil*, the good fortune they had to withstand the former Siege, gave them courage again to stand upon their defence.

The only perplexity he had was for *Paraiez*, being a great Town, not fortifiable, nor well peopled of it self; nor indeed were there enough of the Religion in all *Foix* to man it as it ought: The right course had been to dismantle it; but Men, with whom in Warres of such a nature a man must of necessity comply, are hardly perswaded to things of that kinde: But although this remedy could not be applied, yet he prevailed so far upon the Inhabitants, as to fortifie a quarter of their Town called *la Marcadal*, very conveniently seated, where he designed a handsom fortification; which done he appoints his General Rendez-vous at *Mazeres*, whence he marches by night, and returning the same way he went, comes to *Revel*.

The Duke of *Montmorency* having notice of his motion, goes to wait for him on the great Road to *Montauban*, whence he suddenly retired again to his quarters. The Duke goes from *Revel* to the higher *Languedoc*, where re-assembling the *Colloque* he informed them of all he had done in *Foix*; encourages them to a constant perseverance in their fidelity; and establishes a Council for the direction of their affaires, untill such time, as he could send them a President for the *Colloque*, there being no man among them, that the rest would give place to, for that the Marquess of *Malauze* who had been formerly their President, and would, without dispute, have again been accepted of, was now wholly bent against their Party; the Court having prevailed so farre upon him, as to make him oppose the Duke of *Rohan* in that Province; which that he might the better do, he faines a desire to be reconciled with him, which he signifies by Letter to *Beaufort*; and afterwards, at his first meeting with the Duke, discovering some displeasure, that *Castres* was not yet joyned with the Party, protested that as soon as that Town, and *Montauban*, should do so, and that a General Assembly was formed, he would also publiquely declare for them. This had a pestilent influence on the weaker sort, and gave the dis-affected among them, an opportunity to work much mischief among the people; For neither the Declarations of *Montauban* and *Castres*, nor the convening of a general Assembly wrought any change at all in him, who continued still an enemy to the Reformed

Book IV. *The Memoires of the Duke of* Rohan. 155

formed Party; And dispatches also *Villemade* to *Montauban* to inform them of the cause of his return, to perswade them to declare, and to command the Souldiery, but in subordination to the Consuls: But this last proposition spoyled all the rest; *no man being esteemed a Prophet in his own Countrey*, so that they resolved to assure themselves of a Governour before they would engage in the War.

After this the Duke returns towards the *Sevenes*, and when he came to *Vigan*, received very urgent dispatches from *Vivaretz*, with intelligence that *Brison* had quitted all the higher *Vivaretz*, upon the approach of the Prince of *Condé* (although for want of Canon, he was not in a capacity to force the most inconsiderable Fort there) who had burnt and pillaged that poor Countrey; and that, if they had not speedy relief, it was to be feared that *Privas*, and the lower *Vivaretz*, would make their peace, to which *Brison* earnestly incited them; but upon notice of the Duke's return, and that he was coming in person to their relief, they re-assumed their courages, and maugre all *Brison*'s disswasions, resolved to stand upon their guard; which obliged the Prince to pass into the lower *Languedoc*; whither when the Duke also came, he met with some Souldiers of *Nismes*, who had seized the Castle of *Vauvert*, which he caused them to quit, upon the advance of the Prince, who seemed to have an intention to besiege it; unwilling to give him any occasion to stop there, knowing that his orders were to pass into the higher *Languedoc*, and that his stay would prejudice a design he had upon the Citadel of *Montpellier*, which *Bretigny David*, for six months together, had managed with the Baron *de Meslay*, his Kinsman, and intimate friend; and eldest Captaine of the Regiment of *Normandy*, then in Garison in *Montpellier*.

Now, forasmuch as upon the arrival of *de Fosse*, the Regiments of *Normandy* and *Picardy* were to be drawn out of the Town, and others to be placed there in their rooms; *Meslay* who had there married one of the Religion, seemed much discontented at this alteration; and that he had not left his own to embrace the Reformed Party: *Bretigny*, on the other side, who very well knew his ambition, cherishes him in this humour, and at length tells him, that if he could contrive a way to make himself Master of *Montpellier*, it would be then in his own power to make himself satisfaction, and that withal he would be received into a Party, from which, by that means, he might obtaine whatever his own wishes could suggest to his Hopes. The other listens to him, and demands time to consider both of

the

the thing, and the means to effect it, and both together contrived expedients for mutual Interviews, and conveying intelligence, without suspition, one to the other. Not long after he tells him he was now resolved to undertake the business; Treats with him concerning the advantages and conditions he expected from the Reformed Party, and shews him the way he had to make himself Master of the Citadel; to wit, that being on the Guard every fourth day with his own Company, he could, with much ease, let in as many as he pleased into it: That for assurance of his fidelity he would give his Wife in hostage; and when the design was to be put in execution he would advance an hundred paces from the Citadel towards *Bretigny*, to yield himself up into his hands.

When all these things were communicated to the Duke of *Rohan*, he very well liked of them, for that the two lines of Communication, which conjoyned the Town with the Citadel, being made, and the Town Wall that separated them razed, as they were now at work upon it, the Town would not be able to defend it self; but withal he declared that he would never attempt this design, till that Wall were down, or, at least, great breaches were made in it, that so one and the same action might put them in possession both of Town and Citadel. The design thus concluded on, the Duke, for some dayes, deferres his march: But seeing they proceeded too slowly in raising the Walls, he departs, and advancing a little way from *Roque-Courbe* to pass into *Foix*, *Meslay* sends *Bretigny* word, that the affaire was now in a very good posture, and that it was necessary it should be put in execution, before the Garison in the Citadel was changed; Whereupon he is dispatched into the *Sevenes*, and the lower *Languedoc*, with all necessary instructions tending to the executing of the design, and an express charge particularly to impart it to *Montredon*, and to none else: But all was delayed till the arrival of the Duke of *Rohan*, to whom they then made new Propositions, that, at the same time the Citadel should be attempted without, he should storm the Town with two thousand Men, and also scale the Walls of Communication, alledging, that when they should be Masters of the Citadel, the time they must have to pass three or four thousand Men, through one gate, would give the Town too much leasure to arm themselves. This made him somewhat more cold in the business, and gave him great suspicions of the treachery intended; whereupon he continued firm in his former resolution; in so much as *Bretigny* complained that he found him so refractory in a business able to revive their drooping Party: But he demonmonſtrated to him the danger of this laſt propoſal, and that being once Maſter of the Citadel, nothing could hinder his taking of the Town alſo.

While the Prince of *Condé* was upon his March towards the higher *Languedoc*, the Duke of *Rohan* Rallies his Forces, appointing the Rendez-vous to be on the 19th. of *January* a little above *Claret*, five leagues from *Montpellier*; where about two of the clock in the Afternoon, there met ſix thouſand fighting men : Thence he ſent a party of Horſe to advance before the reſt of the Army, as far as the Bridge of *Saleſon*, which is about a league from *Montpellier*, to intercept all ſuch as might give any notice of his approach : And then commands *Bretigny*, chief of the enterpriſe, to march with the Van, conſiſting of fifteen hundred Men, and divided into ſix Squadrons; the three firſt were compoſed each one of thirty armed men, called out of the Voluntiers, and out of the beſt of the Cavalry, with Halberds and Piſtols; and of fourſcore others, half-Pikes, half Muſquitiers; every ten armed Men had their Officer, and carried with them Petardes, and Ladders, to force the Court of Guard in the Citadel; and two great Forks to keep up the Portcullis; the other three Troops were compoſed of four hundred men, each one; and were ordered for a Reſerve to the other : After theſe, marched the Duke with his Men at Armes, followed by all the other Squadrons, the biggeſt of which conſiſted not of above four, or five hundred men. When they came to the Bridge of *Saleſon*, they found there the Baron *de Meſlay*'s Man, who aſſured *Bretigny* that all went well; whereupon, leaving all their Baggage on the other ſide of the Bridge of *Saleſon*, with a hundred Souldiers only to guard it, they advance as far as the Bridge called *Juvenal*, which is about a Canon ſhot from *Montpellier*: *Bretigny*, by a bold Souldier, gives notice of his arrival to his Couſin, who ſo well knew how to fool him, that he returned with an aſſurance that all was well, and in a good condition, and that there was no difficulty in the matter : Whereupon he proceeds, not minding at all what had been ſo often recommended to him, not to enter the place untill *Meſlay* was come forth to him, and had put himſelf into his hands; but his impatient deſire to execute ſo brave a deſign, animates him, without this precaution, to enter the Citadel with ſix or ſeven and thirty men; thoſe within not daring to let any more come in : For as ſoon, as they ſaw them plant their Forks to ſupport the Portcullis, they cut a cord, by which means the Bridge was drawn up, and a Trap-door opened, whence moſt of thoſe that were gotten in, fell down into a Trench, where they were all harque-buſiered, the Muſquitiers at the ſame time

time playing on those without; *Montredon*, who in *Bretigny*'s absence was to command, and had received a charge to be at the Gate, and see them all enter in good order, drew off the Troops, and gave the Duke notice of their success, who had drawn up his whole Body in Battaila on the right, and left hand of the great Road-way, which he had left open for the retreat of those of the Van; who when they were all passed, he returned to the Bridge of *Saleson*, where making an Halt, he Rallied his Men, and then drew off into the Plains between *Montpellier*, and *Lunel*, quartering his Men in the best Villages thereabouts; not any one stirring out of *Montpellier* to pursue him, or observe his March. The next day he gave leave to the Troops, that came from the *Sevenes* to depart; and marched with those of the lower *Languedoc*, to *Saint Gilles*, where he thought to have made an attempt upon that Garrison, but the violence of the cold forced him to send his Men into quarters.

This was the issue of that enterprise, in which *Bretigny*, and his brother were slain, with about twenty others, and sixteen or seventeen more were taken prisoners.

This Winter was the Duke of *Rohan* hardly pressed both in the upper *Languedoc*, and in *Vivaretz*; in the former of which was the Prince of *Condé*; who whil'st he prepared to invade the Province by open force, endeavoured also by secret practices to undermine the constancy of those Towns that had declared for the Reformed Party; so that the Duke of *Rohan's* presence there, with his Forces, was absolutely necessary: And on the other side *Vivaretz*, since the Prince his March through it, was in a miserable condition; the higher *Vivaretz* being lost, with all that the Duke held upon the *Rhone*: And besides all this, the Duke of *Ventadour* in his Seigniories, and *Missargues* in those he held in right of his Wife, used extream cruelties, and violences against those of the Religion, seizing on their Estates, torturing their Bodies with Whips, and Bastinadoes, driving them to Masse; so that there came thence, to the Duke, frequent dispatches, and Deputies, one upon the heels of another, to implore his presence, and the assistance of his Forces, to restore them to their liberty, which otherwise they should be inforced to purchase at any rate; considering also the divisions between all the Nobility of that Countrey, and *Brison*; assuring him also that they had taken care for the quartering of his Troops, as long as their necessity should require their stay there.

There happened yet another accident, which much obstructed this Voyage; to wit, the unexpected death of *Brison*, which
much

Book IV. *The Memoires of the Duke of* Rohan. 159

much enlarged the former divisions; for if the Nobility refused to submit to *Brison*, who had been already twice Governour of the Province, much more would they oppose his brother *Chevrilles*, a young man, of small experience, and far short of his brothers conduct to govern the Province: On the other side the faction of *Brison*, which was the most prevalent in *Privas*, and *Privas* the most considerable place of all *Vivaretz*, chose *Chevrilles* for their Governour; for that, being conscious of his weakness, they thought to rule all more absolutely, than under his brother, and to allow him what part they pleased, in the administration of the Affairs: To which must be added, that the Province of the lower *Languedoc*, which was to advance the Leavy-money, being highly interessed in the preservation of *Vivaretz*, and blocking up the *Rhone*, it being a River that with great facility and speed could convey all sorts of Arms, and Ammunition to the enemy, preferred this design, before that of the higher-*Languedoc*; for which place *Rohan* had raised two Regiments, of five hundred Men apiece, which was all they desired, in case he could not come himself in person: But the untoward humour of *Faucon*, to say no worse, much retarded this relief; for being designed for that expedition, after he had promised to go, and for that reason had received more Advance-money than was usually allowed; he endeavoured to corrupt his Captains, that so he might reject his merited blame on them; but being not able to prevail on more than one, he was at length constrained to declare openly that he would not go at all; so that the Duke could send but eight of those Companies with *Caumette-Chambaud*, who commanded the other Regiment: But by reason of these difficulties, protractions, and the artifices used by *Faucon* to withdraw both Officer, and Souldier from this Voyage, those eight Companies could never amount to more than eight hundred men in the whole. The Duke thereupon caused *Faucon* to be secured, and tryed at a Councel of War, where he found more favour, than justice. 'Tis one of the greatest calamities that attend the Generals of Parties poor, and composed of Voluntaries only, that they have no capacity either to reward the Noble, or punish degenerous and unworthy actions.

But to return to the Voyage of *Vivaretz*: The Duke of *Rohan* raises four thousand Foot, and about two hundred Horse: But before he began his March thither, dismantles *Saint Geniez*, and other small places upon the River *Gardon*, within the Diocess of *Usez*, lest the *Romanists*, in his absence, should possess themselves of them, and by small Garrisons take off the contribution of all that Country which was full of good Towns; and

prejudice

prejudice the passage from the lower *Languedoc* to the *Sevenes*: And then engages the aforesaid Provinces in a resolution not to hearken to any particular Treaty, but to communicate all occurrences to him, as on his side, he promised the like, and never to consent to any without the privity of them, all the other Provinces, *Rochelle*, and the King of *England*.

When he had taken this course, he comes about the beginning of *March*, with all his Forces to *Aletz*, where he was sollicited (even to a sedition) by the Inhabitants, to employ his Forces in taking in of *Vizenobre*, and *Monts*, two Garrisons that incommoded them; but having cleared himself of this importunity, he advanced. His first work was to secure the Castle of *Rousson*, lying between *Aletz*, and *Saint Ambroix*; and afterwards, in his March, takes in *Tharque*, and *Saint John de Marne sols*, two places belonging to the Marquess *de Portes*, which yielded at sight of his Canon; the latter of these he dismantled, but not the former, being but a small Castle, and the usual residence of the said Marquess: Having cleared his way as far as *Bariac*, and being now upon the Confines of *Vivaretz*, he thought it necessary to secure a Pass upon the River *Ardeche*, for the advantage both of his advance and return. To this end he besieged the Castle of *Salvas*, situate on that River, which he blocked up with part of his Forces, whiles the other part, under the command of *Aubais*, passed the River, both for the convenience of quarters, and provisions, as also that at the same time he might block up the Castle of *Valon* also: The Siege of *Salvas* lasted five dayes; for that the Canon, and other necessaries, to force it suddenly, were not yet come up; so that they contented themselves with breaking some of their Out-works, and then had recourse to two Mines which they sprung, and to good effect too; the base Court being taken, the Garrison retreated to the Tower, which was stormed on every side: Those within behaved themselves bravely, killed and wounded many of the Assailants, and among others, the Colonel *Goudin* was hurt; but the Canon came up, and did such execution on them, that they were constrained to yield the next day after the assault.

Their example drew the Tower *de Moulins*, and the Castle of *Valon* also to a submission: The Duke caused the two Castles to be razed, preserving only the Tower of *Moulins*, which of it self was strong, and tenable by a small Garrison. To secure this pass, and clear all the way of *Vivaretz*, there remained only *Ville-neufve de Berg*, where the Governour *Montreal* had gotten together twelve hundred men; but notwithstanding that, the Duke was resolved, had it been possible, to attempt it; that so he might not leave any thorns behinde him: But he wanted Ammunition, having spent his small store at the Siege of *Salvas*; where the scarcity of provisions, and the nearness of some of his men to their own homes, had much diminished his Forces; and, which was worse, so little care had the Province taken in it, that there was nothing for them about *Ville-neufve*, so that he was fain to leave his Canon at *Goree*, and for conveniency of quarters, to March with all his Troops to *Privas*, the Countrey having not had the least thought of any thing, but how to retort the blame of their want of Provisions one upon another, so that he had much ado to keep together those Souldiers he had left. The first exploit after his arrival in the Province of *Vivaretz* was the Siege of *Choumerarg*, performed by *Chevrilles*, and the Country Troops, whil'st his own refreshed themselves; it lasted three dayes, and then their Works being all battered, the place was yielded on the second of *April*.

The Duke of *Rohan*'s designs in *Vivaretz*, were to place a Governour, and to compose all the divisions there; but principally to secure a good pass upon the R*hone*, both to draw the Tribute of the River to himself, and to facilitate the March of those Forces which the Duke of *Savoy* had promised him: For which end some proposed to him *Sujon*, others *la Voute*, others *Bajes*, and *Pousin*; the inconvenience of the first was its situation, being in the higher *Vivaretz*, and so remote from *Privas*, that it could not be easily removed from thence; that of the second was, that it was a place belonging to the Duke of *Ventadour*, and being of it self weak, and not capable to be made good, would drain *Privas* of all its Ammunition, and consequently draw an affront upon that place, which would ruine his reputation, both with the adverse Party, and his own too: Wherefore he pitches on the latter, and begins with *Pousin*, which when *Brison* gave it up, was dismantled; but, to prevent our re-possessing of it, the enemy had fortified a small Tower in the Castle, and raised a little Triangular Fort upon the Rivers side; he commanded *Aubais* by night, to possess himself of that part of the Suburbs which lies towards *Lauport*; and *Leques* at the same time to enter the Town: In the mean time he drew his Canon, whereupon the Fort was given up; but chiefly for that *Leques* had already taken the Tower, and from the advantages of it, and the Castle, played so furiously into the Fort, that none durst stir to shew himself in it.

Chevrilles with the Forces of the Province, at the same time besieges and takes *Saint Auban*, which obstructed the passage from *Privas* to *Pousin*; and *Malmoirac* was commanded to possess himself of the Town of *Bajes*, to secure it with Barricadoes, and seize on all the Boats in the Port, which he happily effected: This done, *Aubais* received command to attempt the two Castles of *Bajes*, which after their dismantling, had been again repaired; but upon the approach of the Canon, yielded: Which done, the Duke taking into his consideration the situation of both places, conceived that of *Pousin* to be the most convenient, both for the facility of being fortified, and the advantage it had to command the River; thither then he commanded to be brought all the Boats, and sent *Leques* with twelve hundred men into *Dauphine*, which brought so great a terrour on them, that many Towns sent him in voluntary contributions of Corn, Meal, and Bread, which was a great relief to his men, whom the avarice, and disaffection of *Privas* had exposed to great extremities; and, that he might lose no time, sets about the Fortifications, to which the Countrey contributed so little, that he was fain to make Collections among his own Officers to pay the Souldiers that wrought in them.

The Duke, during his abode here, sollicites those of the Religion in *Dauphine* to joyn with him; but in vain, the Count of *Soissons* amusing them with hopes that he would shortly appear himself in the head of them; whereupon he sent the Count some overtures to joyn with him, with four thousand Foot, and three hundred Horse, in any part of *Dauphine*, he should please to appoint; and that if he would bring but as many, he would engage himself in a short time to make him Master of the greatest part of *Dauphine*; but he had no other return than empty words, and complementary thanks, which made him think that the Count had rather make an inglorious peace with those he declared to be his enemies, than engage in an honourable War against them.

Whil'st he stayed at *Pousin*, he also received intelligence from the Duke of *Soubize* by *Carlincas*, that the Fleet designed to bring the Corn to *Rochelle*, would be there towards the latter end of *May*; but the other, from which they expected their entire deliverance, not till after the Harvest. *Chevrilles*, who saw the streights the Duke of *Rohan*'s Forces were in, for want of provisions, proposes him to an attempt upon *Cheilard*, a small Town, belonging to the Duke of *Ventadour*, and seated upon the Confines of *Vellay*; It has large Suburbs, and a Castle, that commands them: All the Inhabitants of this, and the neighbouring places, are of the Religion, and till now had been severely persecuted by their Lord, even in times of peace; in order to the effecting of this design, he demands of him two Regiments, which were granted him: The Town he took with Petardes,

tardes, and with the two aforesaid Regiments invested a Castle, called *La Chezé* which is about a Canon-shot distant from *Cheilard*, and upon the sight of two Faucons that were drawn up to it, was given up; with these Gunnes he begins to play upon the Works of the Castle of *Cheilard*; but the Pieces being not sufficient for Battery, he was fain to send to *Privas* for some bigger.

During this Siege, the Duke had intelligence from all parts, of the Duke of *Montmorency*'s arrival in the higher *Languedoc*, who raised all the Forces he could to set upon him in his Marches, or to cut off his passage by taking *Barjac*: This newes made him resolve, no longer to defer his return; wherefore he writes to *Chevrilles*, that in case the Castle of *Cheilard* was not taken by a day, which he prefixed, he should send back the two Regiments; which so quickned his diligence in the enterprise, that the place was taken within the time limited him: And the Duke having given order for the razing of all the places he had taken, except *Pousin*; and left *Chevrilles* in a firm possession of his Government, sets out from *Privas* upon *Easter* day, and encamps that night below *Mirabel*; and as he was marching thence the next Morning by break of day, *Aubais*, that led the Van, informed him that the enemy appeared, both Horse and Foot, about *Saint Germain*, a large Town, indifferently well fortified, and distant about a quarter of a league from *Ville-neufve*; whence they also drew out fresh Souldiers: They were all the forces that *Ventadour* and *Montreall* could make in that Countrey, which alarmed not the Duke at all, while he was employed about those small Sieges. They made choice of that place, as the most advantageous for them, the passage being strait, and the Dukes Forces of necessity to pass within a Musquet shot of the Town, the passages to which, were very commodious to lodge Musquetiers in: But the Duke of *Montmorency*, being half a dayes March short of them, they only made a little skirmish, which made the Duke of *Rohan* desirous to pursue them, and force the Town, which he might have done, but was happily disswaded from it, lest the Duke of *Montmorency* with his fresh Forces should surprize him, while he was engaged, which would certainly have happened; for he came to *Ville-neufve* about two houres after they had gotten over the pass, which was done with very good conduct and order; in this Rencontre there were some slain, and wounded on both sides: After this no enemy appeared; but the Duke when he came to *Gorce*, took his Canon, which he drew back to *Anduze*, where he gave his Troops some refreshment, which they very much wanted.

Mean while the Prince of *Condé* and the Duke of *Montmorency* joyning their Forces take the field, and march into *Foix* to attempt *Pamiez*, a great Town, but of no strength: The ill destiny of *Beaufort* impelled him to a resolution of defending it; to which end he calls in all his own, and most of the Forces of the Countrey; but, a breach being made, their confusion was too great to give them leave to think of any further resistance; those that were false among them, using all means to augment the others fear: *Beaufort* seeing this disorder, endeavoured to save himself by flight, together with *Anros*, but they were both taken, carried to *Thoulouse*, and there put to death: The town was pillaged, and all manner of licentious cruelties imaginable from Souldiers under such a Commander, were exercised in it: The taking of this Town much dismayed the whole Countrey, where no place escaped the attempts either of threats, or promises; but the courage and fidelity of *Rousseliere*, whom the Duke of *Rohan* had made Governour of *Saverdun*, together with his sedulous industry to encourage others preserved the Province; and the Prince marched back, with his Army, into the upper *Languedoc*: Then was the Duke of *Montmorency* fain to return to *Vivaretz*, to the assistance of his Partisans there; and the Duke of *Rohan* was with no less instances sollicited by the higher *Languedoc*, to the same purpose.

The Prince his first exploit was the Siege of *Realmont*, a Town whose situation rendred it very considerable; well stored with Souldiers, and all sorts of Provisions, and which might have held out much longer, and very well expected the relief preparing for it: But neither did he begin the siege, till he had Treated with *Maugis* who was Governour of it; who, having corrupted the first Consul, the Colonel *Chaumette*, and his Sergeant Major, and made some shew of opposition for ten or twelve dayes, without any breach made, or consulting with his Captains, or the people, contrary to the Oaths they were mutually engaged in, at the enemies first coming before it, not so much as to make the least mention of surrendring, enters into a Capitulation, signes it, and presents it to the Town; who refusing to approve of it, he lets in the Besiegers at a Port, which was at his own devotion, whiles the rest were every one at their respective posts; so that great was the confusion there, and though by the Capitulation the Defendants ought to have marched off with their armes, yet was that violated, and they disarmed. *Sigalon*, and *Huguet*, two of *Chaumett's* Captains, with some other honest Inhabitants of the place, maintained a Bastion, resolutely declaring to the World, that they had rather dye than

than quit their armes, which they carryed off, and with them as much honour due to their bravery, as the others did infamy, merited by their baseness. Great were the miseries of this poor Town, whence Men, and Women stript, and without any other covering than their dischevelled haire, came to *Roque-Courbe*; where *Saint Germier*, and *L' Espuguet*, who had the conduct of the affairs of those of the Reformed Party in those parts, by means of the Correspondents they had in *Castres*, made use of this Barbarisme to provoke the people to an Insurrection, which had so prosperous an event, that notwithstanding the opposition of the President *Montespieu*, of the Advocate General, the Consuls, and their adherents, the Walls were scaled, and the Town without the effusion of any blood taken, and the President, and the Advocate banished thence. *Chavagnac* at the same time came very opportunely into the Countrey, sent thither by the Duke of *Rohan* to command in chief there, where he was received, and, even in *Castres* it self, with an universal Joy.

For besides the delight all Novelties usually bring with them, the present state of affaires required a Governour; otherwise the Prince had carried all the Mountain of *Albigeois* before him; whereas now the greatest mischief suffered there was the loss of *Cauze*, which the Marquess of *Malauze* caused to be delivered up to him, in which place, contrary to his promise, he left a Garison: After this he made an offer at *Viane*, blocked it up, and raised a battery against it; but seeing that neither his threats nor promises made any impression on the Besieged, and that the Governour *Eseroux*, and *Assas*, whom the Duke of *Rohan* had sent thither with four hundred men, seemed to be such as would give him a smart opposition, he raised his siege; and thence goes to attempt *Castelnau* and *Brassac*, places of no strength, but surpriseable even by unarmed men; Nevertheless the former gave him the trouble to draw down his Canon, where the obstinacy of some, occasioned the loss of forty or fifty good Souldiers, who chose rather to submit to all extremities, than to observe the Orders given them by *Chavagnac*, to draw off as soon as they saw the Enemies Canon, which they might have easily done: This done, the Prince, not daring any more to look towards *Viane*, sends *Linas* to *Saint Sever*, a place of which he himself was Lord, to perswade the Inhabitants to submit before he drew down his Canon; but seeing how ineffectual all his perswasions proved, he stayes there with them; where, after they had endured many Volleys of Canon shot, themselves made a breach in the Wall, and escaped by night. Thence he goes

goes to a Conference with the Duke *d' Espernon*, at which they resolved on the Siege of *Saint Afrique*.

But before we pass into the higher *Languedoc*, it will be expedient that we speak a word or two of *Montauban*: This Town, though it was then governed by Consuls, and other Magistrates that were great Enemies to the Reformed Party, had nevertheless great inclinations to joyn with them: This, the Duke of *Rohan* himself at first hindred, being not willing they should declare before he came to them; and when after his return from the voyage of *Foix*, he desired them so to do, nothing obstructed it, but their want of a Governour: Whereupon the best part of the Town casting their eyes upon *Saint Michel*, a younger brother of *La Roche Chalais*, and of Kin to the Duke of *Rohan*, who applauded their choice, they received him into their Town about *May*, and there, after that *de Bergues*, and *Saint Foy*, through many difficulties, and great dangers, had conducted thither, from the lower *Guienne*, fourscore, or an hundred Horse, and *Viant* a Company of Foot, and that he had all his necessary Provisions ready, on the four and twentieth day of *June*, they put him in possession of his Command. The first thing he did, was to order all things in a Military way; raising a Regiment composed of Voluntiers, such as had Asyled themselves there; and inrolling also in the establishment, those Horse that *de Bergues* had brought thither.

But before he could well settle himself in his authority he met with many rubbs, having for enemies, not only those that were of a contrary Party, but, even among his own, many rivals for the place, who under-hand did him many ill Offices: Some of these he surmounted by prudence and dissimulation; and to others he was fain to apply open force, and the extremity of rigor: The most eminent example of which, was occasioned by three young Souldiers, Natives of the Town, whose names were *Cartié*, *La Fo est*, and *Brete*, who disgusted at a denial of some Offices they sued for; or else set on by some others, envious of his honour, entred into a conspiracy against his person, and to compass their design make a Party in the Town, to which they drew in many Giddy braines, and among them some of quality, as the sonnes of the Advocate *Clerk*, and the Counsellour *de la Rose*, which gave greater suspitions that this business was fomented by other persons, who, though they appeared not at all in it, yet were they the principal Agents. The pretence of this conjuration was the publique liberty, by which means having raised many of the people, they shew themselves in the head of them, with their Swords and Pistols in their hands, and in that

equi-

BOOK IV. *The Memoires of the Duke of* Rohan. 167

equipage march to the Governours quarters, crying out *Liberty*, *Liberty*! and that it was high time to rid themselves of those that oppressed it: When they came near to his door, they were stopped by some of his guard, who so gallantly behaved themselves in the defence of it, that they killed five or six of the Mutiniers, and among others *Clerk*, and *La Rosse*: The tumult spreading it self in the Town, the Consuls, with a great number of the Inhabitants, haste down to the Governours; to whom when *Saint Michel* had recounted the Action, and justified the procedure of his Souldiers, all were well satisfied; and the Consuls causing the said *Cartie*, *La Forest*, and *Brete*, Authours of the sedition to be apprehended, they were tryed, and condemned by the Council of Warre, which in favour of their relations in the Town, instead of hanging, caused them to be shot to death.

Saint Michel, whom this example of Justice had now fixed in his authority, thinks of enlarging his quarters; and conceiving himself strong enough in Souldiers, by reason of those that were fled thither for shelter, he undertook to put the Town of *Caasade* in a posture of defence; and having put *Chastillon* a Gentleman of *Angoulmois* with eight hundred good men into it, he used such diligence in his fortifications, that in a very short space the place was made tenable; This the Prince, and the Duke d' *Espernon* had intended to besiege, but were diverted by the Siege of *Creseil*, which drew away the Prince with his Forces, so that the Duke d' *Espernon* was unwilling to engage alone in the Siege, but endeavoured to contrive some intelligences, and correspondencies within, that might help him to surprize it, in which even the Minister of that Church, whose name was *Le Grand*, who had deserted it in the very beginning of the troubles, was his great Assistant, informing him of the condition of the Town, and perswading him, as much as in him lay, to attempt it; but finding his design not feisible that way, he contented himself only with an assault, which he caused to be made on the out-works, where he was so generously received, that, leaving many dead upon the place, and some Garisons in the adjacent Towns, he drew away again.

But return we now to the Duke of *Rohan*, who, from the beginning of the Siege of *Realmont*, was extreamly importuned to relieve it, for which he was diligently preparing himself; but after it was taken, he was as earnestly sollicited to march towards the higher *Languedoc*, so that there passed not a week in which he received not two or three dispatches, to that effect: On the other side he found he should have much ado to gaine his Souldiers

diers consent to it; for that their late sufferings in *Vivaretz* gave them cause to fear they should meet with no better entertainment in this Voyage; so that to allure them to it, he resolves on a design upon *Mirveis*, a place upon the Borders of *Roüergue*, strong, and of great concernment to the *Sevenes*, where he knew all the Countrey would come in to him; assuring himself withal, that, whatever his success should be in the attempt, having by this means drawn his men half way, he should with more facility perswade them to adventure on the rest.

Wherefore he sends for *le Fesque*, who first moved this design to him, and perswaded him, that in taking the Town, he should also surprize the Captain of the Castle, and at one stroke carry both: He gave him Orders to take as many Souldiers as he thought he should have occasion for; but at the time appointed for the execution of it, so violent and tempestuous was the weather upon the Mountain *de l' Espernon*, the place of Rendez-vous, that many of the Souldiers (though it was then Summer) died of the cold; so that they were faine to put it off till another time; which gave the enemy some jealousie of their intentions, and those in the Castle leasure to furnish themselves with many necessaries, and especially to recruit their garisons with Souldiers: Notwithstanding all which *Le Fesque* returnes thither again within two dayes, and fixing four Petardes to it, carried the Town: But, instead of presently investing the Castle, and securing the Corn for the nourishment of the Army, every one fell a pillaging, and in the mean time the *Chevalier Chambour*, with fifty men, got into it.

The Duke of *Rohan* in the mean time expecting the issue of this design at *Nismes*, gave Orders for the raising of the Militia of the *Sevenes*, and principally of the two Regiments of *Valescure*, and *La Roque*, and sent away those of *Lassayre*, and *Brenoux*, commanding them by several wayes to march towards *Mirveis*, and, upon the first notice of the taking of the Town, to invest the Castle, and draw thither the small Canon that was at *Vigan*: He sent away also *Goudin*'s Regiment to *Barjac*, which the Duke of *Montmorency* hovered about, as if he had some design upon it; with Orders also, in case necessity so required, to march into *Vivaretz*.

This done, he receives advice of the taking of *Mirveis*, and the disorders there committed: Whereupon he departs from *Nismes*, and steering his course thitherward, sent *Leques* post before him to compose and order all things there, When he came to *Vigan*, he met with a dispatch from the higher *Languedoc*,

doc, pressing him more instantly than ever to hasten thither, otherwise the whole Countrey was in danger to be lost; whereupon he sent away *Aubais* with the Regiments of *Sandres*, *Fourniquet*, and *Bimart*, and three Troops of Horse: When *Leques* came to *Mirveis*; conceiving, that that Castle was not to be forced by so mean a Train of Artillery as they had there, he commands the Canon to be drawn to *Nujolls*, to secure a Castle standing upon a pass of great importance, which upon the approach of it presently yielded.

After this, comes the Duke himself to *Mirveis*, and being of opinion with *Leques* that there was no taking of the Castle without a bigger piece of battery: Those that were at *Millaud* were proposed, as the nearest and most easie to be drawn thither: Thither then he goes with a sufficient Convoy for them, but found it absolutely impossible to bring them; wherefore he commands *Leques*, by a Letter, to send with all speed to *Anduze* for the Culverin of *Nismes*; And in the interim determines to go himself to *Saint Afrique*, upon report of the Siege of *Viane*, which the Prince pretended to attempt; but as he was ready to set out, he received a Letter from *Leques*, which informed him, that upon a bruit spread among the Troops at *Mirveis*, that he was going towards *Castres*, and that there was a great relief preparing for the Castle, very many of the Souldiers had left their Colours, that the Inhabitants of the Town had sent away their goods, and that unless his sudden return thither prevented it, he would finde the Siege totally abandoned: This made him face about with all speed; and finding that the Letter he had written to *Leques* was fallen into the enemies hands, he sent another to *Anduze* for the great Culverin; and resolved now to see what would be the event of this Siege: In order to which he plants his Canon, and with them batters the Outworks that he might the more easily (in case there should be occasion for it) come to mining; and as he was giving Orders to storm the Castle-works the night following, there came Newes that there was a very considerable Body forming for the relief of *Mirveis*; that all *Larzac* and *Rouergue* flocked in to them; that there were twelve hundred drawn out of the Garison of *Montpellier*, and that from *Beziers* and *Gignac*, were sent many Souldiers also; and that their Rendez-vous was to be at *Veiros*, two Leagues distant from *Mirveis*: In effect the thing was very true, and moreover the Baron *Puzols*, who commanded the Duke of *Montmorency*'s Life-Guard, was already come thither with three hundred Horse, to undertake the charge of the whole relief which consisted of about two thousand Foot: This

made

made the Duke defer the storming of the Castle, that he might provide to repel these succours; to which end he spent all that night in cutting a Trench across the hill, the only way they had to relieve the Castle, and caused his Canon to be drawn into a Redout; the next morning, the Majors General *Leques* and *Boissiere*, visit all the quarters, cause the Redout, and Trenches to be well-manned, and Ammunition to be delivered out to the Souldiers, and also give all necessary instructions to the Colonels; the Duke of *Rohan* himself stayes in the Parade place with *Montredon*, the Voluntiers, two Troops of horse-men, whom he had commanded to alight, his own Guards, and *La Baume*, with two hundred of his own Regiment, that he might be ready upon all occasions, to send relief to those that should need it; about Noon the *Scoutes* give notice of the *Romanists* approach, and suddenly every one betakes him to his Post, when presently after they shew themselves upon the top of a hill, whence they sent down five hundred men in two divisions, which advanced boldly, and in good order up to our very Canon, which gave them a very harsh salute; besides which, they saw the Trenches well stored with men, and on the right, and left hand, Regiments marching up the Hill to environ them; this put them upon as sudden and nimble a retreat; being followed with Vollies of Musquet shot, up to the top of the Hill, where presently all disappeared, and by the disorder was to be seen among them, might be rather conjectured to flie, than to retreat: The next day every one took his own way, and the Duke returned to the intended assault; battering, the night following, the *Pallisadoes* of the Counterscarfe, all which were broken down; and then drew up to the very Graffe, from whence he beat the Defendants off their Works; who as he was approaching to the Wall, beat a parley, which they obtained, together with very honourable conditions. This Siege lasted three weeks; and when the Castle was delivered, there marched out one hundred and thirty Souldiers, that wanted neither Ammunion, nor provision.

  When the Prince had notice of the reddition of *Mirveis*, and that the fifteen Companies drawn out of *Montpellier*, were upon their March to joyn with him, he resolved with the Duke *d'Spernon*, upon the Siege of *Saint Afrique*; which when the Duke of *Rohan* was informed of, he would have gone to *Millaud*; but the next day, after the reddition of *Mirveis*, finding that he had no more than eight hundred men left, the rest being gone to refresh themselves, he was forced to go to *Vigan*; after he had gotten an engagement from them, that within ten days they should be all ready at any Rendezvous he should appoint them,

them, to go to the relief of *Saint Afrique*; he sent dispatches also to *Nismes*, and *Usez*, from whence he received a very good recruit.

In this interval, the Duke of *Rohan* had notice of what became of the second Fleet, which was dispatched from *England*, to supply *Rochelle* with provisions, untill the greater, designed for its entire deliverance, could be made ready. The story is this, The Duke of *Soubize*, seconded by the Deputies, and Merchants of *Rochelle* that were then in *England*, urges the King with such earnest and assiduous importunities, that he resolved upon the victualling of *Rochelle*; for which, when all things were in a readiness, the Duke of *Buckingham* offered him the command of the Fleet; but understanding that there were but five men of War designed for their Convoy, and perceiving by so slender a provision of ships of war, that he intended to draw an affront, together with the whole blame of the *Rochellers* upon him, he refuses to accept it, but declared withall, that, if he would go in person, he would be ready to accompany him; Upon this his refusal, the Duke of *Buckingham* re-inforces the Fleet with five great ships more, and many other men of War; and being raised to the number of seventy in all, on the 17th. day of *May*, he sent them orders to hoise Sail, which they did under the command of his brother-in-Law, the Earle of *Denbigh*; soon as the enemy descryed them, they weigh Anchor, as if they intended to advance, and fight them; but on the sudden tacked about again towards the same place from whence they came. *Bragneau* took a French Pinnace at *Sablenceau*, where the Earle cast Anchor so near the Shore, that he thence received a Canon-shot into his own ship, which made him weigh Anchor again, and with the whole Navy remove to ride at a greater distance from the enemies Canon. Many dayes were spent in debates, and resolutions never executed; so that some Merchants, that were there, urged him to attempt either to fight, or pass by them; but his Captains stiffely maintained that it could not be done, without exposing the *English* Forces to too great a hazard; only the *Vice-admiral*, and one Captain *Carre*, shewed more forwardness, and loudly exclaimed against the slackness of all the rest: Whereupon the *French* that were then in the Fleet, to the number of two or three and twenty ships, and *Barques* drew up together, and seeing the backwardness of the others to resolve on any thing, come in a Body to the Earle of *Denbigh*, and present him a Petition signed by them all, by which they beseeched him to grant them four Merchant-men fitted for a fight, three fireships, and Souldiers to guard those ships that carried the provisions, obliging themselves with that equipage to get into the town,

and

and promising moreover, both in their own, and the names of the *Rochellers*, that in case any of those ships miscarried in the adventure, they should be payed for, according to a just estimation of their value. But to all this they received no answer, but evasions, and denials; whereupon the *French* sent *Gobert*, to the King of great *Britain*, with their complaints, and withall, to discover to him the facility of the passage, and the offers they had made: Mean while the Captain *Vidau* takes a small Boat, and in it passes the *Bay* by night, carrying to the besieged a letter from *Bragneau*, which advised them not to rely any longer on hopes of relief from the *English*, who, at the same time, without any further attempt made, welghed Anchor, steering their course home-wards: When they came to the Isle of *Wight*, they cast Anchor there, and thence sent their Apologies into *England* before them, grounded upon the impossibility of the enterprise, and the tenour of their Commission, whose most substantial words, and which imported a permission to fight, they pretended were interlined, although it was with the Kings own hand.

These excuses were easily admitted by the Duke, and those of his Gang, though others deduced from them but sad consequences for the *Rochellers*, that poor and miserable people, that with such transports of joy beheld the arrival of the Fleet, with no less astonishment saw it lie idle for eight dayes entire, and then leave them in a greater dejection than before; and yet having received so many promises, and assurances of relief, could they not give credit to their Admirals Letter, but prepare a new dispatch to the King of *England*; who upon the newes of the Fleets return, assembles his Council, and resolves to send back *Gobert* to the Earle of *Denbigh* with new Orders to return again to the Rode of *Rochelle*, and there to expect a Renfort. About which time also came *Bragneau* with newes of the Fleets return, and two dayes after *Clarke*, who was sent to be of the Earles Councel, and Agent for the King in *Rochelle*, who when he had given in his relation of the affair, had his own house for his prison: But to hasten away this new relief for the distressed *Rochellers*, Orders were given to Captain *Manners*, & Captain *Pennington*, to expedite the building of ten great ships, of fifteen hundred, or two thousand Tun-burthen, made purposely to fight near the shore, not drawing more than seven or eight foot-water, and carrying two and twenty Guns a piece: The Duke of *Buckingham*, who desired not that any one should pry too narrowly into the projects he had against *Rochelle*, removed from the Court a Secretary that was very zealous for its deliverance, causing him to be sent to *Portsmouth* to prepare other Vessels, and buy Provisions, and Ammunition there, where he stayed till the departure of the Fleet. But

But let us now see what passed at the Siege of *Saint Afrique*, a small Town, lying between two hills that command it, so that nothing can be done within, that may not from thence be discovered; neither did any till this time, ever think of fortifying it: But yet the importance of the place for preserving the Communication between the higher, and the lower *Languedoc* obliged us to break the ground, which is there very maniable: But never did that Town expect the honour of an assault from the first Prince of the blood: The River *Sorgue* runs under the walls of it, and divides it from that part of the Suburbs, that lies towards *Vabre*, which of necessity was to be fortified also, it being easie for the enemy to make his approaches that way, and for that the River beating against the Walls, would not give way to any nearer fortifications on that side: The whole fortification of this Suburbs was composed of Spurs, and little Flanquers, whose Trenches were four fathom wide, and the Parapet Canon-proof, behind it was nothing but a small bank instead of a Rampart; all that gave us hopes to be able to defend it, was, that there was room enough for us to intrench our selves behind it; besides, so strangely odde was the situation of that place, that without a great Army, there was no hindering of relief from coming to it, both from *Millaud*, *Saint Rome*, *Tarn*, and the Bridge of *Cauvers*.

Aubais, who was advanced as far as the said Bridge, that he might have an eye upon *Viane*, when he saw the Army bind its course towards *Roüergue*, divided his Forces into two parts, reserving the stronger to himself, and sending the other to *Saint Afrique*, which the Prince came before on the eight and twentieth day of *May*; and having viewed it, conceived it intenable, and at that instant condemned it to the fire, and all manner of extremities; nor yet indeed was it to be defended, but by a great number of men: *Aubais* very handsomly did his devoir, sending them from his quarters, as many men, and as much powder as they desired: *La Baume*, whom the Duke of *Rohan* had left with his Regiment at *Millaud*, for the same purpose did the like; so that in the very height of the Siege, there was no want of any thing; but there happening a difference between *Vacaresse*, and *Bimart*, *Saint Estienne*, and *Sandres* were fain to interpose, and reconcile them, who afterwards did very good service in the storm. The approaches, batteries, and breaches, being all made within the space of eight or ten dayes, the Prince commands his men to make ready for the assault, and those within also prepare to give him a brave reception; who, though they had very good Works and Trenches, would not yet lose one inch of ground: There were within the Town, besides the

Foot

Foot, the Baron *d' Aletz*, and *Saint Estienne*'s Troops of horse; the best armed among them were placed at the Breaches, and all the other posts were well manned also: The whole Garrison consisted of fifteen hundred fighting men; the storm lasted five houres, was thrice renewed, and during it, one *Culverin* discharged about sixty shot upon one of the Breaches, which carried off some legs, and armes; but could not save the Assailants from a repulse, who left four hundred dead upon the place, among which were *La Passe*, and *La Magdaline*, two Captains, and fourty other Officers, not comprising those that were wounded; of the Defendants there were slain about eight and twenty, and threescore hurt.

The morrow after the assault was made, came both from *Millaud*, and the Bridge *de Canvers*, four hundred men more to *Saint Afrique*: The news of this quickly flew to the Duke of *Rohan*, at *Mirveis*, where he had three thousand Foot, and made what hast he could thither; having given order that *Chavagnac*, with the Forces of *Albigeois*, should joyn with *Aubais*, and fall upon the enemy on one side, while he did the like on the other; and the besieged, at the same time, were to make a sally upon their Canon: But that which he feared, came to pass, to wit, the Prince his raising the Siege: Then had the Duke a fair opportunity to pursue him, and then thought of nothing that would prevent it: But the affairs of *Castres* summoned him thither, where *Saint Germier*, induced to it, by those that were disaffected to the Reformed party, opposed *Chavagnac* in his command: Those of *Foix* required his presence, to remedy the disorders fallen out there since the death of *Beaufort*; the Town of *Villaude* would by all means that he should sit down before *Cresseil*, and sent Deputies purposely to sollicite him to to that effect; and on the other side, the Siege of *Saint Afrique* being now over, no body would stir a foot further; all alledging the necessity of their return, to look after their Harvests, especially those of *Nismes*, and *Usez*, whose fields were threatned to be ravaged; and besides these, there were in the Army many Citizens, and Merchants, too delicate, long to endure the hardship of an Army: *Vivaretz* also cryed out for help, the Duke of *Montmorency* being fallen into that Province, with a strong power: *Lyonnois* also with *Dauphiné*, *Vivaretz*, and the lower *Languedoc*, importuned him to free the *Rhone*; on which the Duke had already besieged *Pousin*, and battered *Mirabel*.

Amidst these urgent sollicitations on all hands, the Duke, it being impossible for him to divide himself amongst them all, returns to the lower *Languedoc*; sends *Aubais* to *Castres*, to compose

Book IV. *The Memoires of the Duke of* Rohan. 175

pose the divisions there, and designs *Saint Estienne* with his Troop for *Foix*; whiles he with the rest of his Forces, to divert the Duke of *Montmorency* from *Vivaretz*, goes to *Vezenobre*, which by a long March he surprized, so disfurnished of men, that having with one Petard, taken the Town, the night following he raised his Battery, and the next morning began to play upon the Castle, which he took by assault; but gave quarter to all in it.

This Siege wrought the wished effect; for the Duke of *Montmorency*, after he had taken *Mirabel*, instead of continuing his progress in *Vivaretz*, marched off to relief *Vezenobre*, which he thought would have held out much longer; but finding the business already over, he drew off to *Beaucaire*; and the Duke of *Rohan*, when he had given order for slighting of *Vezenobre*, dismissed his Voluntiers, put his other Regiments into Garrisons, and goes himself to *Nismes*, to put them in a posture to prevent the spoil the Duke of *Montmorency* had command to make there; but had written to the Court, that he could not undertake it with less than six thousand Foot, and five hundred Horse; for which care was taken, and he supplied with three Regiments from *Dauphine*, and some Horse drawn out of the Army, the Marquess of *Vxelles* was then conducting to the relief of *Cazal*: These preparations made *Nismes*, and *Vsez* look about them, and promise good quarters to all the Horse and Foot should come in to their assistance: The Duke of *Rohan* writ to those of the *Sevenes*, to this effect; but they came not so soon as they promised; nor did those of *Nismes* gratifie them as they ought; Nevertheless he goes to see what might be done, and promises to preserve all their Corn, within a League of their Town, to wit, that which lies upon the *Vistre* (which is the richest land about *Nismes*) a small, but dangerous River; all whose passes he spoyles, and in all places of danger caused good Redoubts to be built; but as for the rest of their Fields, there was no possibility of preserving them: And yet, had the Peasants observed what was commanded them, which was, to leave their Sheaves scattered upon the ground, they had saved a great part of them; which being made up in stacks, and the enemy coming to forrage at the time they usually thresh out their Corn, (which is there done in the Fields) they were all easily consumed.

The Duke of *Montmorency* takes up his first quarters at *Saint Margueriete*, a good league from *Nismes*; and the next day leaving it on his left hand, came and lodged at *Chaumette*, and *Saint Genies*, three leagues distant from *Nismes*, and as farre from *Vsez*: Thence passes through the Towns upon

the

the *Gardon*, and so gets into *Vauvage*, and took up his last quarters at *Bernis* and *Vehas*.

In this march, which lasted six or seven dayes, he burnt much Corn, and also many Villages; which done, he retires to *Beaucaire* (having not at all entred into the Territories of *Nismes*) and the Troops of *Dauphine* returned to joyn with the Marquess of *Uxelles*, all the Volunties went home; the forces of the lower *Languedoc* were sent into Garisons, and the Duke of *Montmorency* himself went to *Bezieres* and *Pezenas*.

About this time came a Gentleman from the King of *England* to the Duke, which dispatch was occasioned by an apprehension given him, that since the return of the second Fleet, there were two Deputies with the Duke of *Rohan*, in order to a Treaty for peace; to divert which, he was commanded to tell him, that though that Fleet after an ineffectual Voyage were returned, yet there was now so strong a one prepared, and ready to set Saile, that he was confident it would be the entire deliverance of *Rochelle*; and that though God should not favour him in that attempt, yet would he never forsake the rest of the Reformed Party; Nay, although there should be no more left than the very person of the Duke, he assured him he would hazard all that he was Master of, for the preservation of that alone; desiring further to know of him what hopes he had of assistance from *Italy* and *Spaine*, that in case the King should press him too hard, he might be directed by him how to assist him, either by a diversion or otherwise: *David*, one of the Deputies of *Rochelle* was present at the delivery of this Message: To which the Duke replied, that he was so far from any thoughts of a Treaty, that he had again caused the Oath of Union to be renewed, to this effect, that none should hearken to any peace, but conjoyntly with him; and that he had already made known to him, the means he had to assist him.

This done, the Duke seeing the Duke of *Monmorency's* Troops lay scattered and dispersed in several parts, takes his turn also, and burnt all the Corn, and Countrey Houses belonging to the Inhabitants of *Beaucaire*, within Musquet shot of their very walls: And when he thought to make another inrode into the *Marish-Countrey* for Salt, he met, in a narrow place upon the *Rhone*, nearer home, two Barques convoyed by a Frigote, and laden with four and twenty thousand *French* Bushels, so that commanding some of his Souldiers to swim to the other side for a Boat, he transported many of his Foot to *Camargues*, that he might on both sides attaque the Frigote; but she soon forsook her Merchandize, which was as quickly carried away: Besides

sides this booty, they drove much Cattle from *Camargues*, and did much spoyle there also by fire. When the Duke of *Montmorency* heard of these excursions, he made haste to rally his forces, appointing them their Rendez-vous at *Lunel*. The Duke, in this expedition, going, and returning, marched above fourteen long Leagues, without making any long stay in any place; and got home again before any of the enemy could be gotten together; And happy was it for him; for he was but in an ill condition to fight; every Souldier being so laden with pillage, that he could never get any more to march in order, than three hundred souldiers, of *La Baume*'s Regiment, which brought up the Rear.

When this expedition was over, the Duke was in great perplexities, not knowing how to dispose of his Forces, especially his Horse: For he could now raise no more contribution for their maintenance, by reason that the Villages were all burnt: And the *Sevenes* was no Countrey for Horse: If he should go towards *Castres*, there was the Prince with his Army in the higher *Languedoc*, who had particular Orders to impede his passage; and the Duke of *Montmorency* had also a strict Command, with his Forces to follow him, whither ever he should go: For it was feared lest he should go to *Montauban*, and raise those of the Religion in *Guienne* in favour of the *English*, whose coming they feared: If he went into *Rouergue* to no other end but to eat them up, it would not be long ere their cryes would be heard; so that necessity now obliged him to undertake the siege of *Crescil*.

But before we go thither, it will not be amiss to say something of *Aubais* his return to *Castres*; who though he made but a seeming accommodation between *Saint Germier* and *Chavagnac*, the cause of the misunderstanding still remaining, and fomenting their conceived rancour one against the other, so that the pretended reconciliation lasted not long; neverthelefs his being there was to great purpose to oppose those that came to forrage and plunder those parts, where his brother *Saint Estienne* was unhappily slain, by their own Canon, which being not well spunged, as they were re-charging it, the Powder took fire, and killed him: He was a Gentleman of great courage, and zeal for his party, and was the next day to have gone into *Foix*, where they stood in great need of him.

The Marquess of *Ragny*, who commanded the Prince his Army, and had much ravaged the Countrey, goes, for his last exploit, to burn *Mazamet*, and to besiege *Hautpont*, whither *Dupuy*, a gallant Souldier, with the Inhabitants of *Mazamet*, were retired; but having, to no purpose, lain before it for the space of twelve dayes, he drew off to *Brugiere*, where he dyed.

And here it will be expedient to infert a word or two concerning *Claufel*, who coming from *Piedmont*, made the Duke of *Rohan* some propositions of assistance from *Spaine*; which, if demanded, he was confident he might have freely, and in a large measure; for that having conferred about it with the *Spanish* Embassadour in *Piedmont*, he had given him very good hopes of it; telling him moreover, that it was the Interest of *Spaine*, to endeavour a prolongation of the Civil Wars in *France*; that they might with more ease compass their designs in *Italy*; that the Abbot *Scaglia*, the Duke of *Savoy*'s Embassadour, was now in *Spaine*, and would contribute his utmost power to assist him in it; having already in *England*, and elsewhere, declared himself a great favourer of the Reformed Party, out of his implacable hatred to those that govern now in *France*.

The great exigencies the Duke was in for want of money, the Countrey being unable, and the Towns unwilling to furnish him any more; neither could he expect any from *England*; nor had he received any thing from the Duke of *Savoy*, but empty promises, enforced him to seek out some way or other to supply his wants; and in effect he saw none but this; which yet he durst not pitch upon, without the King of *England*'s leave, fearing lest it might give him an offence, and consequently an occasion to defert him: Notwithstanding this doubt, yet would he not reject *Claufel*'s proposals; but deferres his dispatch, till he could give notice of it to the King of *England*, and to his Embassadour then in *Piedmont*; from both whom he received very favourable answers; and then sent *Claufel* into *Spaine*; Injoyning him to declare to the King of *Spaine*, that if the continuance of the War in *France* might be serviceable to his designes, upon condition he would afford those of the Religion a speedy and round supply of money, he would engage himself to protect it, as long as it should be agreed upon between them; but that otherwise he should be constrained to make his peace; that he should have the whole Winter to provide it, and that he would expect his answer till the next March: And forasmuch as that, immediately after the departure of *Clanfel*, there came news of the loss of *Rochelle*; he sent two Messengers after him to let him know, that that accident had not any thing shaken his resolutions; but that he continued constant to his former proposals. *Claufel* passes through *Foix* into *Spaine*, where he was very well received, and heard; and had very advantageous Propositions made him also; All which good news he imparts to the Duke of *Rohan*; giving him good hopes of a prompt, and powerful assistance: At length having concluded the Treaty, he goes into *Piedmont*, to facilitate and expedite the execution of all things; and as he went, landed a Gentleman belonging to the King of *Spain*, who was to have brought the Duke a Copy of the Agreement; But he suffered himself to be taken at the Gates of *Lunel*, when he had but half a League more to go beyond all danger, of which *Rohan* advertised *Clausel*, who when he came to *Piedmont*, gave the *English* Embassadour an account of all his negotiation.

Return we now to *Crescil*, a place about a Canon shot distant from *Milland*, having a treble inclosure of Walls, one whereof environs the Town, and the two others the Castle, which must be forced one after another, for that there is no coming at the Castle, but through the Town; the farthest part of it being built upon a Rock of a vast height: It is true, the Walls that inclose the Town are not worth any thing, being ruinous, and full of breaches, so that it were a shame to lie eight dayes before it, and not to take it: But he that has to deale with a people, to whom no design seems difficult, and when they come to put it in execution, make no provision of necessaries to effect it, will want no incumbrances: *Rohan* gives notice of his intentions to *Alteyrac* and *Gueriu*, that without any noise, they might put all things in a readiness to effect them; and gave *Alteyrac* also Orders to block up the place, a day before he came with his Troops; that so he might surprize it at a greater advantage, when meanly furnished with Souldiers; which he did, but yet all their diligence could not prevent the entry of supplies into it.

When the Troops were all come up, the Siege was formed, and a battery of two Guns raised, which had not discharged six shot, before the Carriage of one of them flew all to pieces; and when that was mended, the like accident befell the other; so that the whole time, almost, was spent in repairing the Carriages of the Guns; and with such untoward Timber, that when all was done, they did but little better than before; so that the breach being not made large enough in one day, they were fain to remit the prosecution of their battery till the morrow, which gave the besieged leasure to repaire, and make it better than before: Nevertheless urged by the shortness of his time, the Duke commanded an assault to be made, in which he was repulsed. In the mean while the Duke of *Montmorency*, who with his Army, had still waited on the motions of *Rohan*, joynes with

with the Prince; and having diswaded him from his intended attempt upon *Causade*, and gotten together all the Forces of that Countrey, came with eight thousand Foot, and six hundred Horse to lie at *Saint Geo ges*, distant but a league from *Creseil*; of which, when the Duke of *Rohan* had intelligence, that very night he drew off his Canon, and the next day, having left *Creseil* again at liberty, drew up his whole Army in Battailla near *Millaud*; where about noon, the Prince appeared with his whole Army, which, when *Montmorency* had recruited the Garrison with men, and all other necessaries, marched off to their quarters.

This Siege did at least this good, that it preserved *Causade*, which was not yet in a condition to withstand so great a power: The night following *Rohan* sends his Foot into *Saint Rome* upon *Tarn*, and into *Saint Afrique*; and seeing that both Armies were so near him, he thought with his Cavalry, having no baggage to incumber them, he might reach *Castres* in one night: This he proposed to his Officers, who were of opinion, that it would be convenient to stay one day longer, to observe the countenance of the enemy, which totally frustrated his intentions of passing that way; for as he was about to attempt it the next day, he found that *Montmorency* had prevented him, and waited for him on the way both with Horse and Foot; which made him instantly resolve to take with him all his Forces, and by great Marches got into the higher *Languedoc*, to besiege *Aimargues*, which he was confident (in case he found but the ordinary Garrison in it) a few dayes would make him Master of; It is a Town of an indifferent bigness, distant about four leagues from *Nismes*, and one from *Lunel*, seated in the best part of that Countrey, and upon a Flat, no wayes to be commanded, the mold also being soft, and tractable; and in short, accommodated with all things necessary to make it a very brave place; it is also inclosed with fair Free-stone Walls, flanked with small Towers, and a large and deep Trench, full of water, on the outside of which were two or three half Moons, little, and ill made. To this end he sent *Aubais* to *Nismes*, to get the Canon in a readiness, and that he might the better conceal his design, divides his Forces, and marches thither two several ways; he himself, with that party which he conducted, came thither first, and presently invests the place; the next day arrived the others also, and then he assigned every one their post, and entirely blocked it up: And without further delay sent to *Nismes*, to hasten away the Canon, which came also in good time: The night following, he plants them upon the Battery he had raised,

and

and the next day, without the loss of one man, made a fair breach; and having made provision of ladders, for that the Walls, being but low in many places, are easily scalable, and the Trench in many parts passeable, he disposed his men for a general assault: When the Governour, the Marquess of *Saint Sulpice*, a younger brother of the house of *Vsez* saw these preparations, conceiving he had not men enough to defend himself against the storm, he demands a parley; the Duke of *Rohan* sent him word, that he was much troubled that a young Gentleman of his quality should be so unfortunately engaged in a place where from his first Essay he could derive nothing but disadvantage and dishonour: Nevertheless out of regard to the amity between their houses, he offered him as honourable conditions, as he himself could have desired, which he accepted, and within an houre after marched out with his Garrison.

    The Duke of *Montmorency*, while he was yet at *la Caune*, at the same instant received intelligence, both of the Seige, and taking of this place, and upon the re-iterated importunities made him, presently repaired thither to settle the Province, which the so sudden taking of *Aimargues* had much disordered. The Duke of *Rohan* mean while employes that little leasure he had in clearing the Countrey of those Paltry Forts, and Towns, which lay about *Nismes*, and *Vsez*; as the Castle of *Vauvert*, *Mainne*, *Sargnac*, *Saint Bonnet*, *Resmolins*, *Ves*, and *Chastillon*, which yeilded upon the approach of his Canon: All which he demolished, except *Resmolins*, which he was desirous to keep for that it might be useful to him when he should have occasion to look towards *Ville-neufve* by *Avignon*: But the conservation of *Aimargues*, and the Fortifications he had there begun, made him relinquish all other designs for the present, to apply himself wholly to that.

    Whiles he was thus occupied, survenes the Duke of *Montmorency*, threatning to besiege *Aimargues*, and preparing his Canon, and all other necessaries for it; which obliged the Duke of *Rohan* to draw towards it, and clap in twelve hundred Foot, where he designed also a Counterscarfe, Curtains, and half Moons, to be made for the security of those places which were weakest, and most liable to danger; and having summoned in the Militia of the *Sevenes*, he put six or seven hundred of them into the great *Galarguis*, whither he caused ammunition-bread to be sent them daily from *Nismes*, commanding them to defend it against a party, but not to stay till the enemy drew down their Canon. Some weeks passed they in this posture; in the mean time the Duke of *Montmorency* despairing to do any good upon

Aimargues, turns his design upon the Forces in *Galargues*; appoints his Rendez-vous by break of day at the Bridge of *Lunel*, and that morning goes thence to invest them. The two that commanded there, were *Valescure*, and *la Roque*, both gallant Gentlemen, the former very stiffely persists in a resolution to see their Canon, thinking by night, to draw off into *Vauvage*, a good Countrey for the Foot, and where all the Inhabitants were of the Religion; but this was contrary to the express order of the Duke of *Rohan*; who understanding that they were besieged, with all speed rallies his Troops, and comes to relieve them: The Duke of *Montmorency* on the other side, draws all the Garrison out of *Montpellier*; the Regiment of *Normandy* also, with several others, come to joyne with him. His Army with his Canon, he ranged in Battailla, in a place of great advantage: *Rohan* going to view him, that he might know whether he should attempt this relief by day, or in the night-time, findes him to be four thousand Foot, and four hundred good Horse strong, and so advantageously lodged that there was no coming at him in any good order, nor without passing within Pistol-shot of a dangerous Valley; which made him not discover his Troops, and defer advancing with the relief till the night following: He incamps about half a league from the place, in a Valley near a Wood, leaving a Troop of Horse to observe the motions of *Montmorency*, and to hinder the discovery of his own Forces: About the close of the evening comes a Messenger from the besieged, to demand some assistance, whom he sent back again with another with him, to tell them, that when they should hear the Alarme on the other side, they should be ready to sally out at such a place as they should direct them; that they should finde five hundred selected men to receive them within Musquet-shot of *Galargues*; and that he, with the rest of his Army, would be within a quarter of a league ready to bring them off; that if they knew any better way to save themselves, they should acquaint him with it, and care should be taken of them; but, if they approved of this course, that they should make three fires upon the top of the Tower, that it might be accordingly followed. The Messengers got very well in, and the besieged also approve of the design; In witness whereof they give the signal of the three Fires, and prepare themselves for the Sally: The Duke of *Rohan* sent the five hundred men he had promised within two Musquet-shot, caused the Alarme to be given thrice, and yet no body stirred in *Galargues*, but all stayed till day; which being now pretty well advanced, he drew off his five hundred men, who by a Volley of shot at their departure, let them know how near they had come

to.

to fetch them off: The Duke underſtood afterwards, that ſome of the Captains, who had bad legs, or lame courages, hindred their coming forth; whoſe fears flattering them with falſe and deceitful hopes, made them chooſe rather to ſubmit to their enemies, than run the hazard of marching three or foure hundred paces with ſeven hundred men, with their Swords in their hands, which when they had done, they were ſure to be received by five hundred more, and a quarter of a league farther by two thouſand. In great choler, and with an extream regret did the Duke draw off again, the next day, knowing they had yielded themſelves to be diſpoſed of at the diſcretion of their Conquerours, if they procured not the ſurrender of *Aima gues*; which if they effected, then were they all to be ſet at liberty, and have their baggage reſtored to them: *Valeſcure*, and *Baviere*, were choſen Deputies, and ſent with this goodly meſſage to the Duke of *Rohan*, who made them both priſoners; but *Valeſcure* eſcapes, and gets into the *Sevenes*, to incite the Communalties there to an inſurrection, in caſe *Aimargues* were not given up again; others alſo went thither privately from *Montpellier* to the ſame end; *Rohan* fearing ſome commotions in that Province, goes thither too himſelf, and takes with him the Deputies of *Niſmes* and *Vſez*, aſſembles both the Provinces at *Anduze*, where he brought them to this reſolution, that *Aimargues* ſhould not be re-delivered, and that all thoſe priſoners they already had, or for the future ſhould take, ſhould be treated with the ſame rigour as was uſed to thoſe of *Galargues*; and that he might have his revenge, he ſits down before *Monts*, with but two thouſand men at moſt; five dayes did he lie before it, for that the inceſſant rain that fell, retarded the arrival of their great Canon from *Anduze*, for the ſpace of three whole dayes together: But though the bad weather miſchieved him on that ſide, it abundantly recompenſed that Injury on another, ſwelling the two *Gardons*, ſo that four or five Regiments, which could they have come the direct way, had reached him in one dayes march, not able to paſs the Rivers any other way, than by a Bridge, were fain to make four or five dayes of it; and he to prolong their journey, cauſes all the Boats, and Ferry-boats upon the Rivers to be broken, and a ſtrong Guard to be kept at *Saint Nicholas Porte*; ſo that immediatly upon the arrival of his Canon, without further fear of any diſturbance, he batters the Caſtle, and reduces the beſieged, a hundred and fifty in number, to ſuch ill terms, that they yielded upon condition to undergo the ſame puniſhment as ſhould be inflicted on thoſe were taken at *Galargues*, perſwading themſelves ſtill, that *Hannibal*, to whom the houſe belonged, and who was

Baſtard-

Bastard-brother to the Duke of *Montmorency*, would be able to prevail with him to save his Friends, and Allies: But *Montmorency*, to make his action more eminent at Court, having sent word that he had taken the prime Officers and Souldiers of the *Sevenes*, the King commanded that all the Colonels, and other Officers should be hanged, and the common Souldiers sent to the Gallies; which the Prince having notice of, would not give him leasure to let the Court know what had happened at *Monts*; so that he caused threescore and four to be hanged, which indeed were not all Officers; but many that were well clad, stiled themselves so, out of hopes to finde better usage; see how many times men gull themselves: The Duke of *Rohan* also, for his part, caused the like number to be hanged, not sparing any for their quality, except some few, which he reserved, to fetch off some others, which *Hannibal* had gotten to himself, who were afterwards exchanged.

In the mean time *Montauban* goes on luckily with the War, in which that Town, without the assistance of any other, alwayes behaved it self best of any of the Reformed Party. *Saint Michel*, before he engaged in any other enterprise, looks after the preservation of *Caussade*, upon some jealousies he had of the Governour *Chastillon*; for that in all Military actions he discovered too much effeminacy, and too much disregard of things relating to the security of the Town; but principally for that he held too frequent correspondencies with those of the adverse party, under pretence of procuring the enlargement of his brother, who had been a prisoner ever since the last peace: Neither was he without some suspitions of the others aime to out him of his Government, which made him begin to think upon some way to preserve himself in it, to which end he Courts the affections of the Souldiers, and people of the Town; but before he had well made his Game, he most imprudently declared publickly, that he would no longer own any subordination to *Saint Michel*, who to prevent, and crush this mischief in its birth, exhibited the Articles he had to charge *Chastillon* withall to the Council; whereupon it was ordered that he should be secured, and tried by a Council of War; which was neatly carried by *Saint Michel*, who very privately, and insensibly having gotten many Souldiers into *Caussade*, and coming thither himself unthought on, without any the least commotion, seizes upon *Chastillon*, and carries him to *Montauban*, where he was for a time kept prisoner, and examined: But whether it was, that the proofs against him were not clear enough, or that they feared lest the punishing of him would be a discouragement to other strangers; he was set at
liberty

liberty again; and *Pontbeton* was made Governour of *Caufade* in his place; who continued in that command untill the Peace.

Saint *Michel* having thus secured this Town, thinks upon taking in of many small Forts, and Castles, which were a great disturbance to *Montauban*; having now a fit opportunity offer'd him by the plague, that had driven away most of the Garrisons the Duke *d' Espernon* had left about him; in pursuance of which he drawes his Canon into the Field, and begins with the Castle *de la Motte d' Ardne*, and having battered, and taken it by assault, fired it on the second of *September*: When he came back to *Montauban*, he had intelligence of a great body drawing up, composed of the Countrey Forces, and some other Regiments also, sent for purposely to oppose his designs: On the 6th. of the same Moneth he lays an Ambuscade for them among the Vineyards of *Dieu-Pantole*, about two leagues distant from *Montauban*, and with his Horse goes to draw them into it, and meets them in the plain of *Castalans*, and *Saint Porquier*, where the enemy, without expecting till the rest of their men were come up, or indeed staying one for the other, pursue him in disorder up to the very Ambuscade, where being once engaged, he charges them on every side, and leaves some four or five hundred of them dead upon the place, besides a great number of wounded, losing not above three or four of his own: Thence he marches up to the very Towns of *Castalans*, and *Saint Porquier*, and other Villages, and Farms, which he fired, and then returns to *Montauban*. The next day he besieges the Castle of *Ville-Dieu*; which having endured the battery a whole day, yielded the next; those within it had their lives given them, but they remained prisoners of War, and the place was burnt. On the 8th. of *October* he went from *Montauban* to besiege *Escaliez*, about two leagues from *Montauban*; but those of that Garrison stayed no more for him, then did those of *Blavet*, both which retreated to *Salvagnac*; these two Forts he also burnt: And because *Mouliere* Governour of *Villemur*, had now his Regiment on foot, he was very desirous to invite him into an Ambush also, which he endeavoured to do, by firing the Mills of *Villemur*, which were in sight of the Town, whence yet none would stir out; in his return thence he came before the Castle of *Poulauron*, which he forced.

The Garrison of *Salvagnac* being thus re-inforced with those of *Escaliez*, and *Blavet*, began now to grow insolent, and would no longer stand to the Agreement made with those of *Montauban*, to suffer them freely to pass, and repass; whereupon
he

he laid an Ambush for them also; to allure them to which, he sent out sixty Horse, and fifty Foot, when presently came forth an hundred, or six score Souldiers, to gain the Ford upon the River *Tescou*, where they met with such entertainment, as very few of them ever went back again.

About the beginning of *November* sallied out sixty seven Souldiers from the Garrison of *Loubejac*, to lay an Ambush near *Montauban*, upon the great Road to *Negrepelisse*; which *Saint Mich'l* having notice of, drew out some Horse, and layed a Counter-Ambuscade in the way by which they were to retreat; and charging them in an open field, slew about threescore and four of them; and after this, took the Castle of *Bourquet* by Petard. Many other little actions passed there at *Montauban*, in which *Saint Michel* alwayes came off with honour.

It is now time to return to the lower *Languedoc*, whither presently after the taking of *Monts*, came the newes of the Reddition of *Rochelle*, after the long sufferings of that poor people, had given such large testimonies of their invincible constancy.

The *Rochellers* upon the retreat of the second Fleet, sent four several Messengers to *England*, with instructions all to the same effect; *viz*. To represent unto the King, the deplorable condition they would suddenly be reduced to, and minding him of his promises, to beseech his Majesty with all speed to send them some relief, assuring him withall, that how many, and heavy soever their pressures were, they would not submit to them, but wait his answer: *La Grossetiere*, who was one of the four, arrived there on the 15th. of *June*, and was sent back again with many fair promises on the 30th. but in his return was taken, carried to the King, kept a prisoner till the Town was taken, and was then put to death. The 10th. of *July* following came the second, and on the 14th. arrived the third; but the last, who came about by *Holland*, was some-what longer on his way.

Before the arrival of *la Grossetiere*, had the King of great *Britain* dispatch't *la Lande* with two other Souldiers, to give the *Rochellers* notice of the great supplies he was preparing for them; and after him was also sent *Champfleury* with the like assurances, who got into *Rochelle*, but one day before the Fleet shewed it self in the Rode: The ships preparing for this expedition being not yet finished, the Engineers pitched upon a new invention, to wit, the letting out of three ships lined, and the decks covered with brick, and laden with stones of an immense bigness, and stuffed with barrels of powder, to make these Mines play effectually upon the Barricado the *French* had made in the

Port;

Port: But the King of *England* very much unsatisfied with the slow progress of the Fleet, went himself in person on the last of *July* to hasten it, in which journey the Duke of *Soubize* waited on him.

The Duke of *Buckingham* staying behind, sets his wits on work to find out some means to obstruct the sending away of the supplies, and to this end, endeavours by the means of the *Venetian* Residents in *England*, and *France*, to have some overtures for a peace made: But seeing that took not, he resolves upon a journey to *Portsmouth*; but before his departure, sends for *Vincent*, a Minister of the Church of *Rochelle*, and makes him write a perswasive letter to the *Rochellers*, to dispose themselves to accept of the peace the Duke of *Buckingham* was now procuring for them; which the Embassadour of *Savoy* having an inkling of, he plainly demonstrates to *Vincent*, that it was only an invention to retard the departure of the Fleet, and so defeated that project.

At length, on the 24th. of *August*, comes the Duke of *Buckingham* to *Portsmouth*, and on the 29th. arrived there fifty ships, some men of War, and others laden with provision, and ammunition: But on the second of *September*, the Duke of *Soubize* going to visit the Duke of *Buckingham*, as he had newly dined, he told him that just then he had received intelligence of the re-victualling of *Rochelle*, and that he was now going with the newes to the King; and as he was lifting up the Hangings to go forth of the Room, he was stabbed with a Knife, into the great Artery of the heart, by an Officer, whose name was *Felton*, of which he fell, and dyed immediatly: Nor were the Duke of *Soubize*, and his followers free from danger, it being muttered in the Chamber, that it was a French-man had done this act; but *Felton*, who might have easily escaped, if he had listed, having not been observed by any one, voluntarily discovers himself to be the Authour of this Homicide; saying, that it was better that two men should perish, than a whole Kingdom. The next day the King makes the Earle of *Lindsey* Admiral, *Morton* Vice-admiral, and *Montjoy* Reare-admiral; the other commands were not changed, but the same Captains that were in the former expedition, went also in this, with a greater force, but the same resolutions. After the death of *Buckingham*, it appeared that not half of the Ammunition and Provisions for the Fleet were yet shipped; and that should the prosecution of their business answer the slowness of the beginnings, there would be yet three moneths work more to do; but by the care, and presence of the King, more was now dispatch't in ten or twelve dayes, than in many weeks

weeks before; so that all things being now ready, they set saile on the eighteenth of *September*: That which made the Duke of *Soubize* conceive better hopes of this than the former Fleets, was the care and diligence used by the King, and the command he gave his Admiral, in his presence, not to do any thing without his advice; committing the charge of this expedition conjoyntly to them both.

On the nine and twentieth of *September* came the Fleet into the Rode of *Rochelle*, and after a calm, which continued all *Sunday* and *Munday* following, at night the Wind arose, and sate faire for a fight, so that about two houres before day, upon the Admiral's firing of a Gun, they all set sayle, and at six of the clock in the morning began a fight, which lasted about three houres, in which, on both sides, were discharged three or four thousand piece of Canon, and that was all: The next day about the same houre was the fight renewed, but more temperately, and at a greater distance, so that both those fights were concluded without any great loss to either side: On the third of *October* comes up to them *Friquelet* a Captain that had formerly served under the Duke of *Soubize*, and coming, as he said, from *Tremblade*, shews a Letter from the Captain *Treslebois*, desiring him to know of them whether they would hearken to a Treaty of peace or no; to which was answered, that he should shew his pass-port, or else that *Treslebois* should come up in his Shalloup between the two Fleets, and there let them know what he had to say; which, on the seventh of the same moneth, he did, with one whose name was *de l' Isle*, both who were remitted to *Montague* and *Forain*, who, finding that they had no particular Commission, but came only to know whether the *French* would Treat apart, excluding the *English*, answered them, that that could not be, and so both retired to their own Parties: Nevertheless upon occasion of this interview the Admiral sent *Montague* with a Dutch Gentleman whose name was *Kimphausen*, under colour of demanding of some Mariners, that were Prisoners in the *French* Fleet; but his going thither again the two dayes following, pretending they had promised to shew him the Barricado in the Port, and confessing, at his return, that he had not seen it, because the Tide did not serve, bred some jealousies, that he went thither upon some other design; And when, upon a report that there had Articles mutually passed between them, the Duke of *Soubize* complained that they had entred upon a Treaty, unknown to him, and without the Privity of those that were principally concerned in it; it was flatly denied: But when the continual goings to and fro of *Montague*, had confirmed

med their suspicions of a Treaty, it was put off with this excuse, that they treated of things not relating to theirs, nor the Interests of *France*: And not long after, the Admiral sent *Montague* into *England*, with a pass which the Cardinal of *Richelieu* gave him.

On *Sunday* the one and twentieth of this moneth there hapned a remarkable passage; one *Pojanne*, a Captain that had formerly served under the Duke of *Soubize*, a Villain covered with Crimes, and that had now redeemed his life, by the engagements he had passed to the Cardinal, to kill, or burn *Soubize* in his ship, sets saile out of the River of *Bourdeaux*, in a good ship of two hundred Tun burthen, and filled with Combustible matter; and, the better to palliate his design, passes as an enemy, making prize of several *French* he met withal, and so gets up to the *English* Fleet; When he was come in among them, he tells them that he was come to serve the Party of the Religion as he had formerly done, and desires to be conducted to the Duke of *Soubize* who knew him very well: With him was a Gentleman of *Anjou*, who, as he was going to *Rochelle*, had been cast upon the Coast of *Spaine*, there taken, and thence sent to the Cardinal, who finding him to be a bold and adventurous person, promised him not only his pardon, but infinite recompences in case he would accompany *Pojanne* in this enterprize: The desire he had to save himself together with the perswasions of his brother, who was a servant to the Cardinal, made him promise whatever they required of him: But when they came to the fleet, he unfolded the whole plot to *Soubize*, whereupon *Pojanne* was taken Prisoner, his ship and Prizes seized on: And to prove that this Gentleman said nothing but truth, he offered to get through into *Rochelle* with the Cardinal's pass, and to return thence with a true account of the condition of the place: His offer was accepted of, and double Letters were given him, some of which he shewed to the Cardinal, importing a request to permit him to make this Voyage, and a promise at his return to give him a perfect relation of his discovery. Thus he got in, and returned with other private Letters, which truly represented the state of *Rochelle*, which was so sad, that in case they were not relieved within two dayes, there would be none left alive in it, and that they were now upon the point of yielding.

On *Monday* the two and twentieth, about ten aclock in the morning the Fleets made as though they would engage, but the Captains failing of their promised duty, the whole time was spent in *Canonades*, without any prejudice to either party, and all

all the fire-ships were so ill-managed; that they were vainly, and to no purpose consumed: And in the mean time, in sight of that Puissant Fleet, so well stored with all necessaries, while the time slipt away, the passage unattempted, nor the Duke of *Soubize* his offers, to lead the way with the *French*, desiring the Admiral but to follow him only, accepted, nor those of the Count *de Laval*, while the others were engaged in the fight, to conduct the three ships lined with brick, and in which were the Artificial Mines, up to the Barricado; the famine finished its work in *Rochelle*; there being hardly a man left that could support himself without a staff; all that were left alive were so few, and so debilitated, that they had not strength to handle their Armes; so that on the same day the Admiral of *England* had resolved with his Council, once more to attempt the relieving of it, the *Rochellers* capitulated, and yielded on the 28*th*. day of *October*; and on the 10*th*. of *November* following, the whole Fleet left the Rode, and returned towards *England*: The miscarriages of this action being imputed to the refractoriness and disobedience of some particular Captains; some of them were confined to their own houses, and a Commission was issued out for their Trial: But in a short time after, all this vanished, and they received their pay as the rest did.

The Duke of *Rohan's* Mother, nor his Sister, would not suffer any particular mention to be made of them in the Capitulation; lest the occasion of the surrender should be imputed to their perswasions, or the respect borne to them; not doubting however, but that they should equally enjoy the benefit of the Treaty with the rest: But, the interpretation of Articles being commonly made by the Conquerours, it was the Judgement of the King's Council, that they were not comprised in them, since they were not mentioned in them: An unpresidentable severity, that a person of her quality, of seventy years old, coming out of a besieged Town, where she and her daughter had lived three moneths together upon Horse-flesh, and four or five ounces of bread aday, should be detained Prisoners, prohibited the exercise of their Religion, and so strictly guarded, that they had but one servant allowed to attend on them: But all this rigour abated not their wonted courage and zeale to the welfare of their party: For the Dutchess sent to her son the Duke of *Rohan* a Caution, not to give any credit to her Letters; for that in this restraint she might be compelled to write things contrary to her inclinations, and that the consideration of her miserable condition should not impell him to any thing that might prejudice the Party, whatever mischief befell her: A truly
Christian

Christian resolution, and nothing varying from the whole course of her life, which though it had been a continued texture of afflictions; yet, by the assistance of God, with such fortitude comported she her self in them all, that she has justly merited the applause and benediction of all good people; and will yield posterity a most illustrious example of an unparallelable vertue, and admirable piety. Thus this poor Town, once the Cabinet and delight of *Henry* the Fourth, is now become the Subject of the wrath and Triumph of his Son *Lewis* the Thirteenth: It was assaulted by the *French*, abandoned by the *English*, and buried in a grievous and merciless Famine; but in the conclusion, has, by its constancy, gained a more glorious Renown in succeeding ages, than those, whose uninterrupted prosperity makes them the envy of the present.

This newes caused a wonderful and general dejection among the whole Party, every one casting about, how to make his own peace; and many made publick addresses to that end, alledging, that since *Rochelle* was now lost, for whose preservation only they had taken up Armes, it was necessary that they also should make their own compositions, before a greater extremity befell them; On the other side the *Romanists*, by means of the Confederates they had in the Townes of the Religion, infused suggestions into them, perswading them to a speedy compliance, and that their early submission, would procure them a better reception; offering withal, large recompences to those that could induce their Corporations to send their Deputies to the King, who at the same time also, published a Declaration, wherein he premised to receive again into his favour and protection, any particular persons, or Towns that should petition him to that effect.

The people wearied and ruined with the Warre, and whose spirits naturally stoop to adversity; the Merchants discontented at their loss of Trading; the Citizens grieved to see their houses burnt, and their lands lie idle immanured, and untilled, all encline to a peace upon any terms whatsoever: But of all others the distemper of *Castres* was the greatest, by reason of the divisions between *Chavagnac* and *Saint Germier*, who supported by the Consuls, and others, who stayed in the Town purposely to mischieve the whole party, who played their game so well with the Council of *Albigeois*, that they procured Deputies to be sent to the Duke of *Rohan*, to desire his presence, without which their ills were irremediable, and to summon him, upon his promises, to convene a General Assembly, which might, together with him, take care of the publique affairs; giving the Deputies

charge

charge to return with his answer as soon as possible, that accordingly they might resolve on what they had to do.

This resolution, as also the election of the Deputies, was made contrary to the advice of *Chavagnac*, one of them being a Kinsman of *Saint Germiers*, yet was he fain to submit to it for the present. The project of this message was grounded upon the impossibility they conceived of the Duke's being able to come to them; and upon a belief, that were the way open, yet would he never curb his own power by a General Assembly; so that upon his refusal they promised themselves a fair and plausible pretence, to make their own particular peace, or at least, that making the Assembly their own, they should compel him to assent to what they listed: Which the Duke of *Rohan* foreseeing, and having also, before the arrival of the Deputies, reflected on a General Assembly, as the only expedient, to preserve an entire unity among them, he condescended to all their desires; and that he might lose no time, took the Deputies with him to *Nismes*, where they made choice of Deputies for the lower *Languedoc*; thence went they to the *Sevenes*, where they did the like, leaving the time and place for the Convention to his determination: He sent them also Orders into *Vivaretz* to elect their Deputies too; and then, having taken Order for the gallant fortifications he had begun at *Aimargues*, and all Garisons necessary to be kept in the two Provinces, during his absence, he takes all his Horse, and five hundred Foot, and with them comes to *Castres* about the beginning of *December*, where he found *Rousseliere*, whom the Inhabitants of *Saverdun* had driven out of their Town, by means of *La Plante*, his Lieutenant there, who suffering himself to be seduced by their temptations, had drawn the Garison out of the higher Town, and given it up into their hands: This was also much promoted by the mis-intelligence happened between *Mazaribal* (whom the Duke of *Rohan*, upon the death of *Saint Estienne*, had made Governour of *Foix*) and *la Rousseliere*; upon this occasion; for that *Mazaribal* his facility made him too much yield to the sollicitations of some of the Inhabitants of *Mazeres* (whose villainy was not then known to him, as he confessed afterwards, and that he took them for persons well-affected to the Party) to uphold the Enemies of *la Rousseliere* both in *Saverdun*, and *Carlat*; which made him requite his courtesie, by shewing favour also to all against whom *Mazaribal* had any Picque; and to such a height grew their animosities one against another, that *Mazaribal* obstructed, as much as he could, the payment of the Garison of *Saverdun*, and gave free passage to the Souldiers that ran from *la Rousseliere*; which much elevated the spirits of his enemies, who cherished *Mazaribal* with hopes, that in case they could rid themselves of the other, they would receive him into his place; but when, upon the expulsion of the other, he had a minde to go thither to reap the fruits of their promises, they reduced his train to a less number at the first, and shut their Gates upon him the second time; but protested notwithstanding to continue firm to the Party; which nevertheless, when they had sufficiently secured the place, they utterly abandoned it, and presently made addresses by their Deputies, to the King. It was then (but too late) that *Mazaribal* clearly perceived the wicked intentions of *la Rousseliere's* enemies, whose Treachery he could not now sufficiently aggravate.

The first thing the Duke of *Rohan* did, when he came to *Castres*, was to assemble the two *Colloques* of *Albigeois* and *Lauraguais*, to acquaint them with the resolutions of the lower *Languedoc*, and the *Sevenes*, and to incite them, by the others example, to choose Deputies also for the General Assembly; the like was also done by *Montauban*, *Foix*, and *Rouergne*: After this he endeavoured to compose the difference between *Chavagnac* and *Saint Germier*, which was now grown into so formal a quarrel, that mutual challenges had passed between them: But though *Saint Germier* refused not to submit to a reconciliation, yet would he not condiscend to own *Chavagnac*, as his Superiour in the Town of *Castres*: But on the contrary he professed publiquely, and in private, and even in the Council-House, that he would oppose him in all things, and in all places. This made the Duke of *Rohan* think of removing him into the lower *Languedoc*; to which end he offered him a Troop of Horse, and an honourable allowance for himself and his retinue; but his Partisans, seeing that this tended to the dissipation of their faction, disswaded him from it, promising him withall, that if he could find out any way to evade that employment, they would make him Master of their Town.

The Duke also, finding the great scarcity of Corn was in *Castres*, to supply that want, gets them to resolve to borrow ten thousand Crowns to buy some; and offered them, during his abode there, sufficient Convoyes to conduct it safe thither: But seeing that could not be effected, he seeks out some other way to supply the necessities of the Town: And understanding that there was a great quantity at *Saint Amant*, which lies in the Valley of *Mazamet*; he claps a Petarde to the Town, and by that means enters it, and besieges the Castle, which being hardly pressed, yielded also, and at three or four Convoyes, was the greatest part of the Corn carried to *Castres*: This exploit was performed by *Chavagnac*: He sent also for more provisions to some of the Religion, that living as Neuters, hoped by that means to secure themselves against all parties.

He caused *Donaret* the first Consul of *Realmont*, who was a great instrument of the taking of the Town, to be tried, and executed; but with much difficulty, for that having married the President *Montespieu*'s Neece (such persons seldom wanting Intercessours) they were loth to pronounce a sentence of Death against him: After this, the Winter came on so furiously, that he could not proceed in his intended Designe upon *Brassac*.

Whiles he stayed at *Castres*, he also defeated two several negotiations for particular Peaces: The first was carried on by *Dejan* a native of *Montauban*, who having formerly bought the Office of Provost of the Town, which the Corporation opposed as a thing long before abolished, after a long suit, and a great expence of money he was faine to accept of what he had disbursed: This man being at the Court, had fresh hopes given him of this Office, in case he could effect any thing in this negotiation: To this Lure he stoops, and having his Commission dispatched, comes away with two Letters from *Galand*; one for *Montauban*, and another for *Castres*. At the first place he was refused, and referred to the Duke of *Rohan*; and as for the second, he durst not go directly thither, but approaches as near it, as *Bouquiere*, which is about a League from it, and thence Writes to *Dupuy*, to let him know that he was very desirous to speak with him about a business of great importance; but he sent him word again, That he could not do it, unless he would first acquaint him with the nature of it: Whereupon he essayes a second time to prevail with him, but in vain; so that not daring to come into *Castres*, he was fain to return again without any further satisfaction: Thus his Voyage bringing no advantage to the Court, was nothing beneficial to himself neither, who reaped no fruits at all of those many fair hopes were given him.

The other was managed by the Bishop of *Mende*, who was somewhat more zealous in it, as shall be seen in another place; but for the present he discovered himself thus far, and to the Duke of *Rohan* too; that being a servant to the Cardinal, he had received a Commission to Treat with particular persons, and Corporations, either severally, or conjunctively, and especially
with

servant of his own towards the Duke of *Rohan*, to observe what was done, that the intelligence he should receive of the transactions there, might direct him how to steer his course; who, when he saw that the Duke would not listen to a Man not impowered by any Commission, nor admit of any clandestine or particular Treaty, discovered himself, and told him, that he was sent to inform him from the Governour, that the Bishop had made some overtures to him concerning a particular Treaty for *Montauban*, but that he had rejected his Propositions; nevertheless if he had any inclinations to a general Treaty, he was very well acquainted with him, and could do him much service in it.

On the other side, the Bishop nothing satisfied with *Rohan's* answer; and rightly conjecturing, that his presence would be injurious to his design; resolves to have patience, untill his return into the lower *Languedoc*; that in his absence he might the more effectually prevail upon the several Corporations.

There remained nothing more now, than by a Provident fore-sight, to prevent all inconveniencies, might intervene at *Castres*, during his absence: To this end he settles in the Consulate persons of great integrity, and no less fidelity to himself, banishing from the Town three of the old Consuls, and some others also, of whom he had great jealousie; and placed there four Companies of Foot, for whose subsistence he also provided: The business of *Saint Germier* was the only thing he could not handsomely cleare, because he had absented himself from the Town; which obliged the Duke of *Rohan* to make an Order, prohibiting *Chavagnac*, and the Consuls, to give him, or any of his brothers, any admittance into it; and, in case he came not in to them within the space of eight dayes, to Proclaim him a deserter of his Party: He sent also a Company of Foot into *Roque-courbe*, and another into *Viane*; forbidding them also to receive *Saint Germier* and his brothers, and leaves three hundred Men, which he brought out of the lower *Languedoc*, in *Saint Amant*, where, for their maintenance, he allotted them their proportions out of a part of the Corn was found there.

When he had done this, he went with the Deputies of the General Assembly towards *Nismes*, where he saw the storm was like to fall, and where his presence would be most necessary; and conceiving it also a very convenient place for the General Assembly, made no long delays after his arrival there, before he formed it.

The first and most important affair that fell under their consideration, was that of *Castres*: *Saint Germier*, after the departure of the Duke of *Rohan* thence, animated by the Fugitives of *Castres*, and importuned by those of his Faction, that were left in the Town, from his Mother, and his Wife, whose Sex priviledged their stay there cherished in their discontents, resolves to return thither again, and indeed he himself was the fourth man that came to the Gate, and meeting with no opposition there, he goes up directly to his quarters, where thirty or forty persons flocking to him, perswade him to go out into the Market-place, assuring him, that all the people would joyn with him, *Chavagnac*, who was then at Church, having notice of his arrival, raises his Garrison, commands his own Troop to make ready, and resolves to charge him, wherever he should meet him; but his Lieutenant, *l' Espuguet*, being very opportunely mounted with about twenty of his men to go out upon a party, hearing the Alarme, goes directly to the place where *Saint Germier* was, and without taking any other notice of him, charged him bravely; in which action he received five wounds, and lost one of his men; but he slew and wounded many of the others also, whom he so scattered, and dispersed, that they had no more mind to rally again. Upon this rumour, the Consuls and Consistory interpose in the business, and instead of detaining him prisoner, too charitably mediate for his quiet departure again: This is that which usually ruines all publick affairs, the indulgence shewen to offenders, under the goodly pretence of piety and clemency, which in other mens matters every one cries out for, when as their own particular interests will not endure to hear them mentioned.

This mild comportment of theirs towards *Saint Germier*, instead of pacifying, renders him more haughty than before, puffing him up with a vain opinion, that this courtesie was an effect of their fear; so that encouraged by his followers, and by the assistance of many Thieves, and Villains, that had sheltered themselves in *Roque-Courbe*, he gets into it, drives out the Garrison, and makes himself Master of the place; the Assembly General fore-seeing the evil consequences this would produce, sent a Deputy to *Castres*, with order to communicate his

Commission

Commission to *Chavagnac*, and the Council of the Province; and to endeavour to compose this difference, by submitting it to the determination of Arbitrators; to the end they might not provoke *Saint Germier* to give away the Town; which being now in his possession, he laughed at all mentions of an Accommodation; so that the Deputy at his return, reported to the Assembly, that all he had been able to do, was to confirm *Roque-Courbe* in their resolutions for the Reformed party, which they had anew engaged themselves by Oath, never to relinquish; but that for the present it was impossible to dispossess *Saint Germier* of it; but yet that there was great probability that a little patience, together with his imprudence, would give them what they aimed at; and in effect, a few dayes after, when he urged the Inhabitants to declare for the King, who knew well they must then submit to a *Romish* Garrison, they turned many of his Faction out of the Town, which so terrified him, that thinking himself no longer secure there, he leaves the place also, and goes with them to *Cam*, a house not far from it; which when *Chavagnac* had intelligence of, he besieges, and takes him, and one of his brothers, with fifteen, or sixteen others, half *Romanists*, and half of the Reformed Religion, whom he sent to the Duke of *Rohan*: And yet after such actions as these, found he many Advocates, who deemed it too great a severity to detain him prisoner, till the peace, and seemed also much discontented that his whole equipage was not restored him, and a Troop of Horse given him, that he might serve the party as formerly, and this was the conclusion of this affair.

And now the Bishop of *Mende* renewes the pursuit of his design, with an Essay upon *Montauban*, to which end he sent thither *Vieres*, a Gentleman of *Quercy*, who feigned himself to be of the Religion, and wrote to the Town to this effect, that being now going with the Kings Pass-port to wait upon the Duke of *Rohan*, with some proposals tending to the general advantage of them all, he would not proceed in his journey before he had acquainted them with them, which if they pleased to receive from his Relation, he was confident they would approve of them.

It was not thought fit to admit him into the Town, for fear of the danger might ensue; but yet the natural curiosity of the *French*, at such a time, when every one breathed nothing but desires of a peace, made them very sollicitous to know what he had to say: Wherefore they sent four Commissioners to receive his message, whom he told, that being of the Religion himself, he could not but be very zealous for the general welfare of their

party,

party, and that the Bishop of *Mende* having full power to treat, he was going from him, to the Duke of *Rohan*, and the general Assembly, with some propositions to that purpose; which, that they might be the better resented, and that their Town might also have their part of the thanks, and benefit thence accruing, he advised them to send thither some Deputies also, offering the Kings Pass for their safe conduct; when this was reported to the Common-Council of the Town, they approved of the advice, and presently made choice of some Deputies, of which they also advertised the Assembly.

The Duke of *Rohan* had great jealousies of this *Vieres*, whom he had a long time known for a notable cheat; nevertheless, with great impatience was this Address expected; the report of which being generally divulged, suspended all other thoughts, every one hoping to derive some advantage from it; three weeks passed without any further mention of it, at length came a dispatch from *Montauban*, importing, that they had receiv'd intelligence from the Bishop, that he could not obtain the Pass-ports promised by *Vieres*; but that if they pleased to send their Deputies to perswade the General Assembly to accept of such a peace, as the King should vouchsafe to accord them, and in case they refused to comply, that they themselves were resolved to submit to his pleasure, he would engage himself for the safe conduct of their Deputies: This discovered the whole fallacy to the Town, and made them resolve anew to remit all propositions for peace to the General Assembly, which they exactly observed in that, made them by the Marshal *de la Force*, to this effect, that the King was resolved not to issue out any Declaration for a general peace; nevertheless, if they would Treat every one particularly, the King admitting of all such Treaties, and refusing a peace to no Town, it would at last insensibly prove a general one.

When this business of *Montauban* was over, came a very urgent dispatch from *Vivaretz*, grounded upon this occasion, that the Army which lay before *Rochelle*, after the taking of the Town, went under the command of *Toras* into *Auvergne*, to refresh themselves, and that they were now upon a March towards the upper *Vivaretz*, to go thence to *Valence* in *Dauphine*, there to wait the arrival of the King; this their so near approach, gave the whole Countrey a hot Alarme; especially *Sojon*; which *Chevrilles* about six Months before had seized, and fortified; so that with great Instancy they demanded a supply both of men and ammunition. The lower *Languedoc* furnished them with fifteen hundred men, the command of which was given by the Duke of *Rohan* to *Saint André de Montbrun* as his field

Marshal,

Book IV. *The Memoires of the Duke of* Rohan. 199

Marshal, with whom were also sent the Horse belonging to *Cassagne*, who about three moneths before, was taken prisoner; to whom in this place I must give his merited honour, publishing to the World with what generosity he with-stood both the Menaces, and Flatteries of the Court; for, he being the first Consul of *Nismes*, and of great authority, and reputation there; they hoped by his means to raise a powerful faction there, and wholly take off that Town from their adherence to the Reformed Party.

But to return to those of *Vivaretz*, all whose fears the King's Army having transported with them over the *Rhone* into *Dauphine*, they countermand the Troops were coming to their assistance, which turned to their great prejudice; for that being now a burthen to the Duke of *Rohan*, who knew not yet well how to dispose of them, he was feign to seek out some employment for them, between *Vivaretz*, and the *Sevenes*; and to this end he sent *Saint André* orders to make an attempt upon *Saint John de Valle-Francisque*; and for the more convenient prosecuting of a design upon *Villeforte* or *Postes*, to secure *Genovillac*, and *Chamberigand*; he begins with *Saint John*, which he takes, as also the Fort of *Chamberigand*, and some other places, which were like to incommode him, and then takes up his quarters at *Genovillac*; whence he marches with intention to block up *Villefort*; but finding the Marquess *de Portes* upon the way with a greater power than his, ready to dispute the passages with him; he forces him from them, and so advances to *Ville-fort*, thinking to have lodged his men in the Suburbs; but being not able to effect it, he retires to *Genovillac*, and *Saint Germain*, and thence informs the Duke of *Rohan*, that his men would leave all their Colours, unless they were drawn off thence; whereupon he gives orders for their quartering at *Saint Ambroix*, *Barjac*, *Valon*, and *la Gorce*; that they might be in a readiness to march to *Privas*, upon any occasion should summon them thither.

In the mean time came to him new assurances from *England*, that he should never be deserted, nor any peace made, without comprising the whole body of those of the Religion in *France* in general, and his Family in particular; encouraging him also to a constancy in his resolution, and not to be dismayed at the loss of *Rochelle*: Prince *Thomas* also of *Savoy* sent a Gentleman to him, to let him know, that if he continued in his former humour, and would advance towards him, he would give the King a handsome diversion in *Dauphine*, and meet him upon the *Rhone* with ten thousand Foot, and a thousand Horse; to whom he replied, that he was now in a better humour than ever, and

ready

ready to march upon the first summons he should receive from him.

The King in the mean time goes towards *Dauphine*, but because the plague was at *Lyons* Lodges at *Vienne*, and appoints the Rendez-vous to be at *Grenoble*, where preparation was also made of all things necessary for the relief and victualling of *Cazal*; the jealousies these preparatives raised in the Duke of *Savoy*, made him look about him in several quarters, there being an Army in Province ready to fall upon *Nice*; another in *Bressia* to keep *Savoy* in awe, and the King himself marching with the third to the streights of *Susa*, which is the Key of *Piedmont*; so that the Duke was fain to divide his Forces, that he might be ready to defend himself in any part where the storm should fall, and to call in the *Spanish* Forces to assist him in the defence of *Susa*.

The present state of affairs, gave great probabilities that the King would now have employments enough to divert him a long time from looking after those of the Religion; and upon occasion of some reports dispersed among the people of *Nismes*, that if they had any inclinations to sue for a peace, all necessary Passports for their safe conduct should be given them; the Assembly took care to enquire after the Authours, and truth of these Rumours; but finding them to be all fictions, and the inventions of some Counsellours of the Presidial of *Nismes*, or of some of the Inhabitants that had been expulsed the Town; or of some of *Aiguemortes*, some of them set on by the Duke of *Montmorency*, others by the Marquess of *Varennes*, out of an intention to ruine them, by sowing divisions among them, rather than to procure them any good; the Assembly made a Decree, that all persons that had any proposals or overtures to make for a peace, should first bring them to the Assembly, that they might be examined by them, and improved to their advantage; expressely prohibiting also all persons from such clandestine, and malicious buzzing of reports among the people, to take them off from proceeding in the Fortifications they were then upon.

And next they fell upon the consideration of a course to procure a firm and lasting peace; whereupon they laid down this for an infallible ground, that it could not be such, unless it were made conjoyntly with the King of *England*; neither could he himself procure any upon so good terms, without a previous discent into *France*, whither he was now invited by so many considerable emergencies to favour him in the enterprise; the King being now at the other end of his Kingdom with his best Forces, prosecuting a design, was to be executed without it; where he should have to

oppose

Book IV. *The Memoires of the Duke of* Rohan. 201

oppose him, the Forces of the Emperour, the King of *Spain*, and the Duke of *Savoy*. To this effect a letter was written to him in the name of the Assembly, and the Duke of *Rohan*, beseeching him to embrace this offered opportunity, and confirming the protestations formerly made by those of the Religion in *France*, not to engage in any Treaty, but conjoyntly with him: And for as much as their want of money was great, and that without some Forrain assistance, it was impossible to keep their men together, or advance their Fortifications, the Duke of *Rohan* was sollicited to write to *Clausel*, that they could no longer subsist without a supply of money, and that he should let the *Spaniards* know, that the peace of *France* could be no longer prevented, without a sudden recruit. It was also resolved, that they should endeavour to procure some private Pass-ports, that they might with more security send into *England*; upon assurance to be given to dispose all things to a peace: *Du Cros* of *Montpellier*, who, with the consent of the Marquess *de Fosse*, came to give the Duke of *Rohan* a visit, returned from him with the same promise, which was also confirmed by the whole Assembly.

Thus were they careful not to omit any thing that tended either to their own defence, or the procuring of a peace, even at such a time, when they had fairer hopes of good success in their affairs than ever; but God, who had otherwise determined of them, blasted all their projects: For the King, who left not *Paris*, to go to the relief of *Cazal*, till he had privately gotten an assurance out of *England*, which freed him from the fear of any invasion thence, whil'st he was engaged in that expedition, and made him confident of a peace with that Nation, excluding the Reformed Party, would not admit of any addresses from them, fearing lest they might prevail so far upon him, as to induce him to alter his determinations concerning them: To which may be added, that surprizing his enemies by a nimble march, in the dead of Winter, he easily gained the straits of *Susa*, and immediatly after the Town also; which brought so great a terrour on them all, that *Don Ganzales* raised his siege from before *Cazal*; the Duke of *Savoy* also, to prevent the loss of *Piedmont*, sollicited for a peace, by which he was obliged to re-victual *Cazal*. The King, that he might himself witness the performance of all Conventions, remained about a moneth longer in that Countrey: And then leaving *Toiras* with four thousand Foot, and five hundred Horse in *Montferrat*, and the Marshal *Crequi* with the like number at *Susa*, bent all his thoughts, and the rest of his Forces upon the War in *Languedoc*; in order to which he commanded the Marshal *Schomberg* to advance before to *Valence*,

to

to receive the Forces that were coming out of *Bressia*, and the parts about *Lyons*, to cause the Train, and all other necessaries to be made ready, and to conclude a Treaty already begun with *Chevrilles* concerning *Vivaretz*: To the Duke of *Montmorency*, he sent Orders to besiege *Sojon*; to the Duke of *Guise*, that he should deliver up his Army to the Marshal *d' Estrée*, who had a Commission to march with it into the lower *Languedoc*, to ravage the Countrey about *Nismes*; not long after the King comes in person to *Valence* with a few Horse only, and a few dayes after, the Cardinal arrives also with the rest of the Army; out of which were drawn fifteen hundred Horse, and sent under the command of the Duke of *Trimoüille*, to joyn with the Marshal *d' Estrée*.

In the interim of these preparations the *English* Embassadour than residing at *Thurin*, gave the Duke of *Rohan* notice of the peace concluded there; but that it was not like to be of any long continuance; that the Army was now marching towards him, but in so tattered a condition, that if he could but stand the first shock, he would soon find such diversions made, as would be much to his advantage. *Clausel* encouraged him yet much more with promises of a sudden supply both of Arms and Money. *Nismes*, and *Aimargues* went but slowly on in their Fortifications, *Vsez* a little better; but yet no Town would give quarter to any Souldiers, till they were upon the point of being besieged; which drove the Duke of *Rohan* to his usual way of offering to each particular Town to pull out for them, the Thorn, that pricked them: And first he addresses himself to *Sauve*, with over-tures of an attempt upon *Corsonne*, whither he goes; but findes it a matter of greater difficulty, than his information had given him cause to apprehend; for having battered their Works, the Walls were not to be scaled, but with Ladders of a very great length; so that those he had brought with him proving too short, he was necessitated to make all new again; which gave the Marshal *d' Estrée*, (urged by the Marquess *de Fosse*) leasure to march to the relief of it with six thousand Foot, and four hundred Horse; whereupon the Duke drew off again to *Sauve*; and the next day being desirous to view the Marshal's Army as it marched, and who then took up their quarters at *Sommieres*; it was demonstrated to him, that he could not get back again to *Saint Gilles*, but he must pass the *Vistre* near to *Aimargues*; or the *Gardon*, if he intended to go for *Vivaretz*, as it was reported he did, at both which places he might with ease be discovered, and with advantage fought with: The Duke, that he might not lose this opportunity, writes to *Vsez* for some more Forces,

and

and sends *Aubais* to *Nismes* for the same purpose; *Lesques* goes to *Anduze* for others, accompanied by *Goudin*, and *la Baume*; he sent also to *Saint Hippolyte*, and the neighbouring Garrisons for more Auxiliaries, appointing his general Rendez-vous to be at *Vauvage*; and he himself sets out by break of day with two thousand Foot, and fourscore Horse, to secure *Canisson*, a large, but unfenced Town, whence he might be sure to take his advantage which way soever the Marshal should take; but whether it was that he had the same design upon *Canisson*; or that he had intelligence of the Dukes marching thither with so small a Force; he found him also upon his march from *Sommieres* towards *Canisson*; nevertheless the Duke having the advantage of the way, goes on directly to the Town, and there began to secure the avenewes of it with his Van, that the rest, (considering he was pursued by an Army twice stronger than his own) might in good order possess themselves of the Town; but the extream heat of the day, and fame of the good Wine, wherewith that place abounded, had already drawn thither the greatest part of his Officers, so that it was impossible for him to govern them; when on a sudden he heard many Musquets in his Rear, which was then skirmishing with five hundred Musquetiers, which the Marshal had sent before to try if they could break it; whil'st he, with the rest of his Army stayed upon a little Hill which gave him a view of all the Countrey, and what was done even in *Canisson* it self, whence perceiving the great and general confusion there, he gave Orders for a general assault: The Duke of *Rohan* commanded *Montredon* to rally his men, together with *Carlincas*, Ensign of his Guards; whiles he himself draws out a hundred of his own Guard, whom he led up to the Castle of *Canisson*, which being seated on a little Hill, commands the Town, and circumjacent quarters, so that it is not easily assaultable on any side, enjoyning them strictly to look well to the defence of that place. This done, he goes round the Town, which he begins to fortifie with strong Barricadoes; just as he had finished his circuit, he meets with *Leques*, *Goudin*, and *la Baume*, and tells them that of necessity they must resolve to defend the out-places, untill the Barricadoes were finished: *Leques* undertook the affair, goes to the head of his men, and seeing that the Souldiers that were in the Castle, had quitted it, hastes thither with others, whom he placed in their rooms; and so eagerly disputed he his post without the Town, that when he would have retreated thither, he found the enemy had intercepted his passage, so that he was fain to take the Field: *La Baume* was also served in the like kinde; as for *Goudin*, the Duke would not suffer him, by reason

son of his wound, to shut himself up in the Town; but when he had taken the best course he could to preserve his Foot, he drew off with his Horse to *Nismes* to hasten away the relief he had before sent thither to prepare.

In the mean while *Montredon*, the Major General, *la Boissiere*, and *Alizon*, after they had from post to post, disputed the out-quarters, retreated into *Canisson*, where they had no sooner taken their several posts to defend, but they received a general and furious assault; but necessity animating the Defendants, they bravely repulsed the Assailants; and whiles they looked on, perfected their Barricadoes; then got the enemy into some houses, which they began to break through, thinking by that way to open themselves a passage into the Town, but they were soon fired from that attempt; this storm lasted from Noon till Night; the Officers within behaved themselves with much gallantry, both in rallying, and encouraging their men; but *Montredon*, *la Boissiere*, and *Alizon*, who commanded in chief, got most honour in this action; both parties had their inconveniencies; those within wanted ammunition, those without provisions; so that, that very night the Marshal *d' Estrée*, offered the besieged a Parley, which they rejected, telling him withall, that they should soon see the Duke of *Rohan* there with fresh Forces, to make them remove farther off, and indeed that night had he sent two thousand men of *Nismes*, under the command of *Aubais*, to get as near *Canisson* as possible, and to let the besieged know, that he was now come so far to their assistance; but he returned again, without giving them any notice of his arrival, either by Messenger, or other signal made, as he was expresly commanded; none daring to adventure on the employment; and indeed, so straitly were they invested, that it was impossible for any one to get in to them; this much troubled the Duke, who having refreshed his Troops, resolved to go thither in person, and either save his men, or lose himself: To which end he sent *Leques* Orders to have the Garrison of *Aimargues* in a readiness to joyn with him; but whil'st he was preparing for their relief, came newes to him of the capitulation, which was made upon these termes, That the besieged should with all security march off to the *Sevenes*; that the Marshal *d' Estrée*, should not enter the Town of *Canisson* with his Army; but that the said Army should be drawn up in Battailla, at a great distance from the way they were to pass; that the wounded of both sides, which could not be carried off, should with all safety remain in the Town; and that for the performance of these Articles, Hostages should be mutually given, all which was punctually observed on both parts; of the party of those of the Religion

Book IV. *The Memoires of the Duke of* Rohan. 205

ligion were slain about fifty or sixty, and above double the number wounded: of the *Romanists* were there four hundred slain, and eight hundred wounded.

This was the issue of this action, in which the Duke of *Rohan* was very like to have received a check, would have proved fatal both to himself, and his Party too: But now imagining that it was not without cause that the Marshal so earnestly pursued this design; but that his Forces were intended for the Countrey about *Nismes*, he conceived he would again pass the *Vistre* near *Aimargues*, that he might the sooner recover his quarters at *Saint Gilles*, which made him desirous yet once more to see him; for which purpose he took two thousand of the Foot of *Nismes*, and his Horse, with whom he came to *Aimargues*; the next day he drew them up in a place between *Aimargues* and the Pass, with intention to charge him when he should be half over; which the Marshal having notice of, he changed both his design, and road, and lengthning his way a dayes journey, passed the River at *Aiguemortes*; and the Duke returned to *Nismes*: And seeing the preparations were making on all hands for the invasion of the lower *Languedoc*, and the *Sevenes*, he got the Towns of the lower *Languedoc* to receive their Garisons; assignes the Regiments of *Goudin*, *Fourniquet*, and *Bonal*, to *Nismes*; those of *la Baume* and *Faulgeres* for *Usez*; and that of *Sandres* for *Aimargues*; After this, and the taking of the Fort of *Sojon* by the Duke of *Montmorency*, which cost him but three dayes time, though *Chevrilles* had promised to hold it out three weeks, the Duke of *Rohan* having learnt the particulars of the Treaty for *Vivaretz*, made by *Chevrilles* with the Keeper of the seals for twenty thousand Crowns; he thought it now high time to look after the securing of it; and sent *Saint André de Montbrun* with five hundred Foot, and some of *Cassagne*'s Horse, to *Privas*, whither he got very happily, having defeated *Montreal* and *l' Estrange*, who waited for him at some untoward passes in his way, with a farre greater strength than his. At his arrival there, he found the Consuls with the Common Council assembled at the Town House; who told him that indeed they had formerly wished for his company, but that at present, they having no need of any Souldiers, it would be but a burthen to them; and yet, that they might with the better grace refuse to admit his party into their Town, promised to quarter them in the Villages that lay thereabouts; which *Saint André* perceiving, was the more resolute to quarter in the Town: *Chevrilles* who was then at *Cheyla*, was sent for in all haste, and coming thither the next day with those of his Faction, he

Pre-

presently assembles the Council of the Province, and of the Town too, to perswade them to request *Saint André* to return again, and that in case their intreaties were ineffectual, to induce him to it by the ill usage of his Men: which *Saint André* having notice of, he goes in to the Assembly, and there declares that he was sent thither, by the command of the Duke of *Rohan*, who only had power to recall him againe; and that whatever their determinations should be, he would not stirre a foot thence without his Order: When *Chevrilles* saw himself thus fallen from his hopes, he tells *Saint André*, that in case the Town should be besieged, he would do them better service without than within the place; that he would raise fifteen hundred men, and would put as many of them into it, as he should think necessary, and with the rest would forrage and cut off the provisions from the King's Army.

His proposition was well approved of, and on the morrow he departs: And not long after were there three Barques laden with Salt taken upon the *Rhone*: *Saint André* hasts thither, but came not time enough, for that some Frigots had already forced those that had taken them to quit their Prize: Neverthele[s]s in this excursion he learnt that the King was come to *Valence* but with a small guard, believing, upon the information he had received concerning that particular from the Keeper of the Seals, that the Treaty of *Vivaretz* was absolutely concluded; but that finding that the coming of *Saint André* thither had altered the whole face of things there, he was now preparing for the Siege of *Privas*, which was to be blocked up within four or five dayes: Large offers was he tempted with, even to the value of an hundred thousand Crowns, but his generous refusal of them shewed him to be a person full of honour and fidelity: At his return to *Privas* he makes them all resolve to abide a siege, engaging them also by an Oath, that the first man, that should but mention a Capitulation, should be put to death: Then he assignes to every one their respective posts; and Orders the repairing of the out-works, to which, before his coming, nothing at all had been done; nor yet could he begin them, but the very day before the Town was invested, and yet such diligence used he in it, that some of them were made very defensible, and held out bravely.

The siege was scarce begun, when the Cardinal came up with the rest of the Army that stayed behind at *Susa*: He presses *Chevrilles* to the performance of his engagement; who that he might not wholly lose the recompence of his Treason, desires to have a part in the honor of the Siege, offering to bring in with him 15 hun-

hundred men; his offer was accepted, and he comes in, but all alone: The next day came a Trumpet from the King (accompanied with *Argencourt*) to summon the place: *Chevrilles*, who failed not to be at the place, whither the Trumpet was to come, sent one of his Captains to know what he had to say, which when *Saint André* was informed of, he hasted thither with all diligence, and sent him back again without any answer at all: Whereupon *Chevrilles* seeing him resolved not to give them time to deliberate, whether they should hearken to a Capitulation, or no, leaves them again the second time, carrying with him as many men as he could, and was alwayes the occasion that the Souldiers of *Bouttieres* went not thither to their assistance, amusing them still with promises to conduct them thither time enough, by this meanes ruining the endeavours of those whom *Saint André* had sent thither purposely to invite them to their assistance.

He was no sooner gone, but *Brunel* of *Anduze*, who commanded five Companies of the *Sevenes*, confederating with the other Poltrons and Traitours, frames a conspiracy to kill *Saint André* in case he should refuse to surrender the place; and seconded by some of his Faction, threatens to give him up, if he denied to comply with them: Whereupon it was thought fit by the Council, that he should have a conference with *Gordes*, which he had, but they could not agree upon the conditions.

After that the Cardinal was come up to them, they more closely blocked up the place on every side, made their approaches and batteries, and then gave it an assault, from which they were bravely beaten off with the loss of many of their men; yet did this storm so terrifie the besieged, that they instantly urge *Saint André* to give *Gordes* another meeting: But in his room was substituted, and sent *Vennes* a Captain in the Regiment of the Guards, who offered him very honourable terms for himself, and the Souldiers, but nothing at all for the Inhabitants; all which he refused, protesting that he would never desert them: When *Saint André*, at his return, gave the people of the Town an account of the interview, it struck so great a terrour into them, together with those of *Vivaretz*, that they all quit the Town, and flie to *Bouttieres*, leaving *Saint André* with five hundred men only to defend a place, which was not to be maintained under two thousand. In this extremity he conceives it his best course to draw off to the Fort of *Toulon*, where he might Treat with more security; it being impossible to force him there in any short time, or without the loss of a great number

ber of Men: About break of day *Deffiat*, *Gordes*, and *Vennes*, desire a conference with him, which he condiscended to; at which they make him no larger offers than of his own life only, in case he would abandon his Souldiers, which he generously rejected, and returned to embrace the same fortune with them: When they saw this made not any impression on him, they summoned him once more to send some of his Officers to them with his final resolution: *Brunel* of *Dauphiné* offering himself for this employment, was accepted of; three journeys made he to them, in which time being corrupted by the enemy, he returns from the last with an assurance of all their lives; but adding withall, that they would not give any thing under their hands, untill *Saint André*, with some of his Captains had cast themselves at the King's feet to implore his pardon; and moreover that the Count of *Soissons*, who was to present him to his Majesty, had given him a strict charge to tell him, that he should haste to him with all speed, that he must not now lose any time; and that he did with much impatience wait for him: Whereupon he assembles his Captains, who all earnestly importune him to go; which when he scrupled at, they break out into open reproaches against him, charging him with having ensnared them in a danger from which he would not endeavour to free them: Forced by their invectives, he goes out with five Captains; *Saint Preüil* and *Fourille* conduct him into *Saint Simon*'s Chamber, where, the Cardinal coming to him, told him, that since he was come forth, without any parole given him, he was now a Prisoner: Then was he forced to write to those in the Fort, to advise them to yield at discretion, and that they should receive the same usage he did; who, refusing to credit those Letters, or *Brunel*, who was sent with them, desire to see *Saint André*, who was conducted up to the Fort with a strong guard: As soon as they saw him, they imagined themselves sure of their lives, and thereupon resolved to give up the Fort: Those that first entred it, fired some barrels of powder, purposely to colour the cruelty they were commanded to execute upon those that were in it: *Saint André* and his Captains were kept Prisoners: Thus were most that were in the Fort betrayed to their destruction; some of the Prisoners being hanged, and others sent to the Gallies.

I have related the particulars of this affair, to let the world see how that the perfidie of *Chevrilles*, the two *Brunels*, and of the most considerable persons in *Privas* occasioned the miserable destruction of their Town, and a great part of the Inhabitants, ruined the relief of *Languedoc*, and frustrated those of the Religion

Book IV. *The Memoires of the Duke of* Rohan. 209

ligion of an opportunity to obtain a very advantageous Peace; which, since the publication of that with *England* (which was made during this Siege.) they had entred on a Treaty upon with the Marquess *de Fossé*, who was to that end impowered by the King's Commission: But the taking of this place, as little dreamt of by the *Romanists*, as those of the Religion (considering their brave resistance at the beginning of the Siege) quite ruined that affair: For *Du Cros* had procured conference between *Aubais*, *Dupuy*, and *Lucaz*, Deputies of the Assembly general, with the said Marquess; and although at their first interview, he refused to proceed, unless they would recede from their demands, concerning the demolition of the fortifications; yet with more advantage might they have Treated, while the King was further off, and *Privas* held out, than when he should come into the *Sevenes*, and there discover the Factions, weaknesses, baseness, and Treacheries, that were too frequent among those of the Religion.

The loss of *Privas*, from whence was expected a longer opposition, surprized the whole Party with terrour and amazement; and put the Duke of *Rohan* in mind, that it was now high time to go to the *Sevenes*, to take Order for the security of that Province, and to oppose the first attempts that should be made upon it: This Voyage was hitherto retarded by his fear to leave *Nismes* (which many endeavoured to seduce from its fidelity) till he had supplied it with Souldiers, which, untill compelled by necessity, they would not receive; and withall by reason that having resolved to leave *Leques* there to command in chief, in case it should be besieged, he durst not discover his intentions in that particular too soon, because he knew that *Aubais* aimed at the same command, and that he endeavoured by secret practices to render *Leques* odious to the people, and make himself to be desired by them: In the like perplexity was he for *Usez*, where *Goudin* ambitioned the Government, but was absolutely refused by the Inhabitants: Nevertheless, at length he sets out from *Nismes*, goes to *Usez*, and thence takes *Faulgiere*'s Regiment with him to *Aletz*, and thence put it into *Saint Ambroix*, in hopes that the opposition that place would make, would give him more leasure to provide for the *Sevenes*, where he thought to have found a good sum of money ready raised, out of some Farms he had engaged for his Leavies; but the apprehension of the King's coming into those parts, made most of the Farmers refuse to disburse any: Upon their default he proposed another expedient, that the Bayliffs should advance the money for the Leavies, and that, for their re-imbursement both of the Principal

P.   and

and Interest, should be assigned them not only the aforesaid Farms, but also an imposition then newly laid upon the Countrey; but all these inventions, being not of force to extract any money out of their purses, the Duke was fain to address himself to the Communalties.

In the mean time the Marshal *d' Estrée*, and the Duke of *Trimoüille* began to ravage the Countrey about *Nismes*, where there passed many handsome skirmishes, in which, those of the Town (who killed and wounded twelve or fifteen hundred of the enemy) had alwayes the better, except one day, when some of the Inhabitants, too inconsiderately advancing, were surprized by the Horse, who dealt so roughly with them, that, besides those which were wounded, there remained forty dead upon the place, and had not *Leques* come in with fresh Troops, there had been much more mischief done: For his own part he was forced from his Horse, which was killed under him; but the Forragers came not within Canon-shot of the Town.

The King on his side loses no time, but after the taking of *Privas*, sends part of his Army towards *Gorce* and *Barjac*, which were given up into his hands: *Beauvoir* and *Saint Florent* make their peace, and then turn Brokers for the places belonging to the Reformed Party: The former of them comes to *Saint Ambroix*, to perswade the Inhabitants, to imitate the example of *Barjac*; which the chiefest of them were so ready to consent unto, that, had not the Souldiers interposed, the thing had been then done: Neverthelesse they continue their correspondencies, so that upon the King's approach, though he had no Canon with him, nor could have any come up to him within eight or ten dayes, fear united the two Factions in the Town, who before were at mortal odds, and both together force the Souldiery to a compliance with them, so that the Capitulation was agreed on, upon condition that the Souldiers should no more beare armes for the Reformed party: At which Article, when one of the Captains scrupled, the Duke of *Montmorency* told him, that none ever treated with the King upon any other termes, but that it was but a formality only, and obliged no man farther than he pleased himself: And then flatters one, and another, with promises of great rewards, if they would repaire to *Aletz*, and serve the King there, by joyning with the Count of *Aletz*, who had promised to give him up the Town: Thither then marched all the Souldiers from *Saint Ambroix*, where they excuse themselves by revolving all the blame upon the Inhabitants, who compelled them to yield the place; promising withall, that notwithstanding the Treaty, they would serve the Reformed party, wherever they should be commanded. The Duke of *Rohan* was then at *Aletz*, but had no Forces ready for service, but the Regiment of *Foulgieres*, and five or six new raised Companies; the King being then within three Leagues of him with all his Army, the people of *Aletz* very wavering, and uncertain whether they would stand upon their defence or no; and the Baron of *Aletz*, who had promised to deliver up the Town, that he might the better effect it, would by all means be Governour of it; but the Duke was desirous to place *Aubais* in that command, for that being Field-Marshal, every one would have submitted to him, and promised to leave with him all the best men he had; but he excused himself; for that being refused, the Government of *Nismes*, he had taken up a resolution, never to stay within any besieged place. Then offers he it to *Assaz*, to whose age and experience every one would have born an honourable respect; but he also absolutely refused it: Whereupon he speaks to *Boissiere* concerning it, whose modesty, no suffering him to think himself sufficient for it, made him refuse to accept of the charge, as Commander in chief; but offered to stay there as subordinate to *Aubais*, or any other the Duke should think fitting; so that in this extremity he was fain to leave there one *Mirabel*, an old Gentleman of *Vivaretz*, of a weak sight, and as feeble limbs: And when the King came to take up his quarters within a League of *Aletz*, the Duke of *Rohan* took the Baron d' *Aletz* with him, and went thence that very morning before the Town was invested; promising, before his departure, to send them what supplies of Souldiers he could possible; of which he took so great care, that at several times he sent them in above fifteen hundred; besides the Garrison was there before, which at length he raised to five and twenty hundred in the whole.

When the King saw himself frustrated of his hopes of gaining the place without force, he sent for his Canon, and, (that he might lose no time) began his approaches; part of the Town of *Aletz* is seated on a Plain, and the other so near the Hills, that they command above half of it; the River *Gardon* runs so near the Walls, that it is rather prejudicial, than useful to the Fortifications; for that being but a small Torrent, fordable in most places, and running so near the Town, it leaves no space for any Flanker to be made; nor could it be fortified within the walles by reason of the houses which made a part of them; so that there was no way to secure that part of it, but by raising Works on the other side of the River, and Forts upon the little Hills, which command all a good distance from them, and must

be

be joyned by a Line of Communication to two great stone-bridges, which cross the River. In short, it was a work of vast labour and expence, nor could the Town be kept, but by a great number of men, which was the reason it was never till then fortified; But the people now seeing that *Anduze* was fortifying, would needs imitate their example; a malady which raigned in most of the Communalties of the *Sevenes*, and this discovered its infection, when the Duke was absent, and upon his Voyage into *Foix*; who though he well knew there were already more fortifications begun, then they had Souldiers to man, yet would he not cross them in their humour, for fear of vexing and discouraging them; there was yet this further mischief in it, that besides that, they took things beyond their power to accomplish; when once the first heat was over, they would not employ what they had as they ought, nor would they work, but when compelled by their fears; to which I must yet adde this, that when they were most intent upon the raising of these fortifications, it was impossible to perswade them to store themselves with other necessaries requisite to the defence of their Town; for in such designs one expence draws on another; and if one of these four things be wanting; to wit, *Good Works*, *Ammunition*, *Victuals*, and *Souldiers*, all other provisions are but vain and fruitless.

This being the condition of this Town, they were very much surprized, having neglected to raise a third Fort, which omission, the Duke willing to redeem, in great haft makes up one of Barrels, which flew in pieces at the first on-set, and on this side only did the enemy raise their Battery, between the Bridge, and the Duke *d' Engoulesme*'s Garden; this first assault so terrified the Inhabitants, that they thought of nothing now, but how to make a handsome composition, to which they were incited, by the Captains that came from *Saint Ambroix*, and those of the Baron *d' Aletz* his Faction, whose follicitations wrought such dangerous effects, that they made Holes in their Walls to let the Besiegers in; which being discovered, the breaches were repaired, but the offenders not punished; so that the mischief was only delayed, not remedied; and the disaffected made more industrious to conceal their Treacheries: Two or three of the aforesaid Captains upon their own request were sent to the Duke of *Rohan*, to inform him how weak the place was, both in men and resolutions to stand it out, that the numbers of the Garrison there before, and of the recruits sent thither since, hourely decreased, by their continual flight from it; whereunto he replied, that what they had said, could not be; that he very well knew what Souldiers he had left there, and whom he had placed over them, that he would

daily

daily strengthen them with convenient supplies, both of men, and Ammunitions; and therefore perswaded them to return again to them speedily, to animate them by their presence; which they plainly refused, alledging once for all, that it was the next way to be hanged, considering their engagements to the Duke of *Montmorency*, when they marched out of *Saint Ambroix*; whereupon the Duke being informed that they had had secret conference with the Baron *d' Aletz*, and that they had agreed together that his Cornet *Mesengues* should be sent in to *Aletz*, he commanded they should be all apprehended, and sent *Blacquiere* thither with a recruit of five hundred men, and an express command to kill the first man that should but mention a surrender; but the malady was then past cure, the Townsmen having hid away the ammunition, and deserted the most necessary Work of terrassing that part of the Wall which was opposite against the enemies Battery, so that all he could do, was to protect the capitulation two or three dayes longer, and by that means save five and twenty hundred men, which had they been lost, as were those of *Privas*, it would have deterred all others from any future engagement; that which was most fatal in this reddition, was the Article semblable to that of *Saint Ambroix*, which disabled them from evermore bearing Arms against the King.

As soon as the newes of this was brought to the Duke of *Rohan*, immediatly he sent away *Falquieres* the Lieutenant of his Guards to *Sauve*, where the surrender of *Aletz* had struck a general terrour into the Inhabitants; the most considerable of which, out of hopes of obtaining good conditions for themselves, by the favour of their Lord, the Count *d' Aletz*, denied to let him into their Town; but *Falquieres*, being of the place, and having much acquaintance in it, by the means of some Ladders he had procured, got in; but found the people so resolutely fixed upon an accommodation, that having seized upon the Castle, and a Tower which commanded the Town, and served it instead of a Citadel, told him openly, that they were now resolved to seek out some way to preserve what they had left, and not expose themselves to an utter ruine.

In the interim the Count of *Aletz*, invited by those that had privately Treated with him, advances with three or four hundred Horse, within half a League of the Town, where when he understood that the arrival of *Falquieres* with his Souldiers, had prevented his entry into the Town, he sent a Trumpet to them, with offers of fair propositions; *Falquieres* could not by any means disswade, nor hinder them from sending back a Messenger again to assure him, that though they could not give him admittance at present, yet were they Masters of all the Forts; and that if the Duke of *Rohan* did not suddenly conclude a general peace, as he had promised them, they would, by his assistance, make their own in particular, not doubting but their example would allure the greatest part of the *Sevenes* to an imitation of them: To which the Count replied, that it was in vain to expect a General Peace; and that the Duke deluded them with that Airy fancy; but vvhil'st he made his ovvn, and that then he vvould leave them in the Lurch; that if they could be a means to dravv off any other corporations from the party, it vvould be much to the advantage of their cvvn conditions, and that they should have but a Garrison of thirty Souldiers only in their Castle, commanded by himself; they assured him of their zealous endeavours to effect vvhat they had promised, and that vvithin tvvo dayes they vvould send him a further ansvver by a Messenger of purpose: *Falquieres* that had seen all these Envoys, and heard the free, and lond discourses of the people to him, sent the Duke of *Rohan* word, that unless he recruited him instantly with four hundred men at least, he should be turned out of the Town.

The importance of this unexpected newes perplexed him so, that he took aside three or four of his Officers, in whose fidelity he reposed most confidence, to impart it to them, and receive their advice thereupon; some of them at first sight conceived that the business was desperate, and irremediable, induced to this opinion by their experience in the precedent Wars, of the disaffection of that Town to the Reformed party; and that being now Masters of the Castle, they might at their pleasure let in the Enemy; that it would be a thing of great difficulty to send them any Souldiers; for that the people of *Anduze*, that very moment expected a siege, and had not sufficient for their own defence, would be very unwilling to part with four hundred men; that if the Duke of *Rohan* should go in person thither, which was the best expedient for it, they would presently raise, and diffuse a report, that he had abandoned all; so that it was to be feared, least his endeavours to preserve *Sauve*, should prove an occasion of the loss of *Anduze*; so that their advice was to send *Falquieres* and his party orders to defend themselves the best they could; and to promise them a good assistance, in case the King should draw towards them; but that for preservation of their stores, he would not charge them with any more Forces, untill necessity should draw that burden upon them; others were of opinion, that the place was of such consequence, that the loss of

it

it would draw after it all the *Sevenes*, up to *Vigan*, and cut off all communication between *Anduze*, and the lower *Languedoc*; so that the Duke of *Rohan* would be totally blocked up there, without any possibility of breaking through again; that the loss of it; as was that of *Privas*, and *Saint Ambroix*, would be wholly laid to his charge; and that it might be justly feared, lest the people of *Anduze*, who were known to have inclinations seditious enough, and had store of malignant spirits among them, should enter into conspiracies also against him; in short, that this extremity gave them a capacity to betray him, and therefore it were better to attempt to send four hundred men to *Sauve*, to preserve both himself, and the Town too.

This Counsel was accepted of, and thereupon he drew out all the Garrison of *Anduze*, and out of it chose four hundred men, to send to the relief of *Sauve*; but none would undertake the conduct of them, but the Adjutant-General *Randon*, nor he neither; but upon condition that (to secure his own honour) the Duke would allow him the liberty to retreat with them again, in case he saw the King's Army advance towards him; engaging himself nevertheless not to make use of it, unless enforced to it by some extremity; thus was he fain to expose his own, to save the honour of another.

Amid'st these perplexities, which were no small ones, the Court-faction in the *Sevenes* used many subtile inventions to induce the Communalties there to a particular Treaty, excluding the Duke of *Rohan*; the most dangerous of which, were; first, to hinder the march of the relief from *Anduze* to *Sauve*; terrifying them with continual Alarms, that a part of the King's Army was to cross the Countrey, which they would overwhelme with blood and fire, so that not a Souldier could be perswaded to stir from his house; the next was, without his permission to convoque an Assembly, to which were summoned only those they were sure would consent to a Deputation to the Court in the name of many of the Communalties for a particular peace; and the last was to asperse his honour, by scandalous insinuations, that *Privas*, and *Saint Ambroix* were given up by his especial order; that *Blacquiere* was sent to *Aletz* for the like purpose; and that having made his own conditions, he would expose the people to a necessity of accepting such as the King should impose upon them; and in effect these, and the like defamatory rumours spread abroad, by petty, but very factious persons, that hoped by such means to raise themselves a fortune, raised a general murmur against him; for the people, (especially those of *Languedoc*) are naturally prone to believe the worst, of the best, and the best, of the worst

P 4

sort of men; readily complying with such clamorous persons, as condemn the actions of other men, when as themselves do nothing at all, but vail their hypocrisie with an indiscreet zeal, tending only to sedition, and the subversion of their Religion, and liberties.

The Duke was at the same time sollicited by often repeated Messages from the Provinces of the higher *Languedoc*, *Foix*, *Montauban*, and *Roüergue*, both for men, and money. *Mazaribal* sends him word, that unless he were recruited with a hundred good men, and pay for them, it would be impossible for him to preserve *Mazeres*; and that without such a supply, or a peace, he should within one moneth be forced to quit the Countrey: *Saint Michel*, and the Town of *Montauban*, tell him, that the Prince, and the Duke *d' Espernon*, were drawing down to Ravage the Countrey about them, which they would inevitably ruine, unless he sent them some assistance to prevent it; but that with a thousand men at most, and money to pay them, which they earnestly importuned him for, they made no doubt bravely to repulse them. *Chavagnac*, and the Town of *Castres* remonstrate to him, that a Famine would inevitably surprize them, unless they quickly gathered in their Harvest, which they were incapable to secure, without a Renfort of a thousand Foot, and a hundred Horse, payed for two or three moneths; and money also to muster and discharge the Forces of the Countrey; that the Duke of *Ventadour*, who with his Army lay round about them, had made them offers of very advantageous conditions, in case they would incline to a particular peace, which they hitherto had refused, out of hopes of a sudden, and effectual assistance, the want of which would necessitate them to submit to such a Treaty. *Millaud* also presents him with the same doleful Note; and *Alterac*, Governour of the Town, plainly tells him, that without a fresh supply of Souldiers, he could no longer undertake the charge of it; and all the rest of *Vabres* accord in the same demands, either of men, or a Peace.

The Duke of *Rohan* opprest with the hourely increase of such calamities, saw no other expedient for their remedy, but a General Peace, which also was attended with many difficulties; for he conceived that the King, seeing to what a low ebbe the affairs of the Reformed Party were sunk, would not abate one jot of the Article touching the Fortifications; and on the other side he very well knew, that though the people had no resolutions to stand upon, nor inclinations to prepare for a defence; yet would they never digest the demolition of their Works: If he should resolve to stand it out, and struggle with the the threatned extremities,

mities, then he confidered, that if he quitted *Anduze*, all the *Sevenes* would be loft, and confequently all the Garrifons, up to the very Gates of *Montauban*, muft fubmit; if he ftayed there, he fhould draw a fiege upon a place no wayes capable to fuftain it; but if the King, waving that, fhould draw towards *Sauve*, the whole Countrey would come in, and every Communalty having made its peace, *Anduze* would be left all forlorn, and disfurnifhed of Souldiers to maintain it: But the urgency of their affairs obliging him fuddenly to fix up on fome courfe that had leaft of danger in it, he pitched upon a General Peace; which, though accompanied with never fo many difadvantages, would be yet better than an abfolute diffipation of the Edicts, which would be the undoubted confequence of the particular compofitions of the feveral Communalties; in order to which, he fummoned an Affembly of all the Communalties of the *Sevenes* to be held at *Anduze*, to diffolve that which was already convened without his permiffion; and at the fame time fent *Montredon* to thofe that fate at *la Salle*, to demand a particular Peace; to let them know, that a Provincial Affembly, in order to a General Treaty, was convoqued at *Anduze*; and that, if they, notwithftanding his orders to the contrary, obftinately continued their Seffion, he had a command from the Duke to affemble the people of *la Salle*, to make known their refractorinefs to them, and to require their affiftance for the apprehending of their perfons, and carrying them away Prifoners; his perfwafions, with the annexed Menaces, made them at length diffolve; for Fear is oftentimes very perfwafive.

After this the Duke fent for *Caudiac*, a Counfellor in the Chamber of *Languedoc*, who had already made feveral journies to the Court, in order to a Peace, and was now but newly returned thence; where he found that their only aime, and chiefeft hopes now, were, a total diffipation of the party by particular Treaties; him he defires once again to return thither, and to tell the Cardinal *de Richelieu* from him, that he was a faithful Subject of the Kings, that he defired nothing more, than the Tranquillity of the State, and the Repofe of his own party; and withall, that both he, and the greateft part of them, would expofe themfelves and fortunes to all extremities, rather than fubmit to any Peace, but fuch as fhould be General, and Conformable to the former Edicts of pacification; that it was a thing of dangerous confequence to force an armed Party, how fmall foever, from all hopes of fafety, but what they ground upon their defpair of any; and that if the King would vouchfafe to admit of a General Treaty, and allow the General Affembly but four dayes time only to remove from *Nifmes* to *Anduze*, and Pafs ports for the
safe

safe conduct of their Deputies to come, and Treat with his Commissioners; and that in the mean time all Acts of Hostility might be suspended, he was confident they should conclude a peace: *Caudiac* cheerfully embraced the employment, and obtains the allowance of the four dayes, together with the desired Pass-ports, which he himself was commanded to carry back to the Assembly.

In the mean time every one is very sollicitous to draw his own particular advantage out of this small interval: The Kings party continue their practices in the Province; but with greatest ardour prosecute they the design of *Sauve*, whither, when *Randon* came with the four hundred Souldiers, the disaffected, to exasperate the others, oppress them with quartering, and that they might disgust the people with an apprehension of the Duke's undervaluing of them, quarrel at the person of *Randon*, as a man of too mean quality to command them; and when, according to his Orders he would have mingled his Souldiers with the Inhabitants, to strengthen their Guarders in all quarters, they would by no means suffer it in the Castle, but loudly objected their priviledges against that procedure, as an infringement of them; a prevalent motive to work the populace to any thing; so that upon this ill usage of theirs, *Randon*, unadvisedly told them, that in case they refused him the absolute command of their Town, he had Orders from the Duke of *Rohan* to quit it upon the approach of the King's Army: This inconsiderate expression, so indiscreetly let fall by him, and as nimbly taken up by the disaffected of the Town, had like to have ruined all; for they published strange Coments on it to the people, crying out, that the Duke had sent them men to abandon them, when they should most stand in need of their assistance, and that desired only to possess themselves of their strength, at their cost, to purchase themselves better conditions; so that upon occasion of these jealousies they called a Council, at which they resolved, to die all, rather than admit any stranger into their Castle.

In the mid'st of their deliberations came letters from the Duke of *Rohan* to convoque the Provincial Assembly at *Anduze*, to consult upon some Articles for a general peace; which mollified them so, that they nominated Deputies to send thither: But when the Council was dissolved, the disaffected exclaim against this as a trick of the Duke of *Rohan* to defeat their particular Treaty, and to surprize, and detain their principal Citizens at *Anduze*, until they delivered up their fortresses into his hands: whereupon they thought fit to send away the next day, but one Deputy only to sound the forde, and give them notice how things were carried, that

that accordingly they might be directed in their comportments; and at the same time sent they another privately to the Count d' A-letz, to let him know, that the hopes they had newly received of a General Peace, made them yet defer the performance of what they promised; but yet that they suspected it for an invention only to interrupt the progresse of the Treaty they were already upon; wherefore they beseeched him to clear them in that particular, as much as possibly he could, and to believe, that in case it were not real, that *Sauve* should be at his disposal, of which he might assure his Majesty, and that they had received Letters from the Communalties of *Gange*, *Sunieane*, and *Vigan*, impowring them to treat for them also; and that though *Randon* were in the town, yet could they at pleasure let him into the Castle, of which they were still the Masters.

The King conceiving, upon this newes, that with much facility he might now possesse himself of the *Sevenes*, in all haste sent *Caudiac* word, that he should come back again to him, and let alone the general Assembly where it was: This Messenger found *Caudiac*, and all the Assembly on their way towards *Anduze*, so that much amazed, they returned the same way they came, and *Caudiac*, as little satisfied, goes to *Aletz*. In the meane time *Randon*, and *Falquieres* acquaint the Duke of *Rohan* with the final resolutions of the people of *Sauve*, and the frequent Envoyes passing between them, and the Count *d' Aletz*, and that unlesse seasonable preventions were applyed, the place would be certainly lost: whereupon he put his power upon the rack for a new supply of souldiers for them; and that he might the more effectually proceed in the application of his remedies, he sent to have the wound well searched by his Chaplain *Rossell*, who had been formerly Minister of that Church, and of great authority among them: As soon as he came thither, and had gotten the Common-Council of the Town together, he presented them a true state of their affaires, shewing how near they were obtaining of a general peace, if they preserved the union of the Party, which particular compositions would divide and ruine; after all which their condition would be nothing more exempt from fears or hazard; that to introduce into their Castle, a Garison of a contrary Religion, was not the way to preserve inviolate those liberties they seemed so jealous of; that it was ill done to call those strangers, who were their kinred and neighbours, and had forsaken their own Houses, Wives, and Children, to come to their relief; that to refuse the Generals Orders, and to such persons, half the Guard of their Castle, when as they allow them that of their Walls, and Gates, was a diffidence ill grounded,

ded, and probably of dangerous consequence to the Party, considering the present condition of things; that he very well knew it was publiquely reported, that the Duke of *Rohan*'s forces had not acquitted themselves of their devoir in the Towns lately taken; but that he was as certain that the contrary of it only was true; that at *Privas* the Inhabitants deserted the relief was sent to them; that at *Saint Ambroix* and *Aletz*, they compelled the Garisons to capitulate; and that all the misfortunes that befell those places, flowed from those who either corrupted by the enemy, or perswaded by their own feares, quickly diffused the contagion over all the rest; that they would do well to beware of such plagues, and for the future to yield a greater observance to the General's Orders.

But all these Remonstrances were not sufficient to open the Castle Gates to give admittance to the strangers, which when *Rossel* perceived, he made a Proposition, that the people should nominate a certain number of them, the third of which should be drawn out by lot to be there upon duty every one in his turn, four and twenty houres together. The Common sort approved of this way; but the Consuls, who disliked it, left the Council in distaste; saying, that since they could be no longer trusted, they would discharge themselves of their Offices: But they were called back again; and before the dismission of the Council, was the Guard established. After this *Rossel* visits *Puyredon*, one of the most eminent of the Town, both for Estate, Wisdome, and Courage, and his particular friend, and one that had discovered a great affection to the Duke of *Rohan*, whom he presses so far, that he at length got from him a confession of the whole negotiation, between the Town, and the Count d' *Aletz*; and upon *Rossels* assuring him, that if they separated not themselves from the Party, a General Peace would be soon concluded; in which should be comprised the business of Reprisals (in which he was interessed to the value of twenty thousand Crowns) *Puyredon* also promised him, that, whatever were the success of the Deputy sent to the Count of *Aletz*, he would order things so, that there should be yet nothing altered for foure and twenty houres.

When he had dispatched with these, he found that *Randon*, nothing pleased with the Agreement, threatned to be gone; but when he told him, that he could not be yet besieged for four dayes, that if he would have patience but for two of them only, he should be furnished with all things he could desire, he was then better satisfied; and *Rossel* departed from *Sauve*; and meeting on the way with the Deputy that had been with the Count of
Aletz,

Aletz, he imparted to him the great hopes conceived of a General Peace, to which he gave no other reply than only, *God grant it*; but turning his discourse to the Captain, that convoyed *Rossel*, he told him, that the Duke of *Rohan* had too long abused them by his policies, and that he endeavoured yet to amuse them with hopes of a General Peace, but only to frustrate their Communalty of the advantageous conditions they might receive from a particular Treaty; but that they were now resolv'd to give no further credit to him, knowing that all his talks of a General Peace was nothing but meer delusion, whereupon the Captain took him prisoner, and carried him with him to *Anduze*.

When *Rossel* came back to the Duke of *Rohan*, he gave the Duke an account of his negotiation, telling him, that all his endeavours had no other effect than only somewhat to asswage the tumour, untill he in person should provide a better remedy for it; whereupon he immediately departed thence, and went towards *Sauve*: His arrival there much daunted the disaffected party; but they were now so farre advanced, that they knew not well, how to recede from their engagements: The second Consul fled to the Castle; the Duke sent to command him thence, which summons he durst not disobey: When he was come thence, and the rest of the Council were assembled, the Duke acquainted them with the four dayes liberty he had obtained, for the adjourning of the general Assembly to *Anduze*; that he hoped to procure them such a peace, as should redound to their general welfare, provided, that, renouncing all diffidence and jealousies one of another, they preserved an entire unity among themselves; that he had borne armes these eight years past, upon no other design, but the defence of their Religion and Liberties; for which he had as cleare a zeal, as any of them; but that now he was to know of them, whether they would own him for their General or no, and as such would obey him; whereupon the people crying our, that they would submit to him, he resumed his discourse, telling them that he would then go to the Castle, and place there such of the Inhabitants as he should think fit: The Consuls at first refused to follow him, pretending, that since they were not confided in, they would quit their Offices; neverthelesse when they saw him go up to the Castle, and that all the people flocked after, they stayed not long behind him, who, when he had turned out, the Guard was then in it, made choice of such a number of the Townsmen, as he thought sufficient to keep it, obliging them by Oath to maintain it under the authority of their Consuls, and for the general good of the whole party, against all persons whatsoever; which gave great satisfaction to the people;

and

and when he had left in their Town a thousand men, drawn from *Saint Hippolyte*, *Vigan*, and other places, he returned the same day to *Anduze*.

The news of this came to *Aletz* as soon as *Caudiac*, and so netled the King's Council, that they exclaimed against the Duke of *Rohan* for breach of promise, saying, that the King had not stirred from *Aletz*, but that the Duke had been at *Sauve*, where he had secured, and furnished the Castle, and the Towers, with souldiers; nevertheless they gave him Orders to return with all speed to the Assembly, but told him withall, that the King would not be obliged to any further stay at *Aletz*; *Caudiac*, who clearly saw that all this choler flowed only from the defeat of their design upon *Sauve*, replied, that the Duke had not bound himself by any engagement not to stir from *Anduze*, but not to make any attempt upon the Towns of the adverse Party; and that to provide for his own, could not be interpreted any breach of promise: After this he went to the Assembly, whom he found much perplexed about the Article concerning the demolition of their fortifications; for that, besides the Deputies formerly sent by them to the Assembly, the Towns of *Nismes* and *Usez* had sent others purposely to oppose that Article, and, if it were possible, to draw in those of the *Sevenes* to fortifie them in that opposition.

Whereupon it was thought fit, before they proceeded to any conclusion, that they should have the opinion of the Provincial Assembly of the *Sevenes*, that accordingly they might order their resolutions; But that Assembly would determine nothing in it, without the advice of the Common-Council of the Town of *Anduze*, which they looked upon as a place the most concerned in the subsistance of the new-raised buildings, and fortifications, and most resolute to defend them: The Council reported their opinion to the Provincial, and the Provincial to the general Assembly; the sum of which, was, that considering the absolute necessity that lay upon them, they should choose Commissioners to Treat about a peace, and that the management of the Article concerning the fortifications, should be referred to their discretions.

The Assembly general, unwilling to undergo the whole burthen of the Treaty, associate with them the new extraordinary Deputies of *Nismes* and *Usez*, and a like number of the Provincial Assembly of the *Sevenes*, who altogether resolved to send their Deputies to the King to demand a peace, and to moderate that Article the best they could.

The Deputies haste away to the Court, where after several conferences had, they agreed on many things, but at the proposal of the aforesaid Article, the King's Commissioners would not endure the mention of any mitigation of it; but thereupon sent back the Commissioners, who reported all to the Assembly, to whom they plainly discovered that it was in vain to hope for any qualification of that Article, which seemed to be thrown in as a stumbling block among them; whereupon the Town of *Anduze*, and the Province of the *Sevenes*, being again consulted, they demonstrated the inevitable ruine of their Province, unless a sudden conclusion of a General Peace prevented it; for that otherwise every one was fully resolved to compound for himself apart; and that the loss of their Province would certainly draw after it that of the lower *Languedoc*; that the fire was now at their doors, and that they had rather submit to that Article, than fail of a Peace.

Whereupon after a full debate of the business, it was at length concluded that they should admit of that Article; and thereupon the Deputies were returned fully impowred to Treat, and conclude a peace: Which done, the Duke of *Rohan* desired the Assembly to give their Deputies an express charge, that when they had perfected their Negotiation for the Publick, they should then mind his particular concernments also, which they did.

Thus was the Peace concluded at *Aletz*, the 27th. day of *June*, in the year, 1629. The substance of the principal Articles of which, was as followeth.

1. That a General Pardon be issued out.
2. That the Edict of Nantes, and all other Edicts, Articles and Declarations registred in the Parliament-Rolls be put in force.
3. That their Temples, and Places of Burial be restored to those of the Religion.
4. That all Contributions imposed, during the present, or precedent Broyles, be taken off.
5. That they be also acquitted of all Arrears of Impositions, and Taxes laid by any Governours upon those of the Religion, to exempt the Romanists.
6. That they be restored to all their Goods moveable, and immoveable, notwithstanding any Gifts, or Confiscations.
7. That every one be permitted to re-possess, and re-edifie his own house.
8. That all Judgements, both Civil and Criminal, given by those of the Religion, be confirmed.
9. That the ancient Orders used before the Wars be observed, both concerning the Consulates, and other Political Assemblies of the particular Towns.
10. That they be also discharged of all Accounts, so that the Chamber of Accounts may not demand any review of them.

11. That

11. That all *Courts* of *Justice*, *Offices of Receipt*, and others, be restored again to those places, whence they were transferred, during the late Wars.
12. That the Chamber of Languedoc be re-established at Castres.
13. That the *Assembly of Estates* in Foix be convened at the usual times.
14. That the *Inhabitants* of Pamiez be restored again to their Estates.
15. And that all *Fortifications* be demolished.

 The Deputies Extraordinary of *Nismes* protested against this Peace, Declaring, that if they should accept of it, their Act would be disowned, and themselves killed, when they came home; and at their return, threw the blame of the whole business upon the pretended perfidy of the Duke of *Rohan*, and those of greatest trust about him, by whom they said they had been all sold; and having assembled the chief Officers, both Military and Civil, cause them to oblige themselves by Oath to stand it out to the last, and then sent to the *Sevenes* for some fresh Troops; when they had by this means drawn the Kings Army before the Town, the same persons, who were the Authors of this mutiny, to purchase themselves a reputation at the expence of their Fellow-Citizens, got themselves impowred as Commissioners to Treat for their Town, which derived no other advantage from it, than the spoiling of their Fields and Vineyards; and that which accrued to the Deputies themselves for disposing the Town, to supplicate the King to honour them with his presence.

 The Town of *Vsez* without any hesitation at all, accepted the Peace at first; so did all *Roüergue*, the higher *Languedoc*, and *Foix*; nor was any place suspected to refuse it, but *Montauban*; where the Prince of *Condé* would not cease his plundering, untill the King had sent him a second Order to that purpose; and the Town it self, as the Cardinal marched that way, declared their acceptance of the General Peace.

 This is an account of what passed in this last War, in which the assistance the Town of *Rochelle* had from *England*, served only to consume their provisions, and draw a Famine on the City; and the vain, and illusory hopes with which *Spain*, and *Savoy*, abused the lower *Languedoc*, had like to have proved the ruine of the whole Party.

 God, of his infinite mercy compassionating his poor Churches, hath yet intermitted their sufferings, that by a serious repentance of our faults, and a sincere amendment of our lives, we might at length attract as many benedictions, as our sins have pulled down calamities on them.

The End of the fourth Book.

FINIS.

A TABLE

Of the most REMARKABLE THINGS Contained in this History.

A.

AN Assembly permitted at Chastelraut. pag. 3
Adjourned to Saumure. 6
Du plessis chosen President, which vexed Bouillon. 7
The Assembly send their Deputies to the Court. 10
Their Success. ibid.
Articles signed by Bouillon, Lesdiguieres, Rohan, Sully, Soubize, la Force, and Du plessis. pag. 18
An Assembly of five Provinces convenes at Rochelle, opposed by the Marshal Bouillon. 19
Articles accorded to the Assembly at Rochelle, by their Majesties. 20
Ancre, the Marshal d'An-cre,

The Table

cre, sowes, and foments divisions among the Nobility. pag. 21
An Assembly permitted to be held at Jergeau, removed to Grenoble. 26
Adjourns to Nismes. 31
Removes to Rochelle. 33
Sends Deputies to conclude a Peace. 34
Ancre, his ruine contrived by the Marshal Bouillon. 38
Perswades the Queen to secure the Prince, and others of the Nobility. 39
His house pillaged, and razed by the people. 40
The manner of his death. 42
His Lady with others, arrested at the same time. ib.
An Assembly-General called at Rochelle, the King commands them to dissolve; most of them are inclined to obey, but by the contrivances of la Force, and Favas are disswaded. 56
The Assembly in Languedoc averse to the Election of a General. 67
Great complaints of the Provinces against the Assembly. pag 68
They apply themselves to Chastillon, but are disappointed by Rohan, whom they calumniate to Lesdiguieres. ibid. & 69
Saint Antonin re-inforced by their Neighbours of Montauban, but taken by the King. 77
Saint André de Montbrun makes his way bravely to Montauban. 77
An Assembly called at Lunel by the counsel of Languedoc. 80
Dissolved by Rohan. 83
Articles of the Peace before Montpellier. 88
Violated after the Rendition of the Town. 92, 93, 94, 95
Azil besieged. 106
Bravely defended. 110
An Assembly called at Nismes to ratifie the Act of Acceptance of the Peace. 114
The Duke of Anjou averse to the Marriage with the Princess of Montpensier. 122
The Duke of Anjou marries the Princess Montpensier. 128
Saint Afrique besieged by the Prince of Conde. 173

It

Is stormed, and the Prince repulsed. pag. 174
Aimargues *besieged by Rohan.* 180
Is yielded upon composition. 181
Saint André de Montbrun, *sent to secure Privas his entertainment by the Consuls.* 205
Is made a Prisoner. 208
Saint Ambroix, *the Garrison there forced by the Inhabitants, give up the place.* 210
Aletz *besieged.* 211
Treachery of some of the Officers. 212

B.

Bouillon *ambitious to gain the administration of the publick Affairs.* 2
Designs the ruine of the Duke of Sully. 3
Procures an Assembly to be held at Chastelraut. ibid.
Which he afterwards caused to be adjourned to Saumure. 6
Bouillon *takes a journey to* Sedan, *and for what reasons.* 5, & 6
Attempts to withdraw the Duke of Rohan *from his Father-in-Law, the Duke of* Sully. pag. 8
Berticheres *urges his Restoration to his Governments, is favoured by the Duke of* Sully; *but to arrive at his aims, complies with the Marshal* Bouillon, *and obtains a re-admission to* Aiguemortes. 9 & 10
Bouillon *juggles with the Assembly.* 10
Bullion *sent to the Assembly.* 11
Bouillon *applies himself to the Duke of* Rohan. 13
Bouillon *contrives to out the Duke of* Rohan *of his Government of Saint* John d' Angelis. 14
Bouillon *labours to frustrate the negotiation of the Deputies.* 17
Sollicites the King of England *his success.* 17, & 18
Berticheres *denied entry into* Aiguemortes, *and why.* 19
Bouillon *raises new broyles,* &c. 25
Bouillon *and* Maine, *urge the Prince to make a Peace.* 32
Bearne, *new troubles raised*

sed thereby, du Vaire.

The Lernois *being devested of their priviledges, occasioned the first warre against the Protestants.* 55, 56

Blaccons *made Governour of* Baye. 70

Brison *joyns with the Deputies of the Assembly of five Provinces to calumniate the Duke of* Rohan. 74

Bouillons *overtures to the Duke of* Rohan. 79, 80

Botru *sent Embassadour into* England, *obtains a renvoy of new Embassadours thence.* 114

Brison *refuses to be comprised in the peace* 117

Gives up Pousin *to* Lesdiguieres. 118

Buckingham *arrives with a great Fleet in the Roade of* Rochelle, *and is refused admittance into the Port.* 132

Saint Blancarle *slain in the Isle of* Ree. 135

Bragneau *sent by the Rochelers to buy provisions, furnishes himself, but neglects his opportunity to return to them.* 152

Brison *endeavours to betray* Vivaretz *to the Prince of* Conde. 153

Buckingham *killed at* Portsmouth. 187

C.

The Prince of Conde *upon the instigation of* Bouillon *leaves the Court, with others of the Nobility.* 22

Writes to the Queen, and sollicites the Parliament of Paris, *and the Nobility to joyn with him* ibid.

Concludes a peace upon conditions. 23

Desires a meeting with the Duke of Rohan, *which was assented to.* 23, 24

Writes to the King, Queen Parliament, &c. 28

Upon summons to wait upon the King into Guienne, *changes his pretences.* 29

Sollicits the Assembly at Grenoble *to joyn with him, who sent Deputies to the King at* Tours. 29

Signes the Peace. 35

The Princes *his return to Court opposed by* Bouillon, *and others; he privately makes his peace with the Queen.* 38

Is arested by the Queens order

order. 39

Chinon *seizen on by the Marshal* Souvre. 41

The Prince of Conde *sues to* Luynes *for his liberty.* 45

Chastillon *proposes the recalling of his forces with the Duke of* Rohan, *the Assembly oppose him.* 67

Du Cros, *assassinated in* Montpellier. 70

Chastillon *takes* La Tour, L'Abbe 74

Chauve *a Minister creats with* Rohan *about* Chastillon, *the Dukes answer to him.* 78, 79

Chastillons *restablishment moved in the Assembly at* Lunell, *opposed generally, and particularly by* Dupuy. 80

And by the Deputies of the Sevenes. 81

Chauve *sollicites* Dupuy *concerning* Chastillon. 81

And treaty with Banstillon. 82

The Consulate of Montpellier *contrary to the Articles divided between the Protestants and Papists, by* Valence. 93

Castres *bravely preserved by the Duchesse of* Rohan.

han. 102, 103

Chaligny *miraculously preserved* 109

The Princesse of Conde *ambitious to marry her daughter to the Duke of* Anjou. 123

Chalais *kills de* Lude *in a duel, the consequence of it.* ibid.

Embraces the interests of the Duke of Anjou. ibid.

*The Chancellour's seale taken from him, for not daring to own his Counsel for the commitment of the Marshal d'*Ornono. 125

Chalais *leaves the Duke of* Anjou, *and becomes a servant to the Cardinal.* 127

He deserts him again, and is sent Prisoner to Nantes. 127

Is tried, condemned, and executed. 128

The Duchesse of Chevreuse *flies into* Lorraine. 128

Chevrilles *chosen Governour in* Brisons *place.* 159

Chaumerarguo *taken by* Chevrilles. 161

Clausel *proposes to* Rohan *relief from* Spaine: *the effect of it.* 178, 179

Q 3 Ca-

The Table.

Canisson *bravely defended.* 203

Yeilded upon composition. 204

Chevrilles *treachery concerning* Privas. 206, 207

D.

Dupuy *charged by the Duke of* Rohan, *to see that nothing were concluded concerning* Chastillon, *unlesse he would consent to give up* Aigue-morts. 79

Which he duly observed. 80

Divisions among the Protestant party occasion the losse of many towns. 84

Divisions in Rochelle. 100

Deputies General, viz. Galerande *and* Bazin, *chosen by the command of the King.* 102

The Earle of Denbigh *sent with a Fleet to the reliefe of* Rochelle 171

Divisions in Castry *between* Chavagnac *and St.* Germie. 177, 191, 192

The issue of them. 196

E.

Espernon *wrought to attempt the Queens deliverance, which he effects.* 47, 48

Espernon *ravages the Countrey about* Montauban 107

Embassadors *mediate a peace between the King and his Subjects.* 113

The English Embassadors are caution for the observation of the Peace. 115

Forraign Embassadours signe the League at Paris. 115

Are discontented at the Peace afterwards signed with Spain. ibid.

English *Secretary his Speech to the* Rochellers. 132, 133

With their Reply. ibid.

The English descent into the Isle of Ree, *the issue of it.* 134, &c.

The English draw off from the Isle of Re. 149

Are defeated in their attempt upon the Fort. 150

And in their retreat to their ships. 151

F.

France, *the state of* France *after the death of* Henry *the Great.* p. 1

La Ferte *servant to the Duke of* Rohan, *committed to the* Bastille, *for endeavouring to serve the Queen*

The Table.

Queen. 47
La Force *left by Rohan in Guienne.* 58
La Force *yields up St. Foy.* 76
France *juggles with the Forraign Embassadours* 155
Fargis *Embassadour in Spain, bears the blame of the peace made with Spain.* 121
Florac *corrupted by de Portes, is taken by Montredon.* 153
Faucon *corrupts his own Officers,* 159

G.
The Duke of Guise *follicited to new engagements by the Marshal Bouillon, but in vain.* 40
Gignac *victualled by Bertichees.* 70
Galand *an enemy to the Duke of* Rohan. 119

H.
Hauvre de Grace *in Normandy bought by the Cardinal* de Richelieu. 128

I.
St. John d' Angely, *attempted, but in vain; reinforced by* Rohan. 57
St. John de Breuill *taken by* Rohan. 191

K.
The King of England *perswades* Bouillon *and* Rohan *to a reconciliation.* 18
The King and Queen meet *at* Tours. 49
The King *levies an Army against the Queen, marches into* Normandy, *thence to* Angers, *and defeats the Queens Forces at* Pont de Ce. 52. 53
The King *besieges* Monheur *and takes it upon composition,* 67
The King *carried from* Paris *to* Orleans, *and thence to* Nantes, *by those who desired a continuance of the war.* 76
The King *descends into the lower* Languedoc. 79
The King *forwards the marriage of the Duke of* Anjou. 123
The King of England *sends a Gentleman to the Duke of* Rohan, *his Message, the Dukes reply.* 130
The King of England *goes in person to* Portsmouth *to expedite the relief for* Rochelle. 187
The French Kings *expedition to* Susa. 200
The peace being made, *sends his*

Q 4

his forces into Languedoc. 201
Longueville possesses himself of the Town and Castle of Peronne. 38, 39
Luynes the Kings favourite. 38, 41. 42
Mangott and Bouillon sent to treat with the Duke of Longueville. 39
Luynes makes Deagent and Modene his chief Councellors, and imposes a Confessor on the King. 44
Confines Mangot to his house: sends the Bishop of Lucon to Avignon, and Barbin to the Bastille. ib.
Calls an Assembly of Notables, at Rouen, and vests himself in the Government of Normandy. 45
Marries the daughter of the Duke of Montbazon. ibid.
Lucon by his brother in law sollicites his return from Avignon, whither he was banished, promising to incline the Queen to such a peace as the King should desire. 49
Luynes seek to ruine the Duke of Rohan. 51
Releases the Prince. ibid.
Lynes and his brothers made Dukes, and Peeres of France, ingrosse all Offices. 52
Luynes sends to sound the inclinations of the Duke of Rohan, and Saubize. 57
Luynes invites the Duke of Rohan to an interview, which he assents to. 64
They meet. ibid. and 65
But to no purpose. 66
Luynes at the siege of Monheur dieth of sickness. 67
Lesdiguieres enters Vivaretz. 70
Besieges and batters Pousin. Blaccons gets in, & defends it bravely: by the Duke of Rohan's mediation is yielded upon conditions 70
Lesdiguieres invites Rohan to a personal Treaty. 71
Languedoc much disheartned at the Kings approaches, sollicites the Duke to come to them; the like sollicitations receives he almost from all places. 77
Lesdiguieres made Constable of France, invites Rohan to an interview, which he assents to. 86
Languedoc jealous of the Duke of Rohan. 94
Lediguires his death, and character.

The Table.

character. 118
Lusignan *beats up* Lescures *quarters in* Trillet. 110
Lynsey *made Admiral of the Fleet designed for the relief of* Rochelle. 187
Arrives in the Rode of Rochelle. 188

M.

Montauban *declares for the Duke of* Rohan. 31
Montigny *made Marshall of* France, *and Governour of* Berry *is sent to his Command.* 41
Montauban *fortified by* Rohan. 59
Besieged by the King. 61
Bravely relieved by Beaufort. 62, 63
The siege raised by the King. 66
Montmorency *takes several places in* Languedoc. 70
Montlaur *taken by the Duke of* Rohan. 71
Montauban *desires a Governour,* St. Andre de Montbrun *is sent, &c.* 77
Malauze *fetches off the Garrison from* Realmont. 85
Montpellier *besieged by the King.* 86
Marmeyrac *secures* Aletz *for the Duke of* Rohan. 111

Montague *sent to the Duke of* Rohan. 131
Montague *sends an express to* Rohan. 104
The Magistrates of Mazeres *refusing to admit the Duke of* Rohan *into their town, he is let in by the populacy.* 146
Malauze, *formerly a friend, now opposes the Duke.* 154
Montpellier *attempted, but the design is betrayed.* 156, &c.
Montmorency, *and the Prince of* Conde *joyne their Forces, take* Damiers. 164
Maugis *Governour of* Realmont *betrayes it to the Prince of* Conde. 164
St. Michel *made Governour of* Montauban. 166
Suppresses a dangerous mutiny there. ibid.
Mervies *besieged, the difficulties the Duke meets with there.* 169
St. Michel *jealous of* Chastillon *Governour of* Causade, *surprizes him in his Garrison.* 184
Takes several Garrisons about Montauban. 185
Mazaribal *upon misinformation opposes* Roussiliere

in

The Table.

in his Command, in Sa-
verdune. 102

N.

A sedition raised in Nismes, by Brison. 74

Nismes *declares against the Government of* Brison, *and desires to live under the Command of their own Consuls, untill they had more occasion for a Governour.* 75

Nismes, *and* Bezieres *endeavour to alienate the affections of the* Sevenes *from* Rohan, *but in vain.* 101

Nismes *declares for the Duke of* Rohan. 111

New divisions there occasioned by Montbrun, *and his brothers.* 113

Nismes *protests against the peace concluded at* Aletz. 224

O.

Oleron *taken by the Duke of* Soubize. 76. 98

Oleron *poorly yielded.* 110

Ornano *courted by the Queen, and those that opposed her, about the marriage with the Princess of* Montpensier. 122

Ornano *secured.* 124

Ornano *dies of the stone.*

P.

Propositions sent from Du Plessis, *to* Bouillon *to be treated on in the Assembly at* Chastelraut. 4

Du Plessis *leaves the Assembly of the five Provinces of* Rochelle, *and draws with him the Province of* Anjou. 19

The Parliament of Paris *by Declaration invite the Prince, and Peers to joyn with them, and present very bold Remonstrances to the King himself.* 26, 27

Pardaillan's *treachery prevented by his two sons.* 66

He is afterwards slain in an Inne. ibid.

Puzieux *the Kings favourite, his character.* 91

Puzieux *opposes* Rohan. 94

Puzieux *disgraced.* 96

Le Parc d' Archiat *makes honourable conditions for his men in the Isle of* Re. 110

Pousin *taken by* Brison. 113

The Marques de Portes *seeks by oppressing them, to excite the people to new commotions.* 118

Pamiers *taken by the Duke of* Rohan. 147, 148

The Protestants barbarously used by the Duke of Ventadour,

tadour, *and others.* 158
Pousin *taken by the Duke of* Rohan. 161
Poianne *suborned by Richelieu to kill* Soubize, *is discovered, and taken.* 189
Privas *besieged.* 206, 207
A general peace concluded at Alezt. 223

Q.

The Queen *changes the Officers of State, and raises several Armies.* 41
The Queens *Guards taken from her.* 42
She is removed to Blois, *where she is closely guarded.* 44
The Queen *meets the King at* Tours, *has* Anjou, *with the Castles of* Angiers Pont de Ce, *and* Chinon *given to her.* 49
The Queen *defeated at* Pont de Ce. 53
The Queen Mother *very desirous to consummate the marriage between the* Duke d' Anjou *and the* Princess Montpensier, *is opposed by many, and why.* 122

R.

Rohan, *the* Duke *of* Rohan *being in* Britany, *is informed of the contrivances to out him of* St. John d' Angelis, *sends thither* Haulte Fontain, *whom immediatly he follows.* pag. 14
Returns from St. John *to the Court, leaving* Haulte Fontain *his Deputy, in* St. John. 15
Returns thence again to St. John. ibid.
Is undermined at Court by Bouillon, *and proposals made of besieging him.* 16
The Issue of that Affair. 17, &c.
Rohan *Courted by the Prince to joyn with him; sends* Haulte Fontain *to observe his actions, and writes to the Queen.* 23
Rohan *at the request of the Nobility, and Governors of the Religion, engages to oppose the Marriages with* Spain. 30
Is sollicited by the Queen to joyn with her. 31
Engages the Assembly, *and*

The Table.

and Body of the Protestants with him. ibid.
Take Lectour, and force the Castle. ibid.
Rohan obtains the Government of Poictou. 37
Applies himself to th Queen. ibid.
Rohan gets leave to visit the Queen, and retires into Piedmont. 43
Rohan seeks to reconcile Luines to the Queen, his reasons to move him to it 45
Perswades the Queen to make her Peace with the King, which she did. 49
Rohan in opposition to Luines, adheres to the Queen, perswades her to remove to Bourdeaux, which she refused. 51
Retz, the Duke of Retz, revolts from the Queen. 53
Rohan, advertized of great losses he had received, marches into the lower Languedoc. 59
Cardinal de Retz, and Schomberg, usurp the management of the State Affairs. 67
Rohan chosen General. ib.

Rohan falls sick at Montpelier. 70
Rohan and Lesdiguieres advertise the Assembly General of the Treaty agreed on between them. 71
Rohan returns to his Army in Languedoc, his actions there. 72, 73
Rohan besiegs, and takes St. Georges in sight of the Duke of Montmorency. ibid.
Rohan forbids the Assembly of the five Provinces to meet at Nismes, and defeats the purposes of Brison. 74
Rohan prevents the design of some discontents at Montpellier. 83
Reasons which moved the Duke of Rohan to conclude a Peace at Montpellier. 87
Rochelle sends Deputies to the King. 92
Rohan performs the Articles of his part. 92, 93
Is made a Prisoner by Valencé, enlarged by the King. ibid.
Richlieu the Kings Favourite, 95. Continues the Treaties begun with Forrain

The Table.

raign States. 97
Rochellers apply themselves to Rohan and Soubize. ib.
Rohan calls an Assembly of the Sevenes at Anduze. 101. Fails of his Levies. 102
Rohan marches towards Realmont. 103
The Dutchess of Rohan appoints a Rendez-vous at Brassac. 104
Rochellers indiscreetly refuse the Peace offered them. 107
The Dutchess of Rohan, her demeanour towards Richlieu, and the English Embassadours. 115
Designes against Rohan, which he frustrates. 118, 119, 120
Richlieu promotes the marriage with Madam de Montpensier. 123
Richlieu understands the contrivances of the Duke of Savoy, and others against him. 125
Endeavours to out Vendosme of his Government of Britany. 125, 126
Rohan's Mother and Sister flie from Paris to Rochelle. 132. his policy to advantage himself by the Letters from Rochelle. 135, 136, 137
Isle of Ré described. 138, 139
Rohan publishes his Declarations. ibid.
Rohan sentenced by the Parliament of Tholouse. 140
Gets into Millaud. 141. obtaines a victory over Montmorency. 145
Ré re-inforced by the King of France. 149, 150
Rohan dismantles veral small Garrisons. 159. and engages the people not to listen to any particular Treaties. 160. and then proceeds with his Army. ibid.
Rohan's care to preserve the Countrey about Nismes. 175. Ravages all the Countrey up to the Wall of Beaucaire. 176. meets and takes a good booty of Salt. ibid.
Rohan besieges Creseil. 179
Storms it, and is repulsed. ibid.
Rises at the approach of Montmorency. 180
Rohan puts a party into Galla.

The Table.

Gallargues. 181. *Who are taken, and put to death.* 183. *He in revenge sits down before* Monts, *takes it, and hangs most of the Prisoners.* ibid. & 184
Rochelle *taken,* 190. *The influence it had on the Reformed Party.* 191
Rohan *takes* St. Amant. 193. *Defeats two Negotiations for a particular Peace.* 194, 195. *Convenes a General Assembly at* Nismes. 196
Rohan *is sollicited on all hands for recruits.* 216. *Resolves upon a General Peace.* 217

S

Sully, *the Duke of* Sully, *his ruine endeavoured by some of the Grandees, and why, together with the means they used to deprive him of his Offices.* 2
Sully *urging the Assembly to interess themselves in his cause, is opposed by* Bouillon. 8
The Assembly declare for him. 9
States General convene at Paris. 25

Soubize *makes his Levies in* Poictou *and* Xaintonge. 31
Sully *perswades the Assembly to a Peace.* 34
Sully *upon the mutiny against the Marshal* d'Ancre, *labours a composure.* 40
Savoy, *the Duke of* Savoy's *success in* Alexandria. 43, 44
Saumure *taken from* du Plessis. 57
Soubize *his attempt on* Blavet, *with his success in it.* 97, 98
Soubize *disowned by several Towns.* ibid
Seven Souldiers of Foix, *their generous Action.* 105
Soubize *defeats* Manti, *and the Admiral of* Holland. 107. *The effect of the victory gained by* Soubize. ibid.
Soubize, *by the folly of the* Rochellers, *and Treachery of some of his Officers, worsted in the Isle of* Ré. 108, 109
Soubize *sails for* England. 109, 110
The Duke of Savoy *seeks the ruine of* Richelieu, *and by what*

The Table.

what means. 124
The Count of Soissons *flies into* Italy. 129
Scaglia *Embassadour from the Duke of* Savoy *into* England, *endeavours the ruine of* Richelieu. 129
Soubize *by the help of his Mother gets into* Rochelle, *together with the English Secretary, his Speech to the* Rochellers. 132,133
Soubize *proclaimed Traytour.* 140
Saverdun *taken by* Rohan. 146,147
The Count of Soissons *hinders the conjunction of the Protestants in* Dauphine *with the Duke.* 162
Sauve *treats with the Count of* Ale z. 213, 214. *Mutinies against* Randon. 218 Rohan *goes thither in person.* 221.

T

Toiras *made governour of* Fort-Lewis. p. 97.
Themines *brings an Army into* Lauraguais *and* Albigeois. 101
Themines *falling upon* Lusignin's *quarters, is bravely repulsed.* 103
Themines *made Governour of* Britany. 128

V

Vendosme, *the Duke of* Vendosme's *escapes into* Britany. 22
Vendosme *deserted by the Prince.* 24
Is forced to submit to the Assembly of the Estates of Britany. 25
Vieuville *the King's Favourite.* 96. *disgraced, and sent to* Ambois. ib.
Vigan *taken by* Rohan. 101
Valence *bravely opposed by S.* Blancart. 102
Vendosme, *and his brother sent Prisoners to* Amboise 126
Valette *refuses to receive the Duke of* Anjou's *party until his fathers pleasure were known.* 127
Vendosme *and his brother sent to the* Bois de Vincennes. 128
Vendosme *ousted of his government of* Britany. *ibid.*
Vicenobre *taken by the Duke of* Rohan. 175
Vieres *sent by the Bishop of* Mande, *to delude* Montauban. 197

W

The grounds of the second Warre. 92, 93, 95

FINIS.

Faults escaped in the Printing.

In the *Memoires*.

Page 3. l. 39. r. Amelioration of, &c. p. 16. l. 41. for determinate, r. terminate. p. 22. l. 18. for not, adde, r. adde *ibid.* for retaining, r. retiring. p. 27. l. 9 for vendible, r. venal. p. 28. l. 40. r. practices. p. 41. l. 6, and 7. r. drawn the Duke of *Guise* and his brothers to her party. p. 42. l. 31. for *Lucon*, r. *Luçon*. p. 43. l. 25. r. first sight. p. 46. l. 41. r. in regard of, &c. p. 49. l. 12. r. suit with. p. 49. l. 8. r. with *Bethun*. p. 52. l. 34. r. whose marriage. p. 71. l. 3. r. attaque. p. 76. l. 19. r. *Poictou*. p. 87. l. 20. r. importunate. p. 93. l. 31. r. razing. p. 114. l. 4. r. to submit to them. p. 115. l. 4. r. she. p. 125. l. 10. r. too great. p. 127. l. 42. for who, r. whilst. p. 139. l. 1. r. built. p. 139. l. ult. for securities, r. severities. p. 156. l. 23. r. razing. p. 157. l. 15. for called, r. culled. p. 161. l. 25. for removed. r. relieved. p. 191. l. 42. r. Irremediable. p. 212. l. 13. r. undertook. p. 213. l. 16. r. protract the Cap—— p. 214. l. 32. for had, r. having. ibid. l. 26. r. Irremiable.

In the *Politick Discourses*.

Page 1. line 10. read effected. p. 15. l. 30. r. Partage. p. 15. l. 38. for impioyed, r. obliged. p. 22. l. 34. for perish, r. persist. p. 25. l. 14. r. never served. p. 28. l. 4. r. heretofore. p. 40. l. 32. for ad. r. omitted. p. 41. l. 12. for use, r. us. p. 60. l. 5. for descry, r. decry. p. 61. l. 33. for ports, r. posts. p. 53. l. 9. for ravished, r. ravaged. p. 69. l. 8. for satisfaction, r. vindication.

DIVERS POLITIQUE Discourses Of the DUKE of ROHAN;

Made at several times upon several Occasions.

Written originally in *FRENCH*; and now render'd into *ENGLISH*.

By G. B. Esq;

LONDON,

Printed by *Thomas Ratcliffe*, for *G. Bedell* and *T. Collins*, at the middle Temple Gate in *Fleetstreet*. 1660.

A TABLE of the HEADS of each DISCOURSE.

I.

Upon the death of Henry the Great. Page 1

II.

At the Assembly of Saumure. p. 6

III.

Upon the State of France, during the persecutions at St. John. p. 11

IV.

Upon the Voyage of the King in July, 1615. p. 21

V.

Upon the Government of the Queen-Mother, made in the year, 1617. p. 25

VI.

VI.

A free Discourse upon the present times, 1617. p. 30

VII.

Upon the occasion of the Divisions in Holland, *made in the year*, 1618. p. 37

VIII.

Reasons of the Peace made before Montpellier, *in the year*, 1622. p. 40

IX.

The Duke of Rohan's *Apology concerning the late Troubles in* France *about Religion.* p. 47

X.

Monsieur the Prince *his Letter to the Duke of* Rohan. p. 56

XI.

The Duke of Rohan's *Answer to the* Prince. p. 58

XII.

The Duke of Rohan's *Manifesto, concerning the late Occurrences in the Country of the* Grisons, *and the* Valteline. p. 60

XIII.

A Letter to Monsieur the Prince *of* Condé. p. 53

DIVERS

DIVERS
Politique DISCOURSES
OF THE
DUKE of ROHAN,
Made at several Times upon several
OCCASIONS.

DISCOURSE I.
Upon the Death of Henry *the Great.*

IF I had ever cause to mix my own, with the general groanes of *France*, it was at the deplorable Fate of *Henry* the Great, full of sad and dismal Consequences to us, but happy, as to his own particular: For though he lived inviron'd with difficulties, yet did he so surmount them all, that in the mid'st of all, he still remained a Conqueror, always injoyed himself, and at length beheld the ruine of his enemies; some affected by his,

B others

others by their own hands, and the rest crying out for help. Thus did their total destruction give him the opportunity to recollect the shattered pieces of this broken State, and by his Wisdom and Prowess, to cement and render it more strong and glorious than ever. After his coming to the Crown, he spent eight years in reducing it to his obedience, which, though full of thorny Traverses, may not improperly be called *the happiest of his life*; every addition to his reputation, proving a firm Bulwark to his State. The true happiness of a magnanimous Prince consists not in the long possession of a great Empire, which many times serves only to plunge him in Luxury; but, from a low and desperate condition to raise and establish his own Throne, enlarge his Territories, and satisfie the nobler Appetite of his Soul and Courage, rather than the sensual suggestions of his body. Our sleeps are many times more uneasie in our beds, than in the field; nor is any repose so sweet, as that which is the purchase of danger. This was the felicity of our late King of immortal memory, who by his indefatigable cares and industry, snatched Peace, even out of the midst of perils, and to compleat his happiness, lived twelve years in a glorious possession of it, still augmenting, strengthning and embellishing his Estate, so that he became no less the dread, then wonder of his Neighbours, and Arbitrator of all Christendome: But in the height of all this greatness, without any apprehension either of fear or grief, yielded to a fate, common to many great persons: But, O Death! more worthy a Tyrant, then so sweet a Prince: Unhappy Death! though not in respect of him, yet of his people, whom he hath left to the tuition of an Infant, of nine years old; surrounded with potent Adversaries abroad, full of *Boutefeus* within, and distracted by the several Interests of the Princes and Religion. Let us justly then bewail the greatest King the world ever knew, who was good to all, injurious to no man; whose death hath bereaved *France* of Him, who made her terrible to her neighbours, preserved her in Peace, and Unity within her self, and enriched her with all sorts of good. But from this happy condition are we fallen under the Reign of an Infant, and exposed to the Conduct of a Princess, little versed in Affaires, and opposed by the Grandees of the Kingdome, ambitious to advance themselves, during the weakness of her Government, in which, private designes suppress the Good and publique interests. The Treasures are profused, the Arsenals embezilled, and all at the disposition of Favourites.

The

The comparison of the present, with our former condition, will sufficiently discover the just cause we have to deplore our Prince: so insensible are we of our good, that we never apprehend it, but by its want and absence. *France*, in His life time flourished with such prosperity, as twelve hundred years before could never parallel. His death hath fatally enhaunsed the price of our Repose: Whil'st he lived, the only awe of Him restrained the mischievous; whom now His death hath encouraged in their wickedness, leaving them at liberty to pursue with a full career their pernicious Machinations. The still fresh memory of his Name, retains them yet in some respect, but every succeeding day that carries us to a further distance from Him, are so many advances in the way to disobedience and rebellion. Those who have seen the Reign of *Charles* the ninth, with that deluge of evils that afterwards overwhelmed all *France*, will make an easie conjecture of her present danger. *Charles* the ninth came to the Crown when he was two years older than our present King, governed by the Queen his mother, a wise and politique Princess, and yet what sad effects attended his Reign? The same Factions, the same Interests, and Pretences are yet in being, though not in the same vigour: For our King *Henry* weakened them, yet have they now opportunity to recruite again. The power of our enemies abroad is nothing lessened, nor their Will to hurt us any thing abated. Moreover, the defects in the management of precedent Actions, are so many instructions, and profitable precepts for this present age, to direct them in the Government of theirs: Then were we Novices in the Art of sowing the seeds of discord, in which every one is become a Master. The ambitious humours of men are rather encreased, than diminished. These considerations are enough to make us sensible of the danger of the State, and of our own loss. 'Tis neither hopes of my own particular advancement, nor fear of the ruine of the Reformed Party, that moves my tears: I too well knew how jealous the King was of persons of my Quality and Religion, and am very sensible, that we were never more considerable, than at present: For that we have now no Princes of the blood amongst us, is an addition to our strength; for when we had them, they were not ours, but we were their support, and did their business at our costs. *France* was then divided by the houses of *Bourbon* and *Lorain*, but the pretence was taken from the difference of Religion; but now since both the one, and the

B 2   other

other profess the *Romish* Faith; the former colour is gone, but the Division of the *Popish* party leaves us at liberty to adhere to which party we please: I deplore in the loss of our invincible King, that of *France* in general: I bewail his Person, and regret the glorious opportunity we have lost; and from the bottom of my heart, grieve at the manner of his end: Our own experience will soon inform us, how just a Subject he is for our Tears: The people murmure already, and seem to prophesie their future calamities: The Townes are guarded, as if they expected a Siege: The Nobility seek their safety amongst the most eminent of their own Order; whose factions give them large apprehensions of danger, but not the least appearance of any security. In short, he can be no true *French* man, whom the loss of this good Genius of *France* doth not even kill with Grief: Together with his person, I deplore his Courtesie and Affability, his sweet and obliging Conversation: The Honour he did me, the admittance he vouchsafed me, even to his most private recesses, oblige me not only to lament him, but even not to love my self in those places, where the sight of my good Prince formerly afforded me such infinite happiness: I regret the most noble and heroick enterprize was ever yet heard of. It is not credible that the Equipage of thirty thousand foot, six thousand horse, a Train of Artillery of sixty Gunnes, and Ammunition for sixty thousand shot, with all other furniture compleat, besides the Army then in *Dauphine*, and the Recruites sent to the Frontier Townes, should be designed for the siege of *Julliers*, which was since attempted with eight thousand foot, and a thousand horse: An opportunity I shall never meet again, at least under the conduct of so great a Captain, and with so ardent a desire to serve and learn the use of Armes under his direction: An Army, such as no preceding King of *France* could ever raise; which yet, had there been occasion, he could have kept on foot ten years, without the least oppression or injury to his People. Have I not then just cause to lament the loss of the only opportunity I ever had, to shew my Zeal, Courage and Fidelity to my King? Seriously, each thought of it breaks my heart: One Push of Pike given in his presence, had been a greater satisfaction to me, than to win a Battle now. Much more should I value the least praise from him, in that Art, of which he was the greatest Master of his time, then the Elogie of all other Captaines now alive. I grieve at the manner of his deplorable death:

A

A Prince composed of Sweetness and Clemency, which never did condemn an Innocent to death; whose very victories were unbloody, contenting himself only to reclaim his enemies to their obedience, whom he hath afterwards cherished as his Friends, and laden them with his favours. A Prince slow to anger, and most prone to pardon, without gall or any revengefull thought, beloved and feared. And yet in the mid'st of his chief City, which he had made the Miracle of the world, attended by two hundred Gentlemen, in his Coach full of Princes and Lords, he received a fatal stab with a knife, by a man, not animated by any desire of Revenge for any disgust received, nor excited by any of his Neighbours, fearfull or emulous of his generous Designes, but instigated only by the Writings and Sermons of the *Jesuites*, who after all this, blush not to call themselves *French men*, and can behold this dismall spectacle without inflicting on themselves the punishment due to that execrable Doctrine, taught by them, which promises Paradise to the *Assassinates* of Kings: Who, that ever lived under this most August Prince, as I have done, can take pleasure in these present times? I will now therefore divide my life into two parts, and call that part of it I have already past, *Happy*, since it was imployed in the service of *Henry* the Great; and that which I have yet to come *unfortunate*, and spend it in Lamentations, Teares, Sighs and Complaints: And out of the honour which I owe his Memory, I will devote the Remainder of my dayes (the Kingdome of God being preserved intire) to the service of *France*, because it was his Kingdome; to the King, because he is his Sonne, and to the Queen, because she was once his dear Companion and Spouse.

B 3   DISCOURSE

Discourse II.

At the Assembly at Saumure.

My Lords and Gentlemen,

ALthough this be not the first Assembly, that hath been held upon the same occasion, yet may it prove the source from whence will flow much good or evill to the Reformed Churches in this Kingdom. We are now happened on a *Cartefour*, where many wayes meet ; but there is only one that leads to our safety. The life of *Henry* the Great was our preservation; which we must now expect from our own vertue. God hath taken him from us, that we might no longer place our confidence in him, whom he had given to us and all Christendome, for theirs and ours Repose : He hath deprived us of him, as unworthy the continuance of that Mercy; or else to become himself our Raiser and Defence, even when all humane helps faile us ; provided that our intentions be good and holy. We must therefore come to this Assembly with a most ardent zeal to preserve the Peace of this Estate, and especially of the Church, and lay aside all Animosities, Passion and particular Interests; that with more Freedome and Alacrity, we may set about his work, and consequently expect a blessing on our actions. What greater glory can we be ambitious of, than every man in his place, to be an instrument to support, confirm and augment his declining, weak, and almost desolated Church? to which every one ought to contribute his assistance, according to the Talent God hath lent him. We have only the use, not property of any thing in this world, where we are only Strangers and Passengers, and not to fix our abode : This mortal is not to be prolonged but in order to an eternal Life : Let us therefore be as carefull in the service of our God, as the wicked are in that of the Devil. Let us imitate them, not in their wickedness, but in pursuing with

an

an equal zeal the Kingdome of Christ, as they do that of Sathan. Let there be only this difference seen between us, that we endeavour our preservation by just and lawfull wayes, while the others use all manner of fraude and treachery to undermine and ruine us. It behoves us to beware of them, it being of great concernment to us.

We must therefore fix upon three particulars, as the most essential, and on which all our other concernments depend. The first is Unity among our selves. The second, Our Admission to all manner of Offices. The third and last, to provide for our places of security. Both Reason and Examples have ever taught us, that Concord is the Cement and Stay of all States and Societies, as Discord is the dissipation and overthrow. Let us be therefore more exact in the practice of this Maxime than formerly, it being the very foundation of our whole Structure. And therefore have I begun with this proposition, as being of the greatest Importance, and most difficult Execution, though it depend entirely upon our own Wills. What Encouragement will it be to our Enemies; to refuse us that, which is in their power, when our own Divisions make so palpable a discovery of our weakness? What advantage shall we give them to break in upon us, when our own Dissentions open them the Gates? And yet this hath been our constant practice hitherto. Is it not strange, that Reason, the only distinction between us and beasts, and which alone gives us light to discern between good and evil, should so mislead us to the preferring the riches of the world, before the advancing of the Kingdome of God: the revenging of our own, before his Quarrel: the vanity of being instruments of mischief to our nearest Relations, before our own salvation? In short, that Avarice, Revenge and Ambition should usurp the possession of our souls, and exclude those vertues whose proper seat they are. Let us make our humble applications to God, that he would please to redress these our failings, and to assist us with his Grace, that our words and promises, which have been hitherto fraudulent and treacherous, may for the future, prove infallible pledges of our Fidelity. Let the care then of this Assembly extend to all persons; Let it receive the addresses of all particulars, and inquire also into the condition of those whose modesty will not give them leave to be importunate. Let it impartially do Justice according to the merits of their causes, that so they may have no cause to seek their Protection elsewhere. In this as the strength of our bonds, for if we are remiss in this point, all will abandon us, and submit themselves to new Protectors. Let us also make an order obliging all the Provinces of this Kingdome to submit and adhere to the resolutions of the Assembly: And to this end we must establish a Council, in which all may bear a part: By this means shall we defeat the hopes of such as pretend to the Protection of the Churches who thrust themselves in amongst us, only to purchase their own ends at our cost. And let us hold for an undoubted Maxime, that, *None pretends to such a Power, but meerly to cheat all Parties.* We can acknowledge no other Protector then our King, since he is our Soveraign, and we his Subjects, who never yet held any correspondence with the enemies of the State, but, notwithstanding all Massacres and tormenting flames, have faithfully served our Prince when he hath commanded us, and therefore with good reason may we demand, and insist upon an admission to all Offices and Dignities under him. It were a most high cruelty, that we who are members of the State, *French*-men born, should be excluded from that which even strangers enjoy, and that by the sollicitation of those who teach, that, *A mortal man can, when he pleases, absolve Subjects from their Oath of Allegiance*, and condemn our Religion for that; on the contrary, it injoynes Obedience to our Princes, though Infidels. It is not to be doubted, but that when such Persons have the Kings ear, we shall meet many difficulties in this Affair: But our Resolution and Unity must surmount them; for unless we obtain it, we cannot live with honour. But such is our baseness, that instead of assisting, we bend all our studies to supplant one another, and are more envious at the advancement of our brethren than our enemies. Hence comes it, that we are so ill treated as we are: Let us all therefore see where we have failed in this particular, and resolve upon such a constancy as may purchase us the satisfaction we justly aim at, else shall we our selves give others cause to believe us guilty of Treason: To us will be imputed all the Murthers the *Jesuites* have committed on our Kings, if in their steed we bear the punishment due to them. But these considerations will be of no validity, unless we look better after our cautionary Towns then heretofore: By a fair and gentle complyance to reclaim our enemies from their malicious designes, is a good way; but to deprive them of all means, to effect them, is a surer: Both the one and the other is feisible, provided

at the Assembly at Saumure.

we conjoyne them; for unless we compass the latter, the former will be of small force. Our amity will be more sought after; when freed from the fear of our enemies, we shall be in a capacity to relieve our friends: To this end we must resolutely insist upon the Article concerning our places of Security, whose continuation is of greater concernment to us now then ever: If the late King conceived it just, how much more profitable is it now for the State during the Minority and Nonage of this, to restrain the extravagant liberty our enemies might take, even in contempt of the Royal Authority it self to rekindle that fire, and open again that issue of blood, which our great *Henry* by his indefatigable pains, and with the loss of his own, hath happily quenched and stopped. The Minority of *Charles* the ninth, ought to be an example to warn all good people, to labour to avoid the like mischiefs; but the same example also animates all *Boutefeus* and Disturbers of the State to make use of their time, and the present opportunity, to execute their malicious intentions against it: We have an Interest in it, as being a part of it, if not the greatest, yet at least the best, and for whose sake, God in Mercy preserves the rest.

And now in order to those places of security, we must first endeavour the regaining those we have lost, or others in their room; that so we may cut off our enemies hopes of diminishing their number for the future: Next we must obtain a confirmation of them for a certain number of years, untill all causes of jealousies be removed, and to remedy all abuses committed in the government of them. But how shall we resolve on these things, or with what face can we demand that, which depends upon the Wills of others, when our own avarice tempts us to convert the Money designed for the preservation of the publique to our own private use, when the garrisons from whence we expect our safety, are miraculously. transubstantiated into Lands and Moveables? Certainly this is a most deplorable condition, and so great is our Lethargie, that the examples and inconveniences of such miscarriages can not yet awaken us. We are just like little Children, who think themselves safe when they have shut their eyes, and are never sensible of their Errours, till made so by the punishment. In such a case Repentance avails neither the Publique, nor particular Interests.

I know these things, though Just will meet with much opposition: They will check our Presumption for asking more then we enjoyed in the late Kings Reign, and tell us, that for the preservation of the Peace, in the Infancy of

this

this, we ought to content our selves with the like usage: To which we may answer, that it is the change of the Government that creates in us these jealousies: What priviledges in many places, have been granted to the Clergy to our prejudice? What fears have terrified us, since the fatal parricide of our *Henry* the Great? the Interests of State are varyed by several Emergencies, nor can there be any certain Maxime prescribed them: That which is necessary for one King, is prejudicial to another. If a King of *France* should now become a Persecutor of our Religion, he would loose the Protection of it in all Christendome, enriching another of his Neighbour Princes with that Title, and gaining no credit at all by it among those of the Church of *Rome*, would utterly ruine his own Kingdome: which cannot happen to a King of *Spain* upon the like occasion, for that he cannot lose the Reputation he hath not, nor can it bring any further troubles upon his States, since in this quarrel, he hath already lost all the *Low Countries*, and hath no more Subjects of our Religion: I say moreover, that the situation of *France*, in the mid'st of many other Kingdomes, and the free exercise of our Religion in it, purchase to our Kings that Reputation and Power, they have among all other Potentates of *Europe*, which they will still continue, while they indulge us with the liberty of Subjects. Wherefore if the King be well counselled, he will accord us the things before mentioned; if ill, it is better to know it timely, then to expect the extremity. Let our only aim be the glory of God, and the security of those Churches, which he hath so miraculously planted and preserved in this Kingdome: Let us cordially seek the good one of another, but by lawfull means; Let us religiously resolve to ask nothing, but what is absolutely necessary for us, and be resolved in the pursuit of our demands; and then let us be assured, that he, that out of the ashes of so many Martyrs hath raised so many of his Elect in *France*, to glorifie him, will preserve and encrease their number daily. Honour and glory be given to the Father, the Son, and the Holy Ghost. *Amen.*

DISCOURSE

DISCOURSE III.

Upon the State of France *during the Persecutions at S*^{t.} *John.*

'Tis with inexpressible grief that I begin this Discourse, with the misfortunes the deplorable death of *Henry* the Great hath brought upon all Christendome, and principally upon *France*: A Prince born in a forlorn and persecuted Party, whom yet God raised to be their Preserver, supported and maintained him against all the powers of Christendome, and conducted Him, as it were, by the hand, to the Government of the *French* Monarchy. His Actions were so many Miracles, and worthy Precedents for succeeding Ages. The Conspiracies and Troubles he broke and went thorow when he was King of *Navarre*, gave him a perfect knowledge of some persons whom he had never discovered as King of *France*. His past-necessities had taught him a generous toleration even of the hardest toyl and poverty, and to bear the discontents both of great and small; and in short, to suffer all the calamities incident to the chief of a Party in a State, where the conveniencies of a whole Kingdome were employed to his Destruction : Having vanquished all these difficulties, and conquered by his Wit and Courage that, which his Birth-right had given him a juster Title to, he became at length a Peacefull King of the most puissant and glorious Kingdome of all Christendome, which yet, by reason of its long and languishing maladies, but for his person, had been inconsiderable ; incapable to assist their Neighbours, nay to subsist without them ; but in twelve years after he came to the Crown, becomes more rich, the Townes better built, and the whole was raised to a more flourishing condition than ever; he himself more absolute, his Treasures and Arsenals better stored, his Frontiers better fortified, his true and solid Allyes more strengthned, and his enemies more

weakned

weakened, then any Prince could either hope or wish: In short, he was the Arbitrator of all Christendome, grasped the whole power of Peace and Warre in his hands; and even all the Affairs of *Europe* had their entire dependance upon him. In this prosperous condition did our great *Henry* leave us: We were the terrour of our enemies, and the *Asylum* of our friends: Our *France*, with its Chief, was then looked on as the most considerable part of the world: But let us now reflect on our change, and consider whence it proceeds. It is true, God raises up and removes good Princes, according as his good pleasure is, either to favour, or to chastise the people of the earth, especially when by extraordinary wayes, he either sends or recalls them, which is apparent in the life and death of *Henry* the Great: For if his actions when living, were so highly conducing to our repose; what fears, with our just plaints may we not conceive from his violent death? A death not according to the course of nature, nor by accident, but upon a diabolical deliberation confirmed by the Sermons and Writings of the *Jesuites*, by a most impious Act perpetrated in the height of all his Conquests, and Magnificence; in the mid'st of his great Town of *Paris*, encompassed with his Nobility and People. Let us not therefore after our sins, impute our change from good to bad to any thing, but the death of our good King, whose Reputation did for some time preserve the Affairs of *Europe* in a pretty good estate; but the farther we remove from his Reign, the greater change shall we discover in them. *Europe* hath now another face; which before was ballanced by the two Powers of *France* and *Spain*: The first having without contradiction all the Protestants under its Protection, or leagued with it, sharing with the other, those of the *Romish* Faith. Powers which cannot suffer the one the other, and whom the strictest bonds of Marriages cannot unite, by reason of their mutual Jealousies and Fears, of the increase or diminution of either; Moreover the equality of these, is the safety of the rest, which are much concerned in it, and which otherwise would be easily the prey of the superiour of the two: But now we may perceive an alteration of that Method: The late Allyance between *France* and *Spain* makes all their Confederates look about them, especially those of *France*, who see clearly, that she hath been only courted but to her own, and consequently their ruine: A cunning Policy was it indeed of *Spain*, to perswade the Queen, that these Alliances would fortifie and confirm her Authority, so that none of the Princes of

the

the blood, nor any other should at any time dare to enter into any contest with her. These indeed were very plausible reasons, but of no depth, nor solidity: For against whom should she fortifie her self, but *Spain*? and with whom, but those of a joint interest with her? and yet we practise the clean contrary, take counsel of our irreconcileable enemies, and enter into Allyances with them, to ruine our friends, or at least to lose them to our selves, while willing to save themselves, they seek their protection else where: These are the effects of the *Spanish* Council, or rather the operations of their double Pistols upon the Council of *France*: These are the fruits we are to expect from this Allyance with *Spain*, who joyning with the Pope, can have no other aim then the destruction of the Allyes of *France*, and the better part of the Nation it self.

But let us now consider, who have been till now the Correspondents of those two great parts of *Europe*, their power, and who is most likely to lose by the exchange of their *Partisans*. *France* hath *England*, the *Venetians*, the States of the *Low-Countries*, *Savoy*, the Protestant Princes of *Germany*, the Duke of *Lorrain*, the *Cantons* of *Switzers*, and the greatest part of the Imperial Townes; all equally interessed for fear of the house of *Austria*, which is that of *Spain*, but for different Reasons. *England* is yet mindfull of the pretensions of *Spain*; witness the great *Armado* in the year 1588. and that design of abolishing the Reformed Religion reflects principally upon that Kingdome. *Venice* is jealous of her Neighbour *Milan*, and of the increase of the King of *Spains* Power in *Italy*; for that undoubtedly his design is to render himself the absolute Monarch of it all. The *Low Countries* have but newly shook off the yoak of his Tyranny; they hate and fear Him; and will rather hazard all than submit again to it. There's none that is not sensible of the sweetness of liberty, and what then will not a people do to continue themselves in the possession of that, hath been their own dear purchase. The Protestant Princes of *Germany* have they not just cause to fear, and even abhor the house *Austria*, and by all means to oppose the farther progress of their ambition, since it hath robbed them of the Empire, which they have almost entailed on their Familie? the broad way to slavery into which they are now declining, and nothing but an extream diligence can prevent their fall. The *Cantons* of the *Switzers*, who for the greatest part have slipt their necks also out of the *Austrian* yoak, are not they concerned to prevent his new conquest of them? especially those of our Religion, against whom he can neither want Pretences nor Assistances from *Rome*.

The

The Dukes of *Savoy* and *Lorain* are seated so near to *France*, that though they have for a long time past embraced the *Spanish* Party, yet now they seem to incline to *France*: The former by reason of his pretensions to the *Duchy* of *Millane*, promised to his Lady in Partage: And the second for the facility for a King of *France* to ruine him at his pleasure: There remain only the Imperial Townes of *Germany*, whose Interest is the same with the other Protestant Princes, I omit *Denmark*, *Sweden*, *Polonia*, and the other more remote States, for that their Interests are not conjoynt with ours.

The *Spanish* Party consists of the Emperour, the Arch Duke *Albert*, who are of the same house: of the *German* Princes of the *Romish* Belief, and the Imperial Townes of the same profession, by reason of their mis-intelligence with the Protestants: of all the Princes of *Italy*, whom fear rather than love associates with them: of the *Popish Cantons* of the *Switzers* invited by their *Pensions* to a conjunction with them; and of the Authority of the Pope, who while with a resolute constancy maintaining our Allyances, we shew our invincible power, keeps himself as *Neuter*, though his inclinations be wholly *Spanish*. For there are two things that exasperate him against us; the loss of his Authority, and his revenew in those places which we possess: which Jealousie the King of *Spain* foments, that so feeding him with the fancy of a spiritual Monarchy over all Christendome himself, under pretence of extirpating Heresies, might gain the temporal. Thus all their designes concenter, to work our destruction.

But let us now examine these two great powers, and see whether of them is the more considerable: *France* is a large and potent Kingdom, abounding in all necessaries; rich in Nobility, good Souldiers, and good Mariners, furnished with good Ports, aptly seated to receive the Supplies of their above named friends. *England*, *Scotland* and *Ireland* make up a powerfull State; being Nations naturally valiant, both by Sea and Land, full of Souldiers and good Ships, and able to raise and entertain a gallant Army. The state of *Venice* exceeds in strength all the other states of *Italy*; hath vast Treasure, and may justly assume the Title of Master of the Sea, there being no other power in *Italy*, nay not all the rest together that can equal it for the number of good Gallyes, and other Vessels. The *Low Countries* is a State, whose strength I infinitely esteem and admire; fourty years have they maintained War against the King of *Spain*, from which they

they are nut newly freed: they have the flower of good Officers and Souldiers, whose entertainment they continue, even in times of Peace, they are well stor'd with money, and keep an Army on foot, consisting of fifteen thousand foot, and three thousand horse, and a Train ready to march upon all occasions. As for the Sea, they are without contradiction the absolute Masters of it, so that they can, when they please, aid their friends, and obstruct the relief of their enemies; witness the Army of the Prince of *Parma* against the *English*, which they stopped in their havens, and other Maritime places of the Arch Duke, which during that War, were continually blocked up by Sea. As for the Protestant Princes of *Germany*, and the Imperial Towns, every one knowes how far their force exceeds that of the *Romanists*: And for the *Switzers*, money commands them at any time. There remains only the Dukes of *Savoy* and *Lorain*; they are Princes, especially the former, able to raise considerable numbers: As for their convenience to assist on the other, a map of *Europe* will plainly discover, that no other power can obstruct it.

And now let us reflect on the other power; and first, *Spain* is a great Kingdome, not well peopled, nor over fertile, seated in a corner of the world, and fitter to maintain, than inlarge its confines; invironed with the Sea and the *Pyrenean* hills; which of it self alone is not comparable to *France*: but it hath large Territories both in the *East* and *West Indies*, whence it derives great Treasures, which puffe it up with ambition of the Monarchy of Christendome. Moreover in *Italy* it hath the Kingdomes of *Naples* and *Sicily*, with the Duchy of *Millan*, and eight or nine Provinces in *Flanders*; for though the *Infanta* have them now in *Portage*, yet hath it the sole and absolute authority and disposition of them. Seriously the Dominions of *Spain* are of a vast extent, and were they all contiguous, would far transcend the Power of *France*: But it is necessitated to spend all the Revenews of *Naples*, *Sicily* and *Millan* in Garrisons and Armyes to preserve them, and to imploy all the profit of the *Indies* for the conservation of *Flanders*, by reason of the continual expences it is imployed to there, both for the transporting and paying of these Armyes: Besides, the King of *Spain* wants men, and hath need of *Spaniards* in more places then he can furnish with them, and is enforced to use great severity to make them march. In short, his Dominions bring him in more Anxieties than profit.

The Emperour, who precedes him in Honour, but comes
short

short of his power, hath a great enemy to struggle with, *viz.* the *Turk*, whom he cannot withstand without assistance, and therefore is he very incapable to relieve others. The *Arch-Duke* is comprehended under the power of *Spain*, and neither dares, nor can attempt any thing without its consent and supplies. The *Germane* Princes and the Imperial Towns which own the *Romish* Church, are very inconsiderable, being far inferiour to the others in strength. Nor are the Princes of *Italy* of any consideration, except the great Duke of *Tuscany*, who indeed wants neither men nor money: As for the *Switzers*, money draws them to any party; nor is the *Spaniard* confederated, but with the *Romish Cantons*, whereas the Allyance of the *French* with them is General. There remains now only the Power of the *Pope*, which heretofore, in times of Ignorance and superstition, was very great, his excommunications routing whole Armies, and transferring Crowns from one head to another, at his pleasure; but they are now growen ridiculous, and hurt only those that are afraid of them; his strength consists only in Fulminations. As for the wayes *Spain* hath to convey relief to its several members, they are very long, and full of difficulties and dangers: For first, *France* separates *Spain* and *Flanders*; and *Province* can at any time obstruct the passage from thence into *Italy*; *Burgundy*, *Bressia*, *Lorain*, and the *Venetian Seigneury* divides the rest of *Italy* from *Germany* and the *Low Countries*: In a word, the Dominions of *Spain* are of a vast and wonderfull extent, and in outward appearance invincible: but they lye so scattered and with such difficulty and inconvenience can they joyn, that it takes off much of their strength; whereas on the contrary those of *France*, are compacted, united, and ready upon all occasions either for defence of themselves, or invasion of their enemies.

These are the two principal Potentates of *Europe*, to wit, *France* and *Spain*; and it is of no small importance to them, both to preserve their reputation with their *Partisans*, which is of no great difficulty to the King of *Spain*; for that all his Subjects and Allyes are of his own Religion, or his own Family, or obliged by interest to exterminate the Protestants. So that none of them can entertain a Jealousie that he should change his Intelligences: But 'tis not so with the King of *France*, for he himself professes the *Romish* Religion, and hath many Subjects of the Reformed, and many confederates that are *Papists*, though the strength of his Party consists in the Protestants: so that if he order not well his

Affairs

Affairs with them, but entring into an association with *Spain*, persecutes his Protestant Subjects, he will utterly lose them all. But perhaps they presume upon a confidence, that the Reformed party cannot joyn with the King of *Spain*: But rather then they will submit to their ruine, they may unite and choose the King of *England* for their Protectour, which would be the absolute destruction of *France*: And can we then be so far infatuated, as to offer up our selves a sacrifice to the insatiable and endless ambition of the *Pope*, and the King of *Spain*? Is it not evident, that this must needs draw a civill War on *France*, which is more to be feared than the fulminations of the *Pope*, who since he cannot ruine *France* by forraign Armes, endeavours to do it by her own.

Certainly it is the Judgement of *God*, punishing us for our sins, that we cannot see, apprehend, nor seek to avoid those evils, which even our own Counsels, resolutions & remedies prescribed for their redress have discovered to us for forty years together, and which have reduced our poor *France* to extremities, from which nothing but a miracle can raise her. The same parties are still in being: The first, the Queen-*Mother*, who seeks to establish her authority in the same manner, as did her Predecessour; and to that end, disgraces and suppresses the Princes of the blood; using the power and assistance of the house of *Guise*, to which is joyned that of Monsieur d' *Espernon*; strengthens her self, not with the real friends of the Crown, but with such as aim and endeavour to weaken it by divisions, as the King of *Spain*, and the *Pope*. This is a strong and considerable Party; but composed of persons that desire rather the destruction, than preservation of the State: That which is their greatest Prop is, that they abuse the royal Authority, authenticating all their dispatches and actions with the name of *Lewis* the thirteenth, although to his prejudice and detriment: The second, is composed of the Princes of the blood; who are sensible of the ruine of their House, but are not in a capacity to prevent or remedy it; having by their revolt from their Religion, lost those who were their Father's greatest support, so that they have Justice, but no force on their side. The third party, is that of the Religion, bound by their conscience to a confederacy with all the Protestants of Christendome: a party able of it self to maintain *France*, as it hath formerly done: having preserved the Princes of that house, nourished and bred up *Henry* the Great, the Restorer of this State, whose enemies knowing that the strength of this Party consists in its Union, Discipline and Places of security, have set all their subtleties on work to subvert those foundations; which evidently

appeared

appeared in the Assembly at *Saumure*, where money, Pensions and Menaces were all employed to corrupt Persons capable to raise a Schism amongst them, and in that division to ruine them; As also by the Pass-port given to the Deputies of the particular Assemblies, by the Declaration which they caused to be verified in the Parliaments, in which they expresly forbid the Discipline ever establisht among us, and without which we cannot provide for our necessities: by the industry they use to get into their hands our cautionary Townes; working on the easiness of some of our Governours, and furnishing other confidents of their own with means to purchase the Governments from honest men; endeavouring, to the violation of the Priviledges of particular Corporations, to make their own creatures Majors, and labouring by all means to supplant and eject out their commands such as oppose their designes, well knowing, that our places of security once failing us, we can no longer subsist: and in all these designes so pernicious and destructive to the State, is the *King's* Authority made use of. Thus have you had a view of the several Parties in *France*, what are their designes, and by whom maintained. The one covers all their mischievous machinations with the Royal Authorities: The other exclaims against the evil Government, but it is not heard: The third complaines of their oppression, but are not eased: and even untill this present time such effectual operation hath their money had upon the degenerous and perfidious souls of the two latter parties, that they have been the scorn and derision of the former; and the Counsels of mean inconsiderable Fellows, Pensioners of *Rome* and *Spain*, preferred before those of the Princes of the blood, and the other Grandees of the Realm: But if the aforesaid Princes, and those of the Religion would but reflect upon their miscarriages, and endeavour to correct them, and unite their just plaints and interests, and like good Christians, never be induced by any promise to forsake the one the other, to the prejudice of either, they would undoubtedly raise both themselves and the State from this abject and ruinous condition, and would one day receive both the thanks and profit of it: But if fear or avarice, or both together, shall impede the union of these two parties, or keep them from embracing such generous and necessary resolutions, this will be the issue of it, and God grant it prove no Prophesie; *France* will be the Theatre on which will be executed all the designes both of *Rome* and *Spain*, upon all good *French-men* and Christians. And when

the

the Evil shall transcend all humane Remedy, those who have yet left some sparks of love to God and their Countrey, will have no other consolation than to bewail their past errors, and to submit to that yoak which their own imprudence hath drawn, and a Forraigner shall impose upon them. For we may not imagine, that that party, which by the assistance of the *Popes* Fulminations, and the Forces of the King of *Spain*, shall subdue the other two, shall enjoy its Conquest: Those Princes take not so much paines for our good. Their conspiracies against *France* are so far from being extinct, that they are now renewed with greater vigour and hopes of every thing succeeding according to their wish: The restoring of the *Jesuites*, the death of *Henry* the Great, the Regency of the Kingdome setled in the house of *Medicis*, the State governed by the ancient Pensioners of *Rome*, all other Officers being removed, and the support of it founded on the house of *Loraine*; the Princes of the blood deprived of the Authority due unto them; and a division made among the Protestants; all which evils being in so short time fallen upon this State, encourages their hopes of effecting their long since projected designes. But if the Princes of the blood, during the minority of *Lewis* the thirteenth, retain any Reliques of Generosity, or those of the reformed Religion any sparks of Piety, they will yet oppose the ruine of the State threatned by theirs: For *France* cannot long subsist, if the Royal Family be oppress, and the Protestants persecuted: whose subsistence also depends upon the preservation of the Crown, whose destruction can neither be effected, but that the Kingdome will be reduced to so weak a condition, that it will remain a prey to the first Usurper, or be brought to an intire desolation: Let these considerations then teach us Wisdome, before an absolute impossibility to redress our evils, leave us no consolation but despair: for not having timely foreseen and prevented them.

And now, you Princes, know, that Usurpers never willingly let goe what they possess; that your greatest crime, is the right you have to the Government of *France*, and that nothing but the fear of you can restore you to what their contempt hath deprived you of: And you, who profess the Reformed Religion, recall to your remembrance, by what means your Fore-Fathers planted the Gospel of Christ in this Kingdome, and the provisions they made both for your security and discipline: Shall we be guilty of so much baseness, as to prefer the empty promises of some pension, which shall no longer be continued, then while you betray your own Countrey, or of some small Estates, which after the ruine of your friends, you shall not enjoy, but by the sacrifices of your own consciences and Religion, before our own and our Childrens liberty, and the prosperity of the Church of God? If then the Princes be desirous to maintain the Crown in their own Family, and the Protestants in the State, they must enter into a firm Union to maintain and support the one the other. Let us imploy all our powers to restore them to their lost Authority; let them make use of theirs, to confirm our Rights, Disciplines and Correspondencies: and let us all joyn, to re-establish the ancient Allyancy of the Crown. I see how they calumniate those of the Religion, pretending that their aim is in imitation of the *Switzers*, and those of the *Low-Countries*, by a particular Discipline to disunite themselves from the State. But neither their dispersed, and remote habitations in this Realm, nor the great number of Nobility amongst them, nor the sence of the honour of their Nation, nor yet their own profit, will suffer any of them to admit of such a thought.

God in his Mercy look in pity upon this declining State; and I heartily beseech him, that if his pleasure be to restore, and preserve it, that the body of the Reformed Religion may be its chief Support; but if in Judgement, he resolve upon the ruine of it; that he would yet vouchsafe to replant his Churches, by the same means he first planted them here. *Amen.*

DISCOURSE IV.

Upon the Voyage of the King, *in* July 1615.

I Conceive my self obliged, both by my Allegiance, and the services I have vowed to the Queen, freely to offer my advice concerning the present, many, and important Affairs of the State; which ought to be the more considered, for that it proceedes neither from hatred, nor desire of revenge against any; nor fear of being rejected, nor hope of being advanced to a share in the administration of them: Passions which many times blind the greatest persons; The freeness of my humour, and the Integrity of my affection drew me to this Discourse; which will clearly discover both my Opinion and Resolution. I confess, that as to the Affairs now in Agitation, I cannot clearly see, that the former actions of the Prince of *Conde* can bring his Fidelity or good Conduct into question. Nevertheless I will take all things at the worst, as if all the expedients heretofore made use of were defective, it being a known Truth, *That the miscarriages we smart for, serve to correct and quicken us,* whereas *Prosperity lulls us into a careless Security.*

Untill the Assembling of the States General, all the Subjects and Officers of the Kingdome kept themselves within the limits of their Duty, reflecting at the same time, both on the favours and damages they might receive; and choosing rather to content themselves with their present condition, than out of hopes of a reformation to expose all to a hazard. But at the Assembly of the said States, the disagreement of the orders upon the proposition of the third Estate, made by the Parliament of *Paris*; the instant urging of the Council of *Trent* by the two first Orders, and the malice the Clergy have discovered against those of our Religion, refusing to approve of our Edicts of Pacification, endeavouring to oblige the King by Oath to ruine us, have opened a large gap for those who attempt to diminish the Queens to inlarge their own Authority.

Next came the Revocation of the *Polette*, which made the Officers, when it was not seasonable, be changed; whose re-establishment will not reconcile them: for though it be that which troubles them, yet will they conceal the ground of their discontents, cloaking their particular interests with the pretext of the publique good. But there is yet more, the Deputies of the said Estates, going thither for the most part, not to pursue the general Welfare of the Kingdome, but to do their own private Affairs, having wholly complyed with the pleasure of the Queen, conceive her obliged to return them large Rewards: so that those which received not that Recompence, they supposed they had so well deserved, return to their respective Provinces, exclaiming against the Government of the State: so that this, being added to the number already ingaged against her, will be far the strongest. All these things having been with great care and subtilty aggravated by the Prince and his *Partisans*, have gained a great reputation to their design, even among forraign Princes, and the best Allyes of the Crown of *France*, whom they perswade, that there is a Confederacy between the Queen the Pope, and the King of *Spain*, to extirpate all of our Religion out of all Christendome; which all good Frenchmen are obliged to oppose: for that it would prove a great weakness to *France*, and all leagued with it against the greatness of *Spain*.

This is the true state of our Affairs, in which, either the Prince must give back, or the Queen yield a little, or else all must break out into an open division.

If the consideration of his private interests inclines the Prince to a complyance, it will be the absolute establishment of the Authority of the Queen, wherefore I cannot conceive he will yet listen to any such motion.

But let us now see, whether will be of greatest advantage to the Queen, that she perish in her Resolutions, though all fall into a confusion, or that she yield a little to the necessities of the times, and afterwards resume her former power againe, and what inconveniences will attend both the one and the other resolution. If she submit and retard the marriage, or change any Officers of the State, or the Exchequer, it is probable that the Prince will reap all the thanks and profit of it, that it will be the enlargement of his, and the destruction of the Queens power, and by consequence the contempt of the one, will be the only effect of the glory of the other. If they proceed in the marriage, and continue things in their

present

present condition, then may they fear the troubles which the Prince, the Parliament, and people of *Paris* may raise in their absence, not only in that Town, but all over *France*; The distrusts and jealousies of the forraign Princes, allyed with this Crown; whose own Interests render them very suspitious of this league between *France* and *Spain*. The War with *Savoy*, and our dereliction of that Prince would be looked on, as an argument, that the end of our amity with *Spain*, was their prejudice and dammage; and the apprehensions of those of our Religion, that the whole storm will fall on us: Wherefore I conceive they cannot without the extream hazard of the Queen's authority, begin the voyage before they have provided Remedies for all these inconveniencies.

If they conclude upon the voyage, then my advice is, that in any case they resolve upon four things. The first is, that they have a power in *Paris*, either in the hands of one person qualified for that charge, and to be assisted with a Council, or else in the hands of the Parliament, to maintain a constant correspondence with the Queen; and to prevent all insurrections of the people. The second is, to make a peace with *Savoy*, or at least not to discover our weakness and disaffection, in expresly forbidding the sending any Relief to that Duke; it being not in our power to prevent it. The third is, by entring into an Allyance with *England*, to satisfie all other our Confederates, who are so jealous of this League with *Spain*. The fourth is, by a good and favourable usage of our Assembly, publickly to testifie to the Protestants, that they are also studious of their preservation.

This is my first advice; but I conceive there is another more profitable, and more secure, if well examined, and free from all fear of creating new divisions: which is this, That the Queen let the Prince know, that having considered the Remonstances of the Parliament, she will make all possible provisions for their satisfaction: before she begin her progress into *Guienne*, and that to the end, she desires his Assistance, in reforming and redressing the grievances of the State: If he come not, it will be the Queen's Advantage; who must not fail also to treat with the Parliament about the same thing; For what good soever shall accrue thence, will no more be attributed to the Prince, since he contributed nothing to it. But in this Unity, the Parliament must upon any terms be satisfied, especially concerning the administration of the *Finances*, and this must also be readily, and without any reluctancy granted: For when a man condescends to things against his Will he must not discover his aversion, but rather pretend a ready inclination to it. If this be managed as it ought, and by persons that only respect the Queen's authority, within six moneths it will be more absolute than ever, and the Prince his conspiracy utterly broken; Believe it, there is strength enough in *France* to support the Queen, without borrowing aid from any place: I will use but one example to confirm it, which is, the War of the Commonweal against King *Lewis* the eleventh, who destroyed that great League by no other means, but dividing it; though at first it seemed to threaten the destruction of his Authority. If you cannot find means out of their particular Interests to disunite the Princes, you must try another way: If the Parliament be close fisted, as they now seem to guard their purse, they must be attempted in their weaker quarters, which they do not at all suspect: you must blow them up with the vanity of assisting the Queen, and re-uniting the divided State. In the mean time the King growes on, and his authority increases with his age, which will augment the power of the Queen, and diminish that of the Princes of the Blood. But she must be very cautious, that the apparent diminution of some particulars bring not a hazard on that Authority which maintains them, which once imputed, would be the ruine of them all.

As for my part, I am resolved faithfully to serve the Queen against *Monsieur* the Prince, to imploy all my power to advance the Grandeur of this Kingdome; and in as much as lies in me, to incline all those of the Reformed Religion to the same resolutions: But if out of any animositie they have against the Protestants, or by the procurement of evill Counsel, they use them as at *Saumure*: I will then declare, that I will never dissent nor disunite from the publique resolutions of our Assembly.

DISCOURSE

DISCOURSE V.

Upon the Government *of the* Queen-Mother.

Made in the year 1617.

THat Rhetorick which touches not the Interests of those we would perswade, hath seldome any operation upon them: Nor had the letter which *Monsieur de Vendosm, de Mayenne* and *de Boüillon* writ unto the King against the Marshall *d' Ancre*, nor the Declaration published in his Majesties Name in answer to it, a neat and well composed piece, hitherto any effectual influence upon any, either to incline them to embrace the discontented Princes Party, or to gain their intire approbation of the present Government: For the prodigious favour of the Marshall *d' Ancre*, was both suspected and abhorred: and they who were silent at it, were either in effect, or by some hopes linked to his fortune: And truly, there was never yet any Precedent of a man honoured with the Dignity of Marshall of *France*, that ever served in an Army; nor of a man, that all at once was intrusted with the tuition of Seals and Purse of the King; that is to say, that grasped his whole Authority: Nor is it less strange, that those whom the late King imployed to discharge those offices, should be now discarded. Though the Chancellour hath been faulty since, yet the Integrity of *Monsieur* the President *Du Vair*, and his abilities are unblemishable, and yet could not those parts which advanced him, secure him from disgrace. To maintain also that the Edicts of Pacification, and all Promises made to particular Communalties have been hitherto inviolably observed, would be but a vain Discourse to those that know the contrary: that is, almost to all. This little draught of a complaint, contains in it the summe of the most importance charges against the Marshall *d' Ancre*, and the present Government.

Where-

Whereupon some say, it were to be desired, not that the Marshall *d' Ancre* should be ruined; for his birth is equal to any that in our memory hath been created, not only Marshall, but Duke and Peer of *France*; and hath raised a Family in this Kingdome; and his Wit and Education, and many other qualities, make him thought worthy of this favour, and to be naturalized to perpetuate his Family amongst us; which would be a great honour to our Nation: But it is to be desired, say they, that this greatness give no just cause of suspition to those who are jealous of the Royal Authority, and the French Monarchy; and that untill the perfect Majority of our King, the power should not be ingrossed by a Single Person, who may more easily abuse it than many, who preserving the State from the unjust usurpation of either, will assist one the other in managing and reserving it for him alone, to whom the Rule of it rightly belongs, untill he himself be able to undertake the administration of it. For no man can tell, untill he hath proved it, how far the Itch of Soveraignty may carry, nor can this Tryal be made by any person whatsoever, without mainfest danger both to the King and Kingdome. It is also to be desired, that the ancient *Pilots* of the State, resume the helm again; that the Edicts of pacification be faithfully observed; and that those abuses, which have a long time raigned amongst us, be reformed; whose visible increase threatens much mischief to this Monarchy. But whether we look upon their Intentions or manner of their procedures, we shall deceive our selves, if we think those expedients, which the discontented Princes have formerly, and now still do use, are capable to effect this Reformation: Their two Treaties of St. *Menehould* and *Loudun* will clearly convince all those who shall examine the particular passages of them, that their greatest aim hath been their own private Interests, and that they had a greater desire to ingage many persons to promote their own advancement, and favour their own particular designes, than to reform the State, as they pretended, or better the condition of those, whom their solicitations had drawn to a conjunction with them: For though they promised us a general restauration of all things by the convention of the States General, they cannot deny, but that they openly made their Parties in the Provinces, to procure the Election of such as they supposed to be of their own faction: Thus did they violate the liberty they promised to restore, and give a Precedent to the Queen-Mothers Disciples to do the like. And
though

though since that, to make their own cause appear more plausible to the people, they have publickly accused many, and principally the Mareshall *d' Ancre*; yet did some of them, and especially of the Reformed Religion, maintain a strict intelligence with the said Marshall *d' Ancre* in the hottest of the War. Thus at St. *Menehould* and *Loudun* did they conclude upon conditions, regarding only their own concernments; never moving any thing that really conduced to the advancement of the publique good. Nor hath the defects of their duty to the State been greater, than their Injuries to those of the Religion; whom yet *Monsieur* the Prince was pleased in his Letter to the Queen to mention as persons concerned. And though that at the Treaty of St. *Menehould* the Dukes of *Mayne* and *Bouillon*, nominated by the Prince, to treat with her Majesties Commissioners were earnestly sollicited by *Monsieur de Rohan*, who sent a Secretary of his own in post to them, to desire them to make it appear, that they had summoned them in good earnest, and with intention to procure their Welfare; yet was the Treaty concluded without any benefit to them, or indeed without any mention made of them. They signed also that at *Loudun*, refusing to expect the resolution of the general Assembly then held at *Rochel*; though they had entred into a solemn engagement, not to do it without the mutual consent and Approbation of all parties. But this was not all: for they obliged themselves by a formal promise under their hands, by violence to force the Deputies of that Assembly, if they did not dissolve themselves within a very short time which they prescribed them; which Promise *Monsieur de Trimouille* and *de Bouillon* signed as well as the rest; which *Monsieur de Plessis-Bellay*, *Monsieur de Trimouill*'s Deputy, confessed to the Duke of *Rohan* in the said Assembly at *Rochell*; to whom also, together with *Monsieur de Sully*, he presented it to be signed by them, which they both absolutely refused to do. And when at several times many *Romanists* have reproached the Prince for coming so easily to an accord; his answer still was, that the fear of advancing the Reformed Party forced him to it. Nor did *Monsieur de Nevers* excuse his refusal to joyne with him in the late commotions, but by this, that those of the Religion were of the Party: And *Monsieur de Mayne* hath alwayes protested, nay at the time of their association, that he would never procure any good to them; and yet when they conceive they may be usefull to them, as at present, they want neither promises, vowes, nor protestations to engage. These

These are some Arguments that the principal end of these Princes is not the general good of *France*, much less of the Reformed Party, and God grant that we have not now a just cause to fear, as hitherto (if they arrive at their purpose) an absolute translation of the *French* Diadem: The mildest censures that shall view their actions, cannot but say, that the remedies they prepare, are worser than the disease, I will not say the Plague and poison of the State. For since they pretend nothing but the restoring of the King's Authority, and the Welfare of the people; is there any thing that so much prejudice either the one or the other, as the Armies which have alwayes appeared as soon as their letters and declarations? Can any thing so easily raze out of Subjects hearts, the Reverence due to their Princes, as the accustoming them to bear Arms against them? For although these Gentlemen will not confess that they raise Armes against the King; yet when mention is made of the King's Party, they understand it of the adverse party to them, for so is the Kings Army called; which I do not alledge as the formal reason of the Justice or Injustice of either cause; but only to shew, that unless a great extremity exact it, such things ought not to be permitted to the people, which may many waies impair their reverence of the Royal Majesty, that Reverence, I say, which is the only Basis, and most firm foundation of it. And as for the people which condemn the present Government, whose errors cannot bring on them in twenty years, so many and heavy inconveniencies, as a Civil War will in ten dayes, since it is yet disputable in whose hands the State is left liable to danger, either in the Queen-Mothers, or the Princes; what reason is there to expose it to an apparent ruine for a thing, which may be probably argued, both by the one side and the other.

Certainly, if their power were so great, and the consent of the people in favour of them so unanimous, that the execution would presently follow the pretention of their designes, we should be constrained to endure it: But they are only capable to provoke and stir the humours, not to expell them; to make a wound, and not to heal it; to open a way for a forraign Invasion, never caring how to redeem the Nation again; thus do they draw upon themselves the maledictions and curses of the people, for the evils they have caused them, and have not the least power to do them any good. To this purpose remarkable is the decree of the Council extorted from them, the last year by *Monsieur* the Prince, who was then President of it, which by all those that paid Contribution in the time of the late troubles, were injoyned to pay it over once more; not without the great amazement of those that assisted at the same Council, though they had no other Interest in the business than what Equity, and a natural Commiseration of their Fellow Subjects gave them: But if these Princes were in possession of the Government, the same complaints might be exhibited against those, that would dispossess them of it, and perswade them to patience, until the King should have a perfect knowledge of his own affairs, whose management he would be obliged to look after, as his chiefest Exercise. And good reason also should we have to complain, if we were compelled to bear Arms: but the choice is now left us, either to do it, or to stay at home; though Commissions are daily refused, and that these Lords proclaim all enemies that come not in to them.

That which is before said may give the *French* cause to fear the Contagion of such Reformers, and to remember, that there was never yet any War raised in *France*, under pretence of the publick good, whose principal aim was not the particular Interest of those that begun it. But especially ought the Protestants to be carefull to stick to their priviledges given them by the Edicts made in favour of them; to have a watchfull eye upon their cautionary places, and to unite themselves more strictly than ever under the name and authority of the King; to whom in this posture, they may be one day capable to render very considerable services, and possibly to preserve his Crown: But if they adhere again to those, who have formerly deceived them, and who desire their Assistance for no other end, than to promote their own affairs, they will absolutely lose and ruine themselves: In the mean time, let us leave the event to God, and incessantly implore him for the preservation, prosperity and long life of the King, the good of the State, and the firm establishment of the Crown. *Amen.*

DISCOURSE

Discourse VI.

Made in the year 1617.

A free Discourse upon the present Times.

I very well know, that the general humour of Mankind inclines them to desire what they have not, and to disesteem and slight what they possess. In the time of *Henry* the Great, every one complained of an avaritious and oppressive Government; but none doth stir against it: since his death we have seen those grievances redressed by liberality: But forasmuch as the number of those who receive no profit by it, far exceeds the other, and that Envy is a vice very common and predominant: The former Reign hath been again wished for: The large gifts and pensions conferred on the great Ones, encouraging them rather to transgress, than contain themselves within the limits of their Duty. And now we murmure, that the only means left to restrain every one, are imployed to that end.

Revolving these so different things in my mind, I have reflected on the changes which have happened, and considered the former miscarriages, their causes, and the wayes to redress, and prevent them for the future. The courage of *Henry* the Great, his Authority, his suppressing the Grandees of the Kingdome, his abounding Treasures, and well stored Arsenals, rendred him so redoubtable, that none durst think of disturbing his Repose. His suddain death subjected us to a King of nine years old; and although the Regency without any opposition fell into the hands of the Queen-Mother, yet was it not without a great disgust to the Princes of the blood who pretended to it. The Councils then most prevalent, were by the power of others of the Nobility, to withstand

stand that Authority, which themselves ambitioned in the Court; and to maintain these two powers in so equal a ballance, that in the mid'st of both, the royal Authority (possess'd by the Queen) might freely exercise its functions, to abase the discontents of either, by a profusion of the Treasures, Arsenals, Offices and Governments. As for the first, I must needs approve it to be as good, as I must confess the latter to be bad: For though our Malady by those means be suppressed for ten years; yet will it prove in the end almost incurable. It is a most certain truth, that in all Kingdomes the Power of the King eclipses that of the Nobility, and that the increase of theirs, doth diminish the splendor of his. It is a ballance that can never continue in so equal a poise, but that one side must sway the other. It is therefore but an ill way to preserve the Royal Authority, to put into the hands of those that endeavour to destroy it, the only means to restrain their ambition. How much more easie was it to have kept the Princes in subjection in that weak and necessitous way, I dare say, beggerly condition in which the late King left them, than now, when we have parted with all our forces to strengthen them with them? It may be well said, that a Kingdome is better secured by Love than Tyranny; but then this love must not proceed from imbecility and want of Power, which only breeds contempt; but must be testified by a constant pursuite of Justice, and earnest endeavours to preserve the people from oppression: It is a dictate of nature, that we avoid all inconveniences, and apply our selves to those that are sollicitous for our good. I must include my self in the same accusations, if I should extend this charge against all the Nobility, who are so much more the fittest Instruments to be imployed by the King, as they have the greatest means to do him service. I know that those, who are of a well tempered spirit, look upon their own as the greatness of their King. And more happy, and secure are the Nobility, under a great and potent Prince, than under those petty Soveraigns, who dare not stir for fear of offending either *France* or *Spain.* But I speak of such as would inforce their Majesties to gratifie them, though they have no merit to justifie their pretences; and who alwayes imploy their goods, gotten by unjust wayes, only to augment their own greatness. Certainly the more you give to such persons, the more do you arm them against your self. It were much better to resolve to distinguish between Reward and Punishment; the good and the bad; to the end,

that

that the one may be encouraged, the other terrified, than still to persist in the practice of the Contrary, rewarding the bad, and discountenancing the good: For Impunity opens a door to all licentiousnes and ingratitude, and neglect of good services, to despair and rage.

The opinion I have of this Counsel, makes me suspect that the Authors of it, gave it only to make themselves the longer looked on, as necessary to the service of the Kingdome; and that their own private Interest, a powerfull Orator, disswaded them from giving such Counsels as really conduced to the preservation of the Royal Authority, in that splendor they found it in.

And now I am entring on a way which gives me fair hopes of an happy accommodation of the Affairs of this State; which must be pursued with as much vigour and courage, as the difficulty, and consequently the honour of the Enterprize require. So firm a resolution must we take, as neither their exclamations, nor any other Artifice they shall use to daunt us, may not divert us from our purposes, what ever accidents happen; which possibly may be such, as that to remedy them, we may be forced sometimes to defer, but must never give off our design. For perseverance joyned with the royal Authority, will easily subvert all their policyes, especially at such a time, wherein that vertue is not to be found in many. I confess, that such a Resolution is not to be undertaken, but upon good grounds; wherefore we will particularly examine the State of our *France*, and diligently consider all things in it:

And first, I observe, that there are two Religions professed in this Kingdome; the one much superiour in strength, and which gives the Law to the other, and would gladly be alone: The other alwayes jealous of an Assault, whose ruine will nevertheless draw after it that of the State also: *Henry* the Great, who was of that opinion, gave an equal influence of his favour to them both, and would not prejudice his own greatness to gratifie the humour of either.

The strength of a Kingdome depends upon the King, and his Allyes, not of blood, but interest. *France* and *Spain* are the two great Powers of *Europe*, and the hinges on which all the other move, who still oppose one another, lest either should gain the absolute Superiority. The Interest of the Protestants, is to uphold the greatness of *France*, and so is it also of many other States which profess the *Romish* Faith: It is a Maxime of State, which the King of *France* ought to observe;

observe; not to persecute his Subjects of the Religion, that all Protestants may not throw themselves upon the Protection of *England*: yet must not the favour he shews them be such, as may raise a jealousie in his other Subjects the Catholiques, which are the main body of his State; but he must oblige them by his Justice, preserving inviolate their Edicts, and by his confidence in imploying them in his service. None but the Enemies of his Crown can disallow of such a Procedure.

From the Religions, I pass to the discontents, who are still very numerous, for that the mind of man is unstable, presumptuous and envious, and is many times more troubled at the wealth and honour which another possesses, than that he enjoyes it not himself. But it is according to the strength or weakness of the State, that they discover themselves more or less. Those who now declare against the Royal Authority, whether of the one, or the other Religion, exclaime against the Government, because it is not in their own hands; accusing their Majesties, if not of Treachery, yet of Folly; and suffering themselves to be led by the fancies of other men, they fall upon the stone, not daring to touch the arm that threw it, and cover as much as they can the pernicious design they have, to usurp the Royal Authority, and make themselves Masters even of their Majesties themselves. Those also that serve the King, for the most part, follow their own, not his pleasure. Every one will command an Army and a Province: and if his Neighbour, or one of the same rank with himself have any Command given him, and he not; he presently is discontented, and dares think even of trampling upon the throat of his Master: Certainly if they had all their desires, we should see Monsters instead of Armies, more Commanders than Souldiers. I confess such disorders are not tolerable, and that such persons are almost as much enemies of the King, as those that are convicted of Treason. Others make their consciences plead for them, and remonstrate, that it were better for the good of all Christendome to satisfie the Catholiques, by making War upon the Reformed Party: Counsel tending to the Eternizing of a Civil War in *France*, and the loss of its most faithfull and powerfull Allyes.

Those of the Religion, that engage in these broils, alledge, that they will not stop at the ruine of the Princes they now decry; but that if we stop not their progress, we shall have our share of the persecution: The King's Council proceeds from *Rome* and *Spain*, one of which incessantly seeks our particular

ticular destruction; the other, that of *France* in general; which is clearly discernable by the inobservances of our Edicts: and though they move different wayes, and for different Interests, yet all the discontents of either Religion, unanimously accord in their desires of a change of the present Government.

And now to come to the Remedies, which by reason of the diversity of humours, cannot easily be particularized; we must know that there are two sorts of Discontents; the open, and the concealed; the former cannot be reduced to their obedience by any other means then force: The other are a sort of people that declare for no Party, but would render themselves considerable by a third: These may much incommode the Kings Affaires, by such Diversions as they can make both with the men, and money they can raise; to these nevertheless must be applyed gentle Lenitives, and not those harsher Corrosives of force.

All expedients necessary for the good of this State, may be reduced to four heads. The first, and main particular is, to force the Princes, now in Armes against him, to an obedience to the King: to this the way is open; and the best policy is, to use no other, but only to be very carefull to keep good Armies on foot, to make a good choice of those that are imployed in them, and to make good provisions for the Payment and Sustenance of the Souldiers. The second consists in general, in the Execution of our Edicts, and in particular, in being carefull to free us from those inconveniencies and jealousies that have been, and still are given us. Which may be done by a just payment of our Garrisons and Ministers, and by a sincere effecting of that, which in words they confess, is necessary for us: and by sending Commissioners into the Provinces, and keeping a constant Correspondence with the Principal of them, which may produce more good than is imagined. The third is, a wary and politique comportment towards all those, that declaring for no party, can yet raise great commotions in the Provinces, as the Dukes *d' Espernon*, *de Sully*, *d' Lesdiguieres*, can by means as different, as their ends. A several Remedy must be prepared for each of these, who must be also made sensible of their dis-union, every one labouring to make conditions with the Court apart. *Monsieur d' Espernon* cannot away with the present Government, because he is excluded from the helm: He aimes at the Government of *Guyenne*, and to be made *Connestable* of *France*;

France; which since he cannot obtaine by fair, he would by foul means. He professes much zeal to the King's service, controulles the Catholiques, pretends to be an enemy to the *Prince*, the Duke of *Boüillon*, and all other the discontents: and yet doth he desire the Government of the the King; will live amongst the Protestants, and will deliver the Prince, and the rest. I leave it to all to judge, whether either the one, or the other, can fix any confidence on a man so mutable. If *Guyenne* be given him, it is the way for him to make himself *Conneſtable*: after which he will become a Tyrant over the King and Kingdome; as he is already over those that live under his Government. See what his dealings are: at the same time, that he vowes all Loyalty to the *King*, he promises his uttermost service to *Madame* the Princess, for the deliverance of *Monsieur* the Prince, and maintains a correspondence with all the other Princes in Armes: As for *Monsieur de Sully*, he is wholly inclined to the good of the State: He is weary of the hard measure he receives, desirous to have his services better regarded, and vexed at the neglect of them: but will never be drawn to oppose the Authority of the King, untill he be forced by the greatest extremities. As for *Monsieur* the Marshal *Lesdiguieres*, he hath great commands in his Government, is wise, and one that would be considered as a person of Power and Authority: but is not at all unreasonable in any thing. The first of these is the hardest to be contented; for that, Humility swels his Pride; Gentleness makes him more Violent, and Toleration emboldens him: yet must be amused with fair words, untill the taking of *Soiſſons*; for the issue of that siege, will make all the pretended third Party change their note. The second, by an indifferent and moderate usage, may not be only restrained, but employed where he is, to retain by his power the Protestants within their due limits: And the last may also by the same means be infallibly kept within his: His age, his Antipathy against the Dukes of *Boüillon*, and d' *Espernon*, and the ill usage he hath had from the Prince his party, are prevalent motives to keep him to his Devoir. If these wayes should fail, the King hath yet Peace, and War in his own hand, which he may make with either of them, when he pleases, and severally too. For all the Princes now in Arms against him, would joyne with him to suppress *Monsieur d' Espernon*, or any other, that should be so Fool-hardy as to oppose him. All of them, as many as they are, must needs fight with great disad-

disadvantage, having no Chief that they will own; being in a continual diffidence one of another, pursuing the advancement of their several particular Interests, and the destruction of the Kings, who can at pleasure disunite them, by tendring conditions to either of them, when he shall see his time. There remains now the last expedient, and that is, to foment their mutual Jealousies, and render them odious both to their own and forraign Nations; which must be done by a particular Demonstration of their design, ever since the death of the late King, to embroil the whole Nation for their own private profit; by discovering also their Confederacyes, Treasons, and their fallacious Pretensions, how they have cheated those of the Religion; how one Party complyed, to make its Peace at the others cost; how that in all their Treaties they have not discovered the least thought of the publick Welfare; What submissions they have all made. to him against whom they just before so loudly exclaimed; What fidelity they have sworn him; how faithfull they have been to him, that the world may know what spirit leads them; and that Hatred and Ambition, and not the Love of their Countrey, or the King's service hath alwayes absolutely governed them: If the first expedient be well followed, and the other three not neglected, I shall see the King most absolute, the Civil Wars all ended, and a fair way opened to the Glory, and *Grandeur* of the King and Kingdome.

DISCOURSE

Discourse VII.

Upon the Occasion of the Divisions of Holland. 1618.

STates and Common-wealths are not formed in an Instant, and the Lawes which they make to redress their present inconveniences, are ordinarily better than those which regard the future: which is a great cause of their multiplicity and change of Lawes from time to time, for that they are obliged to apply convenient Remedies to survening evils, before they grow incurable: I speake this principally in relation to the State of the *Low-Countries*, who in a fourty years War, which they sustained against the power of *Spain*, are so augmented, strengthned and established by that glorious toil, and become so absolute Masters of all Military Arts, that they inforced the King to a Peace. But though during the War, they knew how to establish all necessary Lawes in order to the prosecution of it; yet have they shewed themselves but Novices in their Conduct since the Peace, or to speake more properly, they must confess that the Government of their State hath need of some new Expedients to prevent those mischiefs which threaten it now.

The King of *Spain* finding by the experience of that long tract of years, that he could not ruine them by open force, resolved to work their destruction by intestine Divisions. To which end the calm of Peace and Idleness, which many times lulls such persons, as think no harm themselves, into a security, have given him occasion to rowse those unquiet spirits, whom either Discontent, Envy or Ambition, will not suffer to rest satisfied with their condition. Other Divisions than those of Religion, would have been suspected; and for as much as that is the most advantageous proceeding from a Subject which hath the absolute Dominion over others, he designed to undermine them that way: which may be justified by the Writings and Counsels given these ten years past, and upon the same point which are still controverted:

In which he hath so succesfully laboured, that we see that fair State, which the force of Arms could not move, is now sinking to ruine, unless some speedy support prevent it: which I conceive yet feiseable, if they firmly adhere to, and pursue their resolutions. All the Assemblies which they have had till now, whether particular or general, have been to little purpose; for as much as the constitution of the Government of that State is such, that the particular Provinces will not submit to the determinations of the *States General*; nor yet the particular Townes to those of their own Province; for that they pretend, that their *Republick* is composed of as many Soveraignties, as Townes; and that they have till this present time subsisted so; for that till this present they never met with any considerable accident to disturb that order; but were still kept united by the necessity of their own preservation. But now the malady is such, that they will never find any remedy for it in this order, which real'y was utterly unknown to former ages. Is it possible that the obstinacy of some members, should destroy the whole body, or that the body should be so weak, as to be unable to govern them? To speak freely, it seems to me a great Argument of Self-Love and Presumption, to put so high a value on our opinions, as to sacrifice the publick Peace, and hazard the ruine of the State we live in, to purchase them a reputation.

To redress this, I conceive they must take this course, to wit, to endeavour to compose the divisions in *Holland* concerning Religion, by an Assembly of *Holland* only, if it may be done; that so as near as possible they may observe their ancient Order; and also to use the same procedure in the other Provinces, and to pacific them by the same Expedient.

But if this fail, they must of necessity have recourse to a National *Synod*, which though some particular Townes refuse to send in their Deputies, they must proceed in, and submit the Resolutions of it to the Council of the *States General*; which in so important an Affair, must desire their Neighbours, and good Allyes to assist them, by their Embassadours, with their good advice; by this means will they be engaged also to confirm and maintain their decrees, which they must communicate to them, as also to all their Townes and Souldiers; and I am confident, this course will reclaim most of those that have hitherto dissented, especially if they observe moderation in the decrees they make.

Next

Next I conceive that the States ought to endeavour to reduce to their obedience, those that persist in their obstinacy; and, if God give them grace to compass that design, they will extract much good out of these evils.

As for the *Synod*, it will be necessary, that they establish a Discipline for the Church, that for the future every particular person, may not at pleasure fly from it; which must be also so limited and restrained, that it may not in any wise incroach upon the authority of the States; which may be easily effected, by forbidding all *Synods* and Ecclesiastique *Assemblies*, not to intermeddle with any thing, but what concerns Religion only; and that no such *Assemblies* be held, unless some secular Magistrates be also assistant there, and privy to their consultations.

They would do well also to ordain, that for the future no Minister should be admitted to any cure, that maintained any Doctrines condemned by the *Synod*: and that for the present, those that preach, should be enjoyned, not to touch in their Sermons, upon any points in Controversie. But above all, must they endeavour to bring them all to the same Communion: for as concerning that particular, which is the foundation of our Salvation, and of infinite Efficacy to unite us; there is not any diversity of opinions, as I can learn.

DISCOURSE VIII.
Reasons of the Peace made before Montpellier *in the year* 1622.

THE just regret I have to see my good intentions daily aspersed and calumniated, obliges me, both for my own honour, and to undeceive the credulous, to defend the most just of my actions, and most profitable to those of my Religion, to wit, the procuring of the general Peace of this Kingdome: In which I hope clearly to demonstrate the necessity of concluding it, and that in it I have used all the precautions could be desired to obtain it from our victorious and puissant King. But before I enter upon this Discourse, I must observe that my greatest Censures were such, as with folded Armes were only Spectators of the War, and who under favour of a Declaration, continued in a peaceable Enjoyment of their Estates, while we hazarded our lives to secure their repose: and that among those, the most violent of my Detractors, are such, as being themselves corrupted by the Court, upon false hopes diverted the good affections of such as were inclined to assist us, continually posting up and down to deprive us of the Succours we expected. Envy is a vice base in it self, and yet too well known amongst men. But leaving the only cause of the War, which their unbridled ambition raised, and which their revolts could not appease, they now cast the blame on those who admitted nothing to prevent it, whom no hopes of Profit drew into that Engagement, since they lost all they had; nor yet any thirst of glory, since they cast themselves upon a Party that was bought and sold; but only among other godly men, to find a happy death dying for Christ, or an unexpected deliverance, which they could not hope but from the hand of God alone.

It will be impertinent for me to name him that so unseasonably convened the General Assembly, and when convened,

upon the Peace made before Montpellier. 41

incouraged them to continue their Seſſion, and then betrayed them; and who, after he had made his own peace with the Court, animated the Town of *Rochelle* againſt the Aſſembly: For it is well known who was then the Deputy General.

It is alſo needleſs to ſay, that the Intereſts of *Monſieur de la Force*, and the ſollicitations of *Monſieur de Caſtillon*, were very prevalent to make the ſaid Aſſembly renounce all thoughts of diſſolving. For their Agents and *Partiſans* have ſufficiently diſcovered that they alone impeded their diſſolution: And yet the former perſevered not to the end; but ſhuffled up a Peace by himſelf, and the other during the War, covertly did uſe what miſchief he could; and openly, when the other way ſucceeded not: and yet had we all ſolemnly ſworn by our Deputies, not to hearken to any particular Treaty, nor to make any peace, without the conſent of the general Aſſembly.

Though by their Conduct, both of them have arrived at the honour to be made Marſhals of *France*, and that by mine: I have loſt my Governments, yet ſhall I not envy their good Fortune; but confeſs they are more prudent than I am. My purpoſe in this is not to accuſe any one; but only by the force of Truth to repell thoſe faults they impute to me, and evidently to diſcover the neceſſity of making that peace: having not omitted any thing from the beginning to the end of the War, that might conduce to the advantage of that Party, which I deſired to ſupport. For our War being nothing but a juſt defence of the liberty of our conſciences, and the ſecurity of our perſons under the favour of our Edicts of Pacification, granted us by our Kings, we were obliged to embrace all occaſions might induce the King to grant us a peace.

The firſt Overture was at the Siege before *Montauban*, where the Engliſh Embaſſadour extraordinary came thither for that purpoſe, ſent his Secretary ſeveral times to me, to ſollicit me to it, whom I preſently remitted to the Aſſembly General; at length he preſſed me ſo with the apprehenſion of the loſs of *Montauban*, that I conſented to an interview with the *Conneſtable de Luynes*; which took no effect, for that the hopes he had given him of taking *Montauban*, made him reſolute, not to include in the Peace, neither *Montauban* nor *Rochelle*, unleſs they would ſubmit to have a *Citadel* built in their Townes.

Having

Having thus broken with him upon the first point, which concerned a general Peace; and the difficulties of taking *Montauban* encreasing by reason of the relief I had put into it, the *Connestable* invites me to a second conference, which I refused, but he still urged the renewing of the Treaty; whereupon I demanded permission to send to the *Assembly General* for their consent, to treat, and conclude a Peace; which I obtained, but the *Connestable* dyed presently upon it; and those that were engaged in the Affairs, joyned with *Monsieur* the Prince, who was now come to the King, and so changed the whole design of the Peace, that instead of approving the power, the Assembly had given me to treat of it, and which I had desired of them, they impute it as a Crime to me, as if I aimed to make my self chief of the Party.

This opportunity thus frustrated, and seeing I had now the power of the *General Assembly* in my own hands, I began another Treaty, but with greater confidence of success then before, with *Monsieur de Lesdiguieres*, now *Connestable* of *France*, and commissionated by the King to treat with me: we met; and agreed upon most of the particulars in debate, but remitted the entire conclusion of it to the King, to whom I, and all the Provinces under my Command, sent our Deputies: And at the same time did the *Connestable* and I send Deputies also to the Duke of *Bouillon*, *Sully*, and *Trimouille*, and to the Marshall *de la Force*, as also to the *General Assembly*, and to my Brother, that they might also send their Deputies to the King, from whom they were to expect the final conclusion of the Treaty; informing them withal, that our Deputies had no other Commission, but to consult with them about those Expedients which they should think necessary for the publick Good, and the satisfaction of each particular.

Monsieur the Prince, who unwillingly saw the progress of this Affair, hastens the departure of the King, that by the absence of the Chancellour, and the President *Janin*, who remained still at *Paris*; he might the more easily break the Treaty; and leads him towards *Poictou*, where the Exploits of my Brother had given them a sound Alarm: But our Deputies could not come near the King, till after the Rout at *Riez*, the Treason of the *Baron de St. Surin* at *Royen*, and the overture of the particular Treaty with *Monsieur de la Force*, which absolutely defeated the General, and made the King resolve to dismiss our Deputies, without ever admitting

mitting them to his presence, and to pursue his designes in *Languedoc*, whither the hopes he had given him by *Monsieur de Chastillon* invited him.

After so many Disasters that crossed our intentions, the King marches into *Guienne*, and there concludes the Treaty with *Monsieur de la Force*, and others of that Countrey; and having no fears in any other part of his whole Kingdome, but in *Languedoc*, he draws thither all his Forces. In the mean time I omit no Care, Diligence nor Industry, to raise the dejected hearts, and to compose the dis-united Members of our party there. For the approach of such a Tempest shook the constancy of the most hardy; And as the greatness of the danger diversly affected the spirits of them all; and their zeal to the publick yielded to their own particular apprehensions, so were the factions in our Communalties renewed again; and where I was absent, there were the fairest offers made: In the mean while I posted from one Province to another, according as their necessities required: nor did I neglect the overtures made of forraign assistance: For I gave my servants power to engage all my Estate, to bear my proportion of the charges of the Levye and Conduct of such supplies; and obliged the Provinces under my Command to do the like. I furnished *Montpellier* with a pretty good quantity of Wheat, notwithstanding the ravage that *Monsieur de Montmorency* had made there: And, without vanity may I say it, had it not been for me, there had been neither Mills to grind it; nor Powder, nor Match, nor any other necessaries for a siege: And had they hearkened to me, *Lunel, Maugir, Marseillargues*, and *Hymargues* had been dismantled six moneths before me; and *Montpellier, Nismes, Usez* and *Sommieres* for the convenience of the *Sevenes*, been well fortified. And we should then have had men enough to make a brave resistance: But the Imprudence of the people, and the particular Interests of Governours of those places made them deaf to my advice, which they have since, but too late repented.

It cannot be imputed to me, that the eight Regiments designed for *Montpellier*, could not get in as well as that of St. *Cosme*, and some others; for all the Colonells received their Commissions, and Pay at the same time: Nor was it my fault, if, that after the failing of these Colonels, twelve hundred men of the *Sevenes* got not in neither, since their Commander in Chief had received my Orders for it, and after the Souldiers refused to follow him, went in with fifteen

men

men only, without any hazard or difficulty.

And now was *Montpellier* besieged, where I conceive I did as much as lay in the power of man to do, for the fortifying and storing it with Souldiers, and all manner of provisions in five weeks stay, that I made there; And besides did I imploy all my endeavours and interests to raise four thousand Men more to recruite them, before that the *Conneſtable* and the Duke of *Vendoſm* were joyned with the King's Army; but in vain, for it was impoſſible for me to draw any together, but upon conditions made by the greateſt part of them, not to ſhut them up in *Montpellier*.

I have by experience found, that there is a great difference between popular reſolutions, and the execution of them. For *Niſmes*, which had by letters aſſured *Montpellier*, that they would ſupply them with a thouſand armed men from their own Town, would allow me but fourty two: But it is not Enough to raiſe Troupes, but there muſt be care alſo taken for their ſubſiſtence. From the *Sevenes* I could not get any Corn, it being no Countrey for it, and had not then enough for themſelves. As for *Niſmes*, which was our only Granary, they grumbled at the propoſitions I made for any, and would afford me no more than for eight dayes only, within which time they injoyned me alſo to ſend in the relief to *Montpellier*; and yet had I eight Leagues to march with it, and with two hundred horſe might any Convoy, I could ſend, have been eaſily cut off. All the Commonalties were tempted to particular Treaties: that of the *Sevenes* importuned me to make a Peace, and plainly told me, that they would not ſuffer themſelves to be ruined: All our people were weary of the War, and unable to continue it: There was not Forrage enough left to keep the Cavalry for ſix dayes, which conſiſted but of two hundred Volunteers; which I muſt either diſmiſs, or ſend them into the higher *Languedoc*, and conſequently loſe them: The hopes of the arrival of *Mansfeld* were gone with him into *Holland*, which was a great prejudice to us: For the Army deſigned for his Convoy, was now upon their march towards the King, and were already come as far as *Zion*. The King of *England* inſtantly urged me by Letters (in any caſe) to make a Peace, and to ſubmit to, and wholly relye upon the promiſes of my own Soveraign; preſſing me moreover to conſider the Affairs of his Son in Law, and aſſuring me, that he could not poſſibly give us any aſſiſtance: To which I add, that without a Miracle, *Montpellier* could not have been relieved with any

Troops

upon the Peace made before Montpellier.   45

Troops able to preserve it; for that it was so full of Traytours within, that being obliged to draw off to a greater distance from them, I had two thousand horse in the rear of me for three leagues together.

And now let all unprejudicated persons judge of the necessities that oblige me to make a general Peace, and whether it was possible for me to insist too much upon niceties, without an absolute ruine of it. For I must upon a certain day hazard the supplies, which was the same thing as to expose them to slaughter; or I must see the disbanding of my Troops, the demolition of half our Fortifications, and the King's Entry only into *Montpellier*, without which conditions I could not possibly obtain a general Peace: But all the precautions that a weak and vanquished party could require of a strong and triumphant enemy, or a Subject could demand of a King, I have procured; and such, as if those of *Montpellier* would have unanimously accepted, they had been now in Liberty: For besides the Patent they had from the King in terms clear and free from all ambiguity, *Monsieur de Chevreuse*, and *Monsieur* the Marshall *de Crequi* were delivered up to be kept hostages, and to be committed to some place of Safety, while the King stayed at *Montpellier*; whereupon some of the Town told me, that they would not receive them: for that his Majesty could at pleasure seize upon their Inhabitants, to release them; and that they conceived their presence would be more advantageous to them than their absence.

As to the second particular, I answer, that it is a most strange thing, that my open and professed enemies should omit this occasion of calumniating me, and that those that are of the same Religion with me, should endeavour to make the world believe that, which the actions of our enemies so clearly refute: for the crafts and violences practiced by *Monsieur de Vallence* in *Montpellier* for the space of a whole year, to force them to renounce that Patent, and consent to the raising of a Citadel, had been needless, if there had been any particular agreement derogatory to that Patent, made with me before.

There remains now the third, as absurd as the other; to which I answer; that the Souldiers being at my disposing, who constituted such Officers over them, as I pleased, my Authority in *Montpellier* had been much greater, had I abandoned the publick Interest, to purchase my self more advantageous conditions than I have done; The most severe of my Cenfurers and Detractors must confess that the Peace was necessary and good, had it been observed; and that it was not in my power to change any thing in the Edict, nor can they justly impute it to me, that it is not so well observed now, as in the late King's time.

But they further accuse me for neglecting to take such securities as were requisite for us; and that I refused to retain *Montpellier*, only to necessitate them to accept of the Peace I had made; that the Patent given under the King's hand was but a delusion, and that I had before made other Articles with the King, by which the garrison was to be perpetually continued there, that I had caused *Lunel*, *Mauger*, *Marsillearges* and *Somnieres* to stand out only to amuse, and loose the Soulders, purposely to disfurnish *Montpellier* of them; which things if they were true, they might justly condemn me for the most treacherous and indiscreet person amongst us; that being not the way to obtain conditions tolerable for the publick, or any particular Interest. But besides what I have already said, I will yet shew, that their accusations have not the least appearance of Truth; for if the insufficiency of the security accepted by me, be objected as my only Crime, I answer; that to the last, I withstood the two particulars that concerned it most, to wit, the demolition of our new fortifications, and the Kings Entry into our Townes: But seeing, that the retarding of the Peace, caused a daily decay of our Affairs, I was forced, to do what lay in me, to prevent their utter ruine.

I shall not waste any more time in refuting this Reproach; *That my care to secure my own particular Interest made me negligent of the publick*; for that the whole course of my life, and even this last action of the Peace, doth sufficiently evidence the contrary; having yet no Indemnity as to my Governments; for which I have not shewn my self more sollicitous, than for our publick Concernments. But it is no wonder to me, that those, who durst not adventure any thing for the defence of our Religion, should make their own the Rule to judge of the dispositions of others by. My actions since the conclusion of Peace, must needs appear to those who will vouchsafe them an impartial consideration, as so many Arguments of my Sincerity: I have spared no pain to procure the Confirmation and Establishment of our Articles. I have suffered imprisonment, and have boldly represented to the King, how highly he doth prejudice both his honour and his service, in suffering these *Infractions* of

the

the Peace: But neither the persecutions of our Adversaries, nor the Calumnies of our own party shall ever divert me from the firm resolution *God* hath given me, to devote my self entirely to the promoting of his service.

And now I summon all my critical Observators and Detractors, to shew me a better way than *I* have taken; and promise them, that *I* will second them, better than they have assisted me; and that, laying aside all remembrance of former Actions, I will with a free and cheerfull heart embrace the cause of *God*, and repute it my greatest glory to suffer for his Names sake.

Discourse IX.

An Apologie of the Duke of Rohan *concerning the late Troubles in* France.

'TIs an ingratefull Imployment to serve the publick, especially a party weak of it self, and composed only of Voluntaries: for if any one fails of his proposed ends, they all exclaim against those that had the Conduct of them. This I have very lately experienced; being condemned by the people, for that their grievances have not met with such redresses as they expected, and that by the instigation of false Brethren, who to purchase themselves an esteem with the adverse party, are emulously industrious to brand me with their own just Character, as also by our pretended Pacifiques, who in a zealous tone, deploring our miseries, and cast the blame on such, as according to their report, by their participation have ruined our Affairs. I willingly excuse the ignorant people, who sensible only of their Afflictions, judge of things rather by the event than reason, and lay hold on

that

that lyes next before them, like bruit beasts, that only bite the shaft, never reflecting on the arm that darted it: But I cannot pardon men of reason, and persons versed in the affairs of the world, who continually see that the best contrived designes are not infallibly successfull, and that the hopeless do not alwayes miscarry: *Rochelle* alone, to my great grief, furnisheth us with a notable example to this purpose. Its first Siege was presently after the Massacre, and dissipation of the whole party, being then weak in fortifications, reduced to the last gasp, and abandoned by all: which obliged *Monsieur de la Noue*, a man eminent in Piety, Prudence and Valour to perswade them by a timely submission to prevent an utter desolation: yet was it delivered from that imminent destruction, by means of the Polish Embassadours, who came to demand him for their King, who had then brought it to such extremity. At the second siege it was in a very considerable condition, very well fortified, and strengthened with Confederates both within, and without the Kingdome, and at such a time as favoured them with great hopes of better diversions, and yet did we then see it lost: which should teach us not to judge rashly of any enterprises, either by their good or bad success, much less to condemn them, unless we have good reasons to justifie the Censure; otherwise shall we shew our selves more envious of anothers glory, than zealous for the publick good. Yet could I have born those detractions, had they only reflected upon my Imprduence and Incapacity: and should have only reproached the Authors of them, for not taking my place, and endeavouring by their own actions to correct the errours of mine. But I cannot pass over in silence their other accusation, that to gratifie my own ambition, I had exposed the *Protestant Churches* in *France* to ruine, and that, to fill up the measure of my iniquities, I had delivered them up into the hands of their enemies, to satisfie my avarice: these are the objections I intend to answer, that the world may judge who hath been more carefull of them, those who by an open abandoning, or secret oppugning them, have preserved, and augmented their Estates by the acquisition of fair Offices; or those, who to support them, have resolutely beheld and sustained the confiscation of their goods, the demolition of their houses, the loss of their Governments, the indignation of their King, the dispersion of their nearest kindred, and banishment from their native Countrey.

To understand this affair aright, we must know, that the
source

source of all our evils, was the *Assembly Generall* at *Rochelle*, convened by the *Sieur de Favas*, then our *Deputy Generall*. His pretence was the redressing of the affairs of *Bearn*, which then lay desperate and past all hopes of Remedy: But the true occasion of it, was the deniall he had of the Government of *Lectour*, thinking by this means to make himself considerable, and sought after, for his own benefit: But, as it is easier to put a man upon a precipice, then to withdraw him; so, with much lesse difficulty might this *Assembly* be formed then dissolved; I foresaw the inconveniencies of it, and endeavoured to prevent their meeting, and to dissolve them when assembled, for which I was aspersed, as corrupted by the Court. But it is well known to every one, who was the occasion of their continuance. Had ambition only then governed me, and animated me to make my self Chief of a Party then very considerable, and at such a time, when I had not yet experienced the perplexities that attended the attempt; I should not have lost so fair an opportunity to shew my courage amongst those Zealots, whose flashy zeal expired as soon as they had arrived at their ends.

Thus am I clearly innocent of the greatest fault committed in the management of our affairs: This obstinacy of the *Assembly* drew the *King* upon us, every one submits, and gives him up our Cautionary places: and all from *Saumur* to *Montauban*, yield without any opposition, except St. *John d' Angely*, which my Brother defended as well as he could, To describe the various events of that Warre is not proper for this place. But at length a peace was made before *Montpellier*, in which there were comprized no other Generals of any *Provinces* besides my Brother, and my self; all the rest having before made their compositions apart with large rewards added to their Indempnities: Yet was I then, as now calumniated, as the only betrayer of the Party. But time, and the continued violences I have suffered since the conclusion of the peace, have pretty well silenced those more injurious rumours.

Come we now to the second Warre: The ground of which was a totall infraction of all the Articles of the Peace; especially the not disgarrisonning of *Montpellier*, and *Fort Lewis*, and detaining the debts owing to particular persons, which made them all despair of their condition. As for me, my own private affairs obliged me to endeavour a continuance of the peace; For, being by the favour of *Monsieur* the *Chancellour de Sillery*, and *Monsieur de Pusieux* eased of my oppressions, I had gotten some assignations to recompence the losse of my Governments: But that, which was the most urgent motive to this Warre,

E were

were the publique preparations made at *Blavet*, for the blocking up of *Rochelle*, which made its addresses to me; My Brother also came himself to impart to me the design he had, to divert the storme that threatned it. I approved his resolution, which he prepares to execute with the hazard of his Life and Fortunes, upon this condition, that in case he prospered, I should assist; if he failed, I should disown him. I know not many of our Censurers would have runne the like adventure. The treachery of some of the Religion encreased the peril of the enterprize; and was the reason that it was but half effected: Neverthelesse, he seized on all the Shippes, and made himself Master of the Sea, together with the Isles of *Ré* and *Oleron*, overwhelming all that opposed him, untill the *French* Fleet was re-inforced by the conjunction of the *English* and *Hollander* with them: Whereupon we demanded a peace, which we obtained; and, though it were not so advantageous as we could desire, yet was it better than the former; forasmuch as all our Fortifications were to remain entire; and that the *King* of *England*, by the King's consent, became Caution for the observance of it: who was also promised that *Fort-Lewis* should within a little time be razed.

Let us now reflect upon the third Warre, and consider who were the Authors of it. The revolts and treacheries I had experienced in the two former, made me unwilling enough to runne my self into a new engagement; and, none indeed, that had not proved it, could well judge of the heavinesse of such a burthen. Not, but that I saw that the losse of *Rochelle* would necessarily follow the continuation of the peace, without some extraordinary assistance; Neverthelesse, conceiving the evil irremedible by us, I addressed my supplications to God, for its deliverance; conceiving it a sufficient satisfaction to my Conscience, that I had something advanced the condition of our Churches by the precedent peace, and cast the care of the execution of it upon the shoulders of a Potent *King*, who could not with safety be disobliged, and who only was able to undertake the preservation of *Rochelle*.

Whiles I was in this resolution, came a Gentleman to me from the *King* of great *Britain*; to let me know, that, being surety for our peace, he was equally sensible of our sufferings, to which he would apply all convenient Remedies; that the preparations made against it, assured him of our enemies intentions to ruin *Rochelle*, notwithstanding their engagement to the contrary; Wherefore, he resolved to assist them to the uttermost, and that he was now making provision for that purpose:

upon the Troubles in France.

pose: That, in the mean while he would sollicite our *King*, by his Embassadours, to perform his promises in our behalf; and that, though he had little hopes to prevail, yet he conceived himself bound to try all gentle wayes, before he used any extremities: which if he were forced unto, he would hazard all his Kingdomes, and his own person too, in so just a Warre, to which he found himself obliged both by Conscience, and Honour: provided, that for our parts, we should take Armes with him, and promise, as he did, not to listen to any Treaty, but joyntly with him; That he would entertain his Armies, both at Land and Sea, at his own Charges, untill the end of the Warre; That he had no other aime, than the observation of the peace, for which he was engaged; conjuring me not to abandon my Party, when so just, necessary, and apparent opportunity for its Restauration, was offered. Protesting withall, that if he would not hearken to this offer, that he should hold himself discharged of his engagement, both before God and Man. And for conclusion, desired me with all speed, to dispatch a Gentleman to him, with an account of mine, and the resolutions of all our Provinces.

And here I demand of my Detractors what was to be done in this case. If I should absolutely refuse this offer, and that the *King* of *England* after the taking of *Rochelle*, should declare, that it was my fault alone that it was not relieved, in what predicament had I then been? Had I not been in execration with all those of my Religion? What cause had I then given them to condemn me? And here I challenge every particular person of my Accusers to make my case his own, and to consider, whether I could in conscience be deaf to such Propositions. On the other side, I considered to what a heavy burthen, I now a third time submitted my shoulders; calling to minde the inconstancy of our people, the Infidelities of the better sort of them; the poverty of the Villagers, the avarice of the Citizens, and above all, the irreligion of them all.

All which, were sufficient to shake a more resolute spirit than mine. Neverthelesse, hoping that God, who had been ever my defence, would not now forsake me; I was blind to all other Interests, then that of his Church; and extolling his Piety, and generous Resolution, answered the King's Proposals, with a promise, to take armes, as soon as his Army should make their descent into the Isle of *Ré*, and not before; for that our people would need such a Spurr to quicken them: and that, according to his desires, I would within a few dayes send a Gentleman to him, with most humble thanks for this offered assistance, and to satisfie him

him in all points he desired to be informed. The, now dead *Sieur de Saint Blancart*, was he whom I employed: After which, came my Lord *Montague* with Credentials, to confirm all that is above related.

The English Army landed in the Island, and a little after I appeared in armes: It was not my fault that that Army took not the *Citadell* of *Ré*; nor that the second victualled not *Rochelle*; nor that the third did not rescue it from ruin. For as for me, I had continually two or three Armies upon me, which I still held in play, and which was all the diversion could be expected from me; and God so strengthened me, that notwithstanding our wants and weaknesse, they got no advantage on me.

But there is yet another aspersion layed upon me, for that, seeing *Rochelle* was lost, and the *King* engaged in the Relief of *Cazal*, I let slip that opportunity, to desire a peace; To which I answer, That there was then a *Generall Assembly* on foot, with whom I had a joynt administration of affairs; so, that if there were any fault committed, it ought not to be imputed to me alone: But we held this *Maxime: Not to treat with any but such as were able to make good our conclusions*: For our former experience had taught us, that, such Curiosities had ruined our affairs; For while we fed our selves with hopes of peace, our enemies were not so active to prepare themselves for warre, but the spirits of our Party cooled as fast; so that such Treaties, were but inventions to betray us into a deadly security. Nor did such propositions ever proceed from any but our enemies; to which we answered, that we were alwayes ready to ask it with all submission and honour due to our *King*; that we only desired leave to send to the *King* of Great *Britain*, without whom we could conclude nothing. And as for my part, I professe, that I had rather have endured all extremities, than violated so many religious Oaths I had taken, not to enter upon any Treaty without him. To which I add, that the hopes we had of considerable and speedy supplies from forraign Princes; the reiterated assurances of the *King* of *England*; that he would never conclude a Peace, in which we were not included; and the great diversions the *King* then had, were, methinks, sufficient reasons, to withhold us from so unreasonable pressing for it.

There remains nothing more to be spoken, but concerning the Peace it self; in which we must reflect upon the King's, and our own condition, and how things were then carried; that we may the better judge, whether any thing could be better done: Our Impieties obstructed our deliverance, which God only shewed us, as he did the land of *Canaan* to the Children of *Israel*,

rael, who dyed in the Desert. But if we reform our selves, he will, as he did for them, reserve it for our posterity.

He suffered the *King* to conquer, as soon as he came and saw: For to force the narrow passages of the Mountains, to take the Towne of *Susa*, and revictual *Cazal*, and make a peace with the *King* of *Spaine*, and the *Duke* of *Savoy*, were but one and the same action: This expedition over, and the peace with *England* made, he turned his whole power against us. The Country about *Montauban* was ravished by *Monsieur* the *Prince*, and the *Duke d' Esp.rion*; that about *Castres* by *Monsieur* the *Duke de Ventadour*; that about *Millaud* by *Monsieur de Noüailles*; that about *Nismes* by *Monsieur* the *Mareschall d' Estrée*; And the *King* in person came also with his victorious Army, which he re-inforced with that of the *Duke de Montmorency*.

Thus were we at the same time, environed with six Armies, consisting of more than fifty thousand Men, with a train of fifty piece of Canon, with Ammunition for fifty thousand shot, and other provision sufficient for the nourishment of the Souldiery. 'Twas then that the *Partisans* the *King* had in our Townes, began to shew themselves, making overtures of particular Treaties to defeat a general Peace. Every one of those wasted Communalties, except *Nismes* and *Montauban*, required my presence with an Army; or threatned me with a particular accommodation. By the treachery of the *Sieur de Chevrilles*, was the *Sieur St. André de Montbrune*, with eight hundred Men of *Languedoc*, together with the Town of *Privas* lost. The *Sieur de Beauvoir*, having made his own composition, turned Broker for *St. Ambroise*; and all the Souldiers I had put in there, went thence Oratours to perswade others to the like cowardize and baseness. In all *Languedoc*, and the *Sevenes* could I not find a man would undertake the Command of *Alez*, to endure a Siege there; nor yet in *Alduze*, unlesse I shut my self up with them. Divers Communalties had formed their Assemblies before my face, and in spight of me, to make their own Peace apart; To dissolve which, I was enforced to call a *Provincial Assembly*, and promise them, that, if that proved ineffectual to procure a general Peace, they should then be at liberty to make their own conditions. All the most eminent of our Party, a few only excepted, upon every slight occasion pick quarrels either among themselves, or with me; and many of them treated by themselves; for, none thought of saving any thing but his own goods from this miserable wrack. In short, there was none that had any consideration of the Publique Interest. I should have been then glad to have seen,

any

any of these *State-criticks*, who living at their ease, and out of all danger, so freely bestow their Censures upon others: I believe that in such an extremity, they would have felt no less perplexities than I then suffered.

But this is not all; I saw that a general Peace was inevitably necessary, but found it obstructed by many and great difficulties. The King's Councill very well knew our condition, and were extreamly desirous to proceed in their design; encouraged thereunto by our false Brethren, who daily made them new Proposals, tending to our destruction: and, had not I prevented the execution of the Town of *Sauve's* resolution, we had never obtained a general Peace. On the other side, though not one Communalty, would put themselves in a posture of defence, it being impossible to incline them to disburse one *Denier*, towards the raising of any Souldiers, or drawing any to those places where we feared a siege; Yet, by the instigation of some inconsiderable, but seditious persons, bribed to disturbe and embroyle us, did they murmure, when there was any speech of throwing oft but one stone from their Fortifications.

To remove these difficulties, I let the Court know, that I was resolved with the most of our Party, to dye bravely, rather than fail of a general Peace. That it was dangerous to leave an armed people no other hope of safety than in death; that I would never treat alone; but, that if they would grant me respite but for four dayes with a cessation for that time, and safe conduct to bring the *Generall Assembly* from *Nismes*, to *Anduze*, I durst promise my self a happy conclusion: which was at length, but not without much hesitation: accorded me When the *Generall Assembly* were there arrived, they would not charge themselves alone with the whole burthen of the Treaty, especially at such a time, when it was impossible to obtain a Peace any way correspondent to their desires, and whence the reproaches they were to fear, so farre exceeded any thanks they could hope for; But desires the assistance of the *Provincial Assembly* of the *Sevenes*, and also of that of the Town of *Anduze*, as being most threatned with a Siege, and most concerned in the subsistence of the Fortifications. All conclude that a general Peace was necessary; and that they ought not to insist on any thing, but the qualification of the Article concerning the Fortifications. But the *General Assembly* not satisfied with this, associated to themselves twelve other Deputies extraordinary: six from *Nismes*, and six from *Usez*, sent purposely to endeavour the preservation of the Fortifications and as many more also from the *Assembly*

of

of the *Sevenes*: So that the Assembly consisted then of five and fourty, or fifty persons: who unanimously sent their Deputies to the Court; where they had audience, were received to treat, and many Articles were agreed on; but, as concerning that of the Fortifications, no mention of any modification could be suffered; so that our Deputies returned without concluding any thing, and made their report to the *Assembly*; who thereupon sent to those of the *Sevenes* for their advice. The Town of *Anduze* first vote a peace, with the losse of their Fortifications, next the *Provincials*, and last of all the *Assembly Generall* do the like also, and returned their Deputies to conclude it; charging them moreover to insist upon some satisfaction to be made to me, in lieu of the losses I had sustained. Thus did we obtain a general Peace; and for my particular, they procured me a promise of an hundred thousand Crowns: out of which I assigned more than fourscore thousand Crowns, to such as had either served the Party, or disbursed any summes towards the payment of the Souldiery; so, that there remains not to my portion twenty thousand Crowns to repair my ruinated Houses.

And now I shall submit it to the judgement of all Prudent, and Equitable persons, whether was the occasion of the first War? Whether the second were prejudicial to those of our Religion? Whether I procured the third? Whether that being solicited by the *King* of *England*, to such an engagement, I ought to have refused it? Whether that being obliged not to hearken to any Treaty but conjoyntly with him, I ought to draw upon my self the guilt of perjury? And, whether after the peace was made between *England* and *France*, when I was beset of all hands, I should rather suffer the Extinctions of our Edicts, than preserve them by a General Peace; though with the losse of our Fortifications, which we were no wayes able to defend.

These are the Crimes layd to my charge by our *Pacifiques*, and for which I have been condemned of thousands to be torn with wild-Horses, (which I esteem a glory to me, since they before also presumed to sentence *Henry* the Great, and Harquebusierd him in *Effigie*). I shall wish that those that shall succeed me have no lesse zeal, fidelity and patience, than I have had; that they may meet with a people more constant, lesse various, and more zealous than I have done; and that *God* would Crown their endeavours with more prosperous Events; that at length, restoring the Desolate Churches of *France*, they may happily accomplish what I have attempted. *Amen*.

Discourse X.

Monsieur the Prince *his Letter to Monsieur the Duke of* Rohan.

Monsieur,

THe express pleasure of the *King*, to indulge those of the pretended reformed Religion, with a full liberty of Conscience, hath made me hitherto allow it to all, residing in our Garrisons, Country, and Catholique Townes, that have contained themselves within the limits of their obedience due to his Majesty. Justice hath had its free course: Your Sermons are continued in all places, two or three only excepted, where they were used, not as exercises of Religion, but as Trumpets to Rebellion. The Officers that marched out of the Townes in Rebellion against him, still keep their Offices: In a word, those of the pretended Reformed Religion, that violate not their Loyalty, are treated equally with the Catholiques that have been still faithfull to the *King*. The discreeter sort of your Religion, have cursed your Rebellion, and at length found that the *King* hath done, nor you, nor them any harm, but what you have drawn upon your selves, the Malediction of *God*, and your Soveraigns just indignation against you. By the Letter you wrote to the *Sieur Edmond*, I have learned the resolution of the *Assembly* at *Anduze*. Whether will the rage for your discovered juglings, and your foolish animosities against the Catholiques hurry you? Those that were taken at *Gallargues* were hanged by your own Decree; Since that you preferred *Aymargues* before their lives: Their destruction is justifyable, by all the Rules of War, even between two Soveraigns: But in this case, between a servant and his Master, between a subject, as you are, and his King, and Soveraign; the threats you breath both against the Prisoners, which are of a different Nature from yours, and the Catholiques remaining in the Townes now in
Rebellion,

Rebellion, will fall upon your selves: You blow against the wind; you and your followers, will soon, or late, receive an exemplary punishment for it. For my part, I freely declare, I shall not fail to dispose of the Prisoners taken at *Gallargues*, according, as with good reason, I intended; and, (besides *Savignac*, and thirty others with him in *Thoulouse*,) all the Prisoners of *Traquet*, and *Montpellier*, and all others that are already, or for the future shall be taken, shall undergo the same pains, you inflict on those you now detain; and all the *Huguenots* in the Kingdom, the Ministers and Officers not excepted, shall be payed in the same Coyn, the Catholiques under your power are; And of this be most confident. And now that *Rochelle* is at the last gasp; and that the *English*, discovering your fallacies, have deserted you, let it suffice you, to have added to your former Rebellions, three most notorious Crimes: The first is, the calling in of Forraigners into the Realm, and boasting of it publiquely in your writings. The second is, the creating Officers of Justice. The third is, Your coyning of mony with the Royal stamps: proper only to the *King* himself. *God* reward you according to your deeds, and give you grace to repent. For my part, I could wish with all my heart, that the King's service would give me leave to be

From *Bezieres*,
Novemb. 4,
1628.

Your affectionate servant Henry de Bourbon.

DISCOURSE

Discourse XI.

Monsieur the Duke of Rohan's answer to Monsieur the Prince.

My Lord,

AS your quality of Prince of the Blood gives you a Priviledge to write what you please to me; so doth it debar me of the liberty to answer you with that freedom I should otherwise use. It shall therefore suffice me, that I justifie my self against your principal Accusations. I confess that I once unhandsomly took up Armes, it being not for any interests of our Religion, but of your person only, who promised us a reparation for the violations of our Edicts; yet did nothing at all in it, but shuffled up a Peace, before we could hear from the *General Assembly*. Since that time, every one knows, I never had any recourse to Armes, but when obliged by pure necessity, to defend our Estates, our Lives, and the Liberty of our Consciences. If the English came to our assistance, they had much more reason for it than the *Germanes* you drew into *France*; for that, by the King's consent, they were both Mediatours, and Caution for the observance of our Peace; If we have coyned money, it was with the King's stamp, as it hath been usual in all our civil Warres. I understand my self too well, to pretend to be a Soveraign; nor had I ever my Nativity calculated, to know if I should ever arrive at that height: I confess, I am held-in execration among those who seek the ruine of the Church of God; and glory in it: As for your threatnings, they move me not: I am resolved for all events. I seek my repose in Heaven; and God will vouchsafe me the Grace to enjoy the quiet of my Conscience upon Earth. You put to death the prisoners taken at *Gallargues*; I followed your example, doing the like to those I took at *Mots*, I conceive this practice, will be more prejudicial to yours, than our men; for as much as being uncertain

tain of their Salvation, death must needs be more terrible to them. You taught me to begin an exercise contrary to my own disposition. And yet, I should conceive my self too cruel to my Souldiers, not to immolate some victimes to them. As for the massacres you threaten those of the Religion with, who, under the Protection of the publique Faith, are now among you; It is a fair encouragement to make them trust their enemies, and a just vindication of our lawfull defence: I hope also that the *King* will one day know I have done him no diservice, and will forget his displeasure. You tell me, *God* will curse me: I confesse I am a great sinner, for which I do seriously repent me: but, since the ancient Prophesies are fulfilled, and that I give no credit to those of our times, I do not fear that fire from Heaven shall consume me. In a word, I do not think you bestow these imprecations on me in good earnest, but only to purchase you a great esteem among the Papists; For, as 'tis reported, you have done well enough in this War, which gives me an assurance that you will let us alone in the poor *Sevenes*, since there are more knockes than Pistols to be received. There remaines nothing for conclusion, but to pray *God* that he deal not with you after your works; but, that bringing you yet back again to the true Religion, he will give you constancy to persevere in it to the end: that imitating the examples of your Father and Grandfather; you may prove at length the Defender of our Church; then shall I subscribe that to your person, which I now do to your quality; that I am

My Lord,

Alez. Novemb. 6.
1628.

Your servant
Henry de Rohan.

Dis-

Discourse XII.

The Duke of Rohan's *Manifesto upon the late Occurrences in the Country of the* Grisons, *and the* Valteline.

THe true Causes of the Insurrections of the *Grisons*, would be better concealed than published; and it much troubles me, that I am obliged to discover them: But the Calumnies, which people unpunished, are daily suffered to print against me, and the care taken to descry me both within, and without the Kingdom, constrain me, for the vindication of my honour (which I esteem dearer than my life) to speak the truth, as much, at least, as convenience will give way to: For, there are some things which I cannot resolve to touch, but imperfectly; though *I* have just reason to present them in their own true Shapes. The *King* at the Treaty of *Hierasco*, obtained a demolition of the Forts built by the *Imperialists* in the Country of the *Grisons*, who were also to be re-stablished in the *Valteline*, as they were before the beginning of the Rebellion. I was then at *Venice*, where when *I* thought of nothing, but spending the rest of my dayes in quiet: I was commanded by the *King* into the Country of the *Grisons*, to put that design in execution: *I* presently obeyed, and transported my self into those parts; where *I* found, that by the King's Order there was a Levy made of three thousand Men: and that they had begun the Fortifications of the Bridge over the *Rhine*; which *I* continued with as much care, and diligence, as the money allotted for it would give way. When *I* had thus spent a whole year, *I* was commanded to reduce the Troops to a thousand Men, and to return again to *Venice*; which *I* did to the great dissatisfaction of the *Grisons*, who were much discontented to see themselves frustrated of their hopes of being restored to the *Valteline*, and in arreares great summes of money for four moneths pay. Not long after I received a new Command to return to

the

the *Grisons*, to obserue the Actions of the Duke of *Feria*, that he seized not on it, as he marched with his Army into *Germany*. After that Army had passed the *Valteline*, I had six several Orders to enter it, which were as many times revoked : at length, I received other Orders to go to *Paris*, where I was commanded to go to *Alsace*, and thence to the *Grisons*, to execute the design upon the *Valteline*, in *April*, in the year 1635. I happily passed through *Switzerland*, and seized on the *Valteline*, which I defended in four set Battels, in which the Emperour, and the King of *Spains* Armies, sent thither to drive me thence, were defeated. I used all necessary means to secure all the *Valteline*, and the County of *Bormio* and *Chiavennes* : all which was approved by his Majesty. Then was I instantly urged by the *Grisons* for their re-stablishment in the *Valteline*, according to the many Royal promises made them both by word of mouth, and in writing. But having no order to do it ; and being no longer able to delay them with excuses, I sent Intelligence of all to the Court; proposing also an Accomodation, which, though full of difficulty, *I* doubted not to effect ; I had Orders to attempt it ; which I did, and so pursued it ; that at length I procured a Treaty; with the Ratification of the *Grisons*, and the Consent of the *Valtelines* ; by which I obtained all that was desired, and indeed more than was hoped for, But instead of his Majesties Confirmation, were sent me Modifications, and exceptions which ruined all.

While the *Grisons* expected the effect of the Treaty, divers accidents happened in the Country : to wit, want of money to pay the *Grison* Troops : the Pestilence, which destroyed the *French* Army ; and a violent sicknesse which surprized me. All which encouraged those that were desirous of Innovations, and alienated from us the *Grison* Colonels and Captains, who were before well affected to *France* ; who first presented me with a Petition ; next sent me a Declaration by their Deputies ; and at last resolved to quit their Ports, and the service, unlesse they received some pay.

In the mean while, the *Imperial Partisans*, lost no opportunity to revive those Conspiracies, which the Victorious progress of the King's Army in the *Valteline*, had well near suppressed ; and so farre did they proceed, that there was no small probability that we should then see that insurrection which ensued afterwards. I then kept my bed, having scarce recovered my speech, and consequently was in no fit condition to remedy such distempers : All that I could do, was to desire *Monsieur Lasnier* the Embassadour, to take a journey to *Coire*, which he did, but found the Party in such a posture, that he could by no meanes break off

off the correspondency between the Colonel's and Captains, with the chief of the League, who promised them to leave their posts, and retire to the middle of their Country, and there continue in a body. As soon as I had notice of this disorder, I commanded a *Sedan* to be prepared, in which I was carried to *Coire*; where I caused a *General Council* to be held, for the reducing of these people. I was then of opinion to conceal the Modification sent me from the Court, which *Monsieur Lasnier's* Judgement would not give him leave to assent to; so, that the proposition of the Modification was sent to the Commons, which so exasperated them, that they held another Council at *Illans*, where they privately resolved upon the Deputation to *Impruchts* to treat with the *Imperialists*, and *Spaniards*.

Notwithstanding all this, I came to a Composition with the *Grison* Colonels and Captains, concerning their pay: upon which Condition, and after the payment of the first summe agreed upon between us, they were to return to the service. But all the Remonstrances I could make during these stirres, were not prevalent enough to procure the second payment for those Colonels and Captains, nor any pay for the *Switzers*, nor money to furnish the *French* Souldiers with bread: so that I was left alone, to struggle all at once with the discontents of the three Nations. In the mean time their Deputies concluded their Treaty at *Impruchts*, and obtained of the King of *Spain*, the payment of their Troops from the first of *November*, 1636 the re-stablishment of the *Jurisdiction* of the *Valteline*, exercised by the *Grisons*, without any distinction of Religion; and other Articles farre more advantageous, than those we had accorded them. As soon as I had discovered this agreement, I gave notice of it to the Court, by an express of the 27th. of *December* in the same year, in these very terms: That the King must resolve to accept of honourable Conditions to leave the *Grisons*, and withdraw his Troops, or to give Order for their speedy satisfactions, it being past the power of any Promises, or Treaties, longer to prevent the eruption of their discontents, into an open flame; And, at the bottom of my Letter, I conjured *Monsieur Bouteiller* earnestly to press the consideration of it there, where it was of greatest concernment. But all this produced no effect. In the mean while the Deputies returned from *Impruchts*; Whereupon, I wrote again more earnestly than ever; still hoping, If I could yet obtain any necessary supplyes of money, to effect two things infallibly; One was to reclaim a good part of those who had deserted us: being well assured, that despair, and the ruin of their domestique affairs were the only motives that engaged them *upon the Occurances in* Grisons *and* Valteline 63

them in the contrary Party: The other, which I had also compassed, had I been assisted with money, was, to have retarded the rising: For, in such matters, he that gains time winnes all, and delay is the greatest enemy to all Conspiracies. This was the only reason that hindered my departure towards the *Valteline*; For having determined to stop me, the same day that I should be in a readinesse to go from *Coire*; it had been a great imprudence in me to occasion the eruption of a businesse which time alone could prevent: But these considerations were of no validity. For, so farre were they from furnishing me with the necessaries I demanded, that to compleat our mischiefs, my Messenger returned without an answer; so that being now void of all hopes, I had no other consolation to alleviate these extream perplexities: but to protest before God and Men, against those that had occasioned the ruin of the affairs of that Country; which I did by an expresse, addressed to *Monsieur de Noiers*. Whereupon, seeing that I was now destitute of all hopes of assistance, and that my Letters were not vouchsafed an answer; there was nothing more left for me to do, than with impatience to expect the approach of the tempest, which I had long before foreseen.

At length came the storm, of which I was as certain four moneths before, as the very day it fell. I confesse indeed, that to avoid the sight of so unpleasing a Spectacle, I had desired leave to go to *Venice*, to take order for my affairs there; which was granted me upon condition, that I should be responsible for all accidents in the Country of the *Grisons*, during my absence, but not one word of answer was returned, concerning the means I demanded to prevent the evils I foresaw. The whole Country then being in one day risen in Armes against me; all that I could do was to retire to the fort upon the *Rhine*, and there to Rendezvous the Colonel *Schmit's* Regiment of *Switzers*, consisting of 800 men, with the 200 *French* which were there before, be forced to draw off the Guards from the Bridge over the *Rhine*, and from *Steich*, for that I had not men enough to keep those postes too.

There was I besieged by six *Grison* Regiments, which, with the Spanish money they had compleated, out of the Communalties of the *Grison* League, out of the Neighbour Communalties of *Coire*, out of that of *Tans*, of the Valley of *Pertaus*, and the Troops of *Galas*, who were now drawn down to the *Grison* Frontieres, I heard not any thing from the Army in the *Valteline*, nor could I send to them at all, being inclosed in a Fort, where there was but one Mill, which could scarce grind Corn enough

enough for two hundred Men, and generally so ill provided of all necessaries, that it is a shame to speak it: For it was impossible, notwithstanding all the most instant sollicitations made to that end, ever to obtain any setled stores for the subsistance of the said Fort.

Besides these exigencies, all communication with the *Valteline* was cut off, nor could I long continue my correspondencies in *Switzerland*; For the *Grisons* kept the Bridge over the *Rhine*, which was fordeable but fifteen dayes: In which time I took the opportunity to send *Monsieur de Mehoud* Embassadour to *Switzerland*, a true state of my condition, that he might give both the *King* and *Monsieur de Thullerie*, Embassadour of *Venice*, an account of it. I writ also to the *Canton* of *Zurich*, to try, if I could thence in some short time obtain a thousand or twelve hundred *Switzers*, with which I would have attempted to keep the Field: But *Zurich* conceiving the proposition too full of hazard to be undertaken by them alone, there being an *Assembly Generall* ready to sit at *Baden*, thought it sufficient to advertise their Neighbours of these late accidents, And that *Canton*, with that of *Claris*, sent Deputies to mediate an accommodation between the *Grisons*, and me: to which end a Conference was held: The *Grisons* demand the *Valteline*, so often promised them, and a Million of Livers due for their Colonels and Captains for their Arrears: And moreover declare, that, having called in the King's Forces only to defend them against their Neighbours, they had no more need of their assistance, since they were now come to an agreement with them; and that, in a word, they desired without any further delay, they might be put in possession of that, which did of right belong unto them; that, since the *King* had some reasons which impeded their re-stablishment in that manner as they desired, they had now found means to effect it another way, with which they were very well contented, and satisfied; and, that if all these considerations were laied aside, yet was there one more equivalent to them all; to wit, that they desired not that the King's Forces should make any longer abode in their Country, and that it was a thing never before heard of, forcibly to impose relief on those that desired not, nor had any need of their assistance; That Soveraigns give Lawes in their own Territories, and do not receive them from any other; That, as they should ever acknowledge themselves infinitely obliged to his Majesty for the assistance he had vouchsafed them, so did it seem hard to them, that he should continue his Armies in their Country against their will: To which

which I replyed, that the *King* would eafily condefcend to any reafonable propofitions, if they were demanded as they ought; and that, if they would give me time to fend to the Court, I would affure them, they fhould receive all poffible fatisfaction.

The Deputies of *Zurich*, and *Claris* omitted nothing to incline them to more friendly terms, at leaft, till the Seffion of the *Affembly* at *baden*; but whether, that they feared the disbanding of their new raifed Souldiers, or whether it was by reafon of their nearnefs to the *Imperialifts*, and *Spanifh* Forces, who defired nothing more, than to fet footing in their Country, they would not liften to any Compofition, unleffe I would engage to give them up the Fort upon the *Rhine*; which the *Switzers* Deputies alfo fearing the kindling of a fire fo near their own Houfes, perfwaded me to refign.

This was my Condition, and that which is moft confiderable, is, that the *Switzers* were Mafters of the Fort, who cryed alfo, that they never underftood that the King's Forces came into the *Grifons* Country for any other end, than to aid them, as Allyes of the Crown; that his Majefty was too juft to have any other thoughts; that if it fhould appear to them that he intended any thing, fo contrary to the right of Nations, as to continue his Troops in a Confederates Country, by force, they fhould then confider what they had to do: That fince the *Grifons* declared, that they had no more need of the King's Succours, they could no longer remain there, without contracting on the *French* Nation the eternal blemifh of an unjuft ufurpation: And as for their particular, they could do no lefs than withdraw their Souldiers, that they might not draw upon themfelves the guilt of being acceffories to a thing of fo ill refentment.

I had no time given me to deliberate hereupon; for, when I thought to have kept it twelve or fifteen dayes, which was all I could do; I was perpetually urged to be gone: Wherefore, I took this following courfe; to wit, to leave the Fort in the *Switzers* hands (who were indeed Mafters of it before) and accept of a certain term to withdraw the *French* Troops from the *Valteline*, by which I got time alfo to inform his Majefty of it, which I could not any other way obtain of the *Grifons*. This was all could be done in fuch an exigent as I was in, all other courfes being abfolutely deftructive; For, befides that the Fort was not in my power, the *Switzers* being abfolute Mafters of it: it was, as I have before related, utterly unprovided of neceffaries, nor could be relieved but by the way of *Switzerland*, or the Army in the *Valteline*. As for *Switzerland*, it was impossible to be done that way: First, by reason of the aversion the *Cantons* had declared to the design; and next, for that it could not be effected, without forcing the *Grisons*, who kept the Bridge over the *Rhine*. As for the *Valteline*, it is most certain, that no relief could come thence, it being a thing I could not order, for that it was not in my power, for as much as all communication with that Army was entirely cut off. But, that this might have been done, it had been requisite that the *Valteline* Army should have been then commanded by a Man able of himself to attempt such a thing, without expecting Orders from one, who, as is well known, was not in a capacity to send them: For the Forts in the *Valteline*, and County of *Chiavennes*, being furnished for two moneths, he might have marched to my assistance with eight thousand Foot, and seven hundred Horse, which had been sufficient to reduce the *Grisons*, and to hinder the Entry of the *Germanes* into that Country. This was the only errour committed in this Affair; As for my particular, I value not the vulgars descant on my actions; having as much satisfaction within my self, as a punctual and exact obedience to all the Commands imposed on me, can give; having not drawn off my Troops, nor delivered up the *Valteline* to the *Grisons*, untill I had received his Majesties Commission for it: It is true, that before I had it, I began to treat, but upon such terms, that I had time enough to know the King's pleasure, before I came to any conclusion.

If since that time any other expedients to repair that Affair, were thought on, they came so late, that *Monsieur d' Estampes*, and *Monsieur de Guibriant*, who were then present, found it impossible to put them in execution: which I could more clearly demonstrate; did not my duty oblige me to conceal things of that nature, which even good manners will never give me leave to reveal.

Discourse XIII.

A Letter to Monſieur the Prince of Condé.

Monſieur,

I Had never taken the liberty to anſwer thoſe unhandſome Characters, you would have fixed upon me in the *Aſſembly* of *Guienne*, in *November* laſt, could I imagine you had no other deſign, than to exempt your ſelf from the diſhonour, the King's Armes, and the Reputation of the *French* Nation, received under your Command before *Fontarabie*; and ſhould gladly have preferred the reſpect due to your quality before my own Juſtification; had you not alſo engaged that which I owe, my blood, and to aſperſe me, evidenced how willingly you could deſcend from your Quality of Prince of the Blood, to play the ſcurvy Oratour, as if you better knew how to uſe your Tongue, and Pen, than your Sword. The greateſt Crime I am charged with in your Writing, was, that I refuſed to obey you, which you yet pretend, not conſidering, that ſuch a contempt of your Command, would more reflect upon your ſelf than me, if that fair opportunity of taking *Fontarabie* had been loſt upon that occaſion, ſince you had then the power in your hand to puniſh me for my diſobedience. Pardon me, *Sir*, if I tell you, that you palliate with my pretended obſtinacy, the favour you were willing to gratifie the Arch-Biſhop of *Bourdeaux* with, to my prejudice, and, that they were your own inventions which made you change, and re change the Councils after the two firſt aſſaults I had given, and at length loſe your opportunity, to which you impute the affront, as is well known to the whole Army, to deprive me of the fruit of my labours, and ſnatch the *Lawrell* out of my hands: But, how can that conduce to the defeat received three dayes after, or with what colour can that be laid to my charge; ſince you preſently took me from my Poſt,

ſaying,

saying, it would be better managed by another, and that one houres smart assault would make you Master of the place. I suppose, in this you condemn your self, unless you please to say, also that I tyed your tongue and hands: so, that the one could not command, what the others were unable to execute; and that you were much better seek some more specious pretext to oppress me, than to produce such accusations against me, as only betray your own guilt. It were another matter, yet imputing the miscarriages to me, you think it sufficient for my conviction, to say, that I saw the disorder, and stirred not to ayd you; to this I can justly reply, that, if there were any thing of fortune, or honour to be saved after the wrack, it was I that preserved it, and was also the occasion, that the blood of the whole Army was not shamefully spilt, and that the loss was not greater than the dishonour: You never did me the honour to impart any of your resolutions to my knowledge; nor could I have ever thought, that, to hinder the Enemies forcing your Trenches, you would have removed to draw your Army into Battailla two leagues thence, or that you had need of the Body I commanded; since you never gave me notice of it; It is true, I heard of the disturbance, and disorder in your Camp by the first that fled, who came to my Quarters, and in an instant had all my men in a readiness, expecting some generous Commands from you; in which expectation, I conceived you had rallyed again; and impatiently attended some intelligence from you; the first and most certain newes I could hear, was that of your imbarquing; which, I must confess surprized me with amazement, and that being not able to imagine how that should be, I sought in your Wit, and Courage for those Reasons which I could not find in your misfortune; for that I could not suppose you were circumvented for want of providence; that if you were forced to give way to the greater power of your Enemies, I did conceive, that retreating to my Troops, which I till then believed you had kept as a Reserve, we might rally the rest by your Presence, and turn again upon your Enemies, who had gotten so cheap a Victory; on which I my self had adventured, had I not by experience known, how great an influence the example of the *Generall* hath, either to raise or deject the spirits of the whole Body, and that your so sudden imbarquing had disheartned all our Souldiers; Nevertheless, all the rest of that day, and the night following, did I keep all that were under my Command in Armes: conjecturing that you would take up some noble Resolution in this Disaster, and apply such a remedy to it, as could not be expected from

any

any but your self: I drew not off at all untill I saw my self absolutely frustrated of my hopes, and then retreated in such order, as that the Enemy durst not make any attempt upon me; And, 'tis in this particular alone, that I can acknowledge any just cause you have to complain of me, since I usurped the honour which was due to you; My respect shall incline me to suffer all else your passion shall speak against me; and, I am very sorry, that for your entire satisfaction you should be enforced to say, that I have been much suspected in many other rencontres, but that I have not alwayes behaved my self so ill: I would not, it should be known what I contributed to your passage into *Spain*, which progress you extoll so high, to make the ruines of it fall more impetuously upon me; and could wish you had been more reserved in that accusation, for that the multitude you bring to convince me in that particular, makes the world impute the whole guilt to you: It had been enough that you had Justified your self in a publique *Assembly*, and after your fashion, given the *King* an account of my Comportments, without publishing and crying in the streets of *Paris*, your triumph over me at *Fontarabie*. It would have been looked on, as a Procedure much more beseeming your Quality, had you left the thing wholly to his Majesties consideration, who alone was concerned to absolve, or punish me, if I had offended, and not made your self a Sollicitour, Judge, Party, and Suborner of Witnesses, against an Innocent and absent person, whom your Tyranny only forced to leave the Kingdom.

But what have my Father and my Brothers done to be involved with me in your Invectives, unless perhaps you desire to condemn them for fear they should Justifie me, or that you think your self not sufficiently cleared, unless you raze, and pluck up the very Foundations of our House: Pardon me, *Sir*, if I tell you that the honour my Father hath had, to be raised, esteemed, and caressed by Kings themselves: the Service he hath done the State, and his Age, might have made you spare him for your own sake; since you hate him only for mine; and that, as during his whole life he hath professed himself to be, a Just, and Generous Person, who never betrayed his Friends, nor knew how to flatter his Enemies: he hath still so demeaned himself, that he hath never directly slighted or offended the Parliaments, as you insinuate: nor yet been guilty of so much folly and want of reason, as to stand in need of so poor supports, as flattery to uphold his Quality.

Nor are my Brothers any more guilty of my Crimes than my Father; nor can I imagine why you should seek to make them share in my disgrace, unless you bare them some secret grudge, which you will not discover; But after all these things, Sir, I am sorry you should alleadge past-actions, as reasons to perswade the people of the verity of your present Objections against me; and that you should upbraid me with the Battel of *Espellete*, unless for fear they should reproach you that of *Dolé*; and, that you charge my Father with seditions, which are Crimes, as you say, least pardonable in all States, lest they should call to mind the troubles raised by you in the King's Minority; during which time, we may safely say, that you taught the Nobility Faction, and the yet bleeding people Rebellion; which you never gave off, untill the *Bois de Vincennes*, took away both your Reputation, and the use of it.

I know not, *Sir*, with what Eye you will regard this my just Defence; but I trust in your goodness, that when you come to your self again, you will not take it amiss, that a worm of the Earth should turn against him that goes to crush him: and hope, that those, who have stirred you up to persecute me, will one day more justly bear the penalty of your Indignation than my self.

Henry de Rohan.

FINIS.

www.ingramcontent.com/pod-product-compliance
Lightning Source LLC
Chambersburg PA
CBHW030015240426
43672CB00007B/957